HOUSING AN AGING SOCIETY

HOUSING AN AGING SOCIETY
Issues, Alternatives, and Policy

Edited by Robert J. Newcomer, Ph.D.
M. Powell Lawton, Ph.D.
Thomas O. Byerts, AIA

VAN NOSTRAND REINHOLD COMPANY
————————————*New York*

Library of Congress Catalog Card Number 85-26354

ISBN 0-442-26788-6

Printed in the United States of America

Designed by Paul Chevannes

Van Nostrand Reinhold Company Inc.
115 Fifth Avenue
New York, New York 10003

Van Nostrand Reinhold Company Limited
Molly Millars Lane
Wokingham, Berkshire RG11 2PY, England

Van Nostrand Reinhold
480 La Trobe Street
Melbourne, Victoria 3000, Australia

MacMillan of Canada
Division of Canada Publishing Corporation
164 Commander Boulevard
Agincourt, Ontario M1S 3C7, Canada

16 15 14 13 12 11 10 9 8 7 6 5 4 3 2 1

Library of Congress Cataloging-in-Publication Data

Main entry under title:

Housing an aging society.

  Includes index.
  1. Aged—United States—Dwellings—Addresses,
essays, lectures. I. Newcomer, Robert J. II. Lawton,
M. Powell (Mortimer Powell), 1923– . III. Byerts,
Thomas O.
HD7287.92.U54H66 1986   363.5'9   85-26354
ISBN 0-442-26788-6

CONTENTS

PREFACE

During the past quarter century, widespread recognition of the problems facing the older members of society has resulted in increasingly sophisticated programs and policies for resolving these issues. Despite the frustrations of current cutbacks in federal housing–program and research appropriations, and the sometimes capricious attention federal, state, and voluntary funders have given to services for older people, the national level of concern is markedly higher than it was in 1960.

Increased Social Security retirement benefits, Medicare, Medicaid, the Older Americans Act, and Social Service Block Grants have transformed the national service picture. Programs for the elderly, such as homemaker-chore services, home health, home-delivered meals, adult daytime health care, and service management, are now commonplace. These programs have joined with more traditional services, such as information and referral programs, senior recreation centers, congregate meals programs, and reduced-fare transportation services, to form basic elements in the service environment. It is a virtual certainty that this constellation of services will continue to expand as the size of the elderly population increases and as the proportion of those over age eighty-five becomes ever larger.

In our earlier volume, *Community Planning for an Aging Society* (Lawton, Newcomer, Byerts, 1976), we were principally concerned with presenting a collection of readings that exemplified existing knowledge about the interrelationships between human behavior and physical and social environments. The goal of the book was to help the then rapidly increasing number of professionals in the field of aging to understand and apply this knowledge in physical and social planning. Each service or program was viewed as a discrete aspect of the environment. Relationships or interactions among services and programs were given little attention. In our initial planning of the present volume, we envisioned a simple updating

of this earlier material. In spite of the merits of such a book, two even more compelling issues commanded our attention and redirected the focus of the present volume—the growth of health-care expenditures for the aged and the consequences of this growth for public policy.

A variety of policies have been formulated during the past ten years to contain health-care costs. Many of these efforts relate directly to the health-care industry and take the form of restrictions on the supply or location of health services (hospitals, nursing home beds, home health services), or controls on the use of services (such as limits on days or units of care). Other strategies (such as prospective hospital payments and nursing home prior-authorization screening) seek to develop incentives for less costly service substitutions. One of the remarkable consequences of these various policies is that the continuum of care has come to be seen as an interrelated delivery and financing system. Changes in one dimension often have consequences for many others.

As we observed the innovation and experimentation within the health and social service fields, we were struck by two trends. First, the range of housing alternatives was developing as a component of the system of care; housing was becoming recognized both as a residence and as a service component. Second, and most striking, was acknowledgment of this fact by professionals outside the housing field. Housing specialists, on the other hand, were mainly preoccupied with the traditional concerns of financing, affordability, and design.

In response to newly broadened concepts, we decided to develop a book to communicate information about important housing issues across the health, housing, and human service professions. Our purpose is to raise the awareness of specialists in the housing field about the changing health and social service milieu, and the consequences this change will have across a range of housing types.

Among the most important issues is the increasing number of old and relatively frail people who will be living either in their own independent living units or in various supportive forms of residential care. More adequate means must be explored for designing, financing, and regulating the quality of these facilities. Equally important for housing specialists is the reminder that the evolving needs of older people are certain to cause changes in housing demands. This book tries to map this evolution through a variety of environmental contexts and scales.

Our second objective is to present some discussions of the more traditional housing forms in such a way as to be of interest to specialists in the health and social service fields. This book reviews many specific housing types across the continuum of housing and discusses current knowledge about factors affecting the appropriateness of various types and the satisfaction of the residents.

In planning this book, it seemed wise to include a range of material wide enough to satisfy the diverse interests and needs of those experienced in housing issues, as well as those with only rudimentary knowledge. Thus, the book contains some basic information on the older population; many attempts to translate this background material into housing preferences, choices, and uses; a number of extrapolations of knowledge into emerging housing alternatives and other applications; and some reports on moderately esoteric research methods. None of the chapters is so technical as to cause difficulty in comprehension. Most of the material presented is original. It was sought from individuals known to be among the pioneers within their fields of interest.

The chapters are grouped into four sections, each with an extended introduction. Part 1 is an overview of basic housing issues. Among these issues are the role of housing in the continuum of care, the relationship between individual capability and household characteristics, estimates of future housing demand across the country, special problems facing the rural elderly, and consideration of the many public programs affecting the

availability and demand for specialized housing for the elderly.

The remaining parts step back from the larger needs and policy perspectives to address a series of subissues in depth. Part 2, for example, looks at three major housing types and reviews current knowledge about the preferences and choices of the older population in selecting these alternatives. The benefits and limitations associated with these choices, as well as geographic migration patterns, are also considered. Part 3 moves the discussion outside the living unit into the neighborhood context of housing. Critical dimensions of housing satisfaction and residential quality are presented. Among these topics are criminal victimization, urban displacement, neighborhood behavior, and self-help. Part 4 reviews a number of the emerging nonfederally financed housing alternatives for the elderly. These encompass both independent and semiindependent living units and low to high income groups. These readings explore the strengths and limitations of each approach and identify some of the remaining gaps in public response to the continuum of housing.

The editors wish to acknowledge the early interest in the subject matter of this book that was expressed by Charles Hutchinson, formerly with Hutchinson and Ross Publications. Much of the thread of our concern has developed under the support of the Administration on Aging, U.S. Department of Health and Human Services; the National Center for Health Services Research, U.S. Public Health Service; and the Health Care Financing Administration through individual grants to the University of California, Philadelphia Geriatric Center, and the University of Illinois. We are particularly fortunate to have had the benefits of counsel and commentary of our colleagues on these projects. For this we are especially indebted to Charlene Harrington, Carroll L. Estes, Philip R. Lee, and Juanita B. Wood.

The actual production of this book has been greatly facilitated by Ida VSW Red, who provided technical editorial assistance, and Norton Twite, Barbara Jordan, and Susan Churka-Hyde, who word-processed and edited seemingly countless manuscript pages. The authors are grateful for this assistance.

Finally, we want to thank our friends Thomas O. Byerts and Susan Jenott (formerly Susan Newcomer), who gave us much encouragement and filled us with their energy. Both of these dear people died of cancer while we were finishing this book. They are missed. We dedicate this book to them.

ROBERT J. NEWCOMER
M. POWELL LAWTON

PART I

HOUSING NEEDS AND PUBLIC POLICY

CHAPTER 1 Perspectives on Housing Needs and the Continuum of Care

Robert J. Newcomer • Joel P. Weeden

One of the most widely accepted social policy objectives in the United States and most other countries is the provision of adequate housing. Housing adequacy means different things to different people, but as applied to the elderly, it has generally been interpreted to mean a home in sound condition, at a cost of approximately one-quarter to one-third of one's income, located in a safe neighborhood. Measured by the simple standard of condition, the aggregate quality of housing occupied by older persons is about the same, overall, as that occupied by younger persons, though housing tends to be older and may be in need of repair or upgrading (Struyk, 1981).

A more pervasive problem is the cost of housing. Income determines the ability to pay for good housing. Thirty-eight percent of *all* elderly-headed households spend more than 35 percent of their income on housing. Among low-income elderly renters, more than 58 percent spend over 35 percent of their income for housing. Many of the remaining low-income elderly live in housing with physical deficiencies (Struyk, 1982).

U.S. public policies over the years have responded somewhat to these cost and housing quality issues. The response has been implemented through a series of federal housing assistance programs administered by the U.S. Department of Housing and Urban Development (HUD). Assistance is generally in the form of subsidies to the mortgage via low-income loans, rental assistance payments, or perhaps a combination of these two. At least 1.5 million households headed by elderly persons are being served by HUD rent subsidy programs. This amounts to about 40 percent of all income-eligible elderly renters (U.S. Senate, 1984). There is even a housing voucher program experiment—designed to help give low-income people access to a greater range of private-sector housing units.[1] State and local governments have been involved in these efforts on a more limited basis.

While there are unquestionable benefits arising from the past and current public policy approaches to the housing needs of the older population, there are some limitations, too. One of the more important is that, in the minds of many, subsidized housing programs have come to replace the *means* for an adequate home with the *ends*. Subsidized housing program appropriations and project implementation command much more public, political, and research attention than do discussions of structural reform in the housing industry or the adequacy of the full spectrum of housing supply.

Consider the issues at the forefront of policy attention for more than the past decade:

- The relative merits of section 236 versus section 202 housing
- Proprietary versus nonprofit housing sponsorship
- Housing vouchers versus mortgage subsidies
- Site selection criteria for group housing projects
- Neighborhood impact in terms of property values
- Racial integration/segregation

- Age integration/segregation
- Middle- and low-income integration/segregation
- Minimum property standards regarding such things as roomsize and on-site services/facilities
- Design suitability standards for room fixtures, appliances, and material selection
- The operational problems of housing authorities
- Crime and security, especially in subsidized housing projects
- Admissions standards, and tenant physical and mental capacity
- Families versus elderly-headed households as a housing priority

Without minimizing the situational importance of any of these issues, it should be recognized that each largely concerns a subsidized housing program implementation problem. As a series of events, the political debate around these issues has influenced a narrow conceptualization of federal housing policy.

The critique implied by these remarks has been overdrawn to emphasize the narrowness with which housing problems and solutions are usually debated. For example, it is recognized that a number of other issues, such as the conversion of rental housing into condominiums, the rising costs of property taxes and home maintenance, the physical and social deterioration of some neighborhoods, and homelessness, have been the subject of congressional hearings over the past few years (for example, U.S. Advisory Commission, 1975; U.S. Congress, 1981; U.S. House, 1981; 1982; 1983a, b, c, and d; 1984a, b, and c; U.S. Senate, 1980). Nevertheless, it is only recently that the conceptualization of policy has begun to be extended to legislation outside the Housing and Community Development Acts. The formidable role of income tax laws as incentives for private market financing, housing quality maintenance, property turnover, and as income subsidies to middle- and high-income persons is central among the issues too infrequently discussed or considered in "housing policy" debate.

The purpose of this chapter, indeed the purpose

of this book, is to focus attention on another important gap in the conceptualization of national housing policy—the role of housing in the continuum of care. In working toward this goal, a comprehensive anthology of current knowledge has been compiled. These readings cover the full range of public and private sector housing alternatives, identify the benefits and limitations of this housing for the subpopulations served, and the public policy issues associated with the provision and maintenance of this housing stock.

Defining the Continuum

The housing continuum is characterized both by its physical features and by the attributes of its occupants. This continuum ranges from fully independent to dependent households and includes a variety of housing types. The residents in independent households are capable of their own housekeeping, cooking, and personal care. The housing typically used by this group includes single-family houses, apartments, retirement communities, and mobile homes.

Semidependent households include people who may require assistance in one or more activities of daily living such as cooking, cleaning, or personal care. Residents in single-family homes or apartment houses, or those living with other family members or friends, may be considered semidependent householders if they need and receive personal care or other assistance in their activities of daily living. This group is the principal target for such home-based service programs as adult day health care, homemaker/chore services, home health services, and meals on wheels. Another category of semidependent households include people in such facilities as boarding and care homes, retirement hotels, and continuing-care homes. These facilities may include meals, cleaning services, and some personal care as either required or optional services to their residents.

Dependent householders are those individuals who need assistance in such things as ambulation, personal care, grooming, drug use, or eating. Such persons usually live in intermediate-care or skilled nursing-care facilities, although some could live in other settings if adequate assistance were available.

Financing Services for Semidependent Aged Households

Housing policy, such as that reflected in the Housing and Community Development Acts (U.S. Public Law [PL] 93-383 as amended), typically has ignored the housing continuum. Instead, it has focused on persons living in independent settings. About $12.4 billion was allocated for rent and mortgage subsidy programs in fiscal year 1984. Between a third and half of these funds were used for housing units occupied by the elderly (U.S. Senate, 1984).

Persons in need of semidependent or dependent housing have been accommodated not by housing program allocations but by a variety of health and social service programs. Among the more predominant of these are Medicare, Medicaid (Titles XVIII and XIX of PL 89-97), the Social Services Block Grant (Title XX of U.S. PL 93-647), and the Older Americans Act (U.S. PL 89-73). These programs have helped provide homemaker/chore services, referrals, and in some cases, service management. One intention of this assistance has been to enable people to remain in their own homes or apartments rather than nursing institutions, but a far greater amount of money is used to help pay for care within nursing homes. This is shown in table 1-1, which shows expenditures for the aged under these programs. Most of these public program dollars are expended on various forms of health services, but nursing-home care accounts for about $12 billion. Community-based supportive living services total only about $3 billion, even when the other social service programs are also included. These expenditures are principally for persons discharged from hospital settings. Such care is generally seen as being needed for relatively short-term recovery needs, rather than long-term problem management. In short, the public response to community-based supportive care for the elderly, as reflected in its categorical programs, accounts for about 4 percent of the commitment to the major health, housing, and social service programs.[2]

Another nonhousing program, Title XVI of the

TABLE 1-1. Selected Public Expenditures for Home-based Care, Hospital, and Nursing Home Care for the Aged, 1984

	Total 1984 Expenditures (in billions)	Percent Home-based and Other Services[1]	Percent Hospital	Percent Nursing Home[2]	Percent Physician Services
Medicare	$58.5	5.3%	69.2%	0.9%	24.4%
Medicaid (federal share)	15.3	11.8	17.0	68.0	3.3
Veterans Administration and Other Government	6.7	7.5	73.1	16.4	3.0
Total[3]	80.5	6.8	59.6	15.0	18.5

SOURCE: *Adapted from Waldo and Lazenby (1984).*

1. This category includes home health care in the Medicare and Medicaid program; homemaker/chore service, adult health care, and information and referral services under both the Social Services Block Grant and Older Americans Act.
2. Skilled- and intermediate-care facilities are combined in this category.
3. Two major programs financing in-home care for the aged are not included in these totals: the Social Services Block Grant and the Older Americans Act. About $2.7 billion was allocated nationally in 1984 for SSBG. The state contributions to this program are not known, but they are assumed to range between 25% to 100% of the federal contribution. Home-based services accounted for about 16% of all SSBG services funded in 1979—the last year for which this information is available (U.S. House, 1984d). Assuming that all states had a 100% match to the federal allocation and that all home-based care was received by the elderly, then about $.8 billion of these funds were expended for the elderly in 1984. The Older Americans Act authorized $.35 billion for all support services and senior centers in 1984. It is likely that less than half this amount was expended for home care.

Social Security Act (U.S. PL 92-603), provides a guaranteed minimum income for the aged, blind, and disabled. This program is known as Supplemental Security Income (SSI). States have the option of supplementing the federal SSI income level—thirty states do through a State Supplemental Payment (SSP). The SSI/SSP programs, by putting an income floor under the aged and others have directly aided both independent and semidependent households. While the actual housing arrangements of SSI/SSP recipients is not known with precision, it is generally believed that this program has been particularly helpful to persons seeking board and care, single-room occupancy hotels, and low-rent apartment units. The federal maximum SSI payment was $397 for an elderly couple in 1982. The average state supplemental payment in those states with this program was $95 for an elderly couple living in independent housing and $401 for couples in supportive housing (U.S. Social Security Administration, 1982).

Ignorance and Initiatives in Housing

This superficial presentation may give the impression of a parallel, but somehow integrated, housing system: federal housing programs produce low-income independent living units—health and social service programs provide assistance to persons in independent housing (including those in low-income housing projects) needing assistance—and SSI/SSP enable low-income persons to finance residence in semidependent housing.

Unfortunately, if integration or coordination occurs among those programs within any community, it is more likely by accident than design. Subsidized housing projects are separately planned and located through the combined efforts of housing sponsors, housing authorities, city planning departments, and HUD (Newcomer, 1976). Social service dollar allocations and service appropriations are made through different channels—usually state or county welfare or social service departments. SSI income levels are set by the U.S. Congress. SSP income levels are set by state legislatures (although in some states the levels vary

by region within the state). Medicare and Medicaid program expeditures are largely determined by health care providers and the care they give. There is little communication, much less coordination, in the policy setting among these programs. The planning and regulation of these facilities also varies depending on facility size, target groups served, and the nature of the concern. For example, fire and safety are most often a local responsibility. Service quality may be a state or local responsibility (Harrington et al., 1985).

Why is this fragmentation a problem? There are three basic reasons. First, there is a demonstrable unmet need for semidependent living arrangements. The U.S. Health Care Financing Administration (1981) estimates that in 1985 the number of adults needing but unserved by such housing will approach 1.3 million persons. It has taken thirty years of federal housing assistance programs to develop the capacity to serve an equal number of people in low-income housing.

Second, as noted earlier, are the enormous public and private expenditures being made nationally for dependent housing arrangements—namely, skilled- and intermediate-care facilities. The need and consequent cost of this care is expected to rise as the proportion of the population aged eighty-five years and older grows (Rice and Feldman, 1983).

Thirdly, there is evidence that a sizable proportion of nursing-home residents could be adequately cared for in less costly and restrictive environments. Some studies have put this figure at as high as 40 percent (U.S. HCFA, 1981). More typical are estimates of 10 to 20 percent. However, before these less costly alternatives can be used to substitute for nursing-home care, there must be an adequate supply of beds and funds to finance needed residences.

The health and human services field has responded to these concerns with a variety of demonstration programs, health-care financing-regulation waivers, and preauthorization screening and case management programs (see Palmer, 1984, for a comprehensive discussion of these alternatives). These approaches are all designed to reduce the number of people inappropriately placed in nursing homes and to make more services available within people's own homes. Though these interventions have had varying success in health-care cost containment and reduced institutionalization, they have helped document the need for an expanded array of housing alternatives.

Counterbalancing these cautious, yet innovative, efforts to broaden health and social service financing for noninstitutionalized semidependent populations are the activities within the housing field. Housing advocates and housing policy makers have largely ignored or avoided the issue of how to expand noninstitutional care for the semidependent. The major public effort is the Congregate Housing Services Act of 1978 (U.S. PL 95-557).[3] Private sector efforts include experiments in reverse annuity mortgages, shared or echo housing, and continuing-care retirement communities (these are discussed more fully in chapter 18).

Conclusion and a Look Ahead

It is tempting and perhaps even obligatory after a somewhat polemical discussion to propose answers. The issues in this circumstance, however, are complex: both philosophical and technical. Those involved in housing programs and policy must decide if they are taking into consideration the full continuum of housing needs—from independent to dependent. There is need for the integration and explicit coordination of housing with health and social service financing and policy development because changes in one domain affect the others.

In the structural hierarchy of federal, state, local, and private-sector decision making, there are few explicit points of policy coordination and program impact assessment, yet there are legislative and other arenas for public policy debate. National professional groups (such as the American Planning Association and the American Public Health Association), consumer and advocacy groups (such as the American Association of Retired Persons), and national trade associations (such as the

American Association of Homes for the Aged and the American Health Facilities Association) can act as catalysts for this debate. To do so, these national groups and their state counterparts and members must first broaden their review of legislation and regulations to consider effects across the full continuum of health, social service, and housing care.

Turning to the issue of technical substance—this book attempts to provide a compendium of current knowledge across a full functional and economic spectrum of housing for the elderly. The remaining chapters in part 1 begin this process. These materials provide a background for the more focused discussions in parts 2 through 4. In chapter 2, Beth Soldo discusses the relationships among housing characteristics, household type, and the health status and impairments of the older population. This chapter introduces a theme, recurrent throughout the book: people adapt to their living arrangements as their physical and mental competencies change. An important policy question is posed: to what extent can physical and social environmental compensations be used as an alternative to direct service intervention? In chapter 3, Sandra Newman builds on this discussion and begins to translate some of its implications into estimates of housing demand. An informed public policy response to the housing needs of the older population requires such an understanding and the implications of the growth of the elderly population. Various projections of elderly-headed household growth, housing ownership patterns, and the geographic distribution of this population are presented.

Although the United States is predominantly an urban society, there is a large and vital rural population. In chapter 4 Gary Lee complements Newman's national perspective with a thoughtful review of the various perspectives on housing quality of the rural elderly and examines the appropriateness of strategies for ameliorating the problems that exist within this subpopulation.

Population characteristics and projections and the interrelationship of individual characteristics and housing choices are brought into a more individually focused perspective by Lloyd Turner. In chapter 5 he briefly reviews many of the major public policies affecting the elderly and convincingly argues that housing choices are influenced by these.

Raymond Struyk, in chapter 6, reviews the current context of existing federal housing programs and the likely directions this policy may take in the future. His proposals for desired future changes are presented in the context of recent and past experiences, which are also reviewed.

This book neither asks nor answers all of the important questions about housing an aging society, but it provides a thorough review of current knowledge and areas needing exploration, and, we hope, a stimulus to the further thinking and actions of those in the housing, health, and human service fields.

Notes

1. For more background on housing assistance programs, see U.S. Library of Congress (1984a and 1984b).
2. Another form of housing policy is the income tax codes, which allow for mortgage deductions and investment depreciation. It is estimated that $44.4 billion in federal tax revenues will be lost annually by 1987 because of mortgage interest deductions alone (Greene, 1981).
3. Congregate housing usually refers to multiunit rental housing that includes the provision of supportive services such as meals, housekeeping, transportation, and social activities within the facility. Congregate housing accommodates only independent and semiindependent persons. It excludes any type of maintenance health care. The federal legislation initiating the Congregate Housing Services Program is sensitive to the relationship between housing and long-term care, and it realizes the necessity for interagency cooperation. The Department of Housing and Urban Development (under the authority of the Congregate Housing Services Act of 1978) and Farmers Home Administration (under the authority of its section 515 Rural Rental Housing Loan Programs,) had congregate housing demonstrations in operation at a combined total of seventy-two different sites in 1983. An estimated 3,000 persons have been served by these projects since the programs were initiated in 1978 (U.S. Senate, 1984).

References

Greene, J. M. 1981. *The Tax Treatment of Homeownership: Issues and Options.* Washington, DC: U.S. Congressional Budget Office.

Harrington, C., C. L. Estes, P. R. Lee, and R. J. Newcomer. 1985. "State Policies on Long Term Care." In *Long Term Care for the Elderly: Public Policy Issues.* Ed. C. Harrington, R. J. Newcomer, C. L. Estes, and Associates. Beverly Hills, CA: Sage.

Newcomer, R. J. 1976. "Meeting the Housing Needs of Older People—A Look at Federal and Local Decision Making." In *Community Planning for an Aging Society.* Ed. M. P. Lawton, R. J. Newcomer, and T. O. Byerts. Stroudsberg, PA: Dowden, Hutchinson and Ross.

Palmer, H. 1984. "The Alternatives Question." In *Long Term Care: Perspectives from Research and Demonstrations.* Ed. R. Vogel and H. Palmer. Bethesda, MD: Aspen.

Rice, D. P., and J. J. Feldman. 1983. "Living Longer in the United States: Demographic Changes and Health Needs of the Elderly." *Milbank Fund Memorial Quarterly/Health and Society* 61, No. 3:362–96.

Struyk, R. J. 1981. "The Changing Housing and Neighborhood Environment of the Elderly: A Look at the Year 2000." In *Aging: Social Change.* Ed. S. B. Kisler, J. N. Mergan, and V. K. Oppenheimer. New York: Academic.

———. 1982. "Testimony before the U.S. Senate Special Committee on Aging." In *The Impact of the Administration's Housing Proposals on Older Americans.* Washington, DC: U.S. Government Printing Office.

U.S. Advisory Commission on Intergovernmental Relations. 1975. *Property Tax Circuit-Breakers: Current Status and Policy Issues.* Washington, DC: U.S. Government Printing Office.

U.S. Congress. 1981. Joint Economic Committee. Hearing: *Neighborhood Conditions,* May 20. Washington, DC: U.S. Government Printing Office.

U.S. Health Care Financing Administration (HCFA). 1981. *Long Term Care: Background and Future Directions.* Washington, DC: U.S. Department of Health and Human Services.

U.S. House of Representatives. 1981. Committee on Government Operations. Overview hearings: *Condominium and Cooperative Conversion: The Federal Response,* March 30, 31; April 1. Washington, DC: U.S. Government Printing Office.

———. 1982. Committee on Banking, Finance and Urban Affairs. Subcommittee on Housing and Community Development. *Homelessness in America.* Washington, DC: U.S. Government Printing Office.

———. 1983a. Committee on Government Operations. *HUD Is Not Adequately Preserving Subsidized Multifamily Housing.* Washington, DC: U.S. Government Printing Office.

———. 1983b. Select Committee on Aging. Subcommittee on Housing and Consumer Interests. Hearing: *Elderly Housing: Innovative Alternatives,* Portland, OR, August 12. Washington, DC: U.S. Government Printing Office.

———. 1983c. Select Committee on Aging. Subcommittee on Housing and Consumer Interests. Hearing: *Home Equity Conversion,* Mattydale, NY, October 23. Washington, DC: U.S. Government Printing Office.

———. 1983d. Select Committee on Aging. Subcommittee on Housing and Consumer Interests. Hearing: *Housing the Elderly: Alternative Options,* Erie, PA, October 17. Washington, DC: U.S. Government Printing Office.

———. 1984a. Committee on Banking, Finance, and Urban Affairs. Subcommittee on Housing and Community Development; Committee on Government Operations. Subcommittee on Manpower and Housing. Joint Hearing: *HUD Report on Homelessness,* May 24. Washington, DC: U.S. Government Printing Office.

———. 1984b. Committee on Banking, Finance, and Urban Affairs. Subcommittee on Housing and Community Development. Hearing: *Making Affordable Housing a Reality,* June 28. Washington, DC: U.S. Government Printing Office.

———. 1984c. Committee on Banking, Finance, and Urban Affairs. Subcommittee on Housing and Community Development. Hearing: *Section 8 Rent Adjustments, Elderly Housing, and other Assisted Housing Issues,* February 22. Washington, DC: U.S. Government Printing Office.

———. 1984d. Committee on Ways and Means. *Background Data on Programs Within the Jurisdiction of the Committee.* Washington, DC: U.S. Government Printing Office.

U.S. Library of Congress. 1984a. Congressional Research Service. *Federal Housing Programs Affecting the Elderly: A History and Alternatives for the Future.* CRS Report No. 84-21E. Washington, DC: U.S. Government Printing Office.

———. 1984b. Congressional Research Service. *Housing Assistance to Low and Moderate Income Households.* CRS Issue Brief IB 79058. Washington, DC: U.S. Government Printing Office.

U.S. Public Law 89-73. Older Americans Act of 1965 as amended. Washington, DC: U.S. Government Printing Office.

U.S. Public Law 89-97. Social Security Amendments of 1965. Washington, DC: U.S. Government Printing Office.

U.S. Public Law 92-603. Social Security Amendments of 1972. Washington, DC: U.S. Government Printing Office.

U.S. Public Law 93-383. Housing and Community Development Act of 1974 as amended. Washington, DC: U.S. Government Printing Office.

U.S. Public Law 93-647. Social Security Amendments of 1974. Washington, DC: U.S. Government Printing Office.

U.S. Public Law 95-557. Congregate Housing Services Act of 1978. Washington, DC: U.S. Government Printing Office.

U.S. Senate. 1980. Special Committee on Aging. Hearing: *Possible Abuse and Maladministration of Home Rehabilitation Programs for the Elderly,* Santa Fe, NM, October 8. Washington, DC: U.S. Government Printing Office.

———. 1984. Special Committee on Aging. *Developments in Aging: 1983.* Volume 1. Washington, DC: U.S. Government Printing Office.

U.S. Social Security Administration. 1982. *The Supplemental Security Income Program for the Aged, Blind and Disabled: Selected Characteristics of State Supplementation Programs as of January, 1982.* Washington, DC: U.S. Department of Health and Human Services.

Waldo, D., and H. Lazenby, 1984. "Demographic Characteristics and Health Care Use and Expenditures by the Aged in the United States: 1977–1984." *Health Care Financing Review* 6, No. 1:1–29.

CHAPTER 2 Household Types, Housing Needs, and Disability

Beth J. Soldo

Young and old alike have a fundamental need for adequate housing, defined simply as structurally sound shelter affording the residents protection from the elements, security, and access to basic amenities and services at a reasonable price. Beyond this mere subsistence level of need, additional or "special" housing requirements reflect the personal characteristics of occupants (Welfeld and Struyk, 1978). Among the more important of these characteristics, particularly for the elderly, is health. Physical and cognitive capacities dictate, to a large extent, the makeup of the housing service bundle required by older persons living in the community.

Viewed cross-sectionally, the functional health of the older population spans a broad range, anchored at one end by uncompromised capacity and, at the other, by complete functional dependence on others. The housing needs of older persons in the former group resemble those of other healthy adults while the housing needs of the elderly in the latter group are secondary to their needs for care settings either in the community or in long-term care facilities.

The functional health of most older persons falls between the two extremes. These elderly are the community residents whose capacities for unassisted activity or mobility have been eroded, to varying degrees, by chronic disease, or, more typically, clusters of chronic disease (Besdine, 1981). For this group of older persons, housing and household structure not only define the immediate physical surrounding and social setting but also mediate—positively or negatively—the effects of chronic disease on behavior (Graney, 1973).

This idea is expressed formally in the "environmental docility" hypothesis of Nahemow and Lawton (1973) which posits that the weaker the individual, the more dependent are behavioral outcomes on environmental influences. Environmental factors can either stress already weakened coping abilities or compensate for reduced levels of functioning. Since life space tends to contract as competency diminishes, resources for environmental leverage are increasingly circumscribed by the type, quality, and composition of the occupied household.

Because these factors have inherent potential for ameliorating the behavioral consequences of disability, ecological strategies of compensation are fundamental to almost all assistance efforts undertaken by either the formal support network of community agencies or the informal network of family, friends, and neighbors (Cantor, 1979). Such efforts may involve modification only of the physical environment, for example, the installation of ramps and grab bars or the removal of interior thresholds (Costa and Sweet, 1976; Struyk and Soldo, 1980). Community programs often link relocation to upgraded housing units with increased access to and use of supportive services (Brody, 1978; Lawton, 1980a). Still other strategies emphasize enhancing the supportive capacity of the social environment through the introduction of specific services or care providers, for example, through changes in living arrangements or foster home programs.[1] Regardless of how such efforts are structured, the implicit "common denominator" is an understanding of human behavior within the person-to-environment interaction framework (Kahana, 1974; Carp, 1976b; Lawton, 1980b). Behavior is seen as being jointly determined by characteristics of the individual and of an environment that is inherently multidimensional.

In this chapter we examine the complex relationships that exist among the health status of the elderly and the social and the physical aspects of their environments, as reflected in their living arrangements and the type and quality of the housing they occupy.

Health

Old age in itself is not a disease, but even normal aging usually involves a general decline in overall functioning. Muscle strength gradually diminishes, bones become brittle, response time slows, and the senses dull (Carp, 1976a). Whether as a result of normal or pathological aging, the risk of chronic disease increases markedly with age. This relationship is suggested by the cross-sectional comparisons of the prevalence of select chronic conditions shown in table 2-1. Only 14 percent of older persons in the community are free of any chronic illness (Soldo, 1980).

The simple presence of a chronic condition does not necessarily indicate compromised functioning. One would not expect chronic sinusitis or hay fever, for example, to affect behavior to any appreciable degree. The data in the last column of table 2-1 show, however, that the diseases common to old age are also those that frequently produce activity limitations.[2] About half of all noninstitutionalized elderly—approximately 10.7 million persons—are restricted in their activity in some way because of a chronic disease (U.S. National Center for Health Statistics, 1981) and the proportion of older persons so limited increases with advanced age (Wilson, 1977). The overall percentage distribution of the older population by activity limitation status is shown in table 2-2. The data indicate that men are more likely than women to report severe restrictions in activity. In terms of absolute numbers, however, more women than men experience some type of activity limitation.

While these data are useful for sketching the health of the elderly in broad brush strokes, they do not directly translate into indicators of service or special housing needs, per se. The reliability of respondent reports of health problems pose obvious, but secondary, difficulties for interpretation. Of more immediate concern to the topic at hand is that these reports are generally understood to

TABLE 2-1. Prevalence of Select Chronic Conditions among the Middle-Aged and Elderly and Percent of Each Condition Causing Limitations in Activity, 1979.

Condition	Rate per 1,000 Noninstitutionalized Persons 45–64	Rate per 1,000 Noninstitutionalized Persons 65+	Percent of Conditions Causing Limitations in Activity
Arthritis	252.7	442.7	20.8%
Hypertensive diseases	214.4	385.1	13.5
Hearing impairments	119.2	281.6	4.7
Heart conditions	128.5	274.4	32.3
Orthopedic impairments	117.9	162.1	30.6
Atherosclerosis	21.6	123.5	69.7
Visual impairments	58.2	118.5	52.5

SOURCE: *U.S. National Center for Health Statistics, 1979a, table 22.*

TABLE 2-2. Percentage Distribution of Noninstitutionalized Persons 65 Years of Age or Older by Chronic Activity Limitation Status (by Sex), 1979

Chronic Activity Limitation Status	Total 65+	Male 65+	Female 65+
No limitation in activity	54.0	50.9	56.1
Limited, but not in major activity	6.9	5.2	8.0
Limited in amount or kind of major activity	22.3	15.2	27.2
Unable to carry on major activity	16.9	28.7	8.7
Total[1]	100.0	100.0	100.0
	(23,343)	(9,617)	(13,726)

SOURCE: *U.S. National Center for Health Statistics, 1979b, Table 1.*

1. Base numbers in parentheses in thousands

be performance- rather than capacity-based measures. Thus, it is not possible to distinguish between older persons who function at their highest possible level because of supportive services and a friendly environment and those whose function could be elevated if service were introduced or the built environment modified.

A more relevant, but still imperfect, indicator of the tension between health problems and environmental factors is the mobility restriction measure. Approximately one third of the elderly who are restricted in their usual activity also are limited in their mobility. Since mobility limitations are a more extreme disability, very few of those with such limitations can carry out their normal activities without difficulty. Most of those with mobility problems report that they can get around by themselves only with difficulty or with the assistance of a mechanical aid or another person. Nonetheless, approximately one in twenty elderly persons are confined to their homes because of their mobility problems (Wilson, 1977). The physical and social characteristics of the immediate environment perhaps assume the greatest importance for this segment of the older population in which the household quite literally defines life space.

The use of mechanical aids (for example, canes, wheelchairs, walkers) by the elderly also suggests the degree to which they place special demands on their environment. At a minimum, the built environment affects the extent and ease of mobility for the users of special aids. Although out-of-date, the most recent data on this subject indicate that slightly more than one in five older persons use, singly or in combination, some form of special aid (U.S. NCHS, 1972). Current estimates are likely to be even higher since special aid utilization increases with age and the very oldest age groups (those seventy-five or eighty-five years of age or older) are the fastest growing segments in the older population (Soldo, 1980).

Many older persons have multiple impairments, often in conjunction with some deficiency in their social and economic resource base. As a result, it is difficult to estimate accurately the number who place special demands on their immediate environment, even at a single point in time. Lawton (1978) has argued, however, that the number of those who do not depend on environmental resources for some form of compensation—the truly independent elderly—is very small indeed. If viewed longitudinally, the number of persons who remain fully independent over the course of their life cycle is even smaller. Because the health of an individual is not static over time, the need for special housing and other environmental supports can be expected to shift any number of times in response to changes in health status (Welfeld and Struyk, 1978).

Living Arrangements as Social Environment

An ecological interpretation of living arrangements underscores the significant role household composition plays in determining the social resources available to the elderly (Gubrium, 1973; Lawton, 1981). The data shown in the first column of table 2-3 indicate that most older persons (85 percent of males and 59 percent of females) live with others and, at least theoretically, have "built-in" companions and social resources. The overall distribution of living arrangements, however, masks important age- and lifecycle-related changes in household composition. The proportion of elderly living alone increases with age, as does the relative number of older persons sharing the household of another. These trends need to be viewed within the context of the increased risks of both widowhood and chronic disability at the extremes of old age.

In and of themselves, different types of living arrangements convey no inherent meaning. Rather, their importance derives from the degree of "fit" they provide between the needs and preferences of the older individual and the supportive capacity of the household (Carp, 1977). An independent older woman with financial resources and an active social life outside the household would probably find sharing the home of an adult daughter a stifling situation. In contrast, living alone is likely to be intolerable for another older woman with severe self-care incapacities.

There is fairly strong evidence that, for the most part, individuals sort themselves out into living arrangements consistent with the degree of social supports they require from their immediate environment. Wilson (1977), Soldo (1978), Lawton (1981), and others have all shown that those with activities limitations are overrepresented in multiperson households, particularly households shared with relatives other than spouses. Branch (1980), for example, has shown that those who live with adult children are the most likely to have a need of assistance in four areas of daily life: transportation, social activities, personal care, and food preparation. Data such as these support the inter-

TABLE 2-3. Percentage Distribution of Living Arrangements among Noninstitutionalized Individuals 65 Years of Age or Older (by Age and Sex), 1980

Sex and living arrangements	Total 65+	65–74	75+
Male			
Alone	14.7	11.6	20.9
With spouse	71.8	76.0	63.3
With other relatives	11.1	9.8	13.7
With nonrelatives	2.4	2.5	2.1
Total[1]	100.0	100.0	100.0
	(9,784)	(6,550)	(3,234)
Female			
Alone	40.8	35.5	49.3
With spouse	38.0	48.1	22.1
With other relatives	19.0	14.5	26.0
With nonrelatives	2.1	1.8	2.6
Total[1]	100.0	100.0	100.0
	(13,961)	(8,550)	(5,411)

SOURCE: *U.S. Bureau of the Census, 1980, Table 6.*

1. Base numbers in parentheses in thousands

pretation that "the luxury of living alone is reserved for those who can meet the physical demands of independence" (Tissue and McCoy, 1981).

Because income and functional capacity are positively correlated, however, considerable research of late has focused on whether shared housing is primarily a response to economic need, per se, or to assistance needs. Research supporting an economic motivation for shared households would suggest that the personal needs and environmental supports are not congruent for some unknown number of older persons who live in poverty.

Economic theories of family formation can indeed mount strong arguments explaining multi-person households in terms of efficiency and economies of scale (Becker, 1976). Cross-sectional (Soldo, Sharma, and Campbell, 1984) and longitudinal (Newman, 1976; Tissue and McCoy, 1981) data analyses consistently show, however, that the role of economic constraints is secondary to that of the need for some type of supportive service in accounting for multiperson households. Tissue and McCoy's (1981) findings based on a two-wave panel study of older welfare recipients are particularly significant because they show that even in "a population which by any objective standards is dreadfully poor," it is the sickest who most often reside in shared households. It is of interest to the focus of this chapter to note also that, in this study, housing quality (defined in terms of structural characteristics and the availability of basic amenities) failed to emerge as a significant predictor of changes in living arrangements for all but one type of transition.[3]

Additional, though indirect, support for person–environment explanations of living arrangements is found in the work of McCoy (1979) who reports significantly higher mortality rates for the elderly who lived with others at time of death. He interprets this as indicating that "common circumstances such as declining health and loss of function were antecedents to the living arrangements" observed at the time of death. The rapidly accumulating literature on caregiving also shows that shared living arrangements not only are frequently used as a compensating resource but also that such arrangements are effective in buffering the chronically disabled elderly from institutionalization (Brody, Poulshock, and Masciocchi, 1978).

In spite of the evidence cited above, simply relating living arrangements to health status is an imperfect translation of the person–environment interaction model. The social resources and occupied environment of a disabled older person do not necessarily stop at the doorstep of the household. Recent studies of caregiving in New York City, for example, demonstrate that the informal support network of family and friends outside the household is frequently mobilized on behalf of an older disabled person (Cantor, 1982; Horowitz and Dobrof, 1982). The efforts of care providers who live in another household may in part explain how one in ten older persons who live alone can sustain their independent households in spite of severe activity limitations. Because the environment is recognized as being multidimensional, consideration also must be given to the ways in which other aspects of the environment, particularly characteristics of the built environment, can be modified to accommodate disability in lieu of a supportive social environment.

Housing Quality and Household Types

Although our existing research does not justify causal speculation, it is clear that housing quality varies systematically with type of living arrangement. Regardless of how housing quality is measured, prior studies show that older married couples are better housed than the aged who live alone or reside in other types of elderly-headed households (Lawton, 1981). Married couples are more likely to own their homes, which on average, have fewer and less severe structural deficiencies (Struyk and Soldo, 1980). The units occupied by couples also tend to have more efficient heating and cooling systems and better repair records. In 1980, nearly one-third of home-owning couples had repairs made during the previous year. In contrast, repair activity was reported by only one in four older single-person households (U.S. Senate, 1982). These same living arrangement differentials in housing quality exist among the elderly who rent their homes or apartments, although rental units are usually in poorer condition than owner-occupied ones (Struyk, 1977).

The vast majority of older persons (approximately 70 percent) in all types of households own their homes, but older couples are more likely to own homes of substantial value with paid-up mortgages than unmarried elders are. Based on the value of the owned home and the lack of indebtedness, Welfeld and Struyk (1978) estimate that 54 percent of all home-owning couples have "strong asset positions"—proportionately more than any other types of household headed by an older person. This finding is not surprising since the elderly with intact marriages are overly concentrated in the younger age groups, where many are still employed or only recently retired. Their favorable financial status, in combination with the social advantages that marriage usually provides (Hess and Soldo, in press), suggest that older couples command more resources to cope with the vicissitudes of health. It is ironic that individuals least likely to place special demands on their environments tend to occupy households that are unusually well situated to accommodate such needs.

By the same yardsticks of tenure, housing quality, and financial status, the elderly who live alone often are "environmentally impoverished." The comparatively high incidence of housing defects among older, single-person households is associated with high rates of rental occupancy and constrained budgets. Although poverty rates are higher for older women living alone, their housing is in better condition than that of single-person households headed by older men (Soldo, 1978; Welfeld and Struyk, 1978). Lawton (1981) speculates that older women, even though keeping house just for themselves, are more motivated than their male counterparts to maintain their residences and also are more likely to receive help from others with routine maintenance chores.

Compared with the elderly who live alone,

those who share another's household are poorer individually but are much less likely to live in poverty-level households or to confront the problems of inadequate housing. Older persons who live with nonelderly relatives are well-housed, usually in newer units with fewer structural defects. These shared households also are more likely to provide access to "extras," such as televisions and washing machines (Tissue and McCoy, 1981). It seems clear that elderly who live with others exchange independence and autonomy for enriched physical and social environments.

Reciprocity between Health and Housing

The person-environment interaction between housing quality and health of the occupants is difficult to disentangle for several reasons. Income obscures the relationship because it is negatively associated with both poor housing and disability. Standardized measures of housing quality also are inadequate for assessing the degree of fit between the "supportive quality" of the housing unit and the needs of older occupants. In a report of one comprehensive home-care program, for example, the housing of 29 percent of the clients was judged to be substandard, but nearly double that number lived in units incongruent with their needs (Brickner, 1978). This latter group included older amputees who lived in multistory buildings lacking elevator service and wheelchair-bound clients who could not navigate their chairs into the bathroom. But most important, the relationship between housing quality and health-related needs nearly defies study because of reciprocal causality (Windley and Scheidt, 1980).

In spite of the recognized dialectic nature of the relationship, very little research has examined the health effect on housing. The few studies that have adopted this perspective focus on the extent to which disability causes a household to reallocate personal or financial resources away from repair and maintenance activities (Welfeld and Struyk, 1978; Struyk and Soldo, 1980). Consequent to disability, the probability of older homeowners making or contracting for repairs falls sharply although the likelihood of repairs made by family or neighbors increases somewhat. This increase, however, does not appear to offset the decline in self- or purchased repairs. The housing of elderly who live alone is particularly vulnerable to neglect as the oftentimes barely adequate household income is insufficient to sustain maintenance activity in the face of increased health-care costs.

Considerably more research has examined the effects of housing on health. The quality of the built environment has obvious public health connotations regardless of the age or initial health of the occupants (Richter et al., 1973). Improperly heated units and those lacking adequate humidification increase the risk of respiratory infections for occupants of all ages. Similarly, falls and injuries are more likely to occur on staircases that are poorly lit or lack stair rails.

Most prior studies in the aging literature, however, have focused on the potential prosthetic effect of the immediate housing environment on functionally limited elderly. Our knowledge of this potential is informed primarily by the study of "special populations" of elderly who relocate to age-segregated buildings, service-saturated demonstration projects, or wealthy retirement communities. None of these groups are representative of the total population of older community residents for, in each case, the participants were "self-selected" in some way (Carp, 1976b).

As biased as prior study samples are, they seem to demonstrate positive effects on global or subjective markers of well-being resulting from improved or more congruent housing situations. Although one would expect elderly who are rehoused into more supportive environments than those previously occupied to show improved functional capacity, this is not always the case. In comparing several groups of rehoused elderly with controls in the community, Lawton (1980a) notes a relative and substantial decline in functional capacity among the elderly who moved into five different housing projects. It may well be that the statistical controls used did not equate the vulnerability of the rehoused and comparison groups. Since factors which usually have a positive relationship with

health (morale, social behavior, and leisure-time activity) were negatively correlated with functional capacity in the twelve-month followup assessments, Lawton speculates that the net effect of improved housing environments may be "to buffer the individual against a decline in health, so that attitudes, affect, and even some forms of social involvement, could remain at relatively favorable levels" (Lawton, 1980a, p. 14).

In part because of the nonrepresentativeness of previously studied groups, and related problems of measurement and research design (Lawton, 1977), we still know "very little about the impact of the housing and living environments upon the well-being of the majority of the old" (Carp, 1976b, p. 255). Only recently, Parr (1980) has argued for redirecting research attention back to the fundamental questions of how different types of people actually function in given settings and why they function as they do.

Three Variable Relationships

The network of relationships among health, housing quality, and household type does not yield easily or neatly to analysis. Because the relationships are inherently dynamic, each factor simultaneously affects others and is affected by them. Even though mathematical models can accommodate the assumption of mutual causality, the theoretical linkages among the different dimensions of the environment are not clearly specified as yet (Lawton, 1977). Closing this gap requires deducing from the original theoretical framework propositions which relate the physical aspect of the environment to its other components. One promising avenue for such research concerns the substitutability of different strategies of environmental compensation. Program development, for example, would benefit from research that determines if, at various levels of disability, modification of the occupied physical environment is interchangeable with the introduction of services in terms of outcome and cost.

Informal caregiving is one of the few arenas where three variable relationships are currently being studied in "normal" household settings. In addition to other "enabling factors" (Horowitz, 1982), the housing of *both* the older impaired person and his or her pool of potential caregivers influences the probability of informal service provision and the style of caregiving adopted. Those whose homes are large enough to share with a chronically disabled relative are much more likely to become "providers" of care, while those who maintain separate residences are more likely to assume the role of care "manager" (Archbold, 1982). It also is important to note that the level of need, per se, does not solely determine style of caregiving.

Each style of caregiving is associated with a different constellation of stressors and mediating factors. Care-givers who live apart from their dependent older relatives may have an oasis of peace and quiet in their own homes, but they are, in effect, sustaining two separate households. In such situations, care-givers often are responsible for repair activity at the relative's home as well as personal care tasks (Cantor, 1982).

Noelker (1982) has recently reported on an innovative study of the environmental impediments to caregiving in households shared by the care provider and his or her relative. Both spatial barriers, such as inadequate number of bedrooms, and navigational barriers, such as interior stairs, were found to be prevalent. Spatial barriers were most highly correlated with tension among household members, perhaps stemming from a lack of privacy, while navigational barriers were positively correlated with the number of personal care tasks requiring assistance and the care provider's perception of difficulty in providing such care. This study clearly suggests that aspects of the built environment interact with social aspects in determining the duration and quality of caregiving.

Although most home care programs emphasize service delivery, modifications of the built environments in which care is provided also may be effective in preventing or postponing institutional placements. Because housing seems to affect the style, intensity, durability, and tolerability of caregiving, it is fair to conclude that in this context, housing characteristics function as important intermediate variables. The size, condition, and location of the involved households all indirectly affect the degree of fit between the elderly's need and the compensating social resources available.

Conclusion

This chapter has attempted to describe our current understanding of the intricate relationships that exist among housing characteristics, household type, and disability. To the extent possible, attention has been focused on how the elderly in typical community settings relate to and depend on their environments in adapting to reduced capacity in old age.

Even to the casual reader, it should be obvious that relationships among any two of these components are easier to handle—empirically as well as theoretically—than the complexity of the full model. Further progress in testing three variable relationships within the framework of person–environment models depends on our ability to determine which aspects of the environment are most relevant to the disabled (Lawton, 1977) and to develop specific hypotheses that relate characteristics of the environment to behavior (Parr, 1980). Recent and noteworthy progress on these points has been made by Windley and Scheidt (1980).

Even in the absence of what is, by any reasonable standard, only a preliminary knowledge base, existing research offers some policy guidance. Modifying the occupied environment is a valuable, though often overlooked, part of the program planner's repertoire. In some situations, the amortized costs of such modifications may be less expensive than prolonged service delivery and also may support continued residence in homes or long-standing occupancy. Whether physical and social compensation approaches are interchangeable remains to be seen, but demographic changes, including shifts in the age structure and increased labor force participation of women (the traditional caregivers to the elderly), strongly suggest that alternatives to personnel-intensive strategies be explored.

Notes

1. Altering the impact of the environment on capacity by modifying the immediate physical setting is but one of three general approaches available for minimizing the functional consequences of chronic disease. Alternatively, the innate capacity of the individual can be elevated (e.g., by hip replacement surgery) or supportive services or mechanical aids can be introduced. The three approaches, of course, are not mutually exclusive in practice and often are used in combination, particularly the compensation strategies. The prosthetic service approach dominates publicly financed initiatives designed to assist frail elderly in the community, although Yeates (1979) argues that the environment is potentially easier to manipulate than other factors that influence quality of life of the elderly.

2. Housework is assumed to be the major activity for retired persons. If retired persons report that their major activity is not housework, they are asked if their health now keeps them from working or would limit the amount or kind of work done. Older persons chronically limited but not in major activity are restricted in other activities such as church involvement, hobbies, civic projects, sports, or games (U.S. NCHS, 1981).

3. Deteriorating housing quality did increase the chances that someone other than the older person would move out during the interval of observation (Tissue and McCoy, 1981).

References

Archbold, P. G. 1982. "An Analysis of Parent-Caring by Women." *Home Health Care Services Quarterly* 3:5–26.

Becker, G. 1976. *The Economic Approach to Human Behavior.* Chicago: Univ. of Chicago.

Besdine, R. W. 1981. "Health and Illness Behavior in the Elderly." In *Health and Behavior: A Research Agenda,* Interim Report No. 5. Ed. D. L. Parron, et al. Washington, DC: National Academy.

Branch, L. G. 1980. "Functional Abilities of the Elderly: An Update on the Massachusetts Health Care Panel Study." In *Epidemiology of Aging.* Ed. S. G. Haynes and M. Feinleib. NIH Publication No. 80-969. Washington, DC: U.S. Government Printing Office.

Brickner, P. W. 1978. *Home Health Care for the Aged.* New York: Appleton-Century-Crofts.

Brody, E. M. 1978. "Community Housing for the Elderly: The Program, the People, the Decision-Making Process, and the Research." *Gerontologist* 18:121–28.

Brody, S. J., W. Poulshock, and C. F. Masciocchi. 1978. "The Family Caring Unit: A Major Consideration in the Long Term Support System." *Gerontologist* 18:556–61.

Cantor, M. H. 1979. "Neighbors and Friends: An Overlooked Resource in the Informal Support System." *Research on Aging* 1:434–63.

———. 1982. "Families and Social Networks as Resources in Long-Term Care: Issues of Stress and Strain." Paper presented at the Annual Meeting of the Gerontological Society of America, Boston, November.

Carp, F. M. 1976a. "Urban Life Style and Life Cycle Factors." In *Community Planning for an Aging Society.* Ed. M. P. Lawton, R. J. Newcomer, and T. O. Byerts. Stroudsburg, PA: Dowden, Hutchinson and Ross.

———. 1976b. "Housing and Living Environment of Older People." In *Handbook of Aging and the Social Sciences.* Ed. R. H. Binstock and E. Shanas. New York: Van Nostrand Reinhold.

———. 1977. "The Concept and Role of Congregate Housing for Older People." In *Congregate Housing for Older People: An Urgent Need, a Growing Demand.* Ed. W. T. Donahue, M. M. Thompson, and D. J. Curren. Washington, DC: U.S. Government Printing Office.

Costa, F. J., and M. Sweet. 1976. "Barrier-Free Environments for Older People." *Gerontologist* 16:404–09.

Graney, M. 1973. "The Aged and Their Environment: The Study of Intervening Variables." In *Later Life: Communities and Environmental Policy.* Ed. J. F. Gubrium. Springfield, IL: Charles C. Thomas.

Gubrium, J. F. 1973. *The Myth of the Golden Years: A Socio-Environmental Theory of Aging.* Springfield, IL: Charles C. Thomas.

Hess, B. B., and B. J. Soldo. 1985. "Husband and Wife Networks." In *Social Support Networks and the Care of the Elderly: Theory, Research, Practices, and Policy.* Ed. W. J. Sauer and R. F. Coward. New York: Springer.

Horowitz, A. 1982. "Predictors of Caregiving Involvement Among Adult Children of Frail Elderly." Paper presented at the Annual Meeting of the Gerontological Society of America, Boston, November.

Horowitz, A., and R. Dobrof. 1982. "The Role of Families in Providing Long-Term Care to the Frail and Chronically Ill Elderly Living in the Community." Final report. Washington, DC: U.S. Health Care Financing Administration.

Kahana, E. 1974. "Matching Environments to Needs of the Aged: A Conceptual Model." In *Later Life: Communities and Environmental Policy.* Ed. J. F. Gubrium. Springfield, IL: Charles C. Thomas.

Lawton, M. P. 1977. "The Impact of the Environment on Aging and Behavior." In *Handbook of the Psychology of Aging.* Ed. J. E. Birren and K. W. Schaie. New York: Van Nostrand Reinhold.

———. 1978. "The Housing Problems of Community-Resident Elderly." *Occasional Papers in Housing and Community Affairs.* No. 1. Washington, DC: U.S. Department of Housing and Urban Development.

———. 1980a. *Social and Medical Services in Housing for the Aged.* Washington, DC: U.S. Government Printing Office.

———. 1980b. *Environment and Aging.* Monterey, CA: Brooks/Cole.

———. 1981. "An Ecological View of Living Arrangements." *Gerontologist* 21:59–66.

McCoy, J. L. 1979. "Antecedents of Morality Among the Old-Age Assistance Population." *Social Security Bulletin* 42:3–15.

Nahemow, L., and M. P. Lawton. 1973. "Toward an Ecological Theory of Adaptation and Aging." In *Environmental Design Research* Vol. 1. Ed. W. Prieser. Stroudsburg, PA: Dowden, Hutchinson and Ross.

Newman, S. J. 1976. "Housing Adjustments of the Disabled Elderly." *Gerontologist* 16:312–17.

Noelker, L. S. 1982. "Environmental Barriers to Family Caregiving." Paper presented at the Annual Meeting of the Gerontological Society of America, Boston, November.

Parr, J. 1980. "The Interactions of Persons and Living Environments." In *Aging in the 1980's: Psychological Issues.* Ed. L. W. Poon. Washington, DC: American Psychological Association.

Richter, E. D., S. Jackson, S. Peeples, C. Wood, and R. Volante. 1973. "Housing and Health—A New Approach." *American Journal of Public Health* 63:878–83.

Soldo, B. J. 1978. "The Housing and Characteristics of Independent Elderly: A Demographic Overview." *Occasional Papers in Housing and Community Affairs.* No. 1. Washington, DC: U.S. Department of Housing and Urban Development.

———. 1980. "America's Elderly in the 1980's." *Population Bulletin* 35:1–47.

Soldo, B. J., S. Sharma, and R. T. Campbell. 1984. "Determinants of the Community Living Arrangements of Older Unmarried Women." *Journal of Gerontology* 39:492–98.

Struyk, R. J. 1977. "The Housing Situation of Elderly Americans." *Gerontologist* 17:130–39.

Struyk, R. J. and B. J. Soldo. 1980. *Improving the Elderly's Housing.* Cambridge, MA: Ballinger.

Tissue, T. and J. L. McCoy. 1981. "Income and Living Arrangements Among Poor Aged Singles." *Social Security Bulletin* 44:3–13.

U.S. Bureau of the Census. 1981. "Marital Status and Living Arrangements: March 1980." *Current Population Reports,* Series P-20, No. 365. Washington, DC: U.S. Government Printing Office.

U.S. National Center for Health Statistics (NCHS). 1972. "Use of Special Aids: U.S. 1969." Data from the National Health Survey. *Vital and Health Statistics,* Series 10, No. 78. Washington, DC: U.S. Government Printing Office.

———. 1979a. "Current Estimates from the National Health Interview Survey: U.S., 1979." *Vital and Health Statistics,* Series 10, No. 136, Table 22. Washington, DC: U.S. Government Printing Office.

———. 1979b. "Health Characteristics of Persons with Chronic Activity Limitation: U.S., 1979." *Vital and Health Statistics,* Series 10, No. 137, Table 1. Washington, DC: U.S. Government Printing Office.

———. 1981. "Health Characteristics of Persons with Chronic Activity Limitations: U.S. 1979." Data from the National Health Survey. *Vital and Health Statistics,* Series 10, No. 137. Washington, DC: U.S. Government Printing Office.

U.S. Senate. 1982. Special Committee on Aging. "The Aging Population: Growth and Diversity." In *Developments in Aging: 1981.* Vol. 1. Washington, DC: U.S. Government Printing Office.

Welfeld, I. H., and R. S. Struyk. 1978. *Housing Options for the Elderly.* Washington, DC: Center for Urban Public Policy Analysis, American University.

Wilson, R. W. 1977. The Population to be Served. In *Congregate Housing for Older People: An Urgent*

Need, a Growing Demand. Ed. W. T. Donahue, M. M. Thompson and D. J. Curren. Washington, DC: U.S. Government Printing Office.

Windley, P. G., and R. J. Scheidt. 1980. "Person-Environment Dialectics: Implications for Competent Functioning in Old Age." In *Aging in the 1980's:* *Psychological Issues.* Ed. L. W. Poon. Washington, DC: American Psychological Association.

Yeates, M. 1979. "The Need for Environmental Perspectives on Issues Facing Older People." In *Location and Environment of Elderly Population.* Ed. S. M. Golant. Washington, DC: Winston.

CHAPTER 3 Demographic Influences on the Future Housing Demand of the Elderly

Sandra J. Newman

A growing population is one force behind an expanding demand for housing. But housing demand, like the demand for other goods and services, also grows or shrinks in response to the size and rate of change of the population in specific age ranges (Morrison, 1978). Further, the type of housing demanded shifts in response to changes in the age structure of the population (Morrison, 1976).

In the early part of the century, the growth rate of the population sixty-five and older began to surpass the U.S. population growth rate; during the decade of the seventies, for example, this differential was nearly twenty percentage points (about 11 percent for the U.S. versus 28 percent for the elderly). The unevenness in the growth of different age groups of the population is also likely to be sustained: the prospects for the U.S. through nearly the next half century indicate that the elderly population will grow faster than the total population, with particularly rapid growth among the very old (U.S. Bureau of the Census, 1975; Siegel, 1980a).

An understanding of how the growth of the elderly population is likely to shape housing demand in the future requires an examination of the general growth trends and characteristics of elderly-headed households and their implications for aggregate housing demand. The general increase and attributes of elderly-headed households will create important challenges for housing policy.

Trends in Elderly Household Growth

A first step in the process of understanding the future demand for housing by the elderly is to estimate the number of housing consumers who are sixty-five years or older and the pattern of change in their housing choices over time. While population growth or decline is the underlying source of increases or decreases in housing demand, growth rates in the demand for housing are more appropriately considered in terms of the number of households, the consuming unit.

Data from the last four decennial censuses, together with census projections through 1995, indicate what the rate of formation of elderly-headed households has been in the past and is expected to be in the future. Table 3-1 shows past and projected trends in the average annual growth in numbers of elderly- and nonelderly-headed households. The household projections are based on extrapolations of changes in marital status and household status observed over the 1964 to 1978 period (U.S. Bureau of the Census, 1979a).[1]

These data highlight three main points. First, the growth in the number of elderly-headed households has persisted over the last three decades and is projected to continue until approximately the turn of the century. Thus, for example, in 1990, there will be more than three times as many elderly-headed households as there were in

TABLE 3-1. Number and Percent Average Annual Growth in Number of Households, by Age of Household Head

Time Period	Elderly Head of Household[1] (Number of Households)[2]	Nonelderly Head of Household (Number of Households)
1950/1960	4.6% (6.4 mil.)	1.7% (37.0 mil.)
1960/1970	3.1 (9.4 mil.)	1.7 (43.2 mil.)
1970/1980	3.2 (12.3 mil.)	2.7 (50.6 mil.)
(1980/1990)[3]	2.4 (16.2 mil.)	1.9 (64.5 mil.)
(1990/1995)	1.5 (20.0 mil.)	1.5 (76.7 mil.)
(1995)	(21.5 mil.)	(82.4 mil.)

SOURCE: *U.S. Bureau of the Census, 1974; 1979a.*

1. 65 years of age or older.
2. Number shown is for first year of the decade.
3. Parenthesis indicates projected period.

1950—20 million compared with 6.4 million. Between 1980 and 1995, 6 million additional elderly-headed households will be formed. This figure represents the demographically induced incremental demand for housing by the elderly.[2] Second, the ratio of elderly-headed households to households headed by the nonelderly has grown over time. But third, and at least of equal importance, the rate of growth in elderly households has varied over time: it has slowed since 1950 and is projected to slow down even further between the present and roughly the turn of the century. For example, the average annual rate of increase in elderly-headed households during the 1950s was roughly 4.6 percent. By the first half of the 1990s, it is expected to fall to about 1.5 percent. To a large extent, these fluctuations can be explained by variations in past fertility rates; someone who will be sixty-five in 1995 was born in 1930, in the midst of the Great Depression, when the number of births reached an unprecedented low level.

Taken together, these figures raise two concerns. First, it is clear that elderly-headed households are, and will continue to be, a substantial share of all housing consumers. But counterbalancing this absolute size and growth are the variations in the rate of household growth among the elderly. These fluctuations in past and projected rates of household formations "clearly established the fallacy of assuming that the numbers and proportions of elderly households will continue to grow at past rates or even an attenuated version of these rates" (Siegel, 1980a).

As table 3-1 indicates, these variations over the forty-five-year period between 1950 and 1995 are quite distinct. But they are not nearly as dramatic for projecting housing demand as the fluctuations that will occur during the early and middle part of the twenty-first century. At that time, changing demographics will reflect first, the aging of the baby boom generation, and second, the aging of the baby bust generation.

Thus, one major challenge to housing policy, in terms of aggregate housing demand among the elderly, is to meet the varying levels of demand posed by each cohort of elderly households but to avoid the problems of providing insufficient capacity, on the one hand, or excess capacity, on the other. A vivid example of this type of problem is provided by the extensive school building programs in the 1950s and 1960s to meet the demands of the baby boom that then turned into many vacant elementary schools in the 1970s in response to the baby bust.

Housing Demand and the Characteristics of Elderly-Headed Households

While the total future demand for housing by the elderly will be heavily influenced by the number and rate of formation of elderly-headed households, the demand for different types of housing is more closely related to the characteristics of those households (Pitkin and Masnick, 1980). Estimates by the Census Bureau and others indicate that between 1980 and 1995, 6 million net additional elderly-headed households will be formed, with more of this growth occurring in the 1980s than the 1990s. Four attributes of elderly households promise to have significant effects on the nature of their housing consumption: (1) mortality differences between the sexes, (2) growth in the numbers of older elderly, (3) housing tenure choices, and (4) geographic distribution.

While projections are always characterized by some uncertainty because of unpredictable, "chance" events, projections of characteristics of the elderly to the turn of the century are relatively safe because they concern individuals who are currently at least fifty years of age. Thus, magnitudes depend mainly on relatively stable mortality rates rather than the more imponderable shifts in fertility. In addition, housing consumption patterns established at earlier ages appear to have a strong influence on these patterns at older ages. By the age of fifty, the patterns adopted by each cohort are generally quite clear.

Mortality Differences between Men and Women

Men and women have different mortality rates and life expectancy rates. In 1978, a man at birth was expected to live 69.5 years; a woman's life expectancy was 77.2 years. Of white men and women who were 65 years of age in 1975, women were expected to live 4.4 years longer than men (U.S. Bureau of the Census, 1981a). Another way to visualize the differences in life expectancies is by examining ratios of women to men at different ages. In the late 1970s, there were roughly five women for every four men aged sixty-five to sixty-nine years but twice as many women as men in the eighty-five years and over age group (U.S. House, 1978).

One result of this difference has been the steady increase in the percentage of women among older persons and, of particular importance to housing demand, the number of households headed by elderly women. Over this decade and the next, the annual rate of increase in households headed by elderly women is projected to be higher than the rate for all elderly-headed households. Thus, by 1995, nearly half of all elderly-headed households are expected to be headed by women. This 9 or 10 million households headed by elderly women is roughly twice the number that existed in 1970 (U.S. Bureau of the Census, 1974).

Demographers have pointed to two developments that are likely to ensue from the greater life expectancy of women. First, both the incidence and duration of widowhood will rise. Second, since women who are about to enter old age were in their prime child-bearing years during the Depression when fertility rates were very low, they have fewer children and higher rates of childlessness (Morrison, 1978).

Each of these factors—the increasing percentage of females among older people, the high rate and duration of widowhood, and the relatively high incidence of childlessness among women soon to enter old age—implies an increase in the proportion of women living alone. It also seems likely that living alone will become more economically feasible because of the improved health, retirement, and pension benefits that have increasingly become available to the elderly over the last several decades (Morrison, 1976; U.S. Bureau of the Census, 1974).

Growth of the Older Elderly

Of the roughly 7-million-person increase in the elderly population projected for the 1980s and 1990s, almost three-fourths is expected to be among those seventy-five years of age and older (U.S. House, 1978). As shown in figure 3-1, over this decade and the next, increases in the age groups seventy-five to eighty-four and eighty-five years or older are higher than the increase for the sixty-five-to-seventy-four age group. By the turn of the century, in fact, there will actually be a decline in the number of sixty-five-to-seventy-four-year-olds—the Depression cohort. Thus, in the decade of the 1990s, the number of persons eighty-five years or older will grow by nearly 30 percent; those seventy-five to eighty-four years will increase by about 16 percent; but those sixty-five to seventy-four years will decline by roughly 3 percent (U.S. Bureau of the Census, 1976).

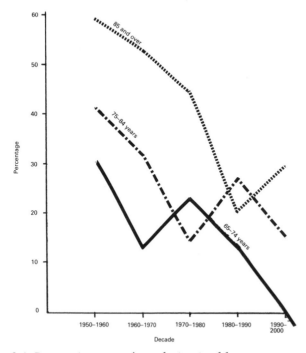

3-1. Percent increase of population in older age groups, 1950–2000. From U.S. Bureau of the Census, 1976.

It is also among the very old that the greatest increase in households will occur between 1980 and approximately the turn of the century. During the 1980s, the average annual rate of growth in the numbers of households headed by persons sixty-five to seventy-four years old is expected to be roughly 1.75 percent; households headed by older persons are expected to grow at nearly twice that rate. During the 1990s, the ratio of growth rates for younger-versus-older households is closer to 1:3 (U.S. Bureau of the Census, 1979a).

The significance of these projections for estimating future housing demand is that it is among this group of older households that special housing needs are concentrated. A large proportion of very elderly households is headed by women who own their own homes, live alone, report some physical ailments, and experience disproportionate rates of poverty (U.S. Bureau of the Census, 1979b). Thus, within the context of U.S. housing policy, there will be more old people who require shelter that meets more than an "average" or "usual" set of shelter needs. Little is known about what older persons do when they become aware of themselves as unable to maintain their dwellings or care for their health needs. Nor is there information about what factors affect how promptly they seek assistance, what types of assistance they seek, and what types they find most effective, or what they find available.

Housing Tenure

A third characteristic that will shape housing consumption behavior of elderly households in the future is tenure choice; that is, whether the householder owns or rents the dwelling. At present, more than 75 percent of the 17 million elderly-headed households in the nation own rather than rent their dwellings (U.S. Bureau of the Census, 1981a). Although this fraction is somewhat higher for white households than for black and hispanic households (that is, 77 percent versus 61 percent and 59 percent, respectively), in all cases a clear majority owns rather than rents.

The relationship between age and tenure is clear

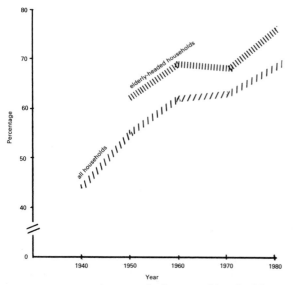

3-2. Home ownership trends, by age of head of household, 1940–1980. (Ownership rates for elderly-headed households, 1940, not available.) From U.S. Bureau of the Census, 1943, 1953a, 1953b, 1962, 1963, 1972, 1973, 1982.

evidence that different types of households display distinct housing market behavior. Empirical research documents the importance of age in determining whether a householder owns or rents.[3] Furthermore, the greater probability of homeownership at older ages has been remarkably stable over the past four decades, even in the face of sizable variations in the mix of housing (single family, apartment, mobile home) produced during this time period (Marcin, 1978). As shown in figure 3-2, although the trend toward increasing proportions of homeowners over time has been similar for all households and for elderly-headed households, the *level* has been consistently higher among older households.

In addition to the increasing trend toward homeownership and the persistently higher levels of homeownership among the elderly relative to all households, a third important attribute of housing tenure is its consistently strong age effect for different types of households: husband-wife

families, households headed by men, and households headed by women all exhibit higher rates of homeownership among elderly-headed households than among households in general (U.S. Bureau of the Census, 1982).

The importance of life-cycle variations in housing consumption patterns, as measured in part by age and tenure, was the central theme of the only set of projections to be found in the literature with estimates for different age groups and dwelling unit characteristics (Pitkin and Masnick, 1980; 1981).[4] In this work, Pitkin and Masnick estimated future housing consumption rates of five-year birth cohorts by projecting the housing choices made by each cohort at an earlier age. Thus, the researchers linked the housing consumption of someone who will be sixty years of age five years from now, for example, to that person's current housing consumption at age fifty-five; thus, the consumption of a cohort at a particular age is associated with its own consumption at earlier ages. This is distinct from age-based projections that estimate the consumption of different subgroups of the population at the same age.

Although Pitkin and Masnick were not specifically concerned with "age effects," or the process by which growing older itself influences housing choices, their results indicate that aging, per se, has an influence. They found that different birth cohorts exhibit different levels of consumption, but that the consumption paths or shapes are similar. One interpretation of this finding is that the cohort effect establishes the level while the age effect influences the shape of the path. Exceptions to these consistent patterns are attributed to a third influence, "period effects": variations in the environment that influence housing choices (for example, the condition of the national economy, the supply of building trades' labor) but are unrelated to life-cycle transitions.

Several combinations of assumptions about household formation and housing choices of total future housing consumption were tested.[5] For the household component of the projections, these ranged from low to high growth in the number of households based on a variety of marriage, divorce, and fertility rates. The housing consumption element is driven by the projected changes in the size and age structure of the population. The main variations in the housing consumption element are the timing of increases or decreases in the choice of particular types of housing units and the level of growth projected for these classes of dwellings.

Figure 3-3 indicates the main components of the Pitkin and Masnick projections and the relationships among them. Housing Consumption, Series A, reflects extrapolations of the estimated actual consumption rates that occurred in 1975. These are derived from following the birth cohort trends observed between 1970 and 1975, while Housing Consumption, Series B, extrapolates from the 1975 consumption rates that are derived from birth cohort trends observed in the 1960–70 decade (Pitkin and Masnick, 1981). Each of these consumption series is then applied to a set of assumptions about future trends in marriage, fertility, mortality, and migration. The fertility level or number of lifetime births for Census Series B, for example, is assumed to be 2.1; for the JC series it is assumed to be 1.8. Mortality assumptions of the census series set the ultimate level of survivorship in the year 2050, while the JC series assumes that survivorship levels are reached in 2025. The marital status assumptions for the census series set the fraction of separated, divorced, and spouse-absent categories at a lower level than the JC series.[6]

We would expect that differences in the characteristics of the inputs—the consumption rates and the household projections—would yield substantially different housing consumption projections. For example, the high rates of homeownership during the early 1970s should result in higher rates of homeownership for the Series A projections, since those are based on 1970–75 consumption rates. Such differences in outputs do, in fact, occur, as shown in table 3-2. For the elderly, as for all households, ownership rates are higher under the two Series A housing consumption projections than under the Series B assumptions. The more general message that the ownership projections convey is that ownership rates are expected to increase between 1980 and 1995. Recent aggregate housing demand projections produce similar findings (Marcin, 1977; Weicher, Yap, and Jones, 1982).

Two features of projections of trends in the attributes of housing consumption by the elderly stand out. First, regardless of the projection series, homeownership is expected to increase among the elderly and, in some cases, substantially so. Moreover, in all cases, elderly homeownership rates are higher than ownership rates for all households and

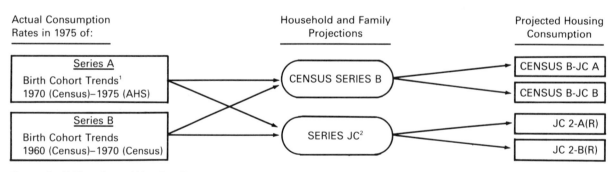

Notes: 1. AHS = Annual Housing Survey
       2. This series assumes lower marriage and fertility rates and higher divorce rates than Series B.

3-3. Pitkin and Masnick cohort-based housing consumption projections. From Pitkin and Masnick, 1981.

TABLE 3-2. Pitkin and Masnick Projected Trends in Ownership and Single-Family Ownership Rates, for Elderly-Headed and All Households

	Census B-JCA		Census B-JCB		JC 2-A (R)		JC 2-B (R)	
	Elderly-Headed Households	All Households	Elderly-Headed Households	All Households	Elderly-Headed Households	All Households	Elderly-Headed Households	All Households
Ownership Rate								
1980	73%	66%	71%	63%	72%	65%	70%	64%
1995	81	69	74	63	80	68	73	65
Single-Family Homeownership Rate								
1980	62	57	60	55	61	56	60	55
1995	67	58	61	53	66	56	60	55
Number of Households (in millions)								
1980	16	80	16	80	16	81	16	80
1995	22	104	22	104	22	105	22	99

SOURCE: Pitkin and Masnick, 1981.

either maintain or increase their lead over the rates for the population. According to the two Series A projections in table 3-2, roughly 80 percent of elderly-headed households would own their homes by 1995. A simplified explanation of this rate that captures the essence of the cohort procedure is that the increase in the rate of homeownership among elderly-headed households over the next decade and a half will reflect the fact that nearly 82 percent of currently middle-aged householders own their homes (U.S. Bureau of the Census, 1981b).

A second important aspect of these estimates is the projected increase in the fraction of elderly households who own single-family homes. While the majority of elderly households began this decade owning single-family homes, this high rate is projected to grow still higher in the future.[7]

The high incidence of single-family homeownership and its growth over time have both positive and negative implications. Homeowners have an accumulated stock of assets that they can draw on if necessary while renters do not. But homeownership also represents the often substantial burdens of upkeep, maintenance, and housing costs for elderly owners (Newman, Zais, and Struyk, 1984).

Geographic Distribution

The uneven distribution of elderly households across the nation and the expected persistence of this unevenness in the future make up a fourth factor that will shape the housing demand of elderly-headed households (McCarthy, Abrahamse, and Hubay, 1982). In 1978, 63 percent of elderly-headed households lived in a metropolitan area, roughly half of them (or 30 percent of all elderly households) in central cities (U.S. Bureau of the Census, 1980). While a roughly equal fraction of black elderly households resided in metropolitan areas, they were much more heavily concentrated in central cities than the white elderly: about 80 percent of the black elderly households in Standard Metropolitan Statistical Areas (SMSAs) resided in the central city. More than three-quarters of hispanic elderly households lived in SMSAs—the highest proportion of all three racial-ethnic groups. About two-thirds of these households were in central cities.

Two facts provide insights into the regional distribution of elderly-headed households. First, at the present time, roughly one-third of elderly-headed households reside in the South, about one-quarter each in the northeastern and northcentral states, and somewhat less than one-fifth in the West. Second, although the very low levels of migration by the elderly have remained stable over time, among the small proportion who move their primary residences, the primary sending areas have been the northern tier of states from Michigan to New York, while the primary receiving state has been Florida, although Arizona and California also have high volumes of older migrants (Rives and Serow, 1981).

At first glance, these two pieces of information may seem inconsistent. High state concentrations, however, result from many factors besides elderly immigration such as the outmigration of nonelderly households, low fertility rates, and immigration of the foreign-born, particularly prior to 1925 (Siegel, 1980b).

Census Bureau projections of the proportions of state populations that will be sixty-five years or older in the year 2000 largely reflect the greater projected growth of the elderly relative to the nonelderly (U.S. Bureau of the Census, 1979c). This conclusion seems inescapable since roughly three-fourths of the states are expected to have greater concentrations of elderly persons in the year 2000 than they did in 1975. But these aggregate data hide substantial differences in the reasons for the growth (or decline) in the concentration of elderly persons across the U.S. One underlying factor that can be isolated easily from the available data is the projected effect of elderly migration. A calculation based on a comparison of two census projection series—one that takes the effects of migration into account and one that does not—shows the contribution that migration is expected to add to (or subtract from) the stationary population between 1975 and 2000.[8] This calculation clearly indicates that Florida leads all states for the effects of inmigration on population growth; net migration of the elderly into Florida leads to a projected population that is nearly fifty times as high as would be expected to occur from the effects of fertility and mortality alone (essentially, the aging of the stationary population). Other states with substantial net elderly inmigra-

tion effects are Arizona, Arkansas, and Maine. The greatest net outmigration effects are projected for New York. Without considering outmigration by the elderly, New York's elderly population is expected to be five times higher than with the effects of migration.

These projections underscore substantial variations in the forces affecting elderly population growth rates across the nation. Of particular salience for future housing demand are two groups of states. The first group includes states that are attracting large numbers of elderly inmigrants who represent new housing consumers with housing needs that may place additional burdens on the existing stock or increase demand for new construction. The nature of these effects will depend, in part, on the growth rates of other demographic groups, the suitability of the existing housing stock for the new elderly migrants, and the like. The second group of concern consists of states that will lose substantial numbers of elderly housing consumers. Again, depending on the level and characteristics of demand from other demographic groups, such states may face serious problems of oversupply and contraction.

Thus, unevenness in the geographic distribution of the elderly means that some areas of the country will experience more stresses on their housing stock and housing-related services than others. The greater the pressures created by this growth on any individual area of the country, the greater will be the need to realign government priorities for serving these areas (McCarthy, Abrahamse, and Hubay, 1982).

Policy Implications

The magnitude and composition of housing demand by elderly-headed households will be shaped by the growth in the number of these households and by their attributes, such as their geographic location, housing tenure, and the age and sex of their members. These characteristics and growth patterns present four important challenges to housing policy.

First, the variations in the rate of growth of elderly households are at least as important as the increase in the number of elderly-headed households over time. Therefore, any housing programs geared to the elderly, especially those involving new construction programs, must take these fluctuations in household formation into account. Otherwise, there are potentials for over- or underbuilding at points in time and problems of expansion and retrenchment over time.

Second, the high rates of homeownership among the elderly combined with projections of even higher rates in the future suggest that some form of assistance directed at this group may be needed. At least two measures of need—income and health status—are appropriate in determining the need for assistance and providing evidence for possible government intervention.

The precarious income situation of elderly homeowners can be illustrated in several ways (Newman, 1981; Newman, Zais, and Struyk, 1984).

1. Elderly-headed households constitute the largest proportion of all households in owned homes with incomes below the poverty level.
2. Among individuals who own homes and do not live in families, the elderly who live alone comprise more than half of all those living in poverty.
3. The median income of elderly females who are heads of households and own their homes is several thousand dollars lower than that of other elderly owners, and is no higher for renters. (It will be remembered that female elderly heads of households constitute a particularly rapidly growing demographic group.)

Consistent with these high rates of poverty is the larger proportion of elderly versus nonelderly homeowners who have excessive housing-cost burdens.[9] Of greater policy interest, however, is that more than 40 percent of elderly homeowners have *persistently* high housing-cost burdens, a figure that is nearly three times greater than that for all homeowners (Newman and Struyk, 1984). Among elderly homeowners with incomes below

$5,000, the fraction with persistent affordability problems is more than two-thirds.

The close association between age and physical health also supports the argument for some form of government assistance to elderly homeowners. National panel data show that individuals who were sixty-five years old or older in 1980 reported, on average, twice as many health limitations as those who were age fifty-five ten years earlier (Newman, 1981). According to the 1980 National Health Interview Survey, roughly 45 percent of the noninstitutionalized population sixty-five years and older had health limitations that restricted activities (U.S. Department of Health and Human Services, 1981). For those seventy-five years old or older, more than half reported activity limitations. Since roughly one-quarter of all elderly owners live alone, and more than half of all homeowners seventy-five or older live alone, there are serious concerns about how the needs of these individuals are being met. These needs include not only health and personal care, but also maintenance and repair of the housing unit, including day-to-day upkeep. Health problems may limit not only the work homeowners would otherwise do for themselves but also their willingness or ability to contract with others to work for them. It seems likely that these problems are related to the additional finding that more than one-quarter of the housing units occupied by elderly-headed households fail the Department of Housing and Urban Development's standard for physically adequate housing (Newman and Struyk, 1984).

The concentration of income and health problems among elderly homeowners, then, strengthens the argument for government assistance targeted to elderly homeowners. The precise form of that assistance will depend on which problem is considered to be most severe or fundamental. Housing allowances or vouchers for owners, for example, are aimed at affordability problems. But the transfer of cash assistance in the form of a voucher may also induce repair activity, assuming the elderly homeowner is willing and able to contract for services. Home maintenance assistance programs (or in-kind services), on the other hand, target on upkeep problems. But here, too, when the cost of the repairs is subsidized, the dollars that may have been budgeted for repair work are freed to defray other expenses.

A third challenge to housing policy concerns the geographic distribution of the elderly. The current and continuing geographic imbalance in the concentration of elderly-headed households will, in turn, create uneven housing demand pressures across regions, states, and localities. In part, the concern is whether the supply and demand will be congruent. There is also the question of equitable treatment by government programs; for the elderly to capture their fair share of revenues that can or must be devoted to housing assistance (for example, general welfare versus energy assistance), geographic disparities must be recognized. The geographic imbalance will come into play even more strongly, however, in relation to a number of housing-related services, particularly health care.

The link between housing and health care is the focus of the fourth implication for housing policy to be derived from the future demographics of the elderly. The larger increases in household formation among the very old, combined with evidence indicating that independent living is preferred by the large majority of older people, suggest that one major challenge over the next several decades will be to determine how housing units can be adapted to allow for the provision of long-term care services. This challenge remains equally strong regardless of whether the provision of health services within the residential environment requires new construction or substantial rehabilitation of existing units, or whether this provision involves the public sector, the private sector, or both.

The demand for housing environments that include, or facilitate, the provision of health services presents a number of practical problems. Two of these problems are so fundamental that unless they are solved, there is little chance that a solid linkage between housing and long-term care can be forged. First, two large and powerful industries—the housing industry and the health indus-try—will have to work together since neither has the expertise to handle this challenge alone. The second problem concerns financing. If there are no radical shifts in the way housing is provided in this country and no comprehensive "income policy" that effectively guarantees all citizens an adequate income, then financing these efforts is a fundamental concern.

Notes

1. The projections shown use Census Series B.
2. Demographically generated aggregate housing demand projections are discussed in U.S. Office Management and Budget (1979).
3. For example, see deLeeuw (1971), Li (1977), Newman and Duncan (1979), Struyk and Marshall (1974), and Struyk and Soldo (1980).
4. This discussion is based largely on Pitkin and Masnick (1980) and Pitkin and Masnick (1981).
5. The specifics of the approach are detailed in Pitkin and Masnick (1980) and Pitkin and Masnick (1981).
6. The reader is referred to Pitkin and Masnick, 1980 and 1981 for the full details of the projection assumptions and methodology.
7. The continued domination of single-family homeownership among the population as a whole is also projected by Marcin (1977) and Weicher, Yap, and Jones (1982).
8. Census Series II-B and II-C.
9. Defined as gross rent above 30 percent of gross family income.

References

Carliner, G. 1974. "Determinants of Homeownership." *Land Economics* 1:109–19.

deLeeuw, F. 1971. "The Demand for Housing: A Review of Cross-Section Evidence." *Review of Economics and Statistics* 53:1–10.

Li, M. 1977. "A Logit Model of Homeownership." *Econometrica* 45:1081–97.

McCarthy, K., A. Abrahamse, and C. Hubay. 1982. *The Changing Geographic Distribution of the Elderly: Estimating Net Migration Rates with Social Security Data.* Santa Monica: Rand.

Marcin, T. 1977. *Outlook for Housing by Type of Unit and Region: 1978 to 2020.* Forest Service, U.S. Department of Agriculture. Washington, DC: U.S. Government Printing Office.

———. 1978. *Modeling Longrun Housing Demand by Type of Unit and Region*. Research Paper FPL308, Forest Service, U.S. Department of Agriculture. Washington, DC: U.S. Government Printing Office.

Morrison, P. 1976. *Demographic Trends That Will Shape Future Housing Demand*. Santa Monica: Rand.

———. 1978. *Overview of Demographic Trends Shaping the Nation's Future*. Testimony before the Joint Economic Committee, U.S. Congress, May 31, 1978. Santa Monica: Rand.

Newman, S. 1981. Testimony before the Subcommittee on Housing and Consumer Interest, House Select Committee on Aging, 97th Congress, 1st Session. July 1981, 108–16.

Newman, S., and R. Struyk. 1984. "An Alternative Targeting Strategy for Housing Assistance." *The Gerontologist* 24:584–92.

Newman, S., J. Zais, and R. Struyk, 1984. "Housing Older America." In I. Altman, J. Wohlwill, and M. P. Lawton. *Elderly People and the Environment*. New York: Plenum.

Newman, S., and G. Duncan. 1979. "Residential Problems, Dissatisfaction, and Mobility." *Journal of the American Planning Association* 45:154–67.

Pitkin, J., and G. Masnick. 1980. "Projections of Housing Consumption in the U.S., 1980 to 2000, by a Cohort Method." *Annual Housing Survey Studies*, No. 9. Washington, DC: U.S. Department of Housing and Urban Development.

———. 1981. *Linking Projections of Households with Housing Consumption: An Exploration of Alternative Series*. Washington, DC: U.S. Department of Housing and Urban Development, Office of Policy Development and Research.

Rives, N., and W. Serow. 1981. "Interstate Migration of the Elderly: Demographic Aspects." *Research on Aging* 3:259–78.

Siegel, J. 1980a. "On the Demography of Aging." *Demography* 17:345–64.

———. 1980b. "Recent and Prospective Demographic Trends for the Elderly Population and Some Implications for Health Care." In *Epidemiology of Aging, Second Conference*. Ed. S. Haynes, and M. Feinleib. Washington, DC: National Institutes of Health.

Struyk, R., and S. Marshall. 1974. "The Determinants of Household Homeownership." *Urban Studies*, 11:289–99.

Struyk, R., and B. Soldo. 1980. *Improving the Elderly's Housing*, Cambridge, MA: Ballinger.

U.S. Bureau of the Census. 1943. *Census of Housing, 1940*. Washington, DC: U.S. Government Printing Office.

———. 1953a. *Census of Housing, 1950*. Vol. III: Farm Housing Characteristics. Washington, DC: U.S. Government Printing Office.

———. 1953b. *Census of Housing, 1950*. Vol. II: Nonfarm Housing Characteristics. Washington, DC: U.S. Government Printing Office.

———. 1962. *Census of Housing, 1960*. Vol. VII: Housing for Senior Citizens. Washington, DC: U.S. Government Printing Office.

———. 1963. *Census of Housing, 1960*. Vol. I: States and Small Areas, Part I: U.S. Summary. Washington, DC: U.S. Government Printing Office.

———. 1972. *Census of Housing, 1970*. Vol. I: Housing Characteristics for States, Cities, and Counties; Part 1: U.S. Summary. Washington, DC: U.S. Government Printing Office.

———. 1973. *Census of Housing, 1970*. Subject Reports HC (7)-2. Housing of Senior Citizens. Washington, DC: U.S. Government Printing Office.

———. 1974. *Current Population Reports*. Population of the U.S., Trends and Prospects: 1950–1990, Series P-23, No. 49. Washington, DC: U.S. Government Printing Office.

———. 1975. *Current Population Reports*. Projections of the Population of the U.S.: 1975–2050, Series P-25, No. 601. Washington, DC: U.S. Government Printing Office.

———. 1976. "Demographic Aspects of Aging and the Older Population in the United States." Special Studies, Series P-23, No. 59. Washington, DC: U.S. Government Printing Office.

———. 1979a. *Current Population Reports*. Projections of the Number of Households and Families: 1979–1995, Series P-25, No. 805. Washington, DC: U.S. Government Printing Office.

———. 1979b. *Current Population Reports*. Social and Economic Characteristics of the Older Population: 1978, Special Studies Series P-23, No. 85. Washington, DC: U.S. Government Printing Office.

———. 1979c. *Current Population Reports*. Illustrative Projections of State Populations by Age, Race, and Sex: 1975–2000, Series P-25, No. 796. Washington, DC: U.S. Government Printing Office.

———. 1980. *Annual Housing Survey: 1978*. Part A. Washington, DC: U.S. Government Printing Office.

———. 1981a. *Statistical Abstract of the U.S.: 1981*. 102nd edition. Washington, DC: U.S. Government Printing Office.

————. 1981b. *Social and Economic Characteristics of Americans During Midlife.* Series P-23, No. 111. Washington, DC: U.S. Government Printing Office.

————. 1982. *Household and Family Characteristics: March 1981.* Series P-20, No. 371. Washington, DC: U.S. Government Printing Office.

U.S. Department of Health and Human Services. 1981. *Vital and Health Statistics.* Series 10, No. 139. Washington, DC: National Center for Health Statistics.

U.S. House of Representatives. 1978. Select Committee on Population. *Domestic Consequences of U.S. Population Change.* Washington, DC: U.S. Government Printing Office.

U.S. Office of Management and Budget, Special Studies Division, Economics and Government. 1979. *Impact of Changing Demographic Patterns on Future Housing Needs: 1980–2000.* Washington, DC: Office of Management and Budget.

Weicher, J., L. Yap, and M. Jones. 1982. *Metropolitan Housing Needs for the 1980s.* Washington, DC: Urban Institute.

CHAPTER 4 Rural Issues in Elderly Housing

Gary R. Lee

Several years ago, the editors of this volume correctly observed that "the gerontological literature is surprisingly thin in its treatment of the special problems of aging in nonmetropolitan areas of the country" (Lawton, Newcomer, and Byerts, 1976, p. 330). Although there has been some progress in rectifying this oversight in recent years (Coward and Lee, 1985), it is still undeniably the case that the problems of the rural elderly receive less attention from the scientific community, the general public, and those responsible for the formulation and implementation of public policy than do the problems faced by their urban counterparts. Part of this imbalance may be because rural problems in general are less visible than are urban problems, a difference that is particularly applicable in the area of housing (McFarland and Thompson, 1975; Bylund, 1985).

Issues related to housing are intimately connected with other aspects of the lives and lifestyles of the rural elderly, as is true for other segments of the population. Research has shown that housing satisfaction is a strong predictor of overall perceived quality of life (Andrews and Withey, 1976; Campbell, Converse, and Rodgers, 1976). In the matrix of factors affecting the quality of life, housing is more than a physical structure; it may enhance or impede elderly persons' abilities to attain their goals, depending in part on its location on the rural-urban continuum. For the elderly, the location of their residences also has a great deal to do with access to services, transportation problems, characteristics of the immediate environment, and the availability of solutions to problems of daily living. Furthermore, for the rural elderly in particular, the quality of their housing may affect their ability to maintain autonomy and residential independence and to live where they want to live.

The object of most immediate concern in this chapter is the well-documented, but little-known, fact that the quality of housing for the rural elderly is extremely problematic. While the focus of this volume and many other recent works is the problematic nature of housing for the elderly, Struyk notes that indicators of housing quality are actually much more strongly related to residence than to age:

> The differences (in housing quality) among elderly households living in rural and urban areas are substantially greater than those between elderly and nonelderly households. The rural elderly, who account for 30 percent of all elderly-headed households, are significantly less well housed (Struyk, 1977a, p. 132).

One of the objectives of this chapter is to document the extent of the comparative disadvantages in housing quality faced by the rural elderly. A second, and equally important, objective is to assess the implications of these disadvantages in an appropriate context. Third, general strategies for ameliorating housing problems among the rural elderly will be addressed. Solutions to problems of housing quality for the elderly that have been applied to urban areas are, for a variety of reasons, not as viable for rural residents; innovative strategies will be required to deal with the contingencies created by rural environments. This chapter will examine some of these contingencies and their implications.

Rural-Urban Differences in Housing Quality

Since 1973, the availability of data from the *Annual Housing Survey* has added greatly to our knowledge of rural-urban differences in housing (U.S. Bureau of Census, 1982). Analyses of these data have uniformly shown the structural quality of the housing units occupied by the rural elderly to be substantially lower than the quality of dwellings occupied by the urban elderly (Bylund, 1985; Morris and Winter, 1982; Struyk, 1977a). The houses of the rural elderly are more likely, in comparison to those of the urban elderly, to lack complete bath and kitchen facilities, water and sewage systems, and central heat. They have more electrical and structural defects. Their roofs and basements are more likely to leak. Rural residents must more often close off some rooms in the winter in order to heat remaining rooms adequately. A higher proportion of the houses of the rural elderly than those of urban elderly are quite old and thus more in need of repair.

There is, of course, no adequate single indicator of housing quality. Bylund (1985) has reported distributions of two indices of housing quality, each of which is comprised of multiple indicators, according to residential location. One indicator is a "Facility Index," which enumerates the presence or absence of key components of housing such as central heating, indoor plumbing, complete kitchens, and so on. The other is a "Condition Index," which rates housing units according to the number of structural problems, such as leaks, sagging floors, or peeling paint, they evidence. On the Facility Index, 68.1 percent of the houses of rural elderly farm residents and 72.6 percent of those of rural elderly nonfarm residents had no deficiencies according to data from the 1975 *Annual Housing*

Survey (U.S. DHUD, 1979). The comparable figure for elderly residents of cities of fifty thousand residents or more was 87.6 percent. Only 4 percent of the homes of elderly urban residents had two or more deficits on the Facility Index, while 18.1 percent of the rural farm homes and 13.4 percent of the rural nonfarm homes had two or more deficiencies. On the Condition Index, only 28.6 percent of the rural farm homes and 46.1 percent of the rural nonfarm homes had no deficiencies, compared with 65.7 percent of the homes of the urban elderly. Data such as these (see also Struyk, 1977a) clearly justify Lawton's generalization that housing for the elderly is "most adequate in urban metropolitan areas, less adequate in towns outside metropolitan areas, and least adequate in rural areas (most often but not always poorer in farm than nonfarm residences)" (Lawton, 1980, p. 58).

There is also evidence suggesting that the relative housing deficit associated with rural residence for the elderly is increasing, although to some extent this is a matter of interpretation. According to Bird and Kampe (1977), the absolute number of "substandard" housing units (defined as either dilapidated or lacking hot running water, toilet, or bathing facilities) occupied by the nonmetropolitan elderly decreased by nearly a million between 1950 and 1975. However, the number of substandard housing units occupied by all nonmetropolitan residents decreased even more dramatically during this period, so that the percentage of all nonmetropolitan substandard housing occupied by the elderly increased from 18.2 percent in 1950 to 35.0 percent in 1975. It is thus clear that, while the overall quality of rural housing has improved in recent years, the rural elderly are experiencing a disproportionately low share of this improvement.

These figures show that, according to virtually any reasonable indicator or indicators of housing quality, the rural elderly live in lower-quality housing than do either the urban elderly or younger rural residents. This is surprising to many people who share in widely held stereotypes of urban blight and rural abundance, but it is true nonetheless. On the other hand, the rural elderly are substantially more likely to own their homes than are the urban elderly and also enjoy lower housing costs than their urban counterparts. These differences appear to favor the rural elderly, but their implications require more careful scrutiny.

Age, of course, is positively related to home ownership: the elderly are more likely than any other age category in the population to own their homes (Lawton, 1980; Struyk, 1977a). Furthermore, among the elderly, rates of home ownership are higher among rural than urban elderly. According to the *Annual Housing Survey* of 1980 (U.S. Bureau of the Census, 1982), over 80 percent of older people in independent residences who live outside of Standard Metropolitan Statistical Areas own their homes. Of those who reside within the boundaries of SMSAs, 76.5 percent of those living outside of central cities and only 57.5 percent of those who live in central cities own their homes. The homes owned by the rural elderly are also more likely to be single-family detached dwelling units (Bylund, 1985; Morris and Winter, 1982; Struyk, 1977a). Morris and Winter (1982) point out that, as indicated by these differences, the rural elderly are more likely than other segments of the population to be able to attain the goals of home ownership and possession of private outside space, which are very pervasive values in American culture (see also Tremblay, Dillman, and Van Liere, 1980). Morris and Winter (1982) conclude that the supply of available housing is more closely aligned with personal preferences in rural than in urban areas. Even among a sample of low-income rural elderly analyzed by Montgomery, Stubbs, and Day (1980), 89 percent of the married couples and 81 percent of the unmarried women owned their own homes. Furthermore, a higher percentage of rural (91 percent) than urban (83 percent) elderly homeowners are free of mortgage obligations (Bylund, 1985).

Largely because of differences in housing tenure status, the housing-related expenses of the rural elderly are lower than those of the urban elderly (Bylund, 1985; Lawton, 1980; Morris and Winter, 1982; Struyk, 1977b). In the most thorough analysis of this issue to date, Struyk (1977b) used data

from the 1974 *Annual Housing Survey* to show that the rural elderly pay fewer dollars, and a lower proportion of their incomes, for housing expenses than do the urban elderly. Struyk (1977b) used a figure of 30 percent of annual income as a distinction between reasonable and "excessive" housing costs for the elderly. He found that housing costs exceeded 30 percent of income for only 19 percent of the rural elderly, as opposed to 31 percent of the urban elderly. This is primarily because most older rural residents own their homes, as noted above, and are thus less susceptible than renters to frequent increases in payments. It is also, of course, caused in some part by generally lower housing costs in rural areas. However, the incomes of the elderly are substantially lower, on the average, in rural than urban areas (Lee and Lassey, 1980), a fact that makes the rural-urban difference in the proportion of income spent on housing somewhat more surprising.

Struyk (1977a) also found that elderly urban residents are somewhat more likely than their rural counterparts to report being affected by undesirable conditions in their neighborhoods: street noise, heavy traffic, crime, litter, pollution, and so on. These are not problems inherent in houses per se but rather problems resulting from the location of homes and the broader environments within which dwelling units exist. Apparently the rural elderly tend to perceive the locations of their houses as advantageous, at least in terms of the absence of environmental annoyances. These locational advantages may compensate, to some degree, for the qualitative deficiencies of the houses themselves. This point is critical to an adequate understanding of elderly persons' subjective evaluations of their housing, and to related issues such as desire to move, which we will examine below.

Implications of the Differences

It should be abundantly clear from the material discussed above that, in general, the housing of the rural elderly is qualitatively inferior to that of the urban elderly. This is, and should increasingly be, a cause for some concern. Older rural residents whose health may be deteriorating and whose finances are probably limited are unlikely to be able to make extensive repairs or improvements to the homes they own. Continued deterioration of their housing, together with other exigencies of old age, may threaten their abilities to maintain residential independence. On the other hand, the rural elderly possess at least three apparent housing advantages in comparison to the urban elderly: somewhat higher rates of home ownership, markedly lower housing costs, and fewer and less serious problems in terms of neighborhood and other environmental conditions.

At this point we need to take a closer look at the meaning of these rural-urban differences, beginning with housing quality. One of the more interesting paradoxes in the study of residential variation in the housing of the elderly is the apparent fact that, in spite of the qualitative inferiority of their houses, the rural elderly seem to be exceedingly satisfied with their housing. In the study of rural housing by Montgomery, Stubbs, and Day (1980), over 95 percent of their sample of low-income elderly reported that their houses fully met their needs. In their full sample, containing low-income adults of all ages, housing satisfaction increased with age even though objective housing quality clearly did not. Virtually no elderly members of this sample expressed any desire to move, and very few saw a need for major improvements in their current houses.

We know that, in general, housing satisfaction tends to increase with age (Lawton, 1980). This may be because the aging process is accompanied by a reduction in aspirations (Campbell, Converse, and Rodgers, 1976), or because of a cohort effect— the current generation of American elderly may have been socialized to lower expectation levels than were younger people (Montgomery, Stubbs, and Day, 1980). It is not because the housing of the elderly is objectively better than that of younger adults, even though objective quality and subjective evaluations are positively correlated (Lawton and Hoover, 1979). Furthermore, Lawton, Nahemow and Teaff (1975) found that the extent to which elderly residents of federally funded housing projects were satisfied with their housing was inversely related to community size. This does not prove categorically that the rural elderly are more satisfied with housing than the urban, since federally funded housing-project residents are hardly representative of rural residents in general. But it is unlikely that the high rates of housing satisfaction among rural residents found by Montgomery, Stubbs, and Day (1980) are exceeded by urban residents.

It thus appears possible that, in spite of the comparatively poor quality of their housing, the rural elderly may be more satisfied with housing than any other age/residence category of the population. This is important, since housing satisfaction is a fairly strong predictor of perceived quality of life, as we noted above. It is not, however, an unmixed blessing: high levels of housing satisfaction may dissuade the rural elderly from efforts to either improve their existing homes or find better homes, in spite of the many housing deficiencies with which they must contend (Bylund, 1985; Montgomery, Stubbs, and Day, 1980). High satisfaction with housing may also, somewhat paradoxically, become very problematic for people who must relocate because of factors beyond their control, such as declining health. Whatever the explanation, the fact that the rural elderly do not feel deprived by the poor condition of their housing may be a major factor in the continuation of the problem, both for themselves and for potential future occupants of the housing.

We should also recognize that the high rate of home ownership among the rural elderly has its disadvantages as well as advantages. Bylund (1985) and others point out that ownership entails problems of upkeep and maintenance that may often be beyond the financial and/or physical means of the rural elderly. This may account in some part for the poorer quality and condition of their dwellings.

Morris and Winter (1978; 1982) contend, with considerable justification, that the American cultural system clearly stipulates the desirability of owning a single-family detached dwelling that includes sufficient indoor and outdoor private space.

They also argue that the content and intensity of these housing norms are quite pervasive across the various subcategories of the population; in other words, almost everyone desires the same kind of housing. Variation from this ideal may be best explained by constraints on personal preferences resulting from resources and available options. Morris and Winter (1982) conclude that the housing stock in rural areas is more closely attuned to preferences than is the case in urban areas.

Data on housing preferences obtained by Dillman, Tremblay, and Dillman (1979) confirm that the substantial majority of Americans do indeed prefer single-family detached dwellings. There is virtually no variation in this preference according to residence, although some variation exists in second choices. If their first choices were unavailable, rural residents are more likely to prefer owning a mobile home on an owned lot, while urban residents would prefer owning a townhouse or condominium or renting a duplex; this suggests that rural residents place a greater premium on maintaining private outside space. Dillman, Tremblay, and Dillman (1979) found that over four-fifths of their sample listed owning a single-family home as their first or (in a small percentage of cases) second choice, and that this preference was indeed quite general. However, they did find two categories of the population in which less than half listed the single-family home as either their first or second choice: the elderly and the widowed. These people were more likely to choose renting an apartment or duplex or owning a mobile home on a rented lot. Unfortunately the data on housing preference reported by Dillman, Tremblay, and Dillman (1979) have not been analyzed according to both age and residence, so we do not yet know whether the rural elderly are more or less likely than their urban counterparts to prefer some housing arrangement other than ownership of a single-family dwelling. However, we know at least that the elderly, who are the most likely to own their own single-family detached homes (particularly if they live in rural areas), are the least likely to prefer this arrangement. Even though older people tend to be highly satisfied with their own homes, they can and do envision other types of housing that may be more congenial with their needs and desires.

The appropriate explanation for this paradox is not readily apparent. Dillman and associates (1979) attach a normative interpretation consistent with disengagement theory: "It appears that the need to conform to . . . housing norms declines with age" (Dillman, Tremblay, and Dillman, 1979, p. 14). The effort and expense involved in home maintenance may also be relevant here; this possibility is supported by the fact that widowed persons (who are predominantly female) are particularly likely to prefer renting a duplex or apartment. The elderly may also consider the greater potential for mobility offered by renting to be advantageous, since moving to be nearer to children, necessary services, and/or desirable retirement locations may be attractive.

Whatever the explanation, the data indicate that a substantial proportion of the elderly, no doubt including the rural elderly, would prefer some form of housing other than owning a home, even though most of them are homeowners. Bylund (1985) speculates that the high proportion of the rural elderly who own their homes may be attributable, in large part, to the lack of available alternatives. There are indeed fewer housing options available to the rural elderly, along with other rural residents. The major option currently available is the mobile home. More rural people of all ages, and the elderly in particular, live in mobile homes than is the case among urban dwellers (Bylund, 1985). We know that this fits the preferences of rural residents to some degree (Dillman, Tremblay, and Dillman, 1979), but it may also reflect the lack of other options.

The lack of options in rural areas may also affect, at least indirectly, the quality of housing for the rural elderly. Since rural areas have not grown as rapidly as urban areas in recent decades, there has been relatively little incentive to build new housing. The existing housing stock in rural areas is thus older than in urban areas, and this contributes to its poorer condition. Furthermore, those rural elderly who may wish to move from their homes have few if any choices of apartments or condominiums, and few options for disposing of their existing houses, particularly if they are in poor condition. As Bylund (1981) has shown, differences in housing quality between the rural and the urban elderly are not entirely attributable to the lower incomes of the rural. Part of the reason for the rural elderly's disadvantage may be that there are fewer competitors for their housing business.

Another factor in the poor housing quality of the rural elderly is the relative unavailability of housing assistance programs for this segment of the population. A very high proportion of the money available for housing assistance for the elderly comes in the form of rent subsidies, a form that is hardly relevant to those who, while they may have very limited financial resources, own their homes, or to those who live in areas where there is nothing to rent (Montgomery, Stubbs, and Day, 1980; Taietz and Milton, 1979). It is not common, in American culture, to think of people who own their homes as being poor, and consequently housing assistance programs are rarely directed toward homeowners. But among the elderly, the highest rates of home ownership coincide with the highest rates of poverty (Lee and Lassey, 1980)—among rural residents.

This brings us to the second apparent advantage of rural residence for the housing situation of the elderly: housing costs. These costs are clearly lower in rural areas. In fact, as Struyk (1977b) has shown, even though the average incomes of the rural elderly are markedly lower than those of the urban, the rural elderly pay a smaller proportion of their incomes for housing than do the urban. This leaves a greater proportion of their (smaller) incomes for other expenses, which is a distinct advantage. But again there are counterbalancing factors that must be considered. One is that lower costs translate into lower values: the houses of the rural elderly are not worth as much as those of the urban (Morris and Winter, 1982), limiting the extent to which they can benefit from the sale or rental of the property they own.

A second factor here is that the data employed by Struyk (1977b) and others to assess the housing costs of the elderly do not constitute complete or exhaustive lists of housing-related expenses. According to Struyk, "the housing expenditure data used in these computations exclude most costs of maintaining and repairing a unit, and hence can easily understate the total resources going to housing" (Struyk, 1977b, p. 452). This understatement is most likely in the case of homeowners (renters pay for maintenance and repair costs as part of rental payments, so these expenses are included for them), and particularly in the case of homeowners whose dwellings are the most in need of repair: in other words, the rural elderly. Thus the cost advantage of rural housing for the elderly is likely to be overestimated because the kinds of housing expenses employed in these estimates (mortgage or rent payments, taxes, and utilities) probably constitute a smaller proportion of their total housing expenses.

On the other hand, it is not clear that the rural elderly spend a great deal on housing maintenance and repair, even though their dwellings are very likely to need them according to general normative standards. Montgomery, Stubbs, and Day (1980), in their study of the low-income rural elderly, found that less than half of their sample had made housing repairs or improvements costing at least $200 in the five years prior to the study. This does not mean that their houses did not need repairs or improvements; data on housing quality and condition showed numerous deficiencies, as we noted earlier. It means instead that the residents simply did not make needed repairs or perceive improvements as being necessary.

Another interesting aspect of the findings of Montgomery and associates (1980) is that virtually none of their respondents expressed any interest in obtaining programmatic assistance to improve their housing. This may be part of the general antipathy of rural residents, and perhaps the rural elderly in particular, to governmental programs (Bylund, 1985; Coward and Smith, 1982). It indicates once again that the rural elderly are not exceedingly concerned about the generally low quality of their dwellings. They would, at least, prefer to continue living in inferior housing rather than to accept financial or other forms of assistance to improve it.

Finally, we need to say a few words about the fact that, as documented by Struyk (1977a) and others, the rural elderly evaluate the properties of their immediate residential environments more positively than do the urban. Apparently the perception that rural environments are more desirable places to live than urban areas is fairly widespread. One indication of this is the "migration turnaround" of the 1970s and early 1980s, in which the elderly are participating to some degree (Beale and Fuguitt, 1978; Deavers and Brown, 1980; Lee and Lassey, 1982). The rate of migration from metropolitan to nonmetropolitan areas now exceeds the rate of nonmetropolitan-to-metropolitan migration. Clifford, Heaton, and Fuguitt (1982) have shown that the older persons most likely to move to rural areas are those who live in independent households (either heads of households or their spouses). Because these people will need homes and are likely to have the necessary resources to obtain them, this may ultimately result in an improvement in the quality as well as the quantity of housing available in rural areas. Clifford and associates speculate that a major motivation of urban-to-rural migrants may involve a search for improvements in the quality of life:

> The positive selection of independent households in elderly migration from metropolitan to nonmetropolitan areas may be more frequently associated with voluntary decisions to seek locations with more favorable climates and better recreational amenities and scenic living environments. This is in line with recent surveys of elderly migrants to nonmetropolitan areas which indicate that quality of life motivations predominate (Clifford, Heaton, and Fuguitt, 1982, p. 154–55).

The general perception thus appears to be that the quality of life is better in rural than urban areas (Dillman and Tremblay, 1977), for the elderly as well as others. On the other hand, Clifford and associates (1982) also found that the elderly rural-to-urban migration stream consisted disproportionately of persons in "dependent" living arrangements (those living with relatives other than the spouse or with nonrelatives). They speculate that outmigration from rural areas by the elderly may result in some part from crises such as deteriorating health or widowhood; these people may need support or services that are unavailable in rural areas.

It appears, then, that those older persons whose personal resources are most limited and who are least able to maintain their autonomy are most likely to move from rural to urban areas. This sort of move is probably not entirely voluntary, since those who have the greatest resources tend to move in the reverse direction. The generally low quality of rural housing and the lack of housing options for the rural elderly may be major contributors to the outmigration of the dependent elderly from rural areas.

Conclusion

It is obvious from this brief review that the quality of housing for the rural elderly is substantially lower than for the urban elderly. This is partially, but not entirely, attributable to the lower levels of financial resources possessed by the rural elderly. On the other hand, norms defining standards of adequacy in housing seem to vary according to residential location: even though the houses of the rural elderly are poor in comparative terms, the people living in them do not seem to be unduly concerned about their condition, eager to obtain assistance for purposes of improvement, or in other ways dissatisfied with the situation.

The elderly who have the greatest objective housing needs in rural communities are, unlike those in urban areas, primarily homeowners. It is not clear that they really want to be homeowners, but the substantial majority are homeowners nonetheless. Those concerned with the development of policies and programs to improve the housing of the rural elderly might most profitably examine two issues. First, can services designed to improve the quality of homes owned by the rural elderly (modernization, weatherization, handy-man services, and the like) be provided in such a way as to make them attractive, as well as affordable, to the intended recipients? Second, is it possible to increase the housing tenure alternatives of the rural elderly, so that those who really do not wish to continue fulfilling the obligations of ownership can actually have some options to exercise?

It is difficult to provide a wide range of housing services to rural residents because of the problems inherent in achieving economies of scale. The efficient and effective provision of housing options requires fairly large numbers of persons concentrated in one locale whose needs may be satisfied in similar ways. Obviously this rarely happens in rural areas. But while housing services are difficult to provide to rural residents in general, and the rural elderly in particular, they are obviously very much needed. This is true in spite of the fact that the rural elderly consistently report high levels of satisfaction with their housing. This high satisfaction may reflect lack of familiarity with alternatives or potential improvements, a sense of pride in ownership, or a variety of other factors, but it does not mean that objective improvements in housing quality would not result in improvements in the overall quality of life for the rural elderly.

Virtually all services for the elderly are less available in rural than urban areas (Taietz and Milton, 1979; Nelson, 1980). Housing services of all descriptions are no different than other services in this regard. But the abilities of older rural persons to maintain residential independence may be heavily contingent on the provision of housing support services. There is a definite need for housing assistance programs for the rural elderly, in terms of housing options, home improvement, and in-house support services. Unlike most programs designed for urban areas, these programs must be geared toward homeowners. If a variety of effective housing services can be provided efficiently to elderly rural homeowners, improvements in the quality of their lives and their abilities to maintain their independence will follow.

References

Andrews, F. M., and S. B. Withey. 1976. *Social Indicators of Well-Being.* New York: Plenum.

Beale, D., and G. V. Fuguitt. 1978. "The New Pattern of Nonmetropolitan Population Change." In *Social Demography.* Ed., K. E. Taueber, L. L. Bumpass, and J. A. Sweet. New York: Academic.

Bird, R., and R. Kampe. 1977. "Twenty-Five Years of Housing Progress in Rural America." *Agricultural Economics Report,* No. 373. Washington, DC: U.S. Department of Agriculture.

Bylund, R. A. 1981. "Housing Quality of the Elderly: The Importance of Size of Place of Residence." Paper presented at the annual meeting of the Rural Sociological Society, Guelph, Ontario, Canada, August.

———. 1985. "Rural Housing: Perspectives for the Aged." In *The Elderly in Rural Society: Every Fourth Elder.* Ed. R. T. Coward and G. R. Lee. New York: Springer.

Campbell, A., P. E. Converse, and W. L. Rodgers. 1976. *The Quality of American Life.* New York: Russell Sage.

Clifford, W. B., T. Heaton, and G. V. Fuguitt. 1982. "Residential Mobility and Living Arrangements Among the Elderly: Changing Patterns in Metropolitan and Nonmetropolitan Areas." *International Journal of Aging and Human Development* 14:139–56.

Coward, R. T., and G. R. Lee. 1985. "An Introduction to Aging in Rural Environments." In *The Elderly in Rural Society: Every Fourth Elder.* Ed. R. T. Coward and G. R. Lee. New York: Springer.

Coward, R. T., and W. M. Smith, Jr. 1982. "Families in Rural Society." In *Rural Society in the U.S.: Issues for the 1980s.* Ed. D. A. Dillman and D. J. Hobbs. Boulder, CO: Westview.

Deavers, K. L., and D. L. Brown. 1980. "The Rural Population Turnaround: Research and National Public Policy." In *New Directions in Urban-Rural Migration.* Ed. D. L. Brown and J. M. Wardwell. New York: Academic.

Dillman, D. A., and K. R. Tremblay, Jr. 1977. "The Quality of Life in Rural America." *Annals of the American Academy of Political and Social Science* 429:115–29.

Dillman, D. A., K. R. Tremblay, Jr., and J. J. Dillman. 1979. "Influence of Housing Norms and Personal

Characteristics on Stated Housing Preferences." *Housing and Society* 6:2–29.

Lawton, M. P. 1980. *Environment and Aging.* Monterey, CA: Brooks/Cole.

Lawton, M. P., and S. L. Hoover. 1979. *Housing and Neighborhood: Objective and Subjective Quality.* Philadelphia, PA: Philadelphia Geriatric Center.

Lawton, M. P., L. Nahemow, and J. Teaff. 1975. "Housing Characteristics and Well-Being of Elderly Tenants in Federally Assisted Housing." *Journal of Gerontology* 30:601–7.

Lawton, M. P., R. J. Newcomer, and T. O. Byerts. 1976. "Conclusion." In *Community Planning for an Aging Society.* Ed. M. P. Lawton, R. J. Newcomer, and T. O. Byerts. Stroudsberg, PA: Dowden, Hutchinson and Ross.

Lee, G. R., and M. L. Lassey. 1980. "Rural-Urban Differences Among the Elderly: Economic, Social, and Subjective Factors." *Journal of Social Issues* 36:62–74.

———. 1982. "The Elderly." In *Rural Society in the U.S.: Issues for the 1980s.* Ed. D. A. Dillman and D. J. Hobbs. Boulder, CO: Westview.

McFarland, C., and M. M. Thompson. 1975. *Current and Future Housing Needs of Elderly Pennsylvanians.* Washington, DC: International Center for Social Gerontology.

Montgomery, J. E., A. C. Stubbs, and S. S. Day. 1980. "The Housing Environment of the Rural Elderly." *Gerontologist* 20:444–51.

Morris, E. W., and M. Winter. 1978. *Housing, Family, and Society.* New York: Wiley.

———. 1982. "Housing." In *Rural Society in the U.S.: Issues for the 1980s.* Ed. D. A. Dillman and D. J. Hobbs. Boulder, CO: Westview.

Nelson, G. 1980. "Social Services to the Urban and Rural Aged: The Experiences of Area Agencies on Aging." *Gerontologist* 20:200–207.

Struyk, R. J. 1977a. "The Housing Situation of Elderly Americans." *Gerontologist* 17:130–39.

———. 1977b. "The Housing Expense Burden of Households Headed by the Elderly." *Gerontologist* 17:447–52.

Taietz, P., and S. Milton. 1979. "Rural-Urban Differences in the Structure of Services for the Elderly in Upstate New York Counties." *Journal of Gerontology* 34:429–37.

Tremblay, K. R., Jr., D. A. Dillman, and K. D. Van Liere. 1980. "An Examination of the Relationship Between Housing Preferences and Community Size Preferences." *Rural Sociology* 45:509–19.

U.S. Bureau of the Census. 1982. *Annual Housing Survey: 1980. Part A: General Housing Characteristics.* Current Housing Reports, Series H-150-80. Washington, DC: U.S. Government Printing Office.

U.S. Department of Housing and Urban Development (DHUD). 1979. *How Well Are We Housed? The Elderly.* Washington, DC: U.S. Department of Housing and Urban Development, Office of Policy and Research.

CHAPTER 5 Public Policies and Individual Housing Choices

Lloyd Turner

The goal of adequate housing for older Americans has been a major public concern over the last half century. Under the authorization of the U.S. Housing Act of 1937, the federal government became actively involved in the provision of "safe and decent housing" for all age groups. Specific responsibilities for the housing of older persons were outlined two decades later in the Housing Act of 1959, which created the Section 202 program to stimulate new construction of units for the elderly and handicapped. The scope of policies for the elderly was further expanded by the Older Americans Act of 1965 and by numerous legislative initiatives granting authority to the Department of Housing and Urban Development and other federal agencies.

Among the general public there is widespread acceptance of the proposition that governmental agencies should bear responsibility for the housing of older persons. At the same time, however, it is widely recognized that public resources are insufficient to meet the diverse housing and service needs of the elderly population. The purpose of this chapter is to establish two basic facts about the evolving role of government in elderly housing: (1) that housing choices are influenced by a wide variety of governmental activities, many of which are not traditionally regarded as housing programs, and (2) that none of these initiatives by

itself is sufficient to meet more than a small fraction of the housing needs of the nation's older population. For these reasons advocates of improved housing for the elderly must understand not only the housing needs and preferences of older persons but also the extent to which their housing choices are promoted or constrained by current policies and programs.

Within this context the present chapter provides an overview of the major public policies and programs influencing individual housing choices. The chapter is divided into two sections. Section one examines the wide range of public involvement in elderly housing during the past half century. It begins with a discussion of direct housing programs and then describes the impacts of other types of policies and programs on housing choices. Section two reviews several recent policy and program changes that affect housing adequacy for the community resident (noninstitutionalized) elderly. This review includes changes in funding levels for individual programs, consolidations of categorical programs into block grants, and the continuing growth of homeowner benefits through federal personal income tax policies. The chapter concludes with a brief summary of the unmet housing needs of older Americans and the emerging role of government in addressing these needs.

This chapter is based upon findings from the Housing Choices of Older Americans Study (1979–82). The study was funded by Grant No. 90-AR-2118 from the Administration on Aging (OHDS), U.S. Department of Health and Human Services.

Major Public Policy Initiatives through 1980

During the last fifty years many separate policy developments have contributed to the housing situation of older Americans. Several of these efforts have been directly related to housing, notably those which encourage new construction, the rehabilitation of existing units, or the provision of subsidized rental housing. Of equal or greater importance, however, are policies and programs developed in other functional areas—income transfers, taxation, health care, social services, community facilities, transportation, energy assistance, and land use.

This author has found that eleven federal agencies and hundreds of state and local governmental units have policies and/or programs which influence housing choices (Turner, et al., 1981). These governmental initiatives are indicated in table 5-1 and are described briefly below. Since very little research has been conducted to quantify the impacts of these initiatives on elderly housing choices, this summary is limited to a qualitative analysis of these policy and program effects.

TABLE 5-1. Major Public Policies Affecting Housing Decisions of the Elderly (by Category and Agency)

	Federal — HUD				Federal — HHS				Federal — Other agencies									State				Local	
	Housing	Fair Housing & Equal Opportunity	Community Planning & Development	Federal Insurance Administration	Social Security Administration	Administration on Aging	Health-Care Financing Administration	Health Services Administration	Department of Agriculture Farmers Home Administration	Department of Justice Law Enforcement Assistance Administration	Department of Transportation Urban Mass Transportation Administration	Department of Energy	Department of the Treasury Internal Revenue Service	Veterans Administration	U.S. Commission on Civil Rights	Community Service Administration	Federal Home Loan Bank Board	State Departments of Revenue	State Housing Finance Agencies	State Agencies on Aging	State Insurance Commissions	General Governments	Area Agencies on Aging
HOUSING PROGRAMS																							
Mortgage Insurance																							
Owner-Occupied Housing (Single-Family, Condominium, Cooperative, Mobile Home)	•								•					•					•				
Multifamily Rental Housing	•								•														
Hospitals, Nursing Homes, Group Practice	•						•	•						•									
Construction, Improvement, and Rehabilitation Assistance																							
Improvement and Rehabilitation Insurance	•																						
Direct Loans and Grants for Construction, Improvement, and Rehabilitation	•		•						•					•					•				

TABLE 5-1. *(Continued)*

	Federal																	State				Local	
	HUD				HHS				Other agencies														
	Housing	Fair Housing & Equal Opportunity	Community Planning & Development	Federal Insurance Administration	Social Security Administration	Administration on Aging	Health-Care Financing Administration	Health Services Administration	Department of Agriculture Farmers Home Administration	Department of Justice Law Enforcement Assistance Administration	Department of Transportation Urban Mass Transportation Administration	Department of Energy	Department of the Treasury Internal Revenue Service	Veterans Administration	U.S. Commission on Civil Rights	Community Service Administration	Federal Home Loan Bank Board	State Departments of Revenue	State Housing Finance Agencies	State Agencies on Aging	State Insurance Commissions	General Governments	Area Agencies on Aging
Public Housing	•																						
Congregate Housing	•																		•	•			
Rent Subsidies	•																						
Relocation Assistance	•																						
Property Insurance				•																			
Home Maintenance Assistance			•		•	•						•				•				•			•
Reverse Annuity Mortgages																	•						
Weatherization												•											
LOCAL HOUSING REGULATIONS																							
Building Codes			•																			•	
Zoning Regulations																						•	
Subdivision Regulations																						•	
TAX PROVISIONS																							
Income Tax Structures																							
Designation of Filing Status													•					•					
Deduction of Interest Payments on Home Mortgages													•	•									
Double Exemption for Elderly													•					•					
Deferred Taxation of Annuity Income													•					•					
Capital Gains Provisions																							
Postponement of gains from sale and repurchase of home within 18 months													•										
One-time exclusion of gains (up to $100,000) from sale of residence for those 55 and over													•										
Deduction of State/Local Tax Payments													•										
Inheritance Taxes																		•					
Wage Taxes																						•	
Property Tax Provisions																							

TABLE 5-1. *(Continued)*

	Federal																	State				Local	
	HUD				HHS				Other agencies														
	Housing	Fair Housing & Equal Opportunity	Community Planning & Development	Federal Insurance Administration	Social Security Administration	Administration on Aging	Health-Care Financing Administration	Health Services Administration	Department of Agriculture Farmers Home Administration	Department of Justice Law Enforcement Assistance Administration	Department of Transportation Urban Mass Transportation Administration	Department of Energy	Department of the Treasury Internal Revenue Service	Veterans Administration	U.S. Commission on Civil Rights	Community Service Administration	Federal Home Loan Bank Board	State Departments of Revenue	State Housing Finance Agencies	State Agencies on Aging	State Insurance Commissions	General Governments	Area Agencies on Aging
Differential Rate Structures																		●			●	●	
Property Tax Relief Programs																		●					
INCOME TRANSFER PROGRAMS																							
Social Security					●																		
Supplemental Security Income					●																		
HEALTH PROGRAMS/FACILITIES																							
Medicare							●																
Medicaid							●																
Home Health Care					●	●		●												●			●
SOCIAL SERVICES PROGRAMS																							
Housing Counseling			●		●	●																	
Protective Services					●	●														●			●
Homemaker Services					●	●														●			●
Nutrition Programs					●	●										●				●			●
Chore Services					●	●														●			●
Adult Day Care					●	●														●			●
TRANSPORTATION PROGRAMS																							
Senior Citizen Transit Programs					●	●					●									●		●	●
Reduced-Fare Transit Subsidies											●									●		●	●
COMMUNITY SERVICE PROGRAMS																							
Police Protection and Crime Prevention					●					●												●	
Multi-Purpose Senior Centers			●		●	●														●			●
ENERGY PROGRAMS																							
Emergency Energy Conservation Service (Low-Income Home Heating Program)												●				●							
ANTI-DISCRIMINATION ACTIVITIES		●													●								

SOURCE: Turner et al., 1981.

Housing Programs

The Department of Housing and Urban Development (HUD) has been the prime source of loans and loan guarantees for the construction of rental units for the low and moderate income elderly. The most notable programs have been Public Housing, Section 236 (Rental Housing Assistance Payments), Section 202 (Multi-Family Rental Housing), and Section 8 (Low and Moderate Income Housing). In recent years congregate housing arrangements for the elderly have also been developed to lessen the economic and physical burden of maintaining a household, giving particular attention to elderly persons who live in public housing projects. In addition several HUD mortgage insurance programs encourage homeownership by moderate-income households. The vast majority of the elderly are homeowners, and few older renters are willing to assume new mortgage debt in order to purchase a home. Thus, mortgage insurance and government home loan programs are primarily attractive to younger, first-time home buyers.

Assistance for the rehabilitation and improvement of existing owner-occupied and rental housing is available to the elderly through a variety of programs administered by HUD, the Farmers Home Administration, and the Veterans Administration. These programs enable elderly households and others to upgrade their housing without moving to another unit, particularly through low-interest loans and grants. Like the mortgage insurance programs, however, the loan programs have limited appeal to the elderly and others on fixed incomes. Another limitation of both the loan and grant programs is that they require the occupant to bring the housing unit up to government standards. In many cases this requirement prevents households from participating in the program because high costs may result from efforts to comply with existing codes.

Other Policies and Programs

From an economic standpoint the most important federal program to house the elderly is Social Security. While this program does not directly provide housing assistance, it is the major source of income for millions of elderly households. Government statistics indicate that the average elderly household spends 23 percent of its income on housing, which is the largest single expenditure category for this population (U.S. Department of Labor, 1976). The central importance of Social Security in promoting independent living is apparent from the fact that over three-fourths of the elderly—or more than 16 million persons in the U.S.—receive Social Security benefits, whereas about one million participate in HUD-assisted rental housing programs (Struyk and Soldo, 1980).

Federal, state, and local tax policies also have major effects on the housing choices of older Americans. The two most important tax provisions are the one-time exclusion of capital gains on the sale of homes and the deduction of interest payments on home mortgages. The capital gains provision encourages older persons to sell their home and move into less expensive housing without incurring a tax liability. The deductibility of mortgage interest payments, on the other hand, encourages households to purchase homes by means of mortgage financing. Double tax exemption for the elderly and exemptions for dependents are two other tax provisions that promote independent living by increasing household income.

State and local property tax relief programs assist low-income households to remain in their homes by improving the affordability of housing. The most widespread property tax relief mechanisms are homestead exemptions (which offer tax reductions for specified types of owner-occupants) and circuit breakers (which place upper limits on the tax liability).

Three additional "safety net" programs indirectly promote independent living by increasing recipients' income: Medicare, Medicaid, and Supplemental Security Income. Medicare and Medicaid are health programs that have their greatest impact on the seriously ill. Medicare, a health insurance program, increases the financial security and independence of older persons by reducing the burden of health-care costs. Medicaid, on the other hand, is an antipoverty program providing medical and health services to indigent or medically needy persons. It is the mainstay of the long-term-care system for the elderly in that it pays for housing and health care in intermediate and skilled nursing facilities; for home health care; and for fees to physicians, hospitals, and laboratories. Originally designed to provide comprehensive and equal medical care for the poor, it has in fact fostered institutionalization of the elderly by allowing higher reimbursements for institutional care than for in-home services, by requiring the poor to "spend down" their assets in order to be eligible for coverage, and by placing control over nursing homes in the hands of health care providers (Butler, 1980). This situation has improved somewhat since 1979, when Medicaid began to reimburse the costs of necessary home health services for individuals living with relatives or in shared housing arrangements.

The last of these three "safety net" programs, Supplemental Security Income (SSI), is a means-tested program for aged, blind, and disabled persons. SSI recipients may live independently, in group homes, or in nursing homes and are automatically eligible to receive various social services and other benefits in any of these settings. SSI ensures a minimum standard of living for about 10 percent of the population over age sixty-five, and in this respect it facilitates personal independence. On the negative side, however, it has been argued that SSI restricts shared living arrangements in that it pays reduced benefits for recipients who live with another person.

The Department of Health and Human Services has provided a wide variety of housing-related services to the elderly through Title XX (now known as the Social Services Block Grant), the Older Americans Act, and other social programs. The various services promoting housing for the community resident elderly can be classified as preventive, supportive, rehabilitative, and sheltered care. Generally speaking, preventive services are designed for healthy individuals and involve such activities as volunteer programs, safe escort services, and legal aid. Supportive services provide limited assistance to persons having one or more functional limitations but who are otherwise able to live independently. Examples of supportive services include meals on wheels and homemaker assistance. Rehabilitative services are offered to individuals who have severe disabilities but who may eventually improve. These services include community mental health centers, sheltered workshops, and rehabilitation centers. Finally, sheltered care provides relatively permanent support for those least able to care for themselves; these services include congregate housing and institutional day care.

The provision of senior citizen centers and recreation facilities is valuable in helping participating elderly to maintain their independence. Proximate access to these facilities enables participation in social and recreational activities, congregate meals, and in some cases employment. In many communities services for the homebound are sponsored by senior centers, and the availability of these services reduces the social isolation of individuals lacking personal mobility or initiative.

Current transportation policies emphasize improving the accessibility of transportation for the elderly and the development of senior citizen transit programs in underserved areas. These programs improve the mobility and social life of the community resident elderly by enabling them to reach shopping centers and social activities on their own.

In recent years emergency energy assistance programs have been developed to lessen the impact of rising home heating costs on low-income households. Numerous state and local programs help to protect elderly persons and others from cold weather, but they generally provide no incentive for the household to make energy-saving repairs and improvements. Moreover, very limited funding is available for this type of assistance, which is often as low as $100 per household during the winter heating season.

Finally, the supply and quality of housing for senior citizens are affected by building and land use regulations. In the last few years there has been a significant decline in the supply of rental housing due to the decreasing profitability of property management. During this period increasing energy costs and real estate taxes have led to deferred maintenance and abandonment of older units and to the conversion of new units to condominiums. The tenants affected by such changes are frequently elderly persons and others living on fixed incomes, and the withdrawal of their residences from the housing stock forces many to relocate to units that are more expensive or of lower quality. This problem is particularly serious for the elderly, since involuntary relocation of older persons may lead to depression and/or a shortened life span. In response to this problem many communities, especially large urban centers, have adopted condominium conversion legislation or are considering such legislation to protect older residents. The most common responses to this problem have been laws granting first right of purchase to current tenants or guaranteed lifetime tenancy to the elderly in units undergoing conversion.

Local building and land use regulations also restrict the development of new housing for the elderly. In some communities there has been intense opposition to proposals for multifamily housing, not only public housing for low-income groups but also senior citizen highrise apartments. While recognizing that a growing number of elderly require housing, neighborhood residents frequently oppose the construction of multifamily housing because they feel that this type of development will lead to reduced property values. Community zoning regulations may also impede attempts to produce shared living arrangements. Persons who live alone in large homes frequently find that they are not permitted to convert their residences to accommodate lodgers or companions due to such legislation. Attempts to construct new housing for shared living have also been blocked by restrictive local zoning regulations (Day-Lower, Bryant, and Mullaney, 1982).

Policy Changes since 1981

Virtually all federal social programs have been affected by policy changes instituted by the Reagan administration. The housing and human service cuts resulting from the 1981 Omnibus Budget Reconciliation Act (U.S. PL 97–35) and subsequent legislative and administrative actions have received widespread publicity in news media and in professional journals. It is important to note, however, that these budget cuts have had relatively little financial impact on households at or above the national median income level. Furthermore, total federal expenditures for housing and related services have actually *increased* during this period. The total change in expenditures in these areas is the net result of three components: (1) reduced appropriations for some categorical programs; (2) consolidation of other categorical programs into block grants, with or without funding restrictions; and (3) increased tax losses resulting from homeownership provisions in the federal personal income tax structure. Clearly, the net effect of these components of change has been to lower the standard of living of less-advantaged older persons. Each of these three changes in expenditures will be discussed in turn.

Appropriations for Categorical Programs

The most visible changes in housing expenditures have been in the area of direct housing programs. Subsidized housing programs grew rapidly during the 1970s and were the third largest category of welfare programs in 1981, behind Medicaid and food stamps. In order to curtail the growth of expenditures for subsidized housing, the Reagan administration has made major modifications in the Section 8 new and existing housing programs and has proposed a less costly and less generous housing voucher program.

Between fiscal years 1975 (when Section 8 was started) and 1982, federal commitments for public housing and rental assistance programs grew from $61 billion to approximately $225 billion (U.S. President's Commission on Housing, 1982). (These figures represent budget authorizations for newly constructed housing projects. Section 8 new construction projects funded since 1975 will receive federal assistance for an average of twenty-four years.) Assuming that no new projects are authorized under these two programs, the annual outlays will rise from $5.5 billion in fiscal year (FY) 1982 to $7.8 billion in FY 1986 due to the completion of projects currently under construction. The 1981 Omnibus Budget Reconciliation Act raised tenant rents to a maximum of 30 percent of the family's monthly adjusted income, compared to a maximum of 25 percent under previous legislation. The administration also proposed a freeze on authorizations for new Section 8 projects and has cancelled some projects that were approved during the Carter administration.

Although the president's FY 1983 budget proposals were rejected by Congress, the figures contained in those proposals demonstrated the administration's desire to reduce expenditures for assisted housing programs. A 98 percent reduction in the budget authority for all HUD-assisted housing programs was proposed between fiscal years 1981 and 1983—from $33.4 billion to $685 million over this three-year period. Budget authorizations for Section 8 and public housing, which totaled $25.0 billion in FY 1981, were set at *minus* $5.2 billion for FY 1983 due to scheduled revisions (Nenno, 1982).

In a similar vein, the president's proposed budget authority for Section 202 housing for the elderly and handicapped was $286 million for FY 1983, a 65 percent reduction from FY 1981 (Nenno, 1982). In a continuing budget resolution, however, Congress decided to fund the Section 202 program at $635 million for FY 1983, representing an increase of $181 million from the FY 1982 funding level. This change from the administration's original budget proposal was made possible through the advocacy efforts of the Ad Hoc Coalition for Housing for the Elderly and local religious groups.

Consolidation of Categorical Programs

A second major policy shift since 1981 has been the development of new block grants, which are intended to control the growth of federal expenditures while increasing the states' discretion in program administration. In addition to the pro-

gram cuts described above, the Omnibus Budget Reconciliation Act consolidated twenty-five federal programs into eight new block grants: Social Services; Community Services; Low-Income Energy Assistance; Alcohol and Drug Abuse and Mental Health; Primary Care; Preventive Health and Health Services; Education; and Maternal Child Health (Adelman and Oriol, 1982). The first three of these new block grants have significant housing effects and will be described briefly.

The Social Services block grant supplants the Title XX program, which provided counseling, home maintenance, and other supportive services to the elderly and to other subpopulations. The level of funding for programs included in this block grant was reduced by 20 percent as a result of this consolidation. States were granted authority to transfer up to 10 percent of their health or energy block grant program allotments to social service programs.

The Community Service block grant was designed to replace many of the functions of the Community Service Administration (CSA), which attempted to ameliorate the problem of poverty in American communities. Many of the CSA programs were eliminated as a result of this change, including home maintenance and repair programs. States were granted broad authority to use this block grant to meet housing, community development, and other needs; but their ability to make improvements in these areas was reduced by sharp funding cuts. A subsequent budget proposal by the administration called for a 79 percent reduction in community services funding between fiscal years 1981 and 1983.

Finally, the Low-Income Energy Assistance block grant combined two federal initiatives in regard to energy: the Low-Income Energy Assistance Program and the Emergency Crisis Assistance Program. Under this block grant up to 15 percent of the state allotment was permitted for low-cost weatherization, and 10 percent could be transferred to the Social Services block grant. Modest funding cuts were made when the Low-Income Energy Assistance block grant was created, and larger cuts have been proposed by the administration in subsequent budgets.

In summary, the consolidation of these programs into block grants has had two major effects on housing. As a result of these changes, states now have greater flexibility to address housing and community development needs. At the same time, however, their ability to improve housing adequacy has been hindered by the 20–25 percent cuts in social service and energy assistance funding levels which resulted from the passage of the Omnibus Budget Reconciliation Act.

Indirect Subsidies through the Personal Income Tax

While the Reagan administration's budget changes significantly reduced the level of funding available for assisted housing, total federal housing expenditures have continued to increase due to the rapidly growing tax "losses" (or expenditures) permitted by the Internal Revenue Service. In contrast to the two types of changes mentioned above, these tax losses result from provisions of the federal personal income tax code and are not subject to annual review through the budget and appropriations process.

According to a study by the U.S. Congressional Budget Office (U.S. CBO, 1981), homeownership benefits under the individual income tax amounted to more than $31 billion in FY 1981 and are projected to increase to over $82 billion by FY 1986—a growth of more than 250 percent during this five-year period. As indicated in table 5-2, most of this growth will be in the category of itemized deductions by households owning and occupying their own homes. Based on present tax laws, the Congressional Budget Office report estimates that homeowner deductions for mortgage payments and property taxes will rise from $29 billion to $78 billion by 1986 as a result of rising property values. In addition a modest increase in tax expenditures is anticipated under provisions for deferred taxation of gains on the sale of owner-

TABLE 5-2. Major Tax Expenditures for Homeownership, Fiscal Years 1981–86 (In millions of dollars)

Provision	1981	1982	1983	1984	1985	1986
Deductibility of mortgage interest on owner-occupied homes[1]	$19,805	$25,295	$31,115	$37,960	$46,310	$56,500
Deductibility of property taxes on owner-occupied homes	8,915	10,705	12,740	15,160	18,040	21,465
Deferral of capital gains on sales of owner-occupied homes	1,110	1,220	1,345	1,480	1,630	1,790
Exclusion of capital gains on sales of owner-occupied homes for persons aged 55 and older	590	650	715	785	860	950
Exclusion of interest on state and local bonds for owner-occupied housing	840	1,220	1,600	1,855	1,890	1,810
Total	$31,260	$39,090	$47,515	$57,240	$68,730	$82,515

SOURCE: *U.S. Congressional Budget Office, 1981.*

1. Does not include the deductibility of interest payments for home improvement loans or loans on investment property.

occupied homes (from $1.1 billion to $1.8 billion during the same time period).

The federal personal income tax also provides indirect subsidies to homeowners through two types of exclusions: (1) capital gains on sales of owner-occupied homes by persons aged fifty-five and over and (2) interest received from state and local bonds to finance owner-occupied housing. The capital gains exclusion is a one-time benefit option for older households, which was increased from a $100,000 ceiling to $125,000 in 1981. Tax losses from this exclusion are anticipated to increase from $590 million to $950 million between 1981 and 1986. The exclusion of income from tax-exempt mortgage bonds is the newest type of tax benefit for homeowners. In 1978 state and local governments began issuing these bonds to meet the need for more affordable housing, both for owners and renters. In 1980 federal legislation banned new tax-exempt bond issues for single-family homes after 1983. Despite these restrictions, federal tax losses from this exclusion are projected to increase from $840 million to $1.8 billion between 1981 and 1986.

These various deductions and exclusions have been developed and expanded over several decades and have permitted millions of American families to purchase their own homes. Nevertheless, these benefits constitute a major fraction of the current federal budget deficit and favor households above the median income level. In 1981, for example, less than $2 billion of the $21 billion in tax expenditures for home mortgage interest deductions went to households earning less than $20,000 a year (U.S. CBO, 1981). Currently, these tax benefits for homeowners are much more costly than Section 8 and all other low-income housing programs combined.

Conclusion

At this time the vast majority of households over age sixty-five are adequately housed, according to government statistics and data from private sources (U.S. Department of Housing and Urban Development, 1979; Struyk and Soldo, 1980;

Lawton and Hoover, 1981). This fact notwithstanding, millions of older persons still live in housing that is poorly maintained, too expensive relative to their income, or inadequate in other respects. Previous research by the author, for example, found that more then 3.1 million elderly households spent at least 40 percent of their income on housing and related expenses in 1980, and 1.3 million believed that their residence was in need of major repairs (Turner and Mangum, 1982).

During the past fifty years the public sector has assumed major responsibilities for the housing of older persons. Despite the recent budget cuts for housing and other social programs, total federal expenditures for housing will continue to rise unless major changes are made in the deduction and exclusion provisions of the personal income tax. For this reason public debate about the role of government in housing should recognize that low-income housing programs account for a much lower fraction of the federal budget than do the indirect housing subsidies resulting from the tax codes.

Finally, it should be reemphasized that the public sector role in elderly housing should not be limited to tax and expenditure policies and programs. As was mentioned above, the option of house sharing is currently unavailable to many older persons due to restrictive zoning ordinances and eligibility rules for federally assisted means-tested programs (Day-Lower, Bryant, and Mullaney, 1982). Although shared living is not the preferred living arrangement for the majority of older Americans, a liberalization of these zoning regulations and program eligibility rules could significantly reduce the number of older persons in need of alternative housing.

Federal and state governments can also have important roles in the emerging area of home equity conversion. As was recognized by the U.S. President's Commission on Housing (1982, pp. 54–56), the federal government should initiate and support various financing mechanisms to facilitate the conversion of housing assets into an income stream. Unlike the traditional second mortgage, which requires the borrower to repay the loan after a fixed time period, equity conversion options such as reverse annuity mortgages and sale-leaseback plans permit the household to receive monthly income for life or until the sale of the home (U.S. Senate, 1982). Because these mortgage instruments have been in existence for less than a decade, they have had a very limited impact on the problem of housing affordability to date. Nonetheless, it is widely recognized that home equity is the largest unleveraged source of capital in the United States and that older persons control a major fraction of all housing assets. For these reasons the federal and state governments should work closely with the private sector to develop innovative home equity conversion plans that would promote better use of this financial resource while protecting the borrowers against the risks of fraud and foreclosure.

Home equity conversion, like house sharing, is only a partial solution to the housing problems of older persons. Existing equity conversion plans are primarily attractive to households in areas where housing prices are experiencing a rapid appreciation, and they are obviously unavailable to renters. For these reasons equity conversion should not be viewed as a substitute for housing assistance programs. Both equity conversion and shared housing can address the housing problems of specific subgroups of the elderly, but special assistance for low-income older persons is needed to further the goals of the Older Americans Act and the Housing Act of 1937.

References

Adelman, I., and W. Oriol. 1982. *1982–83 Chartbook of Federal Programs on Aging.* Bethesda, MD: Care Reports.

Butler, P. A. 1980. "Legal Problems in Medicaid." In *Legal Aspects of Health Policy.* Ed. R. Roemer and G. McKray. Westport, CT: Greenwood.

Day-Lower, D., D. Bryant, and J. W. Mullaney. 1982. *National Policy Workshop on Shared Housing: Findings and Recommendations.* Philadelphia: Shared Housing Resource Center.

Lawton, M. P., and S. L. Hoover. 1981. *Community Housing Choices for Older Americans.* New York: Springer.

Nenno, M. K. 1982. "The President's HUD Budget." *Journal of Housing* 39:43–50.

Struyk, R. J., and B. J. Soldo. 1980. *Improving the Elderly's Housing: A Key to Preserving the Nation's Housing Stock and Neighborhoods.* Cambridge, MA: Ballinger.

Turner, L., and E. Mangum. 1982. *Report on the Housing Choices of Older Americans: Summary of Survey Findings and Recommendations for Practitioners.* Washington, DC: National Council on the Aging.

Turner, L., et al. 1981. "Review of Policies Affecting the Housing Decisions of Older Americans." Iowa City, IA: The Institute of Urban and Regional Research, The University of Iowa.

U.S. Congressional Budget Office (CBO). 1981. "The Tax Treatment of Homeownership: Issues and Options." Washington, DC: U.S. Government Printing Office.

U.S. Department of Housing and Urban Development. 1979. "How Well Are We Housed? The Elderly." Washington, DC: U.S. Government Printing Office.

U.S. Department of Labor. 1976. "Consumer Expenditures Survey Series, Average Annual Expenditures for Commodity and Services Groups Classified by Nine Family Characteristics, 1972 and 1973." Washington, DC: U.S. Government Printing Office.

U.S. President's Commission on Housing. 1982. *The Report of the President's Commission on Housing.* Washington, DC: U.S. Government Printing Office.

U.S. Senate. 1982. Special Committee on Aging. "Turning Home Equity into Income for Older Homeowners." Washington, DC: U.S. Government Printing Office.

CHAPTER 6 Future Housing Assistance Policy for the Elderly

Raymond J. Struyk

Housing policy in the United States for the elderly as well as the nonelderly has been changing rapidly under the spur of dramatic reductions in the level of resources the country believes it can allocate to federally supported social programs. This chapter hazards a look into the future for government housing policy, and hence programs, for elderly Americans. This view is from the vantage point of what government interventions could be. As such they look beyond the immediate federal budget woes, although they are tempered by the probable realities of the 1980s. Judging from the manifest disenchantment of Americans in the late 1970s with high taxes and activist government, fewer federal resources are likely to be available regardless of which party is in the White House (Palmer and Sawhill, 1982).

This presentation takes four objectives of an enlightened housing policy as its starting point. Policies should be designed to:

- provide the elderly with a range of choice in their living arrangements. Hence, equivalent assistance should be available to otherwise similar householders who choose different living arrangements.
- facilitate timely adjustments in housing consumption and living arrangements as they become necessary and the household wishes to make them. So, for example, impediments to living in single-family units such as restrictions about taking in boarders should be removed.

- improve the housing circumstances of those receiving assistance—both upgrading housing quality to a minimum standard and reducing housing expenditures to a reasonable level—at the lowest cost possible.
- treat all similarly situated households in the same way; this implies moving toward making housing assistance available on an entitlement basis, for at least some segment of the population.

From previous chapters, it is clear that housing policy to date has not been formulated so as to have achieved these objectives. Moreover, the changes enacted by Congress since early 1981 are not fully consistent with them. Thus, the gap yawns wide between where we are and where we should be.

The material presented assumes that the reader begins with a working knowledge of federal housing assistance for the elderly as it existed at the beginning of the 1980s. (See chapter 5 for a recapitulation.) Prior papers have also described the current housing situation of the elderly in some detail and others have examined some projections for the future (Newman, Zais, and Struyk, 1984). With this background information in hand, the next section of the chapter summarizes the initiatives taken by the Reagan administration and comments on them briefly as to whether or not they are consistent with the four objectives stated earlier. The following then deals with preferred government interventions via housing assistance to elderly renters and homeowners. The discussion here concentrates on major policy thrusts. Small-scale approaches such as shared housing and reverse annuity mortgages are covered in later chapters.

The Reagan Initiatives in Housing Assistance

A number of legislative actions taken during the first Reagan administration provide a pellucid picture of the administration's philosophy about housing assistance. The goals of this administration were to halt the growth in the number of households receiving assistance, to target the available assistance to poorer households, to reduce benefits, and finally, to emphasize use of the existing stock over building new housing projects.

Program Size

The administration took the position in its fiscal year (FY) 1983 budget that holding the number of households receiving housing assistance to 3.8 million—the number that should be receiving assistance at the end of FY 1985—is "essential to the administration's effort to control long-term federal government spending" (U.S. Office of Management and Budget, 1982, p. 110). In later years, a less stringent position has been evident, but the goal seems clear. The first Reagan administration was able to hold the increases in assisted households to about 70,000 per year, compared with the 200,000-unit programs of the Carter administration.

Sharper Targeting and Reducing Benefits

Since 1981 Congress has enacted several important changes to the housing assistance programs in an effort to achieve better targeting of limited resources, greater equity among participants in public housing and other housing assistance programs, and greater equity between participants in housing programs and nonparticipants. Three changes were enacted:

- The contribution by a tenant receiving housing assistance was increased from 25 to 30 percent of its income.
- Eligibility for assistance has been restricted by limiting the share of all recipient households who have incomes between 50 and 80 percent of their area's median incomes (adjusted for family size). Now a maximum of 10 percent of the units are available for occupancy by this group. Other recipients must have incomes below 50 percent of area median (about 133 percent of the poverty line on a national basis).
- The definitions of income used in computing the tenant's contribution was made uniform for the Section 8 and public housing programs. Traditionally, local authorities had wide latitude in defining incomes; now more of a household's gross income will be counted by some authorities in computing benefits.

There is no doubt that "very low-income households"—those with incomes below 50 percent of local median income—have more severe housing problems than other households. Changes enacted to achieve greater equity among this group are, by themselves, on the mark. Participants have had the share of their incomes devoted to housing lowered dramatically by the subsidies compared to nonrecipients, some of whom would participate under an entitlement program. In 1977, for example, about 80 percent of unsubsidized very low-income renter-householders spent over 30 percent of their incomes on housing. Subsidized renters, on the other hand, were required to contribute only a quarter of their incomes for the housing they consumed.

Emphasizing Use of the Existing Stock

Extending a pattern initiated by Congress in 1980, both the executive branch and Congress have continued to deemphasize new construction. The FY 1982 housing budget has a mix of 88 percent existing and 12 percent new construction and substantial rehabilitation. In the subsequent budgets the administration has maintained this breakdown—an 80 percent-existing, 20 percent-new-construction mix. The main justification for building fewer new units to house low-income households is the great expense of these units. In the early 1970s it cost about twice as much to provide a unit-month of housing services from a federally assisted newly built unit than it did to lease a privately owned existing unit, according to very careful analysis done as part of the Experimental Housing Allowance Program (Mayo et al., 1979). On efficiency grounds, existing housing dominates, as long as it is in adequate supply.

The administration has also achieved enactment of a "housing voucher" program on a demonstration basis which embodies two types of change. One type will make the program more efficient; these changes are based on favorable experience in the Experimental Housing Allowance Program. In particular, changes would cease treating the Fair Market Rent (FMR) as the maximum for which a unit could rent and still be in the program, although the subsidy would be calculated using the FMR; and they would increase the incentive to participants to occupy units renting for less than the FMR. (The FMR is the rent upon which the government's subsidy is based.)

The effects of the second type are less clear but they may make the program less successful. These modifications reduced the fair market rent somewhat. Coupled with a rule limiting the amount of increase in the FMR over the five-year life of the voucher, these provisions may have made the benefits insufficient to induce families living in dwellings failing the program's physical standards to relocate to a unit that would meet these standards. In short, the program may not be capable of achieving the objectives of housing policy as they have been articulated.

Initiatives versus Objectives

On the positive side, some of the actions enumerated above do move toward focusing aid on those most in need and toward greater equity in the treatment of those participating in rental programs. They also move to lower the differences between participants and nonparticipants and to shift housing assistance to a more efficient mode by stressing use of the existing stock.

The negative side of the ledger is longer. By capping the number of participants, differences between the "haves" and the "have nots" is perpetuated. By continuing the separate forms of assistance to renters and homeowners, inequities will persist here as well. Indeed, aid to elderly homeowners through exclusion of up to $125,000 in gains on home equity at the time of sale is quite likely an inefficient way to provide assistance. Benefits to participants in the rental programs are sharply cut.

Finally, only limited choice is provided in these policies. Granted, housing vouchers provide considerably more choice among dwellings than do project options; and exclusion of the capital gains tax cuts the penalty of shifting to renter status. However, limited entitlements restrict participant mobility to remain within the jurisdiction where the person first gets his voucher, and poor owners who become renters have no assurance of being able to receive aid as renters.

Housing Assistance Policy in the Future

For several reasons it is sensible to begin a look at the future by considering the implications of housing assistance available on an entitlement basis to qualifying renters and homeowners. Then, specific issues in program design for renters and for homeowners are discussed.

The arguments in favor of entitlement are formidable. First, an entitlement approach ends the inequities in treatment that presently exist between recipients and would-be recipients. Second, it removes impediments to housing adjustments that may exist because those receiving assistance in a particular unit or jurisdiction fear that in relocating they risk losing them. Third, for poor elderly homeowners, the specter of encountering uncontrollable rents if they move from their unmortgaged home will dissolve. Fourth, the general availability of housing assistance would permit housing assistance to be merged with the balance of the social welfare system to help limit the broader inequities in the system; this, in turn, would enormously facilitate thoroughgoing reform. Finally, housing assistance could be viewed as an integral element in the system of long-term care that must be developed in the next few years to handle the rapidly increasing number of elderly.

Who could participate and what would the program be? Very briefly, the program is a housing voucher program—a program quite similar to the Section 8 existing program—in which the income cut-off for eligibility for a family of four is set at 50 percent of local area median income. Participants contribute 30 percent of their adjusted income for housing. Renters and homeowners can participate; counted as income is the return on most assets, actual or imputed, including the return on home equity.[1] Subsidies for both homeowners and renters are calculated using the same rent levels as an estimate of reasonable housing costs in local areas, based on the size of the rental unit needed. Thus, equity between the two tenure groups is achieved.

Three questions immediately come to mind when considering an entitlement program: (1) how many households will participate, (2) what will it cost, and (3) how will it be financed?

The figures in table 6-1 give a rough idea of participation, based on the open-enrollment portion of the Experimental Housing Allowance Program (EHAP). It is only a rough idea because the income cut-off was higher in EHAP than in the proposed program, meaning that participation rates are somewhat downwardly biased (Struyk and Bendick, 1981). On the other hand, benefit levels were higher in EHAP than those likely to be in effect in a voucher program in the future, judging from 1981 congressional action and the Reagan initiatives. Among the elderly about 2.3 million additional householders—70 percent of them owner-occupants—would participate if they could; another 3 million additional nonelderly would participate as well.

Judging program costs in the future is extremely difficult. We have estimated that under the 50 percent-of-median-income-eligibility rules the

TABLE 6-1. Estimated Participation in an Open-Enrollment Housing Voucher Program (Millions of Households)

	Elderly-Headed Households		Nonelderly-Headed Households		
	Owners	Renters	Owners	Renters	Total
Eligible to receive housing assistance (1979)	5.0	2.9	4.7	8.4	21.0
Currently receiving assistance (1983)	—	1.5[1]	.7[2]	2.4[1]	4.6
Eligible but not receiving assistance	5.0	1.4	4.0	6.0	16.4
Likely to participate in voucher entitlement program[3]	1.6	.7	.7	2.3	5.3

1. Estimates of eligibles are from Zais, Struyk, and Thibodeau (1982); estimates of current participants are from the same source applied to figures in the HUD FY 1983 budget (HUD, 1982, p. H-20). Same elderly–nonelderly split as for HUD programs is applied to aggregate figures for the Farmer's Home Section 515 program (exclusive of Section 515/Section 8); figures on FmHA programs are from Drews (1982), p. 8.
2. HUD programs plus Farmer's Home Administration Section 502; we have assumed no assistance in these programs to the elderly.
3. Participation rates are from the Housing Allowance Supply Experiment; Kingsley and Schlegel (1982), table 5-1.

average annual subsidy payment under the Section 8 existing program in 1983 would be about $2,400 if the program continued as it was in 1981. However, for purposes of these calculations, we think that a total cost of about $2,000 per household in 1983 is a realistic figure, in light of changes already made.[2] Using this figure, the incremental cost of assisting all the additional elderly participants is about $4.6 billion in 1983; assisting all of the incremental nonelderly participants would cost about another $6 billion.[3]

An additional $10.6 billion in government expenditures in the current environment appears at first encounter to be a ludicrous suggestion. But these need not be additional expenditures; in fact, these costs should be met through reductions elsewhere in the budget. Of course, making cuts is difficult because of the competing interests of congressional committees. Nevertheless, three sources in particular could be used. First, the $1.3 billion budgeted for weatherization and heating assistance could be replaced with vouchers. Recipients could use voucher payments for these purposes if they wish, or to meet other more urgent needs. Second, the $550 million in exclusion of capital gains tax on home equity for those over age fifty-five should be repealed; the largest beneficiaries of this provision are households who need it least. Third, mortgage interest deductions from the federal income tax should be contained. The tax losses from these reductions are expected to double from 1982 to 1987 to a staggering $44.4 billion; it is well known that these benefits accrue disproportionately to high-income families (Greene, 1981). A reduction of only 35 percent in the 1983 tax losses, combined with the other cuts, would finance vouchers. The overall effect of substituting vouchers for the other expenditures would be a dramatically improved targeting of housing assistance for the poor.

Renters: Do We Need New Construction?

The traditional bellwether of the federal government's concern for housing for the elderly has been the number of units proposed for construction by

nonprofit sponsors for exclusive occupancy by the elderly and by the nonelderly handicapped under the Section 202 program. Among all programs, elderly-designated projects now house over half of all elderly assisted households and are widely thought of as the primary approach to assisting the elderly. A radical transformation to emphasizing the leasing of existing units is in the offing, driven by the high cost of new construction projects.

In the years ahead the construction of new projects for the elderly beyond token levels will occur only if these projects have a well-defined role in the long-term care system. In short, they will have to be (or should be) congregate housing facilities—housing offering a number of services in addition to shelter—that can be demonstrated to be cost-effective alternatives to both intermediate-care facilities *and* to providing support services to the elderly in the dwelling units they would otherwise be inhabiting.

The evidence on which to base such an argument is certainly not presently at hand. Under a congressional mandate HUD is now conducting the Congregate Housing Services Program as a demonstration to determine if the provision of support services in housing projects has a significant impact on the rates of institutionalization and mortality. Detailed comprehensive analyses of cost-effectiveness compared to intermediate-care facilities are not included. Also omitted is a comparison of congregate facilities with the alternative of providing services to those living in the community. Thus, the requisite knowledge base for informed decision making is at least several years distant, and in the meanwhile new construction may be discontinued altogether.

On a conceptual basis, however, one can define the test that newly constructed congregate facilities would have to pass to dominate the provision of services to the elderly living in the community (Strassen and Holohan, 1980). The economies of scale in the provision of support services would have to be greater than the additional cost of leasing a new dwelling (in the project) compared to leasing an existing one in the community. The difference in the cost of leasing new versus existing units is on the order of $300 per month, which places the burden of proof on those favoring new projects. Savings estimates would certainly be sensitive to the number and mix of support services that households needed. It is clear, however, that for such large economies to be realized, those admitted to the projects would also have to need multiple services. This in turn means that the population housed in new projects would have more health and mobility problems than those now housed in elderly-only projects.

Homeowners: Options to Vouchers

Ignoring tax advantages to homeowners (which are unimportant to those with low incomes or no mortgage), then impoverished homeowners have largely fallen through the housing assistance net. The issue here is how to aid this group efficiently. It was suggested earlier that the exclusion of capital gains tax on home equity at the time of sale embodies problems of targeting and program integration, and would better be replaced with help to owners while living in their homes. In this section we examine two front-running options: housing vouchers and the provision of in-kind home maintenance services. Vouchers provide a cash grant to income-eligible homeowners on the condition that the dwelling meets minimum physical standards. The grant itself can be spent on housing or for anything else. Under the in-kind maintenance services approach, by contrast, an agency provides services directly to the household; the household, which typically is required to pay a fixed small fee (such as $25) to join the program, can spend money (or time and effort) it would have otherwise devoted to dwelling upkeep on other things.

So both approaches make it possible for the household to substitute publicly provided resources for its own, and the extent of such substitution is one important criterion for assessing the two approaches. Policy should favor the approach that transforms more of the federal expenditure into additional services of the type being targeted. A second criterion is the administrative cost and simplicity of the approaches. A final criterion is the likelihood of participation of households in the two programs. The following paragraphs present the evidence for these three areas available from the Housing Allowance Supply Experiment (HASE) and a HUD demonstration of the in-kind services approach in seven cities (Lowry, 1981; Ferguson and Moss, 1982). The reader is warned that the data on the two approaches are not very comparable, so that the comparison is only rough.

The evidence on the amount of repair activity induced by housing vouchers—that is, activity above the normal—is quite convincing. Homeowners in Green Bay and South Bend spent $178 and $153 more per year on repairs, respectively, due to vouchers.[4] These expenditures represent about a 60 percent increase in repairs. Another way to express the effect is to say that the elasticity with respect to an incremental income from allowance payments was 4.8 and 2.9, respectively, in Green Bay and South Bend. These are large increases indeed.

The figures for in-kind services are less easily dealt with. On average, the program delivered $208 per client in repair services (Ferguson and Moss, 1982). However, some of these expenditures may have substituted for work that would have been done in the absence of assistance; alternatively, it may have induced more. My intuition is that the $208 can be interpreted realistically as an upper bound. As such, it is certainly no more than the voucher figures which, when adjusted for inflation for the same period as those for in-kind services, are $247 and $213, respectively. Hence, the amounts for induced repairs are roughly comparable, with vouchers possibly having a modest edge.[5]

The comparison of administrative simplicity and cost for the two approaches is more conclusive. Vouchers are certainly easier to administer since they do not involve the direct provision of services. Both approaches require the standard tenant intake functions, such as outreach and screening for eligibility. The greater administrative simplicity of vouchers is borne out in the cost figures. In the Supply Experiment, sixteen cents of every program dollar goes for administration (Kingsley and Schlegel, 1982), the average for the seven sites providing in-kind services is about thirty-five cents.[6] Beyond these costs it seems probable that the in-kind services approach would require more HUD oversight, meaning higher costs in this quarter as well.

On the other hand, total costs are important; a year of allowances would cost about $1,400 compared to about $800 for in-kind services. Much of the allowances are spent by recipients on things besides housing, even though they result in substantial repairs and are cheap to administer. In contrast, in-kind services are cheaper, but much of the total cost goes for administration.

Participation is more difficult to judge because of the lack of any information on an open-enrollment in-kind services program and because of the general differences in outreach. Using a variety of means, but emphasizing the media, the voucher program (HASE) was able to notify the vast majority of eligible elderly households about the program. Homeowners had to apply for the program and qualify their homes with little or no aid from the administering agency. Under these conditions, one-third of the income-eligible elderly homeowners participated in the program (Kingsley-Schlegel, 1982; Wendt, 1981; Coleman, 1981).

In contrast, the typical pattern of outreach and enrollment for the provision of in-kind services has been much more intense. Neighborhoods are generally the target area and outreach has even included door-to-door canvassing. Enrollment interviews often are done in the client's home. All of this means that more households may participate and that some "hard-to-reach" elderly may join this program who would not have attempted to enroll in a voucher program. Likewise, participation should be higher under the in-kind services approach because generally there has been no minimum physical standard that the home must pass in order for the household to receive in-kind maintenance services. On the other hand, the small-area approach may make comprehensive spatial coverage a problem; if so, clear inequities will arise between those with access to the services and those without.

Looking at the two approaches for assisting elderly homeowners comprehensively, there is no clear winner. Housing allowances do at least as well inducing dwelling upkeep, and they are dramatically less complex and administratively costly. Low participation is a problem, but more detailed analyses indicate that the more needy households participate at higher rates. Yet they are expensive compared to in-kind services. Still, *if* national policy were being made today on the basis of the available analyses, vouchers would seem to be the better choice.

Conclusion

At least the first half of the decade of the 1980s will be characterized by great tumult and probably fundamental change in federal housing assistance for the elderly. In the environment of stringent budget constraints, any successful initiative in this area will have to possess three characteristics:

- It must be "self-financing" in the sense that the initiative replaces a less efficient approach to addressing the same or related problem.
- It must be convincingly cost-effective; a proven track record on cost will be essential.
- It must move housing assistance toward greater cohesion and integration with the welfare and long-term care systems.

Under these conditions the trend will very likely include a greater reliance on housing vouchers to serve elderly renters and homeowners. Their cost-effectiveness is proven, and their integration with the long-term care system seems quite straightforward.

The major impediment to their expansion will be finding the funds somewhere else in the federal budget. As noted earlier, however, the housing-related weatherization and energy assistance program and the tax expenditures on home equity capital gains exclusion would provide a major portion of the funds, with the balance coming from reductions in the generosity of the mortgage interest deductions for higher income households.

At the same time, tighter targeting of vouchers should be pressed. In particular, assistance should be concentrated on the long-term or permanently poor and not used as supplemental unemployment compensation (Newman and Struyk, 1983). Tighter targeting of this type would disproportionately favor the elderly. Indeed, one might begin the move to entitlement by enfranchising the elderly first.

To be sure, the choices ahead are difficult. Each produces losers as well as beneficiaries. Above all, the overriding goal must be greater equity in the treatment of similar households and a greater use of housing assistance to expand the choices available to elderly Americans in general and the poor in particular.

Notes

1. Homeowners participating in the Housing Allowance Supply experiment in Green Bay, WI, and South Bend, IN, had benefits computed this way. For more on this, see Lowry (1974).
2. In particular, these changes are the increase in tenant's contributions from 25 to 30 percent of income and modest reductions in the Fair Market Rents. The $2,000 figure is probably too high for homeowners because it ignores counting their imputed income on home equity in calculating benefits.
3. In the jargon of the federal budget, these are outlays. Budget authority figures would be larger, how much depends on the length of the contract period, i.e., the number of years for which funds are appropriated and committed to administering agencies that is specified in the legislation.
4. These figures are from Lowry (1981), table 5-6. They are for all homeowners, not just the elderly. However, the elderly constitute about two-thirds of all homeowner housing-allowance recipients. Note that they *exclude* the value of unpaid labor used in making these repairs.
5. Another important point is that the variance among the seven sites in the level of services provided under the in-kind program was very large indeed, with a range of $108 to $337 per year. Different levels of services

were provided by the agencies despite quite strong guidelines from HUD. This raises the issue of equitable treatment of participants in such a program.
6. This calculation is based on the figures in table 3-5 of Ferguson and Moss (1982). The calculation was made to give a fairly conservative estimate of administrative costs. Project development and planning costs are excluded; participant intake costs are amortized over two and a half years, costs for referral and counseling are deleted; and fringes for staff in the project development and referral activities (valued at 10 percent of full costs) are excluded. Half of all fringes are allocated to service delivery.

References

Coleman, S. B. 1981. *How Enrollees Respond to Allowances and Housing Standards.* WD-1037-HUD. Santa Monica, CA: Rand.

Drews, R. 1982. *Rural Housing Programs: Long-Term Costs and Their Treatment in the Federal Budget.* Washington, DC: U.S. Congressional Budget Office.

Ferguson, G. D., and S. Moss. 1982. *The Seven City Home Maintenance Demonstration for the Elderly: Preliminary Findings Report.* Cambridge, MA: Urban Systems Research and Engineering.

Green, J. M. 1981. *The Tax Treatment of Homeownership: Issues and Options.* Washington, DC: U.S. Congressional Budget Office.

Kingsley, G. T., and P. M. Schlegel. 1982. *Housing Allowances and Administrative Efficiency.* N-1741-HUD. Santa Monica, CA: Rand.

Levine, M. 1982. *Housing Assistance Program Options.* Washington, DC: U.S. Congressional Budget Office.

Lowry, I. 1981. *Experimenting with Housing Allowances.* WN-8715-HUD. Santa Monica, CA: Rand.

———. 1974. *Equity and Housing Objectives in Homeowner Assistance.* WN-8715-HUD. Santa Monica, CA: Rand.

Mayo, S., S. Mansfield, D. Warner, and R. Zwetchkenbaum. 1979. "Part 2: Costs and Efficiency." In *Housing Allowances and Other Rental Housing Assistance Programs.* Cambridge, MA: Abt Associates.

Newman, S., and J. Reschovsky. 1984. *Federal Policy and the Mobility of Older Homeowners: The Effects of the One-Time Capital Gains Exclusion.* Ann Arbor: University of Michigan, Survey Research Center

Newman, S., and R. Struyk. 1983. "Housing and Poverty." *Review of Economics and Statistics* 65, No. 2 (May):243–53.

Newman, S., J. Zais, and R. Struyk. 1984. "Housing Older America." In *Elderly People and the Environment*. Ed. I. Altman, J. Wohlwill, and M. P. Lawton. New York: Plenum.

Olson, E. O., and D. R. Rasmussen. 1979. "Section 8 Existing: A Program Evaluation." *Occasional Papers in Housing and Community Affairs*, 6:1–32.

Palmer, J., and B. Sawhill. 1982. *The Reagan Experiment*. Washington, DC: Urban Institute.

Scanlon, W., E. DiFederico, and M. Stassen. 1979. *Long-Term Care: Current Experience and a Framework for Analysis*. Washington, DC: Urban Institute.

Stassen, M., and J. Holohan. 1980. "A Comparative Analysis of Long-Term Care Demonstrations and Evaluations." Washington, DC: Urban Institute.

Struyk, R., and M. Bendick. 1981. *Housing Vouchers For The Poor*. Washington, DC: Urban Institute.

U.S. Department of Housing and Urban Development. 1982. *FY 1983 Budget*. Washington, DC: U.S. HUD.

U.S. Office of Management and Budget. 1982. *Major Themes and Additional Details, Fiscal Year 1983*. Washington, DC: U.S. Government Printing Office.

Wendt, J.C. 1981. *Why Households Apply for Housing Allowances*. WE-1037-HUD. Santa Monica, CA: Rand.

Zais, J., R. Struyk, and T. Thibodeau. 1982. *Housing Assistance for Older Americans: The Reagan Prescription*. Washington, DC: Urban Institute.

PART II

HOUSING PREFERENCES AND CHOICES

CHAPTER 7 Housing Preferences and Choices: Implications

M. Powell Lawton

Informed planning and design must take full account of the characteristics, needs, and preferences of groups of people as well as economic resources. Traditional planning has been concerned with maximizing the congruence between people as aggregates and resources as aggregates. This megalevel of "planning" is normally accomplished in the marketplace, with a minimum of intrusion by professional planners. That is, the economic capability and personal preferences of the majority of people form a natural equilibrium with the housing supply and its characteristics so that on the average, people's needs are reasonably met.

The congruence accomplished in such an easy manner has deficiencies, however. First, the ways in which needs are matched are not necessarily the optimum: the housing supply may have developed as it did because of economic or other constraints (for example, bad public housing may be fully occupied only because it comes closest to many people's economic needs). Second, allowing naturally achieved congruence to be the only mode fails to provide for change or growth in a positive direction. If diversity is not actively fostered, consumers will be less likely to experiment with improved housing varieties. Third, and most important for the present purpose, there are inevitably minorities that are not served by the free-market consensual types of housing. This fact has been recognized by the federal government in its designation of specialized housing programs for the poor, the disabled, and the aged. These minorities,

however, may themselves be treated as aggregates, with the same unfortunate leveling of the individual.

The chapters in this section may be viewed as contributions to the idea that knowing about individual needs and preferences, in all their diversity, is essential if planning for aggregates is to proceed effectively. That is, planners must know how many different needs and preferences there are and how many people experience each. Only then will the variety and numbers of resources required be clear.

It is not always easy to separate the demand and supply sides. The chapters in part 2 review current knowledge about individuals in housing settings. Part 4 contains more detailed treatment of environmental resources with some discussion of individuals in those settings. Since studying the aggregate provides information about the individual, consideration of such housing variants as retirement communities or congregate housing can lead to the characteristics that must be determined for planning purposes.

Personal and Situational Determinants of Housing Choice

A naive view of housing choice might see a person's wish as the only determinant of choice. The models of housing choice discussed by Longino in chapter 9 make clear the complexity of the process and the substantial contributions of extrapersonal factors to decisions and moves. In much research on mobility, individual factors have been relatively neglected. The model advanced by Wiseman (1979) and discussed by Longino does not neglect the individual. Many of the factors included in the model are characteristics of the individual—for example, independence loss, personal resources, and personal needs. It is important to note that the construct "residential satisfaction" brackets all the predecision factors.

Residential satisfaction has been extensively studied in both general environmental and gerontological research. Since the chapters in this section deal only in passing with residential satisfaction, a few words on this important topic may be useful. Residential satisfaction represents one domain of the set composing perceived quality of life. Perceived quality of life may be defined as the evaluation a person makes of the adequacy of life in areas such as job, family, friends, activities, or housing.

Understanding the factors that lead to residential satisfaction or dissatisfaction provides the necessary tool for planning environments that maximize satisfaction. A few background characteristics associated with high residential satisfaction are known. Not surprisingly, homeowners and people of higher socioeconomic status are more satisfied with their housing and neighborhoods (Lawton, 1980). One of the most stable findings is that reported satisfaction is greater as chronological age increases (Campbell, Converse, and Rodgers, 1976). The meaning of this finding is still being probed. Another possibility is that older people maintain their mental health by preserving a balance between their aspirations and feeling satisfied with their housing. Campbell, Converse, and Rodgers also suggest that the homes people have attained by this stage of life may in fact be so close to their ideal that aspiration and reality are the same. In any case, the high level of satisfaction cannot be written off as an artifact. Rather, a justified assumption is that at least some part of this satisfaction comes from both active attachment to the residence and the feeling that a change to a new residence might be more risky

than the status quo. The relatively low mobility rates of the elderly discussed by Wiseman in Chapter 8 attest to these reasons for remaining in place. The phenomenon of emotional attachment to place is not well conceptualized at present and certainly not adequately researched.

The objective quality of one's housing is directly related to residential satisfaction, even though the relationship is not as strong as one might hypothesize. For example, in the national sample of older people represented in the *Annual Housing Survey*, the multiple correlation between the incidence of housing deficits and the resident's housing satisfaction was 0.44. The adequacy of the heating system was the strongest predictor (Lawton, 1980). Among older tenants in planned housing, those living in smaller communities, those whose housing was considered conducive to visiting, and those whose units fostered easy maintenance were most satisfied (Lawton and Nahemow, 1979). Neighborhood characteristics such as low crime risk and interviewer-related neighborhood quality were also related to housing satisfaction (Lawton, Nahemow, and Yeh, 1980).

An examination of the characteristics of people who make moves to desirable areas of the country ("amenity moves," in Wiseman's terms, 1979) gives insight into the idea that residential relocation among the aged may represent a continuing effort to improve the "fit" between personal need and environmental context. For example, interstate moves are known to be more frequent among the younger old, the affluent, married, and healthy. These characteristics represent abilities and other resources that people may require in order to be willing to take risks involved in moving during the later years.

Preferences are influenced by intrapersonal and environmental factors acting in concert. A great deal more study is needed of people who have made various choices in order to determine just how much of the remaining-in-place behavior of older people is an active choice made on the basis of preference and how much is a negative choice born of a paucity of personal resources or environmental alternatives.

The Chapters to Follow

Specific residential choices are, of course, evident in where people live. The dynamics of residential choice are better revealed by analyzing changes in location. In chapter 8 Wiseman reviews, first, the geography of residential relocation. This chapter shows clearly the importance of climate and probably the attraction of critical masses of age peers in attracting new migrants. Fine-grain analysis reflects the growing numbers who are seeking sites with topographical interest (e.g., mountainous area) or recreational possibilities for retirement.

Wiseman's analysis of older people's reasons for moving as reflected in the *Annual Housing Survey* represents the first presentation of this important information. Wiseman demonstrates again with his data on migration that many older people move for positive reasons, most falling into the general category of a search for an improved living environment.

Finally, he calls attention to the important phenomenon of aging-in-place. The decision *not* to move is also an active choice and much more frequently made than to move. Wiseman's detailing of how strongly aging-in-place affects the social context of geographic locations now needs to be complemented by a similar analysis of how the individual older person comes to the decision to remain in place.

In chapter 9, Longino approaches the topic of housing choice from the viewpoint of the individual. The model of the migration process is, broadly speaking, applicable to all housing decisions. Far more than any of its predecessors, the Wiseman (1979) model presented by Longino acknowledges the complexity of both personal and environmental determinants. Like Wiseman, Longino shows evidence that, far from being pawns in residential decision making, older people show strong self-determining motivation in this process. Nonetheless, the full explanation must include personal, environmental, and marketing factors.

Longino proceeds beyond the decision making stage to consider the consequences of housing choices. He replaces the deterministic conception that a new environment may "affect" the person with the idea that consequences are an inherent aspect of the decision. People construct a plan that assesses their own needs, looks for a hospitable environment, accounts for pushes and pulls, and fashions the outcome into as acceptable a life for themselves as possible. In calling our attention to the several feedback loops in Wiseman's model, Longino makes the important point that successful residential adjustment requires above all that people be aware of intermediate consequences and be able to adjust their behavior to changing conditions.

Although the retirement community represents a single residential "type" in the minds of most people, in chapter 10 Streib, LaGreca, and Folts show the diversity that in fact exists among the many examples of the retirement community. Because the focus of these authors is on the structural characteristics of the community rather than on the people living in the community, this contribution might be viewed as a discussion of the environmental resource like the chapters in part 4. However, their analysis of the organizational characteristics of communities provides further knowledge of the needs of community residents.

The need for access to basic resources, the varieties of housing types from which prospective residents may choose, the degree of integration with the larger unplanned community, the choices of activities, and the age context of the retirement community are all characteristics of the community that are closely related to the need satisfaction of the resident. In chapter 10, Streib and his colleagues note the potential for change in each of these features. If the context changes in any of these respects, the degree to which the community meets a person's needs may also change. Knowing more about how an individual copes with the aging and possible decline of other residents, with changes in the balance of personal versus external administrative control, or changes in political structure will in turn allow better planning, marketing, and housing counseling to be performed. The research reported by Streib, LaGreca, and Folts is unique in its analysis of the natural histories of complex environments.

Finally, in chapter 11, Sherwood, Morris, and Sherwood examine a sector of the residential continuum that places demands on its residents very different from those made by retirement regions or retirement communities. While the other chapters and this introduction emphasize the active, stimulus-seeking role that many older people assume, it is clear that this is not the only stance appropriate to the older client. Regrettably, old age is for some people a time of decline. To accommodate all people's needs, a wide range of environmental choices must be available for those whose competencies are limited by physical or mental impairments. Nursing homes care for only about 5 percent of the older people, with three times as many living in the community with significant limitation in activity.

Sherwood, Morris, and Sherwood address their chapter to residential arrangements that emphasize the supportive aspect of attaining personal-environment congruence. Specifically, they discuss congregate housing and board-and-care arrangements, citing in detail some of their own relevant research. They conclude that this variety of arrangements is successful both in extending the period of relative independence of these people's lives and in not adding to the economic burden of care.

Viewed in the general perspective of chapter 11, such supportive living arrangements could be chosen by older people as well as by other groups.

Early research in this area demonstrated that older people appear to choose protected environments when their skills become impaired (Lawton, 1969). The great problem is that there are too few choices available, especially to the impaired. If such alternatives as congregate housing, shared housing, foster care, or domiciliary care expand, the preferences of people at the more dependent end of the continuum are far more likely to be satisfied, to the net benefit of both older persons and society in general.

References

Campbell, A., P. G. Converse, and W. Rodgers. 1976. *The Quality of American Life.* New York: Russell Sage.

Lawton, M. P. 1969. "Supportive Services in the Context of the Housing Environment." *Gerontologist* 9:15–19.

————. 1980. "Residential Quality and Residential Satisfaction Among the Elderly." *Research on Aging* 2:309–28.

Lawton, M. P., and L. Nahemow. 1979. "Social Science Methods for Evaluating the Quality of Housing for the Elderly." *Journal of Architectual Research* 7:5–11.

Lawton, M. P., L. Nahemow, and T. M. Yeh. 1980. "Neighborhood Environment and the Well-being of Older Tenants in Planning Housing." *International Journal of Aging and Human Development* 11:211–27.

Wiseman, R. R., 1979. "Spatial Aspects of Aging." Resource Paper No. 88-4. Washington, DC: Association of American Geographers.

CHAPTER 8 Concentration and Migration of Older Americans

Robert F. Wiseman

An understanding of the housing conditions, needs, and desires of older Americans should be prefaced by an understanding of where elders reside and the extent to which the distribution of older Americans is changing. The popular notions of the distribution are fairly portrayed as bipolar extremes. On the one hand, it is commonly held that upon retirement, most people move either to "sun-and-fun" retirement communities or to condominium and inner city apartments where home maintenance is reduced and accessibility to services and conveniences is enhanced. On the other hand, those whose opinions have been informed by mobility statistics realize that older Americans move approximately half as often as the "average American" and therefore most move infrequently, if at all. The first opinion would view the distribution of older people as being very fluid, while the second would infer a highly stable pattern. Each view encapsulates a portion of reality, but neither is a sufficiently accurate generalization.

The following pages demonstrate that the distributional pattern at any scale from national to local is fairly complex, but understandable, and although quite dynamic, it is quite predictable. Three related topics are considered: (1) concentration of elders relative to the remainder of the population in an area; (2) two kinds of residential change by older people that affect patterns of concentration: migration or long-distance movements, and relocation or local movement; and (3) reasons given for change of residence. Although

the examples examined for each topic are selected at the national scale, they illustrate the principle and generalizations that apply almost equally to the local level and are needed to understand and predict subnational distributions. What is depicted is a very general picture that can provide a basis for assessment of local circumstances.

Absolute and Relative Distributions

It is now widely known that older Americans constitute one of our largest and fastest growing "minorities." During the twentieth century, the number of older Americans increased sevenfold, from slightly more than 3.1 million in 1900 to more than 26.3 million in 1981. In 1900 only 4.1 percent of the U.S. population was aged sixty-five or over; by 1980 the percentage had risen to 11.2. These absolute and relative increases in the size of the elderly cohort derive primarily from an increase in life expectancy (from an average age of forty-seven in 1900 to well past seventy years today), from a long-standing decrease in the national birth rate, and from a protracted period of very limited immigration. If these conditions remain at their present levels, by the end of the century more than 30 million Americans, or approximately 12 percent of the population, will be classified as elderly (U.S. Bureau of the Census, 1976).

Perhaps less well known is the wide variation in the size of the elderly population from place to place. For example, many more elders reside in

New York or California than in Florida and each of these three has at least five times as many elderly residents as does Arizona (table 8-1). In fact, the ten largest states account for 54 percent of all older Americans. In general, older people are distributed in much the same way as the total population—the largest states have the largest number of elders. This very broad generalization has remained fairly accurate over time. Its validity is weakened more by variations across space than through time; that is, the generalization becomes less accurate as the spatial scale of observation becomes more local.

Implicit in the above generalization is an assumption of proportionality which, although it has some general validity, masks substantial specific variation among places. The concentration of older people within states, and even more so, within local populations, varies markedly from place to place. Table 8-1, for example, shows that people aged sixty-five and over comprise 17 percent of the population of Florida but only 3 percent of Alaska's. In addition, the concentration of older people has changed markedly over both time and space. At the national level this has produced distinctive regional patterns, illustrated in figure 8-1a on page 72.

The dynamic temporal nature of the pattern of interstate concentration is depicted in figure 8-1b on page 73. The increasing proportion of elders in the population can be seen in the progressive darkening of all the maps over time. It is clear that the increase has not been uniformly distributed among the states and that the range of variation has increased over time. In 1910, only northern New England had a considerable concentration; the rest of the country reported fairly uniform and very low percentages. Since 1910, some states, particularly those in the West and Southeast (with the exception of Florida), have consistently reported low concentrations that fall well below national averages. Other states show large increases and have concentrations far in excess of the national averages. Today, there is a marked contrast among regions, with the most notable concentrations found in the central states, the Northeast,

TABLE 8-1. Population by State, 1980

State	Population (in thousands)	Age 65 and Over	Percent Over 65
Florida	9740	1685	17.30%
Arkansas	2286	312	13.65
Rhode Island	947	127	13.41
Iowa	2913	387	13.29
South Dakota	690	91	13.19
Missouri	4917	648	13.18
Nebraska	1570	206	13.12
Kansas	2363	306	12.95
Pennsylvania	11867	1531	12.90
Massachusetts	5737	727	12.67
Maine	1125	141	12.53
Oklahoma	3025	376	12.43
New York	17557	2161	12.31
North Dakota	652	80	12.27
West Virginia	1950	238	12.21
Wisconsin	4705	564	11.87
Minnesota	4077	480	11.77
Connecticut	3108	365	11.74
New Jersey	7364	860	11.68
District of Columbia	638	74	11.60
Oregon	2633	303	11.51
Vermont	511	58	11.35
Alabama	3890	440	11.31
Arizona	2718	307	11.30
Tennessee	4591	518	11.28
Kentucky	3661	410	11.20
New Hampshire	921	103	11.18
Illinois	11418	1261	11.04
Ohio	10797	1169	10.83
Montana	787	85	10.80
Indiana	5490	585	10.66
Washington	4130	431	10.44
North Carolina	5874	602	10.25
California	23669	2415	10.20
Idaho	944	94	9.96
Delaware	595	59	9.92
Michigan	9258	912	9.85
Texas	14228	1371	9.64
Louisiana	4204	404	9.61
Georgia	5464	517	9.46

TABLE 8-1. (*Continued*)

State	Population (in thousands)	Age 65 and Over	Percent Over 65
Virginia	5346	505	9.45
Maryland	4216	396	9.39
South Carolina	3119	287	9.20
New Mexico	1300	116	8.92
Colorado	2889	247	8.55
Nevada	799	66	8.26
Hawaii	965	76	7.88
Wyoming	471	37	7.86
Mississippi	2521	189	7.50
Utah	1461	109	7.46
Alaska	400	12	3.00

Florida, and perhaps an emerging concentration in the coastal Northwest. Since 1950, several states recorded substantial increases in concentration. For example, Florida in 1950 had 8.5 percent of its population classified as elderly, but in 1970 it had 14.5 percent, and in 1980 it had 17.3 percent classified as elderly. During the 1950 to 1970 period, Florida rose from twenty-first position to first when the states were ranked by concentration of elders. Similarly, Arkansas rose from twenty-ninth position in 1950 (with 7.9 percent) to a tie for second position (with 12.4 percent) in 1970, and to third position (with 13.6 percent) in 1980. These and similar changes demonstrate some of the dynamic nature of the pattern of elderly concentration at the national level and of course, suggest one of the processes responsible—migration.

As spectacular as the demographic impact of elderly migration has been in a few places, it is important to focus briefly on evolution of the more general pattern. Close examination over time reveals that there is substantial change nearly everywhere over the span of just a few decades. There has been a westward shift in the largest regional concentration through the Midwest into the Great Plains. This mirrors the shift in the pattern of maximum agrarian settlement fifty or more years earlier, demonstrating the process of "aging-in-place." Aging-in-place, or the effect of the pas-

sage of time on a given immobile demographic population structure, is probably the single most important process in understanding and predicting elderly populations because of the relatively low elderly mobility rates. The impacts that result from the aging-in-place of a population established in an earlier period are often magnified strongly by the relatively high mobility rate of younger cohorts. A particularly good example was the massive rural-to-urban migration of younger Americans during the first half of this century. This migration left an altered rural population structure which aged in place until today, producing the disproportionately large elderly concentrations observed in many rural areas. (This process is particularly clear at the county scale of observation, Graff and Wiseman, 1978.)

Many of the same generalizations and causal processes observed at the national scale apply to distributions of elderly at more local scales. At the intraurban scale, for example, numeric distribution of elders is more similar to, than different from, the distribution of the remainder of the population (Pampel and Choldin, 1978; Smith and Hiltner, 1975). Analyses of indices of concentration conclude that, although neighborhoods or small areas occasionally contain fairly high concentrations of elders, these concentrations seldom reach 25 percent of the level that occurs for other groups, such as blacks (at the census tract and block level); thus the bulk of the urban elderly do not reside in "age ghettos." The most general statement one can make about the intraurban distribution of elders is that there are higher concentrations in many older neighborhoods, often near the central business district, and that this concentration progressively declines as one moves toward the suburban or exurban fringes of the city where their concentration is very low. However, as the dynamics of this pattern are investigated, we learn of the imminent "graying of the suburbs," in which we can expect growing concentrations of older people in these non-central-city portions of metropolitan areas. The processes responsible for this pattern are the same as those in the national example—substantial aging-in-place, magnified by migration of younger people. The actual residential relocation by older people has a fairly small impact on the general patterns of concentrations, although as we shall see below, in some special instances dramatically large concentrations can result from the movements of older people themselves.

Elderly Migration Patterns

The states with the largest volume of elderly inmigration and outmigration are shown in table 8-2. New York is first-ranked in outmigration, the

origin of nearly twice as many migrants as the next largest states, California and Illinois. Although nearly 60 percent of all interstate elderly migrants come from only ten states, examination of the state rates of outmigration reveals that most states have similar rates, averaging 4.4 percent. Thus, the impact of outmigration is experienced quite uniformly, although small places occasionally report heavy losses because of small base populations. It is interesting to note that California and Florida experience substantial outmigration at a rate only slightly below the national average, given their long histories of heavy inmigration.

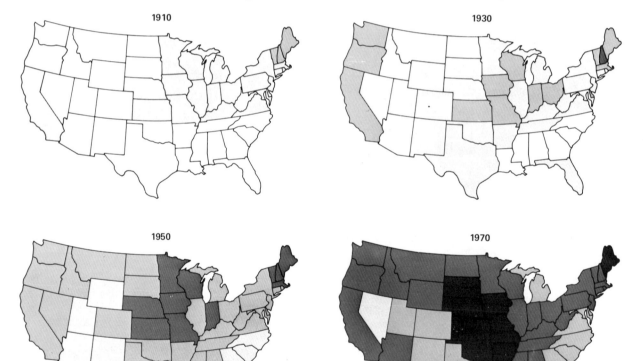

8-1. Concentration of population aged 65 and older, 1910–80.

The pattern of inmigration is much more concentrated than that of outmigration, as shown again in table 8-2. Florida leads the nation as the most popular migration destination, receiving nearly one out of every four interstate migrants. Florida receives more than twice as many migrants as California. Together the two states gather in one-third of all migrants. Arizona is ranked a distant third, rivaled closely by New Jersey, Washington, Texas, Oregon, and others. The concentrated pattern of inmigration makes a heavy impact on these few major destination states. For example, both Florida and Arizona increased their elderly populations by nearly 20 percent during the five-year period, while the average increase among all states was only 5.1 percent.

The general pattern of elderly migration, then, is one of proportionate outmigration with the largest states "contributing" the largest numbers of interstate migrants and highly concentrated inmigration to a few heavily impacted states. This pattern is graphically revealed in figure 8-2 where the major pairwise movements of migrants between a state of origin and a destination state are shown.

The arrows in figure 8-2 depict in their proportionate widths the actual volume of movement between pairs of states. Not all state-to-state movements are shown, only those identified as being disproportionately large. Here, the movement of migrants between states is considered to be unusually large if it is more than might be "expected" to occur by virtue of the state's contribution to or receipt of migrants from the entire pool of interstate migrants. For example, a large receiving state such as Florida (receiving 23.5 percent of all migrants) might be "expected" to receive 23.5 percent of all New York migrants, as well as 23.5 percent of every other state's migrants. This expectation arises because of the vast differences in migration volumes that exist among the states, and the expectation assumes that movement will be in direct proportion to size. Arrows in the figure represent movements that are at least 25 percent *larger* than "expected" (a relative acceptance criterion, RA) and contain more than

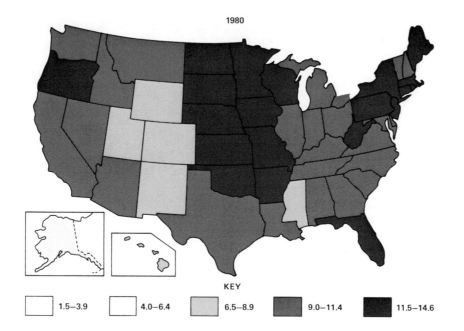

1980

KEY

| 1.5–3.9 | 4.0–6.4 | 6.5–8.9 | 9.0–11.4 | 11.5–14.6 |

TABLE 8-2. Interstate Migration of People Age 65 and Over, 1965–70

Rank State	Migrants (in hundreds)	State's % of elderly migrants	Percent cumulative	Migrants % of 1970 elderly population
Outmigration				
1 New York	552	13.8%	13.8%	5.5%
2 California	885	7.9	21.7	3.1
3 Illinois	882	7.9	29.6	5.9
4 Ohio	543	4.8	34.4	4.1
5 Pennsylvania	537	4.8	39.2	3.2
6 Michigan	530	4.7	43.9	5.3
7 New Jersey	500	4.5	48.4	5.1
8 Florida	464	4.1	52.5	3.6
9 Texas	312	2.8	55.3	2.0
10 Indiana	297	2.6	57.9	4.2
Inmigration				
1 Florida	21,636	23.5	23.5	20.0
2 California	1,070	9.5	33.0	4.3
3 Arizona	479	4.3	37.3	19.9
4 New Jersey	460	4.1	41.4	4.3
5 Washington	412	3.7	45.1	4.5
6 Texas	399	3.6	48.7	2.7
7 Oregon	340	3.0	51.7	6.3
8 New York	328	2.9	54.6	1.1
9 Ohio	323	2.9	57.5	2.1
10 Illinois	228	2.6	60.1	1.9

SOURCE: *Biggar et al., 1982.*

1000 migrants (an absolute difference criterion, AD); these are major movements in both absolute and relative terms. An additional constraint has been applied for inclusion: only states with two or more salient flows are shown. Because of the highly concentrated pattern, very few salient flows have been excluded by the two-or-more criterion. Exclusions are all low-volume flows generally occurring between contiguous states.

The overall pattern is strongly concentrated and unidirectional; there are very few reciprocal flows. As might be expected from the volumetric pattern described above, the spatial pattern is heavily influenced by destination-oriented movements or streams—eleven destination streams as compared to two origin streams. The eleven states that are the focal points of the destination streams account

for more than three-fifths of all migrant destinations, 61.4 percent. The two origin states account for only 12 percent of outmigrants. This highly concentrated and destination-stream-biased pattern differs substantially from the more diffuse and reciprocal pattern found in the nonelderly population (Flynn, 1980).

A simple typology is suggested by mapping the salient flows as in the figure: (1) national streams composed of numerous, large flows which span long distances terminating in the nation's largest inmigrant states (fig. 8-2a); (2) regional streams composed of a few, low-volume, and short-distance flows which terminate in regional retirement/vacation centers (fig. 8-2b); and (3) emerging national streams of a few long-distance flows as well as flows from contiguous states (fig. 8-2c).

Florida and California are clearly national streams (fig. 8-2a). Here we find the longest salient flows, the largest numbers of salient flows, and the greatest absolute volumes of inmigration. The major origins of these extensive destination streams are (1) the eastern states—New York, New Jersey, Connecticut, and Massachusetts—and (2) states in the north central region—Minnesota, Wisconsin, Michigan, Illinois, Indiana, and Ohio. Migrants originating in New England and the eastern Midwest move in disproportionate numbers to Florida, while those bound for California originate only in the Midwest, particularly in its western states. Thus, the source regions of the two streams are quite different, the Mississippi River being a nearly perfect dividing line.

Five regional streams can be identified by the salient flows into seven states (fig. 8-2b). New York, New Jersey, and Ohio each have separate streams while the groupings of Missouri–Arkansas (the Ozark region) and Washington–Oregon (the Cascade region) are the recipients of the remaining streams. Together these streams account for approximately one-fifth (20.5 percent) of all migrants. Only a few salient flows constitute these streams and generally arise in neighboring states. Several of these streams appear to be the result of recent developments, particularly regional vacation centers, although the New Jersey stream to Ocean and Cape May counties may be even older than the long-standing national streams to Florida and California.

At an intermediate scale between the distinctly regional and national streams are what might be termed emerging national streams, Arizona and Texas, (fig. 8-2c). These are fairly recent Sunbelt migration streams with fewer and smaller salient flows than the national streams of California and Florida. They are important, however, with Arizona the third and Texas the sixth largest elderly inmigrant states. They attract nearby migrants to vacation centers like the regional streams, but also receive long-distance migrations from the Midwest to Arizona and from California to Texas.

Unexpectedly, the two national streams are also the only important origin streams to be identified

in the analysis (fig. 8-2d). These disproportionately large outmigration flows suggest the existence of a considerable amount of subsequent movement following an earlier retirement migration. Just as these two streams have very different patterns of inmigration—their origin areas are divided by the Mississippi River in figure 8-2a—their outmigration patterns are different. Although each has outmigrant flows that terminate in neighboring states, a sizable proportion of outward movements terminate in very different regions. Florida's flows are reciprocal with northeastern states', which send disproportionately large numbers of migrants to Florida. This pattern suggests the importance of return migration (Longino, 1979). California, on the other hand, experiences very little return outmigration. Outbound Californians are moving to other Pacific coastal and southwestern states, not to the Midwest where most of California's elderly migrants originate.

The patterns of local relocation have received much less attention than long-distance migration patterns. The spatial pattern found by studies at the intraurban scale appears to be much more diffused than the national pattern, that is, both origins and destinations are highly dispersed. There is a definite outward bias to many of these moves in that a substantial number originate near the city center and terminate in locations nearer the city's suburbs (Golant, 1975; Wiseman and Virden, 1977). In general, these are moves between older neighborhoods of the city and not between city and suburb. Minor concentrations occur in areas with a strong ethnic character and a slight increase in older elders is apparent near the downtown (Rudzitis, 1982).

Numerous differences exist between the people whose movements produce patterns of migration versus those who relocate locally. There is a large difference in numbers alone, with approximately four times as many moving locally as between states. Between 1965 and 1970, 28 percent of the population age sixty-five and older moved at least once; 18 percent relocated within the same county, 4.5 percent moved elsewhere within the same state, 3.8 percent migrated to different states, and

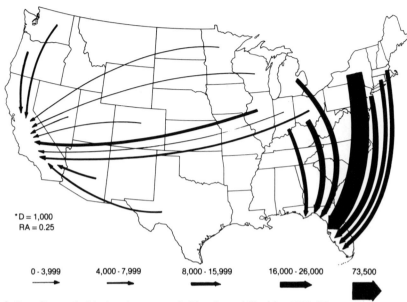

a. Salient flows of elderly migrants to California and Florida, 1965–70.

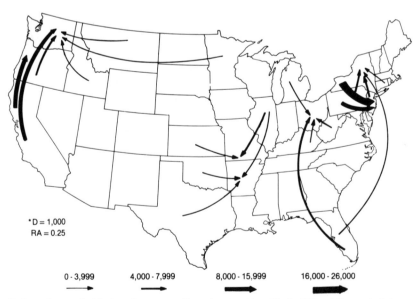

b. Salient flows of elderly migrants to New Jersey, New York, Ohio, Missouri, Arkansas, Washington, and Oregon, 1965–70.

8-2. Interstate migration of population aged 65 and older, 1965–70.

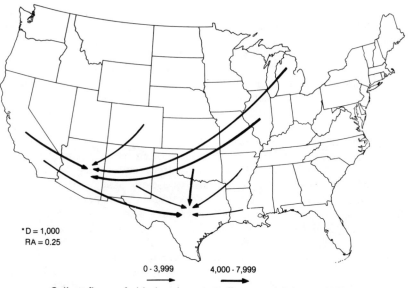

*D = 1,000
RA = 0.25

0 - 3,999   4,000 - 7,999

c. Salient flows of elderly migrants to Texas and Arizona, 1965–70.

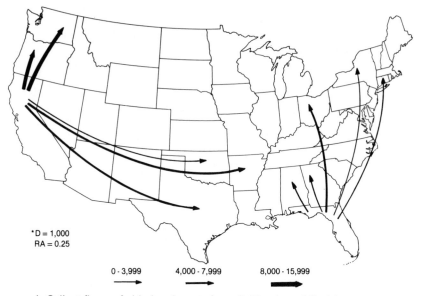

*D = 1,000
RA = 0.25

0 - 3,999   4,000 - 7,999   8,000 - 15,999

d. Salient flows of elderly migrants from California and Florida, 1965–70.

1.7 percent moved to another country. Those who move longer distances (particularly interstate migrants) are, as a group, better educated, wealthier, slightly younger, and generally better housed than those moving locally (Biggar, 1980). It is also commonly thought, although not conclusively proven, that the motivation for moving different distances are markedly different. Migrants are thought to move primarily in response to climatic and recreational amenities that are needed to sustain a leisure-oriented retirement lifestyle. A large proportion, however, are found to be returning to their states of birth; others are thought to be moving to the communities of their children or a relative (likely in search of support or assistance). The reasons for local relocation are thought to be more complex, ranging from positive motivations (such as obtaining one's dream house) to very negative reasons (such as eviction). This complexity is apparent when we examine survey data.

Why Older Americans Move

The *Annual Housing Survey* (AHS) of the Department of Housing and Urban Development provides insight into this question. Each year residents of sample housing units composing the survey population are asked whether they resided in the same unit one year ago. New residents are then asked several questions regarding their former residence and the primary reason why they moved. Because of the low mobility rate among elders, older movers are poorly represented in any year of the survey. This makes it difficult to obtain a sufficient sample of elderly movers for study. However, by aggregating annual samples of movers, one can assemble a file containing several thousand "recent" movers. The following discussion is based on samples taken from 1974 through 1977.

There are many problems associated with employing such a file in general and with these data in particular. This kind of file is sensitive to period effects. For example, during the 1974–77 period, cost of living and inflation soared, housing values increased enormously in most local housing mar-

kets, and Americans in general experienced large gains in real income. By aggregating the annual subsamples it is assumed that such changes have no influence in the aggregated period examined. In addition, these particular data are constrained by the categorical scheme employed to code responses. The scheme was designed to apply to all age groups although there was a clear lack of thought given to the special situations of elders. As a result, elders more than any other age group replied with noncategorical responses—15 percent identified "other reasons" in response to some of the questions asked. Moreover, there are the usual survey research concerns regarding recall accuracy, misrepresentation by the respondent, and a "family" decision being interpreted and reported by an individual. Finally, there is the general problem of looking at only the primary reason for moving. This is troublesome because contemporary theory suggests a constellation of reasons composing a general dissatisfaction with former residential conditions or significant environmental incongruences along several dimensions that motivate a move. It is illogical and naive to assume that only one reason leads to a change of residence in all cases. Conversely, some studies among the general population indicate that as few as 10 percent of all movers voluntarily cite more than one reason. In summary, these data are subject to much legitimate criticism and the qualifiers appended to their use defy precise quantification. On the other hand, the data are some of the best available and provide more direct answers to the questions at hand than do the many indirect and deductive interpretations that predominate in the literature.

Table 8-3 reveals the responses of nearly 4,000 elderly movers to the question, "What is the main reason [head of household] moved from his/her previous residence?" The responses are collapsed into groups which represent fairly cohesive but nonetheless subjective aggregations.

Change of residence for reasons relating to employment does occur with modest frequency—5.6 percent of reported moves. Most of these moves result from obtaining a new job or having an old

TABLE 8-3. Primary Reason for Moving Cited by People 60 Years and Over, 1974–77

Reason	Number in Sample	Percent of Total	Percent Subtotal[1]	Reason	Number in Sample	Percent of Total	Percent Subtotal[1]
Employment-related				**Family breakup**			
Job transfer	51	1.3%		Widowed	141	3.5	
Entered or left armed forces	2	0.5		Separated	21	0.5	
				Divorced	23	0.6	
New job	56	1.4		Total	185		5.8
Change commuting pattern	32	0.8					
Attend or leave school	3	0.1					
Other work	32	0.8		**Change in family condition**			
Total	176		5.6%	Newly married	51	1.3	
				Family increased	5	0.1	
Retired, total	333	8.4	10.5	Family decreased	54	1.4	
				Establish own home	138	3.5	
Climate-related, total	104	2.6	3.3	Other family	222	5.6	
				Total	470		14.8
Housing and tenure adjustments							
Larger unit	120	3.0		**Closer to relatives, total**	372	9.3	11.7
Better home	272	6.8					
Want to rent	30	0.8					
Want to own	122	3.1		**Forced-move**			
Total	544		17.2	Displaced by public sector	61	1.5	
				Displaced by private sector	210	5.3	
Neighborhood adjustments				Displaced by natural disaster	37	0.9	
Overcrowded neighborhood	18	0.5		Lower price or rent	280	7.0	
Racial/ethnic shift	43	1.1		Total	588		18.5
Better neighborhood	144	3.6		Other, total	599	15.0	—
Better schools	7	0.2		Not answered, total	215	5.4	—
More services and conveniences	187	4.7		Total number in sample	3985		
Total	399		12.6				

SOURCE: *Calculated from Department of Housing and Urban Development,* Annual Housing Surveys.
1. Denotes percent of sample excluding "Other" and "Not Answered" responses; here N=3171.

one transferred to a different work place. Not surprisingly, retirement from work engenders more mobility than all work-related reasons combined; approximately one in ten movers cites retirement as the reason.

One of the persistent stereotypes of elderly migration is that of "sun-and-fun"–oriented retirement moves to select Sunbelt states. Although this reason often applies in the limited cases of migration across state boundaries, it is apparent from table 8-3 that such moves compose only a very small percentage of all moves. Only three respondents in a hundred changed residence because of climatic amenities or adversities.

A commonly cited reason for moving among the general population is that of improving one's housing situation; that is, bringing dwelling-unit conditions into a more harmonious balance with one's needs, tastes, and preferences. The same motivation is cited by the elderly, where nearly as many report moving to obtain a better home as report relocation due to retirement. A popular stereotype is that older people often sell the family home and move into a smaller, more manageable rental unit. Given this stereotype, the number of instances of older people doing just the opposite is perhaps surprising. Nearly four times as many move to become homeowners (3.1 percent of all who move) rather than renters (0.8 percent), and a relatively large number are moving into larger units (3 percent). Overall, housing and tenure adjustments compose a substantial proportion of the reasons given for residential change by both older and younger segments of the population.

Slightly fewer move to improve neighborhood conditions than move to improve their dwelling-unit conditions—12 versus 17 percent. Among those moving to improve neighborhood conditions there is a strong desire to improve the environment in terms of services and to be more conveniently situated with respect to activity locations. A few report moving in response to changes in the social structure of their old neighborhoods. Many simply move to a "better neighborhood." Whatever the specific characteristics are, taken together, moves for improving dwelling-unit and/or neighborhood conditions account for more than one-quarter of all moves.

A small proportion of movement results from the dissolution of family structure, that is the death of a spouse, separation, or divorce. Although widowhood appears to be fairly common, it apparently causes few directly related residential changes. Interestingly, as many move because of a new marriage as move because of separation or divorce. In addition, many move to establish their own home, 3.5 percent. Residential change due to changes in family circumstances account for approximately 20 percent of all moves.

Nearly one out of every ten moves results from the desire to be closer to a relative. It is of course impossible to specify here the extent to which this is due to a simple desire for more frequent or closer family ties, or if this reflects a need for more direct support or assistance. In any case, this reason is one of the few more frequently cited by elders than other age groups.

Forced movement of several kinds constitutes a rather large set of reasons cited for moving. Only one percent of the entire sample moved because of a natural disaster such as flooding or fire. Nearly twice as many were displaced by public action, such as condemnation of the building for a public project. Three to four times as many were displaced by private sector actions ranging from foreclosures and evictions to condominium conversions. Of all forced movement, nearly half is due to economic circumstances, that is, seeking a reduction in housing costs. Although it is arguable as to whether or not these moves are forced moves or merely adjustments due to circumstance, it is most likely that given a choice, very few of these moves would be made.

Several findings from these data deserve further mention. First, attention is directed to what is not known about why older Americans move. Besides the obvious 15 percent of responses that could not be placed into the data categories, there are many responses that need elaboration or further specificity, for example, "closer to relatives" and "better neighborhood." As always, there is room for further study. Second, these data do provide some empirical basis for constructing a framework for understanding the phenomenon of relocation. It is clear that there are many dimensions in this framework, many sets of reasons, each creating a general motivation and dimension. It is, however, not at all clear that these dimensions are orthogonal or independent. Third, in a gross way we can begin to assess the size and importance of the various motives for moving. For example, we see that moves motivated by family circumstances compose a very large proportion of all moves, but that the specific aspects of family change responsible for movement are highly varied and not equally important. Fourth, it can be inferred from the reasons cited that although some elders, probably a substantial majority, improve their residential situation in the process of moving, other movers suffer conditions worse than before the move. Finally, it must be noted that there are few if any surprises here. Other studies have found fairly similar results in more localized studies (Lawton, Kleban, and Carlson, 1973; Nelson and Winter, 1975).

Conclusion

The foregoing sections have described patterns of elderly concentration, migration, and movement motivations. Although the examination has been at the national scale, the general conclusions have utility at local levels as well. Here, national patterns can provide a backdrop against which unique features of the local situation can be seen in bold relief. Such features, however, often vary substantially among localities, necessitating considerable informed judgment on the part of practitioners transferring findings from this study to the local level. In general, factors producing national patterns are also operating at the local level. For example, residential concentrations of older people in specific neighborhoods result from the same processes as those producing national concentrations. Just as aging-in-place has produced high concentrations in midwestern states, it is producing the "graying" of suburban America. It is important to note that the dynamics of these processes are often accelerated when viewed at the local level. It is not unusual to find specific urban neighborhoods radically altered in age structure in less than ten years, primarily through inmigration.

Whatever the spatial scale of concern, the foregoing shows that widely held stereotypes are badly distorted in respect to the volume and nature of residential movements and in respect to the interpretations applied to such movement. Contrary to popular views, we see that very few elders migrate long distances and that, although many do move locally, the vast majority do not move at all. Thus, the popular view leads to an overly large and optimistic interpretation of elderly residential movement as being mostly "sun-and-fun" migration or "high-activity-low-maintenance-condo-contentment" relocation. On the other hand, the more informed view, focused heavily on the relatively low mobility rate of older people, often leads to an overly negative interpretation: low rates reflect low desires for moving and therefore, most of those who do move do so reluctantly or only in response to negative changes in their lives.

The contradictory interpretations demonstrate that our views are much too limited. As we have seen, there are many different reasons cited for moving—motivations which span a wide range from negative (such as eviction) to more positive reasons (such as being attracted to better dwelling units and neighborhoods). Appreciation of the breadth and diversity of the reasons given for residential change not only facilitates better targeting of assistance of those moving for negative reasons, but the broader view also stimulates consideration of older people as important and desirable components in the general housing market. Those moving for positive reasons constitute a large proportion of all elderly movers and, as a group, create substantial effective demand in local housing submarkets.

References

Biggar, J. C. 1980. "Who Moved Among the Elderly 1965–1970: Comparison of Types of Older Movers." *Research on Aging* 2:73–91.

Biggar, J. C., et al., eds. 1982. *Elderly Migration Patterns, 1955–1960 and 1965–1970: Final Report*. Washington, DC: U.S. National Institute on Aging.

Flynn, C. 1980. "General Versus Aged Interstate Migration, 1965–1970." *Research on Aging* 2:165–76.

Golant, S. M. 1975. "Residential Concentrations of the Future Elderly." *Gerontologist* 15:16–23.

Graff, T. O., and R. F. Wiseman. 1978. "Changing Concentrations of Older Americans." *Geographical Review* 68:379–93.

Lawton, M. P., M. H. Kleban, and D. A. Carlson. 1973. "The Inner-City Resident: To Move or Not to Move." *Gerontologist* 13:443–48.

Longino, C. F. 1979. "Going Home: Aged Return Migration in the United States, 1965–1970." *Journal of Gerontology* 34:736–45.

Nelson, L. M. and M. Winter. 1975. "Life Disruptions, Independence, Satisfaction, and the Consideration of Moving." *Gerontologist* 15:160–64.

Pampel, F. C., and H. M. Choldin. 1978. "Location and Segregation of the Aged: A Block-Level Analysis." *Social Forces* 56:1121–39.

Rudzitis, G. 1982. *Residential Location Determinants of the Older Population.* Chicago: Univ. of Chicago.

Smith, B. W., and J. Hiltner. 1975. "Intraurban Location of the Elderly." *Journal of Gerontology,* 30:473–78.

U.S. Bureau of the Census. 1976. *Current Population Reports, Special Studies (May).* "Demographic Aspects of Aging and the Older Population in the United States." Washington, DC: U.S. Government Printing Office.

Wiseman, R. F., and M. A. Virden. 1977. "Spatial and Social Dimensions of Intraurban Elderly Migration." *Economic Geography* 53:1–13.

CHAPTER 9 Personal Determinants and Consequences of Independent Housing Choices

Charles F. Longino, Jr.

Why do residentially independent older people move and how do they adjust afterward? Rather than condensing the book that a thorough answer to this question would require, an argument will be constructed in this chapter to show that both determinants and consequences are dimensions of a single underlying process by which independent housing choices may be understood.

The notion that most relocation in old age results in residential dependency should be dismissed at the start. In a careful study of the characteristics of nonmovers, local movers, and migrants over age sixty and using the 1960, 1970, and 1980 census public-use samples, Biggar (1982) and Longino et al. (1984) made it quite clear not only that independent residence was the norm for all of these mobility categories, but that it increased in all categories between 1960, 1970, and 1980. By 1980 nearly three-quarters (74 percent) of local movers and 78 percent of interstate migrants, after their move, were living independently, either alone or with their spouse. Ninety-one percent of those who had not moved in the past five years were maintaining independent households.

Residential independence, though related to it, is not the same as independent housing choice. While the former can be demonstrated in census data, the latter cannot. It has been part of gerontological folk wisdom that children and close friends exert a strong influence on the housing decisions of older people. Perhaps this view is an inevitable consequence of the tendency for research to focus upon the most dependent part of the older population.

A study of retired movers (Peterson, Longino, and Phelps, 1979) recently addressed the question of housing choice. Samples of residents in eight communities were questioned about who participated in the final decision that resulted in their move. Of those who received help in making the decision, that help came mostly from spouses. Children tended to play a relatively minor role. Fewer than one-quarter of the residents, in most settings, turned to children for help with the relocation decision. It was surprising to learn that about half the people acknowledged help from no one. When others did participate in the decision, they primarily did so by giving advice. Practically no one felt coerced by others.

Who actually made the final decision? A handful of women said their husbands decided. Otherwise, couples said they made the decision jointly, and the unmarried said they made the final decision alone. In an urban public housing site, some residents had been displaced elsewhere by urban renewal projects and had relocated there as a result. They admitted that the final decision was not entirely theirs. Are retirement community residents placed there by their children? A few probably are, but the number is almost negligible by comparison to the vast majority who make the final decision themselves or with their spouses. Most do not involve their children in the decision at all.

In England and France this social and psychological independence from children is evidence of a modern rather than a traditional lifestyle and is a middle- rather than working-class pattern (Cribier, 1980; Law and Warnes, 1982). What may have been measured, inadvertently, is the mover's pride and desire for independence, rather than actual freedom from the influence of others. Nonetheless, the degree of expressed independence in making the final housing choice is substantial. It seems fair to assume that independent residence and independent housing choice are both characteristic of elderly residential mobility in the United States in the 1980s, and this assertion provides the context in which the determinants and consequences of relocation are examined below.

Determinants of Relocation

Decision Models

The decision to move has been a theoretical puzzle for a century, since E. G. Ravenstein (1885) set down his "laws of migration." He felt that some people moved for essentially negative reasons, attempting to escape heavy taxes, unattractive climate, or uncongenial social surroundings. These were among the factors he said "pushed" some people out of their original residence in search of another. But, Ravenstein continued, more people were attracted to new locations by the desire to better themselves. That is, the "pull" factors in the migration decision outweigh the "push" factors for most people (Ravenstein, 1885). Lee (1966) added to this formulation the idea that there are intervening obstacles that may prevent a move, even if the motivation is there. Just wanting to move is no guarantee that the move will take place. It may be too costly, too risky, or the idea may not be congenial to other household members.

For voluntary moves, at least, it is probably safe to assume that people do not move when they are perfectly satisfied with their present location relative to others (Simon, 1957). How dissatisfied they have to become before they reach a decision to move (and the particular factors contributing to a high level of dissatisfaction) are hotly debated by migration theorists (Morrison, 1970; Wolpert, 1965; 1966). There is a growing consensus, however, that the decision process is multistaged (Rossi, 1955; Brown and Moore, 1970; Morrison, 1971).

The only multistaged decision model explicitly developed for studying the residential relocation of retirement-age people was recently proposed by Wiseman (1979; 1980; Wiseman and Roseman, 1979). In this model, the decision process begins with a triggering mechanism, that may center on dissatisfaction with one's current location for a variety of reasons or on the attractiveness of an alternative location. That is, the decision process may be triggered by "pushes," such as critical life events or unhappiness with the old neighborhood, or by "pulls" from friends and family members in other places, as well as perceived opportunities for a more pleasant life in a new location.

A second set of factors in Wiseman's model includes indigenous facilitating or inhibiting mechanisms. This idea is an expansion and refinement of Lee's (1966) notion of intervening migration obstacles. Wiseman divides these mechanisms into four categories: resources, past experience, community ties, and perception of likely outcomes. One's personal characteristics and past relocating experience would influence the decision. If one has seldom moved as an adult, there may be considerable resistance to a retirement move (McGinnis, 1968; Morrison, 1967). If the decision is not to move, Wiseman predicts that this will be followed by adjustments that reduce dissatisfaction with the present situation, like repairing the house or reasoning that moving was a foolish idea in the first place.

If the decision is in favor of moving, a secondary decision follows—selecting the new location. Several locations may be considered before one is

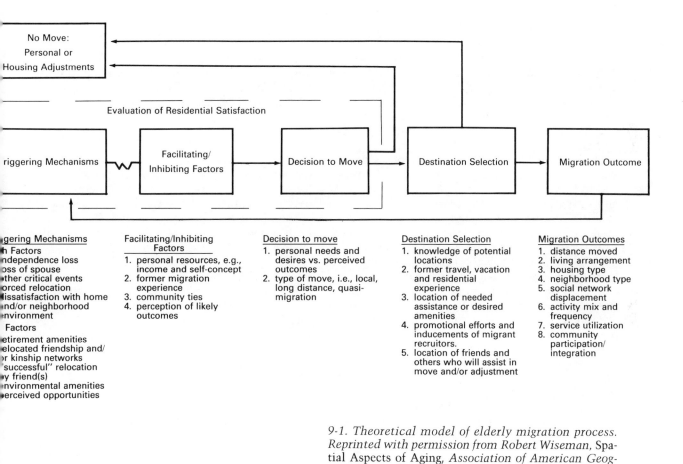

9-1. Theoretical model of elderly migration process. Reprinted with permission from Robert Wiseman, Spatial Aspects of Aging, Association of American Geographers, Washington, DC, 1979.

selected. The move itself contains two inseparable elements: distance and destination. Knowledge about potential destinations is the key to selection. Such knowledge is a necessary but, in itself, insufficient motivation for moving. Knowledge, of course, is facilitated by the location of family members and friends and one's own earlier travel and migration experience.

Samples for Examples

In 1975, the Social Security Administration funded an ambitious comparative study of midwestern retirement communities. This three-year project involved ethnographic field work and extensive interview surveys in eight retirement communities. They were studied by a team of social scientists representing the disciplines of sociology, anthropology, psychology, and economics (Peterson, Longino, and Phelps, 1979). Three communities were chosen from the files of the project for use as examples in the remainder of this chapter. They are briefly described below.

There are several places in the United States that have become popular locations for retirement migration since 1945 (Longino and Jackson, 1980;

Longino and Biggar, 1981). One of these is the Ozark region connecting the states of Missouri, Arkansas, and Oklahoma. By the mid-1970s, older migrants in the Missouri part of the Ozark lakes country represented the dominant group in most of the area's churches, civic and community organizations, and neighborhoods. The towns in this area had become retirement communities *de facto* (Longino, 1980; Golant, 1980). Retired migrants are relatively young, with a mean age of sixty-eight years. The average age at retirement, of course, would be younger. Most (86 percent) are married and virtually all (99 percent) are white. These are middle- and upper-middle-class migrants from large midwestern cities; most are in good health. This Ozark sample provided interviews with 662 persons, all of whom had retired at least once and relocated in the Ozarks after their retirement.

The second study community, Carefree Village, lies in a suburban community near a midwestern metropolitan center. It is explicitly planned for and populated by retired people, offering them a service-enriched sheltered environment with an emphasis upon its health-care system. Its resident profile is substantially different from that of the Ozark lakes country. The mean age in Carefree Village is seventy-six; over three-quarters (76 percent) are women; two-fifths are married; nearly two-thirds rate their health as good, and they are all white. Village residents, thus, are less frequently young, married, healthy, and wealthy than the retired migrants to the Ozarks. Most are older, middle-class white women in good health. Three hundred and fifteen Carefree Village residents were interviewed.

A third sample was drawn from Horizon Heights, a high-rise public housing site located in the center of a midwestern metropolitan center. The residential profile stands in sharp contrast to that of the Ozark migrants. Most are over age seventy; the mean age is seventy-eight. Less than a fifth are married, over four-fifths are women, and three-fifths are black. Only half see themselves as being in good health. The public housing residents are similar to those in Carefree Village in their gender, marital status, and age but quite different in their socioeconomic status, health, and race. The median income is only a third of that in Carefree Village. Horizon Heights residents are mostly older working-class widowed women in their seventies and eighties. The public housing sample includes 162 residents.

Triggering Mechanisms

People in Horizon Heights, Carefree Village, and the Ozarks made their community and housing choices for a variety of reasons. It must be remembered that each community is different in both its attractions and its built-in inhibiting features. The selection from among potential migrants is based on these characteristics and increases the homogeneity of the resident population. Horizon Heights, for example, offers services and safety. Cost of residence is not prohibitive if one is poor, but the financial screening of applicants would discourage or prohibit the admission of a new resident who was too wealthy. Carefree Village advertises its life-care plan, emphasizing health care in particular. The cost of residence would be an obstacle to the poor applicant. The Ozark lakes country offers a beautiful natural setting, but does not have many of the specialized services of Carefree Village. The potential migrant who is in his or her seventies might consider this location too risky.

People in all of the communities were asked for the single most important reason for their move. There is indeed a congruence between personal needs and community selection. The financial advantage of subsidized housing is not overlooked by Horizon Heights residents. Over half of Carefree Village residents listed health needs as the key reason for selecting this life-care community. Finally, there is a congruence between the outstanding natural beauty of the Ozarks and the residents' motivation for moving there. Over half the respondents gave it as their primary reason for moving.

People in the three communities were asked, "How did you come to be living here?" Their answers were taken down word for word and analyzed for evidence of what Wiseman called positive and negative triggering mechanisms in the relocation decision process. There were more "push" than "pull" responses in Horizon Heights, and "push" and "pull" responses were about even among Carefree Village residents, with the edge perhaps given to the "push" responses. Among the Ozark migrants, the "pull" responses were overwhelming (Longino, 1978).

The Ozarks attract people from farther away than do the two types of planned communities; the people that move there are also younger, most are married, and they are in better physical and financial health than those who moved to the two planned communities. Their reasons for moving are also positive. Planned communities, on the other hand, specialize in providing services and meeting special needs for older people. They advertise their advantages to residents, and as a result they tend to attract people who, due to critical events in their lives or unhappy neighborhood situations, feel they must move. Old people who are poor are also more likely to find themselves in critical or unhappy life situations, and this is reflected in a higher "push" level in their explanation of the move to Horizon Heights.

Selective Recruitment

Independent housing choice implies an individual perspective. Decision models generally see things from the ego's point of view. It is, however, the *interaction* between the decision-maker and the environment that is central to the process of housing choice. Wiseman captures these "exogenous factors," such as the housing market, in his model and makes destination selection contingent on knowledge of potential locations (Wiseman, 1980). It is important to consider how one comes to know about potential housing options. Producers of housing do so with the expectation that the housing will be occupied and paid for. Indeed, housing suppliers usually set into motion recruitment efforts for accomplishing their market goals. Recruitment is always selective. At a minimum the supplier wants someone who can afford the housing. Often there are many other characteristics of the targeted "market," and since the housing is designed to meet the needs of the households in the target market, its appeal is thereby limited. "Promotional efforts and inducements of migrant recruiters" is included in Wiseman's decision model as a factor in the selection of a housing destination.

In Horizon Heights, there is a waiting list. Not much open recruitment goes on by the Housing Authority managing the community. Rather, social service agencies, particularly those who have as clients persons with low incomes, refer clients with pressing housing problems to Horizon Heights. This is no less selective recruitment than the effort found in Carefree Village where a large sales force aggressively recruits new residents, using skillfully targeted newspaper, radio, and television campaigns. Unlike Horizon Heights, however, the selective process filters into the community those who can afford a substantial entrance fee and monthly maintenance payments. In the Ozarks, land developers acquire and use large mailing lists of people nearing retirement age, and advertise in selected magazines that are thought to be read by their target market. The advertisements proclaim the pleasures of picturesque mountain life.

Thus, suppliers of housing for an elderly market, with varying degrees of success, selectively search for new residents, just as persons self-selectively search for destinations that will meet their perceived needs. When asked who first talked with them about the living environment they chose, over one-third of the Horizon Heights residents said that community social service providers had done so. Almost one-third of Carefree Village residents said that community sales representatives first talked with them about the village. In the Ozarks, over one-fifth said that developers and realtors first approached them. Selective recruitment, then, cannot be ignored when considering the relocation decision process of older people (Longino, 1982). In addition to people who are involved in official recruitment efforts, there are many informal recruiters in elderly relocation destinations, and their efforts also facilitate self-selection on the part of their friends or family members who are considering a move.

Network Recruitment

Once elderly persons begin moving into a living environment that they like, they tell retired family members and friends about it. This leads to visits and sometimes to being joined by their friends and family members on a more permanent basis.

Residents of the three example settings were asked if they had known anyone living in the community before they had moved there themselves. In each community, about half the residents had known someone prior to relocating. Whether the residents had moved from the same county or from out of the state, the proportion remained about half. How many people had they known? The average is five in Horizon Heights and seven each in Carefree Village and the Ozarks. Most residents characterized these prior acquaintances as friends. Nearly all the Ozark and Carefree Village residents had visited their community at least a couple of times before moving. Network recruitment, like selective recruitment, therefore, is a part of the filtering process of persons and housing options resulting in a general similarity of resident backgrounds within the respective communities. Network recruitment, however, has the greater long-range impact on the area because it initiates and maintains migration streams from one location to another. Perhaps for this reason the Wiseman decision model places such great emphasis upon it, considering network recruitment a "pull" factor among the triggering mechanisms, an exogenous factor facilitating the move, and, finally, a factor in the destination selection (Wiseman, 1979, 1980).

Consequences of Relocation

The process by which communities recruit new members and retired people make housing choices should result in compatability between the person and his or her new living environment (Carp, 1968). The details of how living environments meet the needs of their inhabitants is not clearly understood. Some gerontologists rather expect the adjustment to be a poor one. Brotman (1976, pp. 15–16) asserts, for example, that "many older persons are not very satisfied with the change after it has been made but find a return to a previous residence or another change too complicated." This assertion is not supported by research, but represents the pessimistic attitude shared by some gerontologists that relocation in old age is problematical at the least and often disastrous. For that reason, the literature on housing adjustment often tends to have a dark cast. Residential relocation and institutionalization are often not clearly distinguished. Relocation is considered a stressful situation with which older people must "cope" (Kahana, Fairchild, and Kahana, 1982). Institutionalization, which is only a proportionately small part of residential relocation in old age, may represent a stress-filled crisis, but independent housing choice is generally a far more positive experience. This is not to say that adjustments are not required, but that a crisis model misrepresents these adjustments (Sherman, 1971; 1972; 1979).

Support systems have a dynamic character. Persons build their support systems over time, adding and deleting resources as needs change. There is also a time dimension in the frequency and importance of the support flowing from particular resources to the supported individual. Some relationships become intense in times of crisis, but cannot be maintained for long periods. Thus, they tend to fluctuate over time. This pattern characterizes many primary relationships. Some relationships, particularly secondary ones, can dispense support regularly over long periods of time. The balance, then, between primary and secondary relationships in the support systems of older individuals in new living environments is an important consideration (Lipman and Longino, 1982; Longino and Lipman, 1981; 1983).

The need for support increases with advanced age. Social contact may become more difficult to maintain and even personal services may become more problematical. This increased need for support may upset the balance in the reciprocal relationships between the older person and his supporters and cause him to feel increasingly dependent.

One of the serious threats to the support systems of older people is the loss of primary relations. Parents, uncles and aunts die, then older siblings and one's spouse, then friends and more distant relatives, and finally, perhaps even younger siblings and older children. This loss increases resource deficits at the very time when increasing support is needed. The family is a fertile recruiting ground for primary relationships. If a person starts with fewer family members, as does one with no siblings or one who never married or married but remained childless, the loss of additional primary resources can be painful. As this happens, there is likely to be a search for new resources, especially those that can stave off feelings of dependency.

When the support systems of the residents of the three sample communities were compared, it became clear that people in both planned communities and in the Ozarks were similar in one important way. The average number of resources in the support system of Ozark inmigrants is not very different from those in the planned communities (between eight and ten). The reason for this similarity is found in the balance between primary and secondary relations. Primary relations averaged highest in the Ozarks and lowest in Horizon Heights. Secondary relations were highest in Carefree Village and lowest in the Ozarks. This is predictable from the nature of the living environments and the characteristics of the residents. But the implication of this pattern has to do with instrumental support for the elderly in their living environments. Instrumental, task-oriented support involves specific kinds of help, such as housekeeping, transportation, or shopping, on a more or less regular basis. In all three communities, about half of the primary relations in the support systems of the residents provide no instrumental support. Most of them probably live too far away to help on a regular basis. A few secondary relations provide no instrumental support either, but most do. As a consequence, the average number of relations providing instrumental support for residents of Horizon Heights and Carefree Village is larger than that for Ozark residents.

The reason for this difference is obvious when one remembers that secondary relations are all those who are not primary relations but who do things for the older person. In the interview, each resident was asked what each primary relation on her list does for her on a more or less regular basis that she really appreciates. After each primary relationship was discussed, the resident was asked if there is anyone *else* who does things for her regularly that are also appreciated. At this point, the secondary resources were mentioned. "Yes, the bus driver, the security guard who checks my building every night, the physical therapist, the maintenance man, the golf pro, the chaplain, and the lady down the hall who always smiles at me (although we're not really friends yet)," a resident of the Carefree Village might add. "Yes, the lady who runs the congregate meal operation, the postman, the repair man, the housing manager, and the bus driver," a resident of Horizon Heights might continue. The number of potential secondary relations, therefore, depends upon how many services are provided for residents in the different locations, and how much help the resident needs. Occasionally, other secondary resources are mentioned that are located outside the living environment (such as personal physicians, pastors or radio preachers, social workers or librarians). Secondary resources located outside the living environment, when they are listed, however, almost always provide services that can be used regularly and repeatedly. They are more infrequently mentioned by Ozark residents, when they are mentioned at all. Younger and strongly self-reliant people, and those surrounded by primary relations, seem to need secondary relations less often, even when they are available. More germane to the argument, they seek out sheltered settings rich in such resources less often as well.

In summary, at least in planned living environments, a lower level of primary relations in one's support system can be compensated for by a higher level of secondary relations as it bears on instrumental support (Longino and Lipman, 1981). This compensation is reassuring, and it is a distinctive benefit of this type of housing choice.

The foregoing would seem to imply that residents of planned housing for the elderly are better off than they would be in other environments. But we cannot be certain that this is the case. For one thing, almost all voluntary movers feel better off in their new surroundings than at their former address. For another, while developers and managers of retirement communities claim a special benefit, one could hardly expect them to say otherwise. Finally, retirement communities are specialized living environments and do not attract a cross-section of the general population of older people, as we have seen.

When the Social Security Administration funded the comparative study of midwestern retirement communities, its focal interest was a comparative evaluation of retirement community costs and benefits. In the survey, many of the questions were drawn from the national survey by Louis Harris and Associates that had been conducted recently for the National Council on the Aging. Standardization procedures evolved into a system of shadow sampling (Longino, McClelland, and Peterson, 1981). Shadow samples were drawn in the following manner: (1) a matrix of five or six background variables was created for each community. Each cell in the community matrix represented one particular combination of the background variables of age, gender, marital status, education, and income. Race was also used in the public housing samples where there was racial diversity. (2) Cases in the national sample that conformed to the combination of characteristics in each cell were selected randomly and in the same proportion as in the retirement community sample. The result of this matching technique is that for every widowed black woman over age seventy-five with an elementary school education living on less than $2,000 in Horizon Heights, a person with the same profile of characteristics was drawn from the Harris survey sample and placed in the Horizon Heights shadow sample. The process was repeated for every other combination of the background variables. Shadow samples were drawn to be as large as possible consistent with preserving the correct proportions of respondents with the specified background characteristics. In this way, the study deals with the problem of the unrepresentativeness of retirement community populations and attempts to control for the effect of selective recruitment—at least as far as it relates to background variables. By comparing the quality of life of residents in one retirement community with people similar to themselves in the general population, it becomes possible to assess the relative benefits of this type of living environment for its residents.

The Life-Care Community

Carefree Village provides a living environment with measurable benefits to residents in the areas of medical care, freedom from the fear of crime, and from loneliness and boredom. One would expect people attracted to life-care communities to feel this way. Access to health care, after all, is the community's major attraction. The cost-of-housing benefit is negative; the same tangible housing and services can be purchased more cheaply in suburban areas elsewhere. The intangibles of life-care community living, however, seem to make a substantial difference to the residents. They feel that they are getting a good deal; their morale is higher than their counterparts elsewhere. The consequences of their independent housing choice are positive.

The Urban Public Housing Project

Beneficial living environments, happily, are not reserved only for the affluent. People in the shadow sample were far more likely to complain about "insufficient medical care" than were the residents of Horizon Heights. The residents also scored a significant benefit in their freedom from fear of crime. Many of the residents had moved from high crime areas into Horizon Heights, whose security guards and exclusively elderly residents make them feel safe. Social support seems adequate in Horizon Heights as well.

One major study that was made of the same people both before and after they entered planned living environments was conducted by Carp (1966). She compared nonmovers with movers to subsidized public housing communities, and not only measured the initial adjustment to the move after a year, but conducted a final interview with the movers after eight years (Carp, 1974). The findings of a statistically more sophisticated study of residents of five public housing sites before and after their move by Lawton and Cohen (1974) were similar and more generalizable than Carp's findings. Seen in this context, the finding of positive benefits for Horizon Heights reinforces those reported by earlier researchers. Carp reported that satisfaction with their housing and living environment increased after the move and was higher for retirement community residents after eight years. She concludes that "the factors which predict short-term adjustment in elderly-designed public housing tend to predict long-range adjustment, implying that the new environment will benefit the sample people in the long run as in the short run" (Carp, 1976, p. 248).

Concentrations of Retired Migrants in Small Towns

At this point, the question of relative benefit seems adequately answered for planned communities, at least for those with well-developed service packages. But when the Ozark retired migrants were compared with their shadow sample from the general population, the same pattern repeated itself except in one key finding. The Ozark residents, while feeling safer from crime and more socially adequate in every way than their shadow sample counterparts, were much more likely to complain about insufficient medical care. The characteristics of these migrants are exactly consistent with the stimulus-seeking and risk-taking behavior that results in the trade-offs demanded by rural retirement lifestyles. In addition, the Ozark migrants also had higher morale than their counterparts in the general population, although morale was high in both groups, indicating that

on balance the benefit of this housing choice was also positive.

Conclusion

This chapter has argued that the determinants and consequences of independent housing choice cannot be separated. They are like two sides of one coin. When housing choice is independent, it considers the needs of the decision-maker in its search for a living environment that will meet these needs. The adjustments following the housing relocation are often merely confirmations of the determining factors.

The interface of determinants and consequences is seen in the intersection of migration decision and support systems theory, as they are applied to residents who had relocated to the three example communities. The argument is summarized below. Resource deficits, in the face of rising support needs, can be a powerful triggering mechanism in the choice of housing in old age. Both subsidized (Horizon Heights) and nonsubsidized (Carefree Village) planned communities are service-enriched living environments, designed in accordance with the particular needs of older people. It should not be surprising, therefore, that more of the people who move to these environments feel "pushed" rather than "pulled," and emphasize in their reasons for moving those very areas of support that are the strengths of the planned community. Nor should it be surprising that the retirement-age people who are attracted to planned communities tend to have characteristics that imply greater need and vulnerability. Such people, on the whole, are older, more often widowed, and less healthy than the retired people who move to unplanned, de facto, retirement communities such as the Ozark lakes country. For those who move to subsidized retirement housing such as Horizon Heights, one can add that they are also much poorer. The fit between living environment and individual needs would seem, then, to be reasonably good in such settings. People with a greater need for instrumental support tend to be attracted to communities built to meet that need, and support indeed seems to flow from within the community to the people who more there (Longino and Lipman, 1981, 1982; Peterson, Longino, and Phelps, 1979).

As a final caution against over-simplified conclusions it must be remembered that Wiseman's decision model shrewdly includes three feedback loops. First, the decision to move may not reach closure due to various inhibiting factors. When the individual gives up on the move, there may be an accommodation with her existing situation. Perhaps the house is fixed up somewhat, and she decides that it is not so bad after all. Second, after the decision to move is made, if she cannot settle on a destination, she may abandon the decision altogether and adjust to the present housing community situation. Finally, after deciding to move, deciding where to move, and actually moving, the whole process can begin again. Each feedback loop, whether or not the move is actually made, puts the decision back at its beginning, where pushes and pulls trigger the decision process anew. The planner must not make the mistake of assuming that he or she is planning for the "final move" when the independent housing choice by older persons is the object of the planning.

References

Biggar, J. C. 1982. "Migration Selectivity and Distance Moved, 1955–1960 and 1965–1970." In *Elderly Migration Patterns, 1955–1960 and 1965–1970: Final Report.* Ed. J. C. Biggar et al. Washington, DC: National Institute on Aging.

Brotman, H. B. 1976. "Every Tenth American: The 'Problem' of Aging." In *Community Planning for an Aging Society.* Ed. M. P. Lawton, R. J. Newcomer and T. O. Byerts. Stroudsburg, PA: Dowden, Hutchinson and Ross.

Brown, L. A. and Moore, E. G. 1970. "The Intraurban Migration Process: A Perspective." *Geografiska Annaler* 52 (Series B): 1–13.

Carp, F. M. 1966. "Effects of Impoverished Housing on the Lives of Older People." In *Patterns of Living and Housing of Middle-Aged and Older People.* Ed. F. M. Carp and W. M. Bennett. Washington, DC: U.S. Government Printing Office.

———. 1968. "Person-Situation Congruence in Engagement." *Gerontologist* 8:184–88.

———. 1974. "Short-Term and Long-Term Prediction and Adjustment to a New Environment." *Journal of Gerontology* 29:444–53.

———. 1976. "Living Environments of Older People." In *Handbook of Aging and the Social Sciences.* Ed. R. H. Binstock and E. Shanas. New York: Van Nostrand Reinhold.

Cribier, F. A. 1980. "European Assessment of Aged Migration." *Research on Aging* 2:255–70.

Golant, S. M. 1980. "Locational-Environmental Perspectives on Old Age Segregated Residential Areas in the United States." In *Geography and the Urban Environment.* Vol. 3. Ed. R. J. Johnson and D. T. Herbert. London: Wiley.

Kahana, E.; Fairchild, T.; and Kahana, B. 1982. "Adaptation." In *Research Instruments in Social Gerontology.* Vol. 1. Ed. D. Mangen and A. Peterson. Minneapolis: Univ. of Minnesota.

Kahana, E., and Kahana, B. 1979. "Support Networks of Long Distance Movers: The Cultural and Geographical Transition." Paper presented at the Thirty-second Annual Meeting of the Gerontological Society of America. Washington, DC.

Law, C. M., and Warnes, A. M. 1982. "The Destination Decision in Retirement Migration." In *Geographical Perspectives on the Elderly.* Ed. A. M. Warnes. London: Wiley.

Lawton, M. P., and Cohen, J. 1974. "The Generality of Housing Impact on the Well-Being of Older People." *Journal of Gerontology* 29:194–204.

Lee, E. S. 1966. "A Theory of Migration." *Demography.* 3:47–57.

Lipman, A., and Longino, C. F., Jr. 1982. "Formal and Informal Support: A Conceptual Clarification." *Journal of Applied Gerontology,* 141–46.

Longino, C. F., Jr. 1978. "Pushes and Pulls: Migration Selectivity and Retirement Relocation." Paper presented at the Annual Meeting of the Southern Regional Demographic Group. San Antonio, TX.

———. 1979. "The Unit of Analysis Problem and Network Measures of Changing Support." Paper presented at the Thirty-second Annual Meeting of the Gerontological Society of America. Washington, DC.

———. 1980. "Retirement Communities." In *The Dynamics of Aging: Original Essays on the Experiences and Processes of Growing Old.* Ed. F. Berghorn and D. Schafer. Denver: Westview.

———. 1982. "American Retirement Communities and Residential Relocation." In *Geographical Perspectives on the Elderly*. Ed. A. M. Warnes. London: Wiley.

Longino, C. F., Jr., and Biggar, J. C. 1981. "The Impact of Retirement Migration on the South." *Gerontologist* 21:283–90.

Longino, C. F., Jr., J. C. Biggar, C. B. Flynn, and R. F. Wiseman. 1984. *The Retirement Migration Project: A Final Report to the National Institute on Aging*. Washington, DC: National Institute on Aging.

Longino, C. F., Jr., and Jackson, D. J. 1980. "Migration and the Aged." *Research on Aging*, Special Issue 2:131–280.

Longino, C. F., Jr., and Lipman, A. 1981. "Married and Spouseless Men and Women in Planned Retirement Communities: Support Network Differentials." *Journal of Marriage and the Family* 43:169–77.

———. 1983. "Informal Supports of Residents in Planned Retirement Communities." *Interdisciplinary Topics in Gerontology* 17:107–18.

Longino, C. F., Jr., McClelland, K. A.; and Peterson, W. A. 1981. "The Aged Subculture Hypothesis: Social Integration, Gerontophilia and Self-Conception." *Journal of Gerontology* 35:758–67.

McGinnis, R. 1968. "A Stochastic Model of Social Mobility." *American Sociological Review* 33:712–22.

Morrison, P. A. 1967. "Duration of Residence and Prospective Migration: The Evaluation of a Stochastic Model." *Demography* 4:553–61.

———. 1970. *Chronic Movers and the Future Redistribution of Population: A Longitudinal Analysis*. P-4440. Santa Monica, CA: Rand.

———. 1971. *Unresolved Questions about Population Distribution Policy: An Agenda for Further Research*. P-4530. Santa Monica, CA: Rand.

Peterson, W. A.; Longino, C. F., Jr.; and Phelps, L. W. 1979. *A Study of Security, Health and Social Support Systems and Adjustment of Residents in Selected Congregate Living and Retirement Settings*. Washington, DC: Social Security Administration.

Ravenstein, E. G. 1885. "The Laws of Migration." *Journal of the Royal Statistical Society* 48:165–227.

Rossi, P. H. 1955. *Why Families Move*. Glencoe, IL: Free.

Sherman, S. R. 1971. "The Choice of Retirement Housing among the Well-Elderly." *Aging and Human Development* 2:118–38.

———. 1972. "Satisfaction with Retirement Housing: Attitudes, Recommendations and Moves." *Aging and Human Development* 3:339–66.

———. 1979. "Site Permeability, Service Availability, and Perceived Community Support in Crisis." *Journal of Social Service Research*. 3:139–57.

Simon, H. A. 1957. *Models of Man*. New York: Wiley.

Wiseman, R. F. 1980. "Why Older People Move: Theoretical Issues." *Research on Aging* 2:141–54.

———. 1979. *Spatial Aspects of Aging*. Resource Paper No. 78–4. Washington, DC: Association of American Geographers.

Wiseman, R. F., and Roseman, C. C. 1979. "A Typology of Elderly Migration Based on the Decision Making Process." *Economic Geography* 55:324–37.

Wolpert, J. 1965. "Behavioral Aspects of the Decision to Migrate." *Papers, Regional Science Association* 15:159–69.

———. 1966. "Migration as an Adjustment to Environmental Stress." *Journal of Social Issues* 22:92–102.

CHAPTER 10 Retirement Communities: People, Planning, Prospects

Gordon F. Streib • Anthony J. LaGreca • William E. Folts

Retirement communities are a relatively recent development in the United States and are unique to American culture. One finds few of them in similar urban, industrialized societies such as Great Britain, France, Germany, or Canada. Retirement communities developed from a combination of several factors: the increasing number of retired persons; their higher level of income; and their wish to live in a warm climate and enjoy leisure activities during their nonworking years (Webber, 1954; Gottschalk, 1975). A retirement community is defined as

> a small community, relatively independent, segregated, and noninstitutional, whose residents are mainly older people separated more or less completely from their regular or career occupations in gainful or nonpaid employment (Webber and Osterbind, 1961, p. 4).

Such communities are living environments to which most, if not all, of the residents have relocated since their retirement. These communities seek to provide residents with a lifestyle that revolves around retirement and its increased opportunities for social and leisure activities.

Understanding how retirement communities develop, what threatens their existence, and how they change over their lifespan is vital to urban planners, zoning bodies, and prospective developers and administrators of retirement communities.

Origins and Prevalence

The first retirement communities were developed forty to fifty years ago in Florida and California and somewhat later in Arizona (Kleemeier, 1954; Mangum, 1978; Webber and Osterbind, 1961). In recent years, retirement communities have begun to flourish outside the Sun Belt, because retirees have become aware of the advantages of age-dense environments that provide security, recreational facilities, and economical housing, and may also be closer to one's friends and relatives in nearby cities (Heintz, 1976; Lawton, 1980). Another major change is that whereas early retirement villages were small, with populations of a few hundred persons, today there are retirement communities of thousands of houses and a few with populations of 20,000 or more, the largest having 45,000 residents.

The early history of retirement communities in the United States can be traced back to the trailer parks of the 1920s. An important element

This research was supported, in part, by grant number 5 R01 AG02602-02 from the National Institute on Aging. Portions were presented at the 77th Annual Meeting of the American Sociological Association, September 6–10, 1982, San Francisco, California.

in their historical development was the founding of retirement places for special populations by religious organizations, fraternal organizations, and trade unions (Gottschalk, 1972, 1975). Like so many of the planned communities of the nineteenth and early twentieth centuries, some retirement communities were first founded on utopian or quasiutopian anticipations.

Some retirement communities have endured over long periods of time involving national depressions, world wars, and other changes associated with modern technology and shifting values. The number and distribution of retirement communities is difficult to ascertain because no official or nongovernmental agency has compiled such statistics and only educated guesses can be made.

Retirement Communities as Planned Communities

The contemporary retirement community usually originates from one of two sources: 1) a pre-existing community, usually small and oftentimes made up of mobile homes, begins to change its general renting/ownership policy limiting residency in the community to those age fifty-five and over; or 2) as in the case of most retirement communities, a developer, association, or group of individual investors purchases land for the express purpose of building a retirement community. In both situations, owners, developers, and investors seek to make some financial profit while providing retirees with an age-concentrated community in which the lifestyle is devoted to retirement living. In both of these origins, planning is involved; that is, a systematic plan or policy is established that seeks to maintain an age-concentrated community setting. As in any community development as a profit-making venture, financial considerations are important. There are, however, other design factors that must be adequately addressed: (1) environmental considerations; (2) proximity to social services; (3) political considerations; (4) housing

considerations; (5) social and recreational considerations; (6) the community as a commodity.

Environmental Considerations

The proposed retirement community should be placed in an area that can support its population with regard to land use, water and sewage facilities, basic utility services, and other concerns that affect its position relative to the ecological and environmental concerns of the area.

A related concern is the specific consideration of location; should the retirement community be placed in close proximity to a larger concentration of age-integrated residences (such as near a large town or city); or should it be placed in a predominantly rural area?

Proximity to Supportive Services

The availability of supportive services should be an influential element in the selection of a site for a proposed retirement community. Smaller retirement communities might be placed near larger existing towns or cities that can provide such basic services as medical care or police protection, as well as shopping and other personal amenities. Larger retirement communities usually can stand on their own because they have a residential population sufficiently large to support a basic level of medical and service concerns. The ideal placement of a proposed retirement community would be such that supportive services would be conveniently available to the resident population. Thus, the large retirement communities with well-developed internal support systems may be well suited for location in rural areas where support services are otherwise inadequate. However, many retirement communities, both large and small, have been established on land that is inexpensive in comparison to other lands used for residential purposes. The relative isolation of this low-cost land has meant that community services are sometimes situated some distance away and are often inconveniently located for the residents.

Political Considerations

As with the placement or emergence of any new population settlement, consideration must be given to the "degree of fit" a retirement community will have into the comprehensive land-use plan of the area. Hence, attention should be given to placement of the planned community where zoning and/or land-use regulations are compatible with those of the larger community that will serve the residents. Communities placed in areas adjacent to vacant land zoned for industrial development will undoubtedly face increased future tension as the pursuits of the residents clash with those of the industrialists. In Florida, for example, the placement of several retirement communities was poor because they were located near phosphate mines, which are a constant source of noise and air pollution as well as traffic difficulties resulting from the large fleets of trucks and equipment used in mining.

Housing Considerations

Retirement communities consist of all types of housing, ranging from mobile homes and single detached residences to apartment/condominium structures containing multiple-dwelling units. This array of options allows retirees a wide variety from which to select the type of unit that best meets their needs and financial situation. Some of the factors that the individual retiree must consider include: the cost of the land and/or housing unit, the variation in the degree of ownership/rental options, and the amount of upkeep that an individual resident must perform.

Social and Recreational Considerations

Most middle-sized and larger retirement communities pay close attention to the social and recreational needs of the residents. In these communities planning frequently involves the construction of an activity center or meeting hall, the construction of a swimming pool, and the preservation of small areas as open spaces. Although the middle-sized retirement communities usually have a social committee that organizes and oversees an extensive variety of social and recreational activities, the larger communities often hire a full-time social director.

Community as Commodity

A basic focus in contemporary retirement community development is that of regarding the community as a commodity (Fry, 1977). That is, the basic planning model of the community takes into account the central concern of marketing both the community and its lifestyle in order to make a profit.

Age Concentration

Age concentration is, by definition, one of the essential population characteristics of a retirement community. Two facets of age concentration must be mentioned: (1) the possible outcome of the community's viability if the age-concentration structure is lost with the admission of younger people — especially those with children under the age of eighteen — and (2) the changes that may occur in a retirement community whose population ages so that the majority of the residents are over the age of seventy-five (Neugarten, 1974).

Some insights concerning the possible impact of the loss of age concentration on retirement communities can be gained by comparing retirement communities with certain "new town" experiences in the United States. Knittel (1973) noted that one of the chief threats to the viability of a new town is the loss of stability due to the emigration of too great a proportion of the originally homogeneous population. In his example, the concern was expressed in regard to the possible financial collapse faced by a new town if it lost a key element of its population homogeneity. Knittel's perspective is bolstered by the observation of Kelman (1958) and Kanter (1968) who focused upon major losses of community identity and stability. This concern is especially appropriate to the retirement community.

People choose to live in a retirement community for a number of reasons including the desire to live in an age-homogeneous community. The commodity these people seek is not just a residence, but an environment whose chief characteristic is that of providing a physical/social milieu that celebrates the benefits of retirement living. Therefore, if the community begins to lose its age homogeneity stability, other retirees may not seek to enter the community. Furthermore, many of the younger retirees may begin to "sell out" and move to a community with an age concentration that has not eroded. The community's goal of seeking to create a sociophysical setting "for pleasant living and for private profit" (Knittel, 1973, p. 40) is then lost as far as its being a retirement community is concerned.

Loss of age concentration also raises questions about the economic viability of the community. Most retirement communities, because of their design and location, cannot accommodate or attract younger people with families. While this observation has not yet been tested by any systematic data analysis, there does appear to be a "tipping point" at which time the inmigration of young people sounds the death knell for a community as a retirement community. That is, the initial movement of a few younger families into the community may reduce its attractiveness to the elderly. However, the presence of a still sizable elderly population may inhibit large numbers of younger families from moving into the area. Therefore, the community is unable to repopulate itself since it appeals completely to neither the young nor the elderly.

What happens to the retirement community whose population consists mostly of the "old old" (those over age seventy-five)? The aging phenomenon of the retirement community, is, of course, a natural consequence of a planned community whose initial residents are retirees. If the community is still in development, this aging of the population is not initially a concern since new structures tend to be bought by retirees of varying ages. However, once a community is fully occupied, the community "ages" rapidly over a period of ten to twenty years. As residents age, their ability or willingness to be active participants in the life of the community tends to lessen. Therefore, the owners and managers of these communities are pressed by an increasing demand for additional services to meet the needs of the residents. At the same time, there may be a decline in the use of recreational facilities.

Age Restriction

Age restriction is a subject of interest to researchers of retirement communities and also developers, managers, and residents of the communities (Streib, 1985). The existence of age-restricted communities poses a fundamental question: are occupancy restrictions based solely upon age a legal and socially acceptable means of providing housing for a particular group of people? The social acceptability of such age restrictions seems to be demonstrated by the overall succes of existing retirement communities and by the rapid growth of this type of living arrangement.

Whether this acceptance takes the form of active encouragement of age-restricted communities or of passive tolerance, the result is the same. The legality of age restrictions, however, is less well demonstrated. Several courts have handed down decisions that have the effect of upholding age restrictions as a legal means to limit occupancy. However, the overall issue is by no means decided, and age restriction must necessarily await further judicial scrutiny. An analysis of relevant cases may be found in Doyle (1977).

There are many different configurations and methods for the age restrictions found in retirement communities. For the sake of simplicity they may be grouped into two classes: formal and informal age restrictions. Informal restrictions appear most often as a screening exercise performed by the manager or owner/developer of a particular community. Formal age restrictions are those contained in the legal documents of a particular community and may be divided into two classes: those that are inclusionary, that is, those which include a specific group; and those that are exclusionary, that is, those which exclude a specific group. Inclusionary age restrictions usually place a minimum age requirement on occupants of the dwelling units while exclusionary restrictions usually deny occupancy to a specific group.

Formal age restrictions may appear in any of the legal documents associated with a particular community. The most common practice is for the restrictions to be placed in the deeds where residents own the property, or in the leases, where the residents rent the property. In addition, several states permit special zoning classifications for housing specifically designed as "retirement housing." In the states that create special zoning classifications, violations become a criminal matter, whereas deed restriction violations are entirely a civil matter. Thus, a resident in an age-restricted community in some states could be prosecuted and perhaps put in jail if he or she sold his or her property to a person who does not meet residency requirements.

Informal age restrictions are less obvious and more susceptible to the personal interpretation of a manager or owner/developer. Where informal age restriction is practiced, the manager or owner/developer usually has a preconceived idea of what he or she wants the community age structure to be. Potential residents are then informally screened to assure that they meet the requirements of this preconceived age structure.

In any discussion of age restrictions, the role of economics in the maintenance and revision of such limits should not be ignored. Although formal age restrictions are far less likely to be affected by economic issues, both types of age restrictions depend, to some extent, upon internal economic stability for their continued existence. While the mechanisms of change for the formal restrictions are complex and somewhat cumbersome, a severe decrease in the demand for housing in a particular community, regardless of the type of age restrictions involved, increase the pressure to enlarge the pool of potential residents by expanding the age restrictions beyond their established boundaries. This is especially apparent where the community operating budget is partially dependent upon en-

trance fees of new residents or where budgets are based upon monthly maintenance fees and assume full or nearly full occupancy.

In communities with formal restrictions and where the residents own the property, there is an added issue. When a resident initially joins such a community, the age restriction is a community protection device, but when the resident is trying to sell his or her property, it is, perhaps, a restrictive device. Some residents in these communities, desiring to protect their investments and enhance the resale potential of their property have resisted the further legitimization of age restrictions through zoning ordinances and have started movements to change the deed restrictions that limit sales to a particular age group. An informal, but effective screening device, such as a community admissions committee, would be preferable to deed restrictions to these residents. Notwithstanding the legality of such screening devices, flexibility may be more important than protection in times of low demand.

However, until there is a radical judicial pronouncement to the contrary, age-restricted retirement communities appear to be firmly established as a legitimate lifestyle for an increasingly significant portion of our population. The prevalence and economic viability of these communities will undoubtedly weigh heavily upon social and judicial decisions regarding the acceptability and legality of age restrictions.

Cultural Context of Retirement Communities

Retirement communities are often regarded somewhat negatively by gerontologists and the general public. The reasons for such disapproval range from the attitude that the elderly are "banned" to ghettos to the opposite point of view that they are escaping to a hedonistic style of life. A third objection, focusing on the age-segregation discussion above, is based upon the idealistic view that the old and young should live in close proximity and share a common way of life. These attitudes are held by many, despite a cumulative set of research findings establishing the preferences for and positive outcomes of highly age-dense environments (Barker, 1966; Bultena and Wood, 1969; Malozemoff, Anderson, and Rosenbaum, 1978; Messer, 1967; Rosow, 1967; and Teaff et al., 1978). Another reason for negative attitudes toward retirement communities may stem from the fact that most communities have been commercial developments, and there have been instances of unscrupulous developers taking advantage of residents. This phenomenon, however, is not peculiar to retirement communities—it can occur in developments for any group, regardless of age. In spite of these negative attitudes, increasing numbers of elderly persons are choosing to live in such environments.

Retirement communities must be placed in the broad context of an urbanized and industrialized society characterized by high mobility of both young and old. The desire for separation of the generations is part of a complicated cultural drift which stimulates age-segregated environments. Epitomized by the phrase "intimacy at a distance" (Rosenmayr, 1977), this trend includes the establishment of economic security programs encouraging generational separation.

There is another consideration that may be involved in the choice of age-concentrated environments that has been largely neglected by gerontologists, sociologists, and environmental psychologists. Modern society is increasingly characterized by individualism, competitiveness, and anomie. In the last period of life, when peer status attainment may be over, people may seek a different style of life embodying a more *Gemeinshaft* orientation — a shared community experience characterized by a higher degree of reciprocity, mutual aid, interdependence, and cooperation than would be experienced in the normal, age-heterogeneous community (Litwak, 1985). In addition, there is the question of physical security. Many older persons seek the safety of a more protected environment because they do not want to be compared unfavorably with younger working persons who are participating in the mainstream of competitive economic life. They prefer an environment where they do not suffer status loss because of their retirement from gainful employment. Furthermore, some people choose retirement communities because they believe these settings are characterized by what Atchley (1975, p. 2) has described as rural ideals: "Rural areas are conceptualized as being small in scale and dominated by social patterns which emphasize personalized interaction, informality, simplicity, slow social change, and little social differentiation." This would describe many retirement communities, even some located on the fringes of large metropolitan areas.

Preliminary Research Findings

In the last three decades, a small but important segment of American elderly have chosen to move to retirement communities. Case studies have been conducted on specific retirement communities (Jacobs, 1974; Longino, 1981), as well as two broad-scale investigations of retirement communities located in various parts of the United States (Streib, Folts, and La Greca, 1984; and Hunt et al., 1984). More information, however, is needed on the structure, organization, nature of services offered, and quality of life of communities and on how communities themselves have adapted to changes in the surrounding environs and to the internal demographic trends, namely, the aging of the original cohort. There have been a few studies of the residents, their activities and adjustment in the communities (Osgood, 1982; Bultena and Wood, 1969). However, there has been little research in which the community itself was the focus of the investigation.

In 1978, a pilot study was initiated by the authors to gather data on fifteen older retirement communities in Florida. An aim of the research was to answer several questions about what happens to a retirement community as the residents age. How does an aging population affect the vitality and activities of a community so that perhaps new retirees will not be attracted? Do the residents age in place or do they move out as they become frail or sick only to be replaced by younger retirees? How does the autonomy of a community affect its quality of life?

In 1981 the National Institute on Aging funded a two-year study of retirement communities in three main retirement areas of the United States: the West (California and Arizona), the Northeast (New Jersey), and the Southeast (Florida). A community was considered to be large if it had one thousand residents or more. A community was rated as "old" if it had been in operation fifteen years or more.

The following generalizations or "tentative uniformities" are based on a preliminary analysis of the data of thirty-six communities. The data are both objective and qualitative.

1. The history of each retirement community is idiosyncratic in that it is shaped and colored by the specific persons who developed and managed the community and by the relationships that develop with the surrounding community. In addition, the enthusiasm and willingness of the first residents to adapt to the kind of environment and lifestyle provided by the developer determine the ambience of the community. Despite the apparent diversity of the communities, there are similar patterns that can be discerned in the stages of establishment, marketing, and early adjustment by the residents to the environment (La Greca, Streib, and Folts, 1985).

2. One of the fundamental distinctions that shapes the structure and community history is whether the lots on which the dwelling units are located are owned or rented by the residents. The dwelling units themselves may vary from simple to affluent, and the amenities, facilities, and services may vary widely, but land ownership is the basic differentiating factor, leading to the following generalizations: (a) in communities in which the lots are rented there is no predictable calendar for the stages of ownership and control. The community may be sold because of personal, market, or external factors that are beyond the control of the owners or the residents. (b) In communities in which the lots are owned by the residents the control of the community passes to residents after a certain percentage of lots are sold. In these retirement communities, the calendar is not temporal but spatial for there is no set time for the takeover. This constitutes a clear and predictable developmental stage in the history of these communities. Thus, the more successful the developer is in the marketing of the community, the more quickly the residents will assume some autonomy. Whether this is a burden or a privilege depends on the point of view of the individual. (c) In communities in which the lots are owned by the residents, the owner/developer may retain control of certain commonly used facilities (social, recreational, sports, etc.) and determine the fee system. The charges for these facilities may then become a focus of controversy between residents and the owner. (d) In communities where the residents own the lots, as well as in communities where the lots are rented, the residents realize the owner has considerable control over the community. In some ways, a retirement community is like a benign company town. The owner/developer, of course, must operate within legal constraints defined by the statutes, which vary from state to state.

3. In some cases residents prefer to leave the management and operation of the community in the hands of others (Streib, Folts, and La Greca, 1985). Inasmuch as the control of the future implies stability, the residents of retirement communities generally expressed an interest in controlling the future of their particular community. Some informants in resident-owned communities, however, expressed serious doubts about the ability of their fellow residents to deal adequately with the problems and issues involved. They felt that competent, although perhaps autocratic, outside ownership was preferable to democratic, but perhaps incompetent, resident control.

4. The internal power and decision-making mechanisms elicit ambivalent responses from some residents. On one hand, there appears to

be a desire for democratic participation in the decision making of the community, and on the other hand, a desire to be free of the details of the day-to-day operation of the community. Some residents have a fear of benign incompetence which may result from peer control and are willing to sacrifice self-determination, within limits, if it results in stability.

5. In communities in which the residents own the lots, the residents are able to exercise some power and control over the operations of the community. This may lead to greater stability. In communities in which the lots are not owned by the residents, control is always external to the residents and the low level of resident control is not related to length of residential tenure. The owner can sell the land at any time, resulting in a change in fees charged and services provided. Although there is general awareness of the possiblity of sudden change in ownership, the residents have little influence over the decision.

6. In communities where residents rent the lots, external events or factors may create an economic situation which results in the sale of the community such as: (a) changes in surrounding land use; (b) increased value of the land; (c) inflationary pressures on fixed rentals; (d) the owner's wish to invest capital in a more profitable or more convenient source of income; (e) the owner's desire to sell the property before the structures have aged and depreciated to the point where major repairs are necessary.

7. Most residents are unconcerned about the economic viability of a community until a crisis situation arises, and this may be too late for the residents to have an input into the decision-making process. Regardless of the type of land ownership, kind of dwelling units, or nature of amenities and services, the financial ability of the community is of paramount significance to the continued existence of the community. From the standpoint of the residents, the protection of their investment is paramount.

Conclusion

When seen from a planning point of view, retirement communities are prime examples of the dynamics governing the formation of intentional communities. From the smallest to the largest, these communities can be seen as being "ongoing laboratories" for the study of planning processes and policies.

When regarded from the point of view of marketing, retirement communities are assessed as being sound financial investments provided the investors and developers understand the demand for such communities in a given area. The soundness of the financial investment is also somewhat dependent upon the ability and desire of the developer or owner to maintain an age-homogeneous population. Retirees move to retirement communities not only because they want housing but because they want a lifestyle that encompasses the community as a whole—a lifestyle devoted to retirement living.

When analyzed from a sociological point of view, retirement communities provide a useful social laboratory in comparison to "normal" communities, for in a retirement community, there are a limited number of community functions and essential activities are more restricted than in a more "normal" community. For example, there is no need to be near employment possibilities or to consider school systems.

Retirement communities are recent social phenomena, and thus it is possible to reconstruct the past with some accuracy because the planners, owners, and residents can still be interviewed and the researchers can supplement these observations with conventional historical methods. The research has the advantage of studying community structure, change and processes, such as decision making, from a vantage point not found in most community research.

Few residential choices are made with such care and deliberation on the part of residents as that of a retirement community. Most persons living in retirement communities have weighed the advantages and disadvantages of this lifestyle. The evidence gathered on thirty-six communities suggests that there is a high amount of satisfaction with their choice. Despite problems or uncertainties about land ownership, these communities deliver the kind of environment that their residents desire. What retirement community developers have done that social scientists have *not* done, is to judge accurately and respond adequately to the preferences and power of elderly persons as consumers.

References

Atchley, R. C., ed. 1975. *Rural Environments and Aging.* Washington, DC: Gerontological Society.

Barker, M. B. 1966. *California Retirement Communities.* Berkeley, CA: Univ. of California.

Bultena, G., and V. Wood. 1969. "The American Retirement Community: Bane or Blessing?" *Journal of Gerontology* 24:209–18.

Doyle, M. 1977. "Retirement Communities: The Nature and Enforceability of Residential Segregation by Age." *Michigan Law Review* 76:64–107.

Fry, C. L. 1977. "The Community as Commodity: The Age-Graded Case." *Human Organization* 36:115–23.

Gottschalk, S. 1972. "Fifty Years at Moosehaven: The Lessons of Experience." *Gerontologist* 12 (Part 1): 235–40.

———. 1975. *Communities and Alternatives.* Cambridge, MA: Schenkman.

Heintz, K. 1976. *Retirement Communities: For Adults Only.* New Brunswick, NJ: Center for Urban Policy Research, Rutgers.

Hunt, M. E., A. G. Feldt, R. W. Marans, L. A. Pastalan, and K. L. Vakalo. 1984. *Retirement Communities: An American Original.* New York: Haworth.

Jacobs, J. 1974. *Fun City: An Ethnographic Study of a Retirement Community.* New York: Holt, Rinehart and Winston.

Kanter, R. M. 1968. "Commitment and Social Organization: A Study of Commitment Mechanisms in Utopian Communities." *American Sociological Review* 33:499–517.

Kelman, H. C. 1958. "Compliance, Identification, and Internalization: Three Processes of Attitude Change." *Journal of Conflict Resolution* 2:51–60.

Kleemeier, R. W. 1954. "Moosehaven: Congregate Living in a Community of the Retired." *American Journal of Sociology* 59:347–51.

Knittel, R. E. 1973. "New Town Knowledge, Experience, and Theory: An Overview." *Human Organization* 32:37–48.

LaGreca, A. J., G. F. Streib, and W. E. Folts. 1985. "Retirement Communities and Their Life Stages." *Journal of Gerontology* 40:211–18.

Lawton, P. 1980. *Environment and Aging.* Monterey, CA: Brooks/Cole.

Litwak, E. 1985. *Helping the Elderly: The Complementary Roles of Informal Networks and Formal Systems.* New York: Guilford.

Longino, C. 1981. "Retirement Communities." In *The Dynamics of Aging.* Ed. F. Berghorn and D. Schafer and Associates. Boulder, CO: Westview.

Malozemoff, I., J. Anderson, and L. Rosenbaum. 1978. *Housing for the Elderly: Evaluation of the Effectiveness of Congregate Residences.* Boulder, CO: Westview.

Mangum, W. P. 1978. "Retirement Villages: Past, Present, and Future Issues." In *Back to Basics: Food and Shelter for the Elderly.* Ed. P. Wagner and J. McRae. Gainesville, FL: Univ. of Florida.

Messer, M. 1967. "The Possibility of an Age-Concentrated Environment Becoming a Normative System." *Gerontologist* 7:247–50.

Neugarten, B. 1974. "Age Groups in American Society and the Rise of the Young Old." *The Annals of the American Academy of Political and Social Science* 415:187–98.

Osgood, N. J. 1982. *Senior Settlers: Social Integration in Retirement Communities.* New York: Praeger.

Rosenmayr, L. 1977. "The Family—A Source of Hope for the Elderly?" In *Family Bureaucracy and the Elderly.* Ed. E. Shanas and M. Sussman. Durham, NC: Duke.

Rosow, I. 1967. *Social Integration of the Aged.* New York: Free.

Streib, G. F. 1985. "The Elderly—Victim or Oppressor? A Study of a Court Case Involving Age Segregation." Paper presented at the 38th Annual Meeting of the Gerontological Society of America, New Orleans.

Streib, G. F., W. E. Folts, and A. J. LaGreca. 1984. "Entry into Retirement Communities: Process and Related Problems." *Research on Aging* 6: 257–70.

Streib, G. F., W. E. Folts, and A. J. LaGreca. 1985. "Autonomy, Power, and Decision-Making in Thirty-six

Retirement Communities." *Gerontologist* 25: 403–409.

Teaff, J., et al. 1978. "Impact of Age Segregation on the Well-Being of Elderly Tenants in Public Housing." *Journal of Gerontology* 33:126–33.

Webber, I. L. 1954. "The Organized Social Life of the Retired: Two Florida Communities." *American Journal of Sociology* 59:340–46.

Webber, I. L., and C. Osterbind. 1961. "Types of Retirement Villages." In *Retirement Villages.* Ed. E. W. Burgess. Ann Arbor, MI: Univ. of Michigan.

CHAPTER 11 Supportive Living Arrangements and Their Consequences

Sylvia Sherwood • John N. Morris • Clarence C. Sherwood

Advances in medicine and health care along with changes in immigration and fertility patterns have resulted in escalating numbers of elderly persons in American society. At the same time, because the incidence of chronic conditions increases with age (U.S. GAO, 1979), the graying of America is accompanied by substantial increases in the size of the population requiring long-term supportive services. In 1979, it was estimated that as many as 3.4 million or 18 percent of the population sixty-five years or older had functional deficits sufficient to necessitate long-term supportive services (U.S. GAO, 1979). Exacerbating this problem is the rapid growth of the seventy-five-plus segment of the elderly population. This is the group most likely to need long-term care services and most at risk of institutional placement—about three times more likely to be in nursing homes than persons between sixty-five and seventy-four years of age (U.S. CBO, 1977). Moreover, a significant increase is expected in the over-eighty-five age group. Over 50 percent in this category can be expected to have substantial needs for long-term care services (Sherwood, et al., 1977).

Expenditures for long-term care are rising rapidly, and the demographic patterns indicate that the need for long-term care services will continue to grow in the coming decades. Currently, the major share of these expenditures is devoted to paying for institutional care. Institutional placement, however, is not a necessary concomitant of chronic illness or physical impairment. Estimates from a number of studies indicate that many chronically ill and physically impaired persons placed in long-term health-care institutions could potentially function in less restrictive settings (Pfeiffer, 1973; Moroney and Kurtz, 1975; Gruenberg, 1975; Sherwood et al., 1981). Indeed, a survey of persons in Intermediate Care Facilities (ICFs) conducted in Massachusetts (Gruenberg, 1975) estimated that nearly one-third of all patients residing in ICFs—which account for more than two-thirds of the nursing home beds in the state—could live adequately at a lower level of care, including institutional "rest homes" ("personal care" facilities), small family foster-type "board-and-care" homes, or even less restrictive settings in the community. In a more recent study of Vermont's ICF population, 10 percent were assessed as being capable of residing in board-and-care homes in the community (Morris and Gutkin, 1979). The spiraling costs of institutional care for the elderly and the recognition that many persons have been forced to live in more restrictive and costly settings than necessary have led to seeking other, preferably community-based, alternative sheltered living arrangements for the frail and impaired elderly.

Enabling legislation has played a role in facilitating opportunities to receive service supports in other than institutional settings. Title III of the Older Americans Act (U.S. PL 95-478), for example, provides resources for nonmedical supportive services to needy elderly living in the community. To some extent Medicaid (Title XIX of the Social Security Act) also may have aided individuals to remain in community living arrangements by providing the means for the government to pay for the cost of medical care. (To a large extent, however, Medicaid has run counter to the movement toward independent community living in that it has largely supported nursing homes.) Originally Title XX (of the Social Security Act) and, more recently, social services block grants, have provided for at least some funding of nonmedical services to the especially needy elderly, which can potentially help maintain such persons at a satisfactory level in the community. Community health legislation (for example, U.S. PL 95-622, the Community Mental Health Centers Act) can also be cited as enabling, at least to some extent, the provision of community services to deal with mental health problems of the elderly. Such types of enabling legislation gave impetus to the development of alternative community living arrangements for the impaired elderly (as well as other disabled persons) by supplying a structure for the provision of services in local communities rather than in state institutions or nursing homes.

Discussions of various alternative community living arrangement models have been presented in other chapters in this book. This chapter focuses, in particular, on two types of sheltered community living arrangements: congregate housing and community board-and-care. While still scarce resources, these two types of residential settings have become increasingly available to elderly persons with poor physical functioning and health status.

Congregate Housing as Sheltered Community Living Arrangement

Congregate housing developments provide some level of service to assist tenants with special needs. More specifically, along with barrier-free apartments and common social areas, congregate housing provides its residents with the opportunity to receive, either on-site or in very close proximity, one or more supportive services designed to help maintain independent functioning in a community setting. The level of supportive service varies among such houses, both in the type (such as meal, transportation, homemaker, nursing) and intensity of on-site services.

By themselves, architectural modifications that have for some time been standard in public housing for healthy elderly residents—emergency alarm buttons, grab bars in the bathroom, no door sills, common spaces for social activities—can be viewed as facilitating the physical and social functioning of the frail and physically impaired. In combination with these features, the opportunity to receive support services within or in close proximity to the building can be hypothesized to be a particularly effective living arrangement for maintaining at-risk elderly in a community setting. Functional status of the individual can be perceived as a vector of environmental demands and capacities. Functional limitations are those activities in which the client's performance is deficient to the extent that the individual is unable to meet the demands of the environment or the expectations of society. The less energy required to negotiate the environment, the easier it is to function despite physical impairment. Architectural design, including barrier-free features, and proximity of services and social activities can be seen as environmental supports that can help maintain satisfactory functioning within one's own residence.

In conjunction with more general enabling legislation, the development of congregate housing alternatives for the elderly has been facilitated, in particular, by the passage of various housing acts. Between 1961 and 1978, every national housing act has contained an enabling provision for either specially designed housing for the elderly or for maintaining or expanding existing programs (Thompson, 1982). Affordable housing (with rent supplementation when necessary) as a living arrangement appropriate for persons requiring long-term supportive services was specifically given legislative support by the Congregate Housing Act of 1970, which allowed for the design and building of service spaces within public housing. Congregate housing was given further legislative support: (a) by the Housing and Community Development

Act of 1974, when responsibility for meeting the special needs of occupants through congregate housing was specified (although no funds for operating programs were made available through HUD); and (b) by the Congregate Housing Services Act of 1978, which, on a demonstration basis, specified funding for a Congregate Housing Service Program (CHSP) to selected public and nonprofit (Section 202) HUD-sponsored housing projects applying for these funds. Concentrating solely on nonmedical supportive services, the CHSP offers meals and other ancillary support services to vulnerable residents, presumably to be paid for, at least in part, on a sliding scale by the recipients of these services.

Congregate Housing across the Nation

Based on data from various HUD publications and news releases, it can be estimated that there were some 750 Section 202 projects and about 2380 public housing projects for the elderly in operation across the nation as of September 1980. These housing projects do not necessarily provide supportive services to assist the vulnerable elderly to remain in the residential settings. In fact, some of these houses may have been designed with insufficient common spaces for on-site provision of supportive services or are in areas where it is not possible to establish services in the immediate proximity of the building.

A recent survey of a random sample of 125 *nondemonstration* public and Section 202 housing developments in selected areas across the nation in which CHSP demonstration housing projects are located indicate that at least some of these houses are providing one or more supportive services (Holmes, Alfaro, and Levine, 1983). Of seven types of services—meals, housekeeper/chore, personal assistance, social services, transportation, escort, and health—only 4 percent had all. About 19 percent had no services. Access to transportation one or more days per week was the service most available (66 percent). However, escort services, needed in particular by physically impaired residents, were offered one or more days per week

in only slightly more than one-third of the buildings. Meals were also frequently available, with over half of the nondemonstration buildings in the sample having an on-site meal program one or more times a week. On-site social services one or more days per week were offered by almost half, and health services were available in about a third of the projects. Housekeeper/chore and personal assistance were the services least available, with personal assistance services either being a component of the housekeeper/chore services or not existing at all.

Insights concerning the needs of residents of these buildings are provided by data from samples of residents of some of these buildings as well as in CHSP buildings. Of the approximately 4500 screened residents sixty years or older in these buildings, almost one-quarter can be considered vulnerable, in that they need a package of services in order to remain in the community at an acceptable level of activity. The classification of "vulnerability" is based on a clinically grounded ten-question screening instrument (Morris, Sherwood, and Mor, 1984; Mor, Morris, and Sherwood, 1980), initially developed and tested on a large sample of elderly persons living alone in age-integrated public housing in Boston. Of the vulnerable, about three-quarters could not walk up and down stairs without help and over half had gone out only one day a week or less in the month prior to the screening. More than half of those considered vulnerable could not do ordinary work around the house, about 38 percent needed help in preparing meals, and 33 percent needed help in dealing with trash disposal; only about 9 percent needed help with dressing.

While the majority of the elderly in these buildings cannot be considered vulnerable, there are, nevertheless, sizable proportions of persons currently in public housing who need supportive services, whether from formal or informal sources. Relatively few of these houses, however, provide packages of needed services; for example, a combination of meals, housekeeper/chore, personal assistance, and transportation and escort services are available in only 7 percent of the housing projects in this sample. Even for persons who may need to use only one of the services, availability of the service as part of a package of services may be more important than its availability by itself. In other words, simply knowing that services in general will be available when needed may have beneficial consequences.

It cannot be automatically assumed, however, that the provision of packages of services in the context of barrier-free housing will produce the desired ends. Questions concerning the feasibility and impact of this type of living arrangement on reducing institutionalization must still be answered. In addition, impact on the quality of life and the cost/benefit ratio of this type of living arrangement need to be determined.

Hard data based on carefully controlled studies of the impact on the target population of different congregate housing models are extremely sparse and sorely needed. Such data may result from the national evaluation of the Congregate Housing Service Program currently underway in Boston by the Hebrew Rehabilitation Center for the Aged (HRCA) and future analysis. Meanwhile a previously completed HRCA controlled study of one congregate housing model—medically oriented housing for the physically impaired and elderly (Sherwood et al., 1981)—examines the feasibility, effectiveness, and costs of such models.

Medically Oriented Housing: The Highland Heights Story

Initiated in 1970 and continuing for a period of seven years, a longitudinal investigation was initiated of a low-income, federally sponsored, medically oriented housing project for the physically impaired and elderly in Fall River, Massachusetts —Highland Heights.[1]

Highland Heights is a fourteen-story low-income housing project consisting of 110 studio and 98 two-room apartments designed specifically for physically impaired, largely elderly adults living alone or with one other person. In addition to building design and hardware features, the site location facilitates access to health and other com-munity services. Located in the basement is an out-patient clinic with physical therapy, occupa-tional therapy, and other out-patient treatment rooms. The apartment house also includes space for other ancillary services and social activities. The out-patient clinic therapy team coordinates with several community resources to provide services, including homemaker–home-health aid and visiting nurse agencies. Available on-site are some social services, activity programs, and congregate dining opportunities (the noontime meal, Monday–Friday).

An analysis of comparable construction costs based on 1977 figures indicates that it would have cost a little over $6 million at that time to build Highland Heights on its current location. This is about $500,000 more than if the apartment house had been built for a general population of adults seeking efficiency or one-bedroom apartments. When costs for a manager with specialized training and for additional help to provide chore services to the occupants were taken into consideration, it was estimated that, in 1977, the operational costs of Highland Heights would have been about $40,000 a year more than they would have been for "normal occupancy" in a comparable building. As defined here, "normal occupancy" excludes housing for the "well" aged in which "chore" services are provided.

It should be noted that the basic health services, either provided for in the planning stage of Highland Heights or for which funds in the form of third-party payments are available, have functioned satisfactorily from the time of its opening. Social and other ancillary services for which there was no direct provision either through prior commitment or third-party payments have been slower to develop. Nonetheless, social and recreational services have developed primarily through volunteer programs, as well as by using the staff already involved in Highland Heights (the out-patient nurse for social worker case aide services, for example).

It was hoped that the combination of barrier-free features and readily available medical and other services would foster a "normal" social life, promote psychological well-being, and provide a viable alternative to institutionalization for persons who, while requiring a specialized environment, do not need the twenty-four-hour care of a chronic hospital or skilled nursing home.

The viability of this type of living arrangement for deinstitutionalizing persons from medical long-term care facilities was demonstrated by a longitudinal study of fifty-one persons who moved directly to Highland Heights from a long-term care facility during the first five years after the building was opened. All but one of these persons lived in Highland Heights for more than one year, and some individuals who had been in an institutional living arrangement for many years lived almost totally independently in Highland Heights for over six years. Almost none of the elderly, however, had been in an institutional setting for more than two years when they moved from the long-term care institution to Highland Heights.

These deinstitutionalized persons varied in age from nineteen to eighty-five years; 76 percent were forty-five years of age or older, over 40 percent of whom were sixty-five years or older. Almost all of the individuals moving to Highland Heights were clinically assessed as meeting the Medicaid medical standards concerning nursing home placement (either the intermediate-care or skilled nursing criteria). Demonstrating the vulnerability of this group, an examination of the use of "emergency" services at Highland Heights revealed that, for both years, Highland Heights residents who came from an institutional setting used the emergency services two to three times as much as the remaining residents. Six of the fifty-one deinstitutionalized were found to have been "excessive" users of hospital services; the utilization patterns of the remaining group, however, were quite comparable to national averages for the elderly or disabled.

Pointing to the advantages of the Highland Heights architectural design (including building features and site location) for persons with specific types of impairments are findings from a small substudy of twenty-five Highland Heights residents who represented a variety of types of disabilities. Based on relevant medical data pertaining to medical diagnosis and functional limitations for each sample member, on a case-specific basis a consultant expert in environmental analysis and design assessed desirable features of architectural design that could facilitate functioning (and conversely, the absence of which would constitute an environmental barrier for the individual). Findings indicate that Highland Heights had indeed created a more barrier-free environment than the former dwellings for the majority in the study sample. This held true in particular for those with limitations in stamina and locomotion and for persons requiring the specific medical services of the outpatient clinic such as physical therapy, speech therapy, supervision of medication, and assistance in obtaining appliances.

Impact of Highland Heights on the health and well-being of residents was also studied for up to five years with respect to death, institutionalization, and hospitalization in an acute facility. Other quality-of-life outcomes examined were housing satisfaction, activities, and emotional state variables.

Posttest interview data revealed positive effects for the residents in a number of quality-of-life areas, especially housing satisfaction and participation in formal activities. Moreover, for the first four years, in particular, the death rate of residents was significantly lower than that of a control group of nonresidents. By the end of the fifth year, the gap in the death rate between residents and control group was not as large; but even at the end of the fifth year of the impact study period, the average number of days alive during the five years was significantly larger for the residents than for the control group.

Of particular importance, the impact findings are very positive with respect to the major goal of the intervention—to serve as an alternative to institutionalization. Throughout the five-year impact study period, the residents were significantly less likely to become institutionalized and spent less time in a long-term care facility as compared with their matched controls.

However, by the fifth year, residents had spent

significantly more days in an acute hospital setting than their matched controls had—a factor not significantly different for both groups in the first few years. Despite these potentially additional costs, a three-year cost-savings analysis, based on the periods during which both members of the resident-control matched pairs were alive, revealed a cumulative benefit-to-cost ratio (net savings divided by net costs) of $2.21, with a benefit-to-cost ratio of $2.83 for the first year. In other words, for every dollar of actual costs incurred for a resident, $2.83 was saved in other areas during the first year, with $2.21 being saved cumulatively over a three-year period. For every resident, there was an average dollar savings of $2,986 over the three-year period, or about $995 per year.

It can be seen, then, that medically oriented congregate housing can be a feasible, effective, and financially sound living arrangement for at least some segment of the elderly-frail population. Conclusions from this study, however, cannot be drawn concerning the extent to which the medical orientation is necessary or whether or not medical services are more important than other ancillary supports. It may be that barrier-free housing providing fewer supports than those available at Highland Heights may also have positive effects. It must be emphasized that the control group consisted of persons on the waiting list to Highland Heights, most of whom were not residents of other housing for the aged. It remains for future research to discover the differential effects of different types of congregate housing on different types of impaired adults.

Board-and-Care as a Sheltered Community Living Arrangement

Board-and-care models constitute a different, more sheltered type of alternative community living arrangement for impaired adults than medically oriented housing. By federal standards, to qualify as a board-and-care living arrangement, some type of supervision or protective oversight must be provided in addition to room and board, although the level of care may vary from just general supervi-

sion to intensive nonmedical care. However, board-and-care homes do not qualify as Medicaid-certified facilities. Known by different names in different states (such as board-and-care homes, group homes, foster-care homes, rest homes, residential-care or personal-care homes, to name just a few), they include some relatively institutional settings—"rest" homes and homes for the aged—as well as community sheltered living arrangements, such as foster homes in a family setting or group homes with fewer than five persons. The common element of board-and-care facilities is a focus on meeting the nonmedical needs of clients who, because of their disabilities, cannot function in totally independent living arrangements.

In conjunction with other enabling legislation concerning the provision of long-term care supportive services in community settings, the development of board-and-care living arrangement options, in general, received a major stimulus from the Supplemental Security Income (SSI) Program (Title XVI of the Social Security Act). The SSI program was first implemented in 1974, replacing a patchworklike network of state-administered programs. SSI provides for a federal floor of income for aged, blind, and disabled persons who, based upon uniform national standards, are deemed eligible for benefits. While the payment level is sharply reduced for persons in other shared living settings (such as living with relatives), benefits to needy persons living in board-and-care homes, referred to by the Social Security Administration as "domiciliary-care" homes, are the same as those received by persons living alone.

Supplementation of the federal SSI payment by optional state contributions is encouraged by the federal government, and, at the option of the state, may be either state or federally administered (through the Social Security Administration). In 1981, only nine states did not have an optional supplement to the federal SSI program. States often provide different levels of supplementation to different categories of individuals. In some states higher state supplements are offered to SSI recipients in board-and-care homes, while in others, as is the case for the federal SSI payment, a board-

and-care resident receives the same levels of supplementation as does a person living alone.

Based on an analysis and extrapolation of data
from a variety of sources, Sherwood and Seltzer
(1981) derived and tested estimates concerning the
number of elderly in board-and-care homes. Including those residing in more institutional types
of settings, they estimated that, as of 1980, there
were about 120,000 elderly domiciliary home residents in the United States. There were 70,000
board-and-care homes nationally in which one or
more elderly persons resided.

As board-and-care continues to grow in importance, questions are being raised concerning the
use of this type of living arrangement for elderly
and other adult long-term care target populations.
While hypotheses abound, little is known about
relationships between and among selected features
of domiciliary-care programs and the achievement
of what may be considered to be desired goals of
domiciliary care by one or more governmental,
policy, and professional groups. Summarized below are selected findings from a number of HRCA
studies of domiciliary care that add to knowledge
and insights concerning such issues. These research efforts focused on domiciliary-care programs across the nation as well as an evaluation
of an innovative program of domiciliary care initiated in Pennsylvania in 1976.

Domiciliary-care Programs across the Nation

Mail responses from 142 domiciliary (board-and-
care) state level programs across the fifty states
and Washington, D.C.,[2] in conjunction with census and other secondary source data, yield interesting insights concerning the relationship between residency in small domiciliary homes—
community rather than institutional domiciliary-
care alternatives—and the achievement of two
goals: (1) cost-contained placement and delivery
of appropriate services, and (2) the provision of
personal and support services (Sherwood et al.,
1982).

The large majority (82 percent) of these state
programs include, usually among others, family-
run facilities. Over half also include for-profit,
corporation-owned (54 percent) and nonprofit (63
percent) domiciliary-care homes. Over three-
quarters (118 of 142) are in states with optional
state SSI supplementation. Programs in states with
no SSI supplementation are significantly less likely to require that services be provided or procured.
For the 118 programs in states with this supplement, those in states with special domiciliary-care
supplements are more likely to require individuals
receiving the state supplement to reside in licensed, certified, or approved facilities than those
in states with general supplementation only. Furthermore, programs in states having special supplementation for domiciliary care tend to have
more robust case-management services than programs in states without such special supplementation. Programs in supplemented states are more
likely to use case-management techniques for
placement and follow-up to ensure appropriate
placement, service planning, and provision of
needed services.

The goal of availability of personal and support
services was operationalized in terms of a five-
point scale indicating how many (from zero to
four) of four services—service planning, case
management, supportive service provision, and
monitoring and evaluation—were specified in the
program as available to clients. A scale score for
the cost-contained "placement and delivery of appropriate services" goal was obtained by multi-
plying the availability of personal and support services score by the total number of persons placed
(at the time of enquiry) in domiciliary-care homes,
and then dividing this figure by the program's operating expenses (excluding payments to residents). This score represents person-services per
dollar spent. The higher the scale value, the more
the goal achievement by these programs.

For each of the goals, a series of regression analyses was conducted in order to explore, in a controlled manner, the extent to which various program elements account for program differences in
the operationalized goal achievement measure.
Included among these program elements was fa-

cility size, with large homes representing the more institutionlike facilities, and small homes representing the more familylike community settings. First, contributions of state characteristics (such as size of the population, per capita income, availability of other long-term care such as nursing home beds, age distribution in the state) were extracted from the operationalized measure. The contributions of program elements to goal achievement to remaining variability in goal achievement were then examined.

The role of small homes (usually community-based living arrangements) in goal achievement is worthy of special note. Controlling for state demographic characteristics impinging on goal achievement, multiple regression analysis supports the viability of small domiciliary or board-and-care homes in community settings. In fact, facility size was one of the six most important variables entering the equation for predicting availability of program personnel and support services. The smaller the average size of the facilities, the greater the availability of services. Furthermore, while size of the program (as measured by the total number of domiciliary-care client beds) contributed importantly to the achievement of cost-contained placement and delivery of appropriate services, small facility size did not impinge negatively on the achievement of this goal. In other words, the findings suggest that large programs, not large facilities, may be needed in order to get the benefits of economy of scale.

The Pennsylvania Domiciliary-care Program

Seeking high-quality noninstitutional alternatives for the increasing numbers of chronically ill, physically and mentally handicapped, and marginally adjusted adults in the population, an innovative program of case-managed community-care homes for dependent adults (including elderly, mental health, and mental retardation target populations) was conceptualized by the interagency Domiciliary-Care Task Force of the Pennsylvania Department of Public Welfare. As defined in this program, approved homes were to consist of small

family-oriented foster homes providing sheltered living arrangements for up to three clients, as well as somewhat larger group-home facilities providing sheltered living arrangements for four to thirteen clients. Under the aegis of Pennsylvania's Office of Aging, the program was an integrated effort to serve the target populations of three agencies: Aging, Mental Health and Mentally Retarded (MH/MR), and Income Maintenance. The county offices of these agencies contributed either personnel or funds to the operation of the domiciliary-care program in their areas. In addition to room, board, laundry, and other needed household services, the domiciliary-care home operator must provide the client with personal care and protective services (including up to twenty-four-hour supervision) when necessary. The program was begun late in 1976 in select counties on a pilot basis (currently implemented on a statewide basis). A federally funded, multifaceted evaluation was conducted by the Hebrew Rehabilitation Center for the Aged with the collaboration of the Pennsylvania central office of the domiciliary-care program.[3]

As operated, the program consists of three major components: (1) the state provision of financial supplementation (through the Inverse Maintenance agency) to functionally debilitated financially needy (Medicaid-eligible) clients of certified homes; (2) the certification (or approval) and monitoring of domiciliary-care homes; and (3) case management, including the determination of functional eligibility of applicants for domiciliary care (assessing the applicant's needs and coordinating services for these clients), the placement of eligible applicants in approved homes, and the continual monitoring of needs and coordination of services for these clients. From a combined state and federal SSI payment, a fixed amount is paid to the proprietor of the domiciliary-care home by the client.

While the program includes group homes with as many as thirteen clients, together with small foster-family homes of up to three clients, the latter predominate, as they did in the study sample. More physically impaired and frail elderly were housed in domiciliary-care homes than were mental health or mentally retarded clients. About 42 percent of the applicants studied were part of the Aging agency's target population; 34 percent were MH and 17 percent MR clients. The remaining applicants (7 percent) included non-aged, usually physically handicapped persons. (In general, the characteristics of these persons closely resembled the Aging agency's client population.) Additionally, about half of the MH and about a quarter of the MR study population of domiciliary-care applicants were sixty years of age or over.

Both clinical assessments and self-report data reveal that the applicants considered eligible by program staff were seriously debilitated and in need of supportive living arrangements. Demonstrating the focus of the program on the more debilitated applicants, elderly persons who seem to have less ability to perform instrumental tasks of daily living were more likely to be placed than were the less debilitated. However, domiciliary-care applicants were less likely to be placed if they were judged to exhibit serious personal adjustment problems. Thus, on one hand placing persons with low ability to perform instrumental tasks of daily living was successfully accomplished. On the other hand, special efforts with additional supports to the domiciliary-care home operator need to be considered in order to be more successful in placing technically eligible persons with serious personal adjustment problems.

The program was very successful in deinstitutionalizing elderly persons from long-term care institutions. However, institutionalization for over two years appears to present a significant problem when discharging functionally impaired elderly persons from long-term care institutions to domiciliary-care settings. Only 5 percent of the placed Aging agency's subsample had been institutionalized for two or more years prior to discharge to domiciliary care (as compared, for example, with 53 percent of the placed MH and 50 percent of the placed MR subsample). Thus, the feasibility of this type of sheltered living arrange-

ment for the most debilitated elderly remains to be demonstrated.

The evaluation featured a controlled study of the impact of the domiciliary-care program on the recipients of care and a determination of the cost/benefit of the program. It was not possible to have a randomized experiment. In this case, placed domiciliary-care residents were considered the pool of potential experimentals, and identified vulnerable persons in counties that did not as yet have the program were considered the pool of potential controls. Impact over a period of a little less than one year was studied.

Although not without problems, the results are very encouraging. Not only were quality-of-life impacts observed, but domiciliary care was found to be both a feasible and cost-effective option for the elderly (as well as for other segments of the long-term care target population). When the elderly residents (experimentals) were compared with the comparable types of persons in similar counties in Pennsylvania that did not have the program (controls), positive impacts were observed on quality of life, reduced institutionalization, and costs. In particular, the service needs of the experimentals were more likely to be met; they became more integrated into community life than their control counterparts, and they scored better with respect to emotional status, as well as on selected measures of satisfaction with living arrangement.

No difference existed in the death rates of the experimentals and controls. However, the domiciliary-care program was found to be effective in reducing the number of institutional days, particularly for elderly persons entering the program from an institutional setting (a skilled or intermediate nursing home, or a state or county hospital for the chronically ill). In other words, the program was found to be a viable and successful living arrangement for deinstitutionalizing elderly persons.

In general, the cost comparisons strongly indicate that the Pennsylvania domiciliary-care program has generated and can continue to generate significant cost savings. For the aging client population, the benefit-to-cost ratio (net savings divided by net costs) was found to be $3.85 for those who were deinstitutionalized and $1.59 for persons from the community. That is, for every dollar of actual costs incurred for a deinstitutionalized aging client in the program, $3.85 was saved in other areas; for every dollar spent on an aging client from a community setting, $1.59 was saved. In net dollars saved, this amounted to an average of about $21 per placement day for the deinstitutionalized aging client and about $4 per placement day for aging clients from the community.

Through secondary analyses of these data, as part of a subsequent study carried out by HRCA[4], institutional days and costs of the elderly Pennsylvania domiciliary-care clients entering from a community setting were compared with a comparable group of applicants to intermediate-care facilities (ICFs) in Delaware (Sherwood and Morris 1983; Ruchlin and Morris, 1983). For domiciliary-care clients entering from a community setting, about 8 percent of their time over the next year was spent in a long-term care institution. For comparable persons applying for residency in an ICF in Delaware, about 80 percent or more of their time was spent in an institution. The cost comparisons based on the total societal allocations for maintaining these individuals indicate that at the time it cost about $40 per day to maintain these persons in an ICF as compared to about $31 per day in a domiciliary-care home. These figures include costs for institutional residency, acute hospital care, formal community services, informal community services, and the cost of maintaining the client in the community while a resident thereof. However, if one were to concentrate simply on institutional and other *formal* services, the figure was about $31 for an ICF and about $16 a day, not counting room and board, for domiciliary care.

Conclusion

In summary, data from national studies as well as intensive multifaceted longitudinal studies of particular interventions indicate that vulnerable individuals are in fact being maintained successfully in sheltered living arrangements in the community. Furthermore, while the target groups were not identical (the domiciliary-care group being perhaps the most vulnerable), impact analyses in separate large-scale studies strongly demonstrate that both medically oriented congregate housing and case-managed, foster-family–type domiciliary-care living arrangements can be viable and effective options. Both interventions were shown to have positive effects on the quality of life and to reduce institutionalization of vulnerable elderly persons.

In addition to prevention of institutionalization, both studies indicated that at least a segment of the currently institutionalized elderly can be successfully placed in a less restrictive living arrangement in the community. While recent years have seen a significant movement away from institution-based services and toward community residential care and treatment settings for all long-term care target groups, deinstitutionalization efforts (successful and unsuccessful) have focused primarily on the MH and MR target populations. To date there has been no major movement toward deinstitutionalization of those currently in medically based long-term care facilities. At the same time, the data reported here indicate that deinstitutionalization to community residential options is feasible and appropriate not only for MH and MR clients, but for chronically ill and elderly populations as well. As noted, however, in both studies, almost all of the elderly persons successfully deinstitutionalized had been in an institutional setting for less than two years. Thus, special motivational efforts may be necessary in order to deinstitutionalize elderly persons who may be functionally appropriate for more independent living but who have been in institutional settings for longer than two years.

Finally, effective interventions from a quality-of-life perspective are not necessarily more costly to society than more traditional institutional care. Indeed, data from these impact studies show substantial cost savings along with positive quality-of-life impact.

Notes

1. This study was supported in part by HUD Contracts H-1275, H-2180R, and HEW/NCHSR Grant HS00903.
2. The analyses reported were conducted by HRCA in connection with Contract #600-79-0096 with the Social Security Administration. In conjunction with census and other secondary source data, they represent secondary analyses of data from a mail survey of state-level domiciliary (board-and-care) programs across the nation that were gathered by the Horizon House Institute (Reichstein and Bergofsky, 1980) as part of a previous HRCA study, AoA Grant #90-A-1659. Data-gathering procedures were followed by Horizon House to ensure replies from programs which included at least some elderly.
3. Contract #130-76-12, funded by Region III of the U.S. Department of Health, Education, and Welfare (now HHS).
4. These analyses were conducted by HRCA as part of a study of Alternative Paths to Long-Term Care, supported by AoA Grant #90-A-1666.

References

Gruenberg, L. 1975. *The Massachusetts Department of Public Health Long-Term Care Patient Surveys.* Internal report. Boston: Massachusetts Department of Public Health, Office of Health Planning and Statistics.

Holmes, M., J. Alfaro, and J. Levine. 1983. "Process Report II: Issues in CHSP Planning and Implementation." Mimeo report for U. S. HUD study, Evaluation of the Congregate Housing Services Program (Contract HC-5373). Boston: Hebrew Rehabilitation Center for the Aged.

Mor, V., J. N. Morris, and S. Sherwood, 1980. "An Assessment for Use in Identifying Persons Who Have Benefitted from Use of Lifeline Emergency Alarm Services." In *A Study of the Effects of an Emergency Alarm and Response System for the Aged: A Final Report.* Boston: Hebrew Rehabilitation Center for the Aged.

Moroney, R. M., and R. N. Kurtz. 1975. "The Evolution of Long-Term Care Institutions." In *Long-Term Care: A Handbook for Researchers, Planners, and Providers.* Ed. S. Sherwood. New York: Spectrum.

Morris, J. N., and C. E. Gutkin. 1979. *A Comprehensive Examination of Characteristics and Evaluation of Dischargeability of a Selected Group of Patients in Vermont Long-Term Care Facilities.* Contract with Vermont Professional Standards Review Organization. Boston: Hebrew Rehabilitation Center for the Aged.

Morris, J. N., S. Sherwood, and V. Mor. 1984. "An Assessment Tool Used for Identifying Functionally Vulnerable Persons in the Community." *Gerontologist* 24: 373–79.

Pfeiffer, E. 1973. "Introduction to the Conference Report." In *Alternatives to Institutional Care for Older Americans: Practice and Planning, a Conference Paper.* Ed. E. Pfeiffer. Durham, NC: Duke Univ. Center for the Study of Aging and Human Development.

Reichstein, K., and L. Bergofsky. 1980. *Summary and Report of the National Survey of State Administered Domiciliary-Care Programs in the Fifty States and the District of Columbia.* AoA Grant No. 90-A-1659. Boston: Hebrew Rehabilitation Center for the Aged.

Ruchlin, H., and J. N. Morris. 1983. "Pennsylvania's Domiciliary-Care Experiment: Cost-Benefit Implications." *American Journal of Public Health* 73, No. 6:654–60.

Sherwood, C. C., and M. M. Seltzer. 1981. "Tasks III Report Board-and-Care Literature Review." Research Sequence Subcontract HEW, 100-79-0117. Boston: Boston Univ. School of Social Work.

Sherwood, S., and J. N. Morris. 1983. "The Pennsylvania Domiciliary-Care Experiment: Impact on Quality of Life." *American Journal of Public Health* 73, No. 6: 646–53.

Sherwood, S., et al. 1977. *The Needs of Elderly Community Residents of Massachusetts.* Boston: Hebrew Rehabilitation Center for the Aged.

———. 1981. *An Alternative in Long-Term Care: The Highland Heights Experiment.* Cambridge, MA: Ballinger.

———. 1982. "Domiciliary-Care Programs Across the Nation: Implementing an Option in Long-Term Care." Mimeo report, Social Security Administration Contract #600-79-0096. Boston: Hebrew Rehabilitation Center for the Aged.

Thompson, M. M. 1982. "Enriching Environments for Older People." In *Congregate Housing for Older People.* Ed. R. D. Chellis, J. F. Seagle, and B. M. Seagle. Lexington, MA: Lexington.

U.S. Congressional Budget Office (CBO). 1977. *Long-Term Care: Actuarial Cost Estimates.* Washington, DC: U.S. Government Printing Office.

U.S. General Accounting Office (GAO). 1979. *Entering a Nursing Home: Costly Implications for the Elderly.* Washington, DC: U.S. GAO.

PART III

NEIGHBORHOOD QUALITY, SATISFACTION, AND PRESERVATION

CHAPTER 12 Neighborhoods and the Aged

Lance M. Pollack • Robert J. Newcomer

The concept of neighborhoods and neighborhood units has long held an idealized position in the planning and design of communities (Gallion and Eisner, 1963). Some professions and disciplines have chosen to interpret this concept in physical terms—focusing on population size, density, and distances to needed services (see, for example, DeChiara and Koppelman, 1969). Others have emphasized the social networks and relationships among the residents of specific geographic areas (Keller, 1968; Suttles, 1972). No standards have emerged to define the population, its size, composition, and density, or the physical size of these areas. Those who have chosen to emphasize physical features have been largely concerned with separating residential and nonresidential districts, placing major street traffic around rather than through these areas, and making some neighborhood stores and services available within a reasonable walking distance. In other words, they have directed attention to the urban form and efficiency in the spatial location of land uses. Attention to the social aspects of neighborhoods have generally been directed to the factors affecting community identity and interaction. The presence of these features is thought to enhance safety and mutual support (Jacobs, 1970; Warren and Warren, 1977). An underlying basis for the attention given to neighborhoods is their assumed importance in resident satisfaction.

The concern of this chapter is to explore the extent of current knowledge about the importance of neighborhoods for one subpopulation—the elderly—identifying those features that make an area desirable, and discussing how this knowledge can be used better to guide the development and preservation of neighborhoods. We have approached this issue from both a physical- and social-planning perspective. The syntheses of these perspectives has been facilitated through a person-environment conceptualization of the issue.

Our focus on the elderly stems from several bases. First, households headed by someone aged sixty-five or older constitute about 20 percent of all households in the U.S. (U.S. DHUD, 1979). This proportion varies markedly across and within cities. Second, as discussed by Beth Soldo in chapter 2, the probability of impairments affecting the ability to drive, climb stairs, board buses, and conduct other self-maintenance tasks such as shopping and cooking increases with age. The presence of functional limitations is thought to reduce physical mobility and necessitate a higher dependency on physical (and perhaps social) neighborhood features than may have been present prior to the reduced functional capacity. A third basis of concern stems from the implementation of a variety of public and private actions, including congregate housing site selection, urban redevelopment, neighborhood socioeconomic transition, and changes in commercial and residential land use. Each of these actions has the potential for displacing or disrupting the lifestyle of an area's residents. The elderly are particularly affected by

119

this because they spend a greater proportion of their time at home and in their immediate neighborhood (Struyk, 1981).

Environment and Aging

Several models of person-environment interactions have been conceptualized in recent years (for a review of these, see Windley, Byerts, and Ernst, 1975; Lawton, 1977; Newcomer and Bexton, 1978). All of these assume that behavior represents some aspects of the individual interacting with the environment. One of these, the Lawton-Nahemow (1973) transaction model, is especially useful for the clarity of its dimensions and their applicability to program and design decision making (see fig. 12-1).

The basic premise of this model is that individual behavior and satisfaction are contingent upon the dynamic balance between the demand character of the environment (press) and the individual's ability to deal with that demand (com-

petence). Press can be positive, neutral, or negative and may reside in the physical or social environments (the people present and the modal characteristics of those people) or the sociological environment (societal norms, values, and institutions). Competence can be operationally defined as the ability to perform tasks in the areas of life maintenance, functional health, perception and cognition, physical self-maintenance, instrumental self-maintenance, and social role performance. When competence and press are basically in balance, the resulting behavior is characterized as adaptive, and satisfaction is experienced by the individual (*center*, fig. 12-1). When competence and press are not congruent, the result is maladaptive behavior and dissatisfaction. In situations in which competence far outstrips press (*upper left*, fig. 12-1), the model posits that behavior is maladaptive as evidenced by boredom and an accompanying atrophy of unused or unchallenged skills. When press overwhelms competence (*lower right*, fig. 12-1), the individuals are expected to cease or limit their exposure to that environment.

The schematic model also illustrates a theory of aging called the "environmental docility" hypothesis (Lawton, 1970). This hypothesis contends that high competence is associated with relative independence from environmental press, while low competence is associated with a greater vulnerability to environmental press. Put another way, a small change in press has a greater impact on the behavior of a low-competence individual than on the behavior of a high-competence individual. As an individual ages, aging-related deficits and decrements contribute to a deterioration in level of competence. Thus, the aging individual becomes increasingly susceptible to changes in environmental press, and in order to maintain the dynamic balance desired, the individual is confronted with having to ameliorate press, bolster competence, or withdraw from the environment.

From a practical standpoint, this model defines virtually any planning and service delivery problem as one in which it is necessary to identify those individual abilities and perceived environmental demands that are creating a current or po-

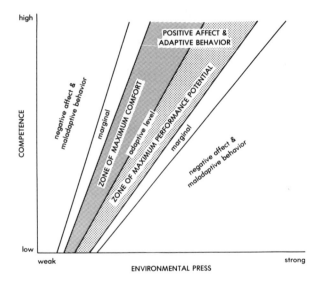

Source: M.P. Lawton and L. Nahemow, 1973.

12-1. Ecological model. From M. P. Lawton and L. Nahamow, 1973.

Point of application	The Individual's role	
	Respondent	Initiator
The environment	A Social and environmental engineering	B The individual redesigns his environment
The individual	C Rehabilitation, therapy	D Self-therapy growth

Source: M.P. Lawton and L. Nahemow, 1973.

12-2. Environmental change model: the older person as initiator and responder. From M. P. Lawton and L. Nahemow, 1973.

tential problem in the individual's functioning. Once problems and their antecedents have been identified, the task of maintaining congruence between the individual and the environment may be accomplished through the four types of ecological change depicted in figure 12-2. In other words, intervention can occur in attempts to change the individual or the environment. Typically, within health and social service programs, interventions are directed at raising the individual's competence. Design and city-planning approaches on the other hand, are more often directed at environmental factors. Each approach can have validity if appropriate to the presenting circumstances. In looking at the issue of neighborhood suitability for the aged, it is important to appreciate that a range of interventions is possible and that no set of solutions will likely be applicable in all situations.

Consider, for example, the issue of functional self-maintenance. The ability to climb stairs, walk distances, cross busy streets, board buses, or drive a car are all related to the ability to leave one's house. Functional competence within a particular environmental context would be defined not purely by the individual's ability, but by the necessity to perform these tasks. Whether one can or cannot drive is relatively unimportant, for example, in defining competence if walking or buses can be substituted. Hence the individual could be seen as having a competence level adequate to the press of the situation. This congruence would be expected to result in adaptation and satisfaction with the living situation.

Demand Character of the Neighborhood Environment

The study of neighborhoods and aging has largely focused on two concerns—influences on neighborhood selection and residential satisfaction. Within this context four aspects of neighborhoods have been identified as being particularly important: aesthetics and amenities, transportation and access, safety and fear of crime, and social characteristics of neighborhoods. We briefly review these dimensions to provide a basis for further exploring approaches to planning and intervention. Neighborhood aesthetics and amenities have been studied both in terms of reported quality (Lawton, Brody, and Turner-Massey, 1978) and physical condition (Bohland and Davis, 1979). Regardless of the approach, these attributes have been found to be important predictors of residential satisfaction among those aged sixty-five years and older. This influence does not necessarily mean that people will relocate if aesthetics and amenities are not satisfactory (Gutowski and Field, 1979). Thus, aesthetics/amenities appear to affect satisfaction, but not necessarily behavior.

Access, measured in terms of distance and other physical and social barriers, affects both satisfaction and behavior, particularly the use of resources (Lawton, 1977). This has been shown for inner-city neighborhood residents (Cantor, 1979) and among national samples of subsidized housing residents (Newcomer, 1976). The relationship of distance to the pattern of service use varies somewhat with the nature of the service. Convenience and recreational services such as supermarkets, department stores, parks, senior centers, and pharmacies are used more frequently if located within reasonable proximity (usually up to ten blocks). On the other hand, frequency of use of medical services such as physicians and dentists does not appear to vary with distance to facility. A developed public transit system also is seen as promoting convenience and use of other services such as health care.

The absence of sufficient access to needed services can constitute a significant negative influence on residential satisfaction (Regnier, 1982) and has been associated with an expressed desire to move among elderly-headed households (Gutowski and Field, 1979; Carp, 1980). While this indicates a direct connection to neighborhood selection among those who move, a variety of circumstances mediates this effect. Paramount among these is that the living arrangements of most older people were chosen at a younger age when criteria such as proximity to work or schools were more salient than proximity to convenience shopping, and when driving compensated for distance. Although many older people may express dissatisfaction with their current access to services, relatively few actually relocate because of this fact alone. Should relocation occur, however, it becomes more likely that the choice of the new residence will include consideration of service access.

Crime and fear of victimization have been designated as the major problem in the community environment by the elderly (Louis Harris and Associates, 1975; Toseland and Rasch, 1978; Gutowski and Field, 1979; Regnier, 1982). As discussed by Liang and his associates later in part 3, expressions of fear and safety derive more often from individual perceptions than objective reality. The lack of environmental control due to physical, sensory, economic, and social limitations of the aged have been posited as contributing factors in these negative perceptions (Lawton et al., 1976). The effects of crime in both its physical and psychological dimensions can be mediated by the designed environment through creation of zones of territorial influence called "defensible space" (Newman, 1972). These zones of territorial influence can be induced through environmental modification by providing surveillance opportunities, clearly defining the function and ownership of various spaces, limiting access, eliminating conflicting uses, providing amenities, and improving area aesthetics. Residents tend to maintain a surveillance over such territories that reduces both crime and fear of crime. Additional support for the defensible space concept is found in a study of elderly homeowners. Those who displayed more territorial behavior were less fearful than elderly

homeowners who displayed little territorial behavior (Pollack and Patterson, 1980).

The social characteristics of neighborhoods, although varyingly defined in previous studies, have tended to encompass issues of social participation (such as the presence and number of friends and relatives) and social homogeneity of neighbors (similarity of age, race, and socioeconomic characteristics). Less tangible dimensions, such as social cohesion and a sense of belonging, have also been considered. Status similarity between neighbors and older residents has been shown to be positively correlated with activity participation by older residents (Lawton, Brody, and Turner-Massey, 1978; Regnier, 1982). The presence of a family member or close friend in the neighborhood has been found to be as desirable in terms of residential satisfaction as the presence of any service or amenity (see, for example, Cantor, 1979). Neighborliness, defined to include social cohesion and a sense of belonging as well as friendship, has also been identified as a significant predictor of residential satisfaction (Bohland and Davis, 1979). This quality could even ameliorate concerns for safety.

Tying the social characteristic concept more directly to the Lawton/Nahemow transactional model is the suggestion that localized social networks may have particular importance for older persons who as a group have limited mobility, play fewer roles, have less interaction, experience a smaller number of social contacts, and suffer significant social disruption resulting from role loss and poor health (Ward, 1979).

To recapitulate briefly the general literature on neighborhoods and the aged, an underlying assumption seems to have been made that the aged as a group have a higher proportion of members with impaired functional ability than is true of younger age groups. As a result, many elderly are assumed to be at risk of becoming increasingly dependent on their residential environment for the regulation of behavior and satisfaction. Four general aspects of the neighborhood environment have been found to have special significance for the elderly. The quality and condition of the physical plant of the neighborhood contributes to the comfort of the elderly resident but does not appear to affect residential satisfaction negatively, at least to the point of relocation. Access to services is of more critical importance in that lack of access or transportation to services precludes use of services and negatively affects comfort and satisfaction. The aged appear to prefer having most convenience services within walking distance. Crime and concern for safety form the single biggest problem confronting the elderly resident. While crime is usually considered a social problem dealt with through institutional means, it appears that the associated fear may be modified by the presence of a sense of territory and community. Social aspects of the neighborhood are also of more significant importance to older than to younger residents. Perhaps this is because of the loss of social roles and opportunities for social interaction characteristic of old age, and because of more limited activity.

These findings suggest a variety of possible environmental interventions which can positively or negatively affect the residential satisfaction of the elderly. The type of intervention and the quality of its effect depends upon whether the goal of the decision maker is to support or inhibit maintenance or growth of an elderly subpopulation in a given neighborhood. Supportive strategies for elderly neighborhood residents vary according to whether a given population is aging in a constant neighborhood, an aged population is living in a changing neighborhood, or an elderly population is relocating to a new neighborhood.

Planning and Policy

Public policies are usually adopted and implemented in response to highly visible problems. Because there is often uncertainty about the consequences arising from these actions, decision making tends to build incrementally on the experience of previous action (Lindblom, 1980). Issues of neighborhoods and neighborhood quality for the elderly, such as site selection for new housing units, dislocations, condominium conversions, and victimization, can generate immediate and incremental public policy response.

Cities, for example, have traditionally used their authority to affect traffic volume, traffic patterns, street lighting and maintenance, public transit routes, location of public-financed services, housing type and quality, management of open space, public health standards, loans, and taxes. Such authority can have important and often immediate effects on many of the conditions which have been found to enhance neighborhood satisfaction for the elderly. Manipulating traffic flow can influence neighborhood aesthetic values by affecting ambient noise and air quality. Control over the volume and speed of traffic flow can also affect pedestrian safety. Street lighting and maintenance carry implications for both aesthetic and safety concerns. Emergency rescue and police outreach can also enhance perceptions of and actual safety. Transit routes and location of services have a direct impact on access and the patterns of neighborhood-based activity. Zoning laws can be used to influence the level and type of commercialization and the variety of housing types available in a given neighborhood, thus affecting aesthetics, access, perceptions of safety, and social characteristics among other considerations. Housing quality regulations and public health laws affect the type, quality, and cost of dwelling space, while taxes and loan programs affect the income and ability to pay for housing and other services and the social mix and socioeconomic characteristics of neighborhoods.

The interventions noted here provide tangible examples of the range of choices available to local government and community groups to affect potentially important short- and long-term changes in neighborhood conditions. Interventions, directed more explicitly at changing individual competence, are also widely available. They may occur in health-care system services as attempts to accommodate for loss (for example, physical therapy and eyeglasses) or as preventive strategies aimed at reducing the cause of physical and mental limitations. They might also take form in self-help programs.

This enumeration of intervention mechanisms, while illustrating potential means of influencing neighborhoods, also serves to point out that both public and private changes and adaptations in neighborhoods are constantly occurring. In other words, decisions and actions are being taken daily to affect the physical and social form of an area, and over time these may also affect the age, racial, and economic composition and household size that are characteristic of the area's residents. The actions taken or not taken can have potentially important consequences for the older population. In the balance of the chapter we explore some of the options and questions that city planners and others might consider as they formulate "policy."

Neighborhood Planning Models

A basic consideration is a decision about the groups intended to benefit from a course of action. One planning strategy, termed the *constant model* approach (Lawton, Greenbaum, and Liebowitz, 1980), attempts to preserve as far as possible the original character of the residents and the general housing environment. Under this model, as individuals decline in competence (physically, mentally, economically), policy implicitly or explicitly encourages them to move to a more congruent environment. Replacements for these individuals similarly would be sought to match the functional ability and demographic background of the continuing residents. Such an approach maintains a constant social and physical community environment. It does not necessitate much social or physical intervention, except perhaps to help people relocate from or into this setting. Moreover, it precludes the elderly from freezing housing stock sought by others (Myers, 1978). An alternative strategy has been termed by Lawton, Greenbaum, and Liebowitz (1980) as the *accommodative model* approach. This model develops the necessary social, physical, and service interventions needed to maintain the aging individual (or other target groups) in their residences. These interventions can be made purposefully by public

action or through the operation of local market forces.

A variation on these "pure" models has been proposed by Regnier (1975) through what he calls *reinforcement by redefinition*. This approach calls for targeted intervention in neighborhoods that have a high concentration of elderly residents (or other target groups) or those areas where high concentrations might either be expected or desired. The intervention would involve the provision of improvements in the form of a core or critical mass of services near the greatest concentration of the target residents. The implication is that others who need such local support will seek out these neighborhoods.

The importance of delineating these broad strategies is that they clarify the public policy choices available. Each strategy can be applied on a neighborhood-by-neighborhood basis with the local government consciously acting to achieve planned consequences in the urban form and composition. In other words, public actions can be made to create and maintain age-mixed neighborhoods, develop and maintain age-segregated neighborhoods, keep people in their single-family homes, or encourage relocation to more supportive housing.

Characteristics of Elders in Neighborhoods

In selecting a strategy for action regarding the elderly there are several specific factors that should be considered. Perhaps the most important is that the vast majority of these people have become "old" within their residential locales. In other words, most residents moved into their current residences during earlier periods in their lives. Even among the elderly who do move, most tend to relocate within a relatively short distance, often in the same town, and in similar neighborhoods (Molozemoff, Anderson, and Rosenbaum, 1978; Myers, 1978). For people in this situation a determination should be made regarding the constancy of the environment. If the environment is remaining relatively constant while individual competence may be declining, one possible approach would be to reinforce this competence through individually targeted support or prosthetic services. Another, perhaps complementary, approach would be the introduction of environmental enhancement, designed to reduce the demands from the environment. Transportation service would be one example of this approach.

Another group of elderly may be those living in neighborhoods that have changed markedly. This change can take many forms—some of which enhance living quality, others detract from it. The direction of change needs to be determined and decisions made regarding the appropriateness of remedial action. Such action, as in the preceding scenario, could be aimed either at affecting individual competence or environmental press.

A third group of elderly are those who have relocated to different living situations perhaps as an attempt to achieve a better match between their current or anticipated competence levels and the demands of their environment. An identification of the areas attracting in-moving elderly is a necessary first step for public action regarding this population. Public action might be taken to help protect and maintain those locations which are desirable for their amenity, safety, and other dimensions. On the other hand, for areas not meeting these criteria, efforts might be adopted either to enhance area quality or to deflect the elderly population migration into other locations.

Interrelated Neighborhood Issues

Of course, selection of a specific plan of action demands consideration of a wide variety of other factors, such as the population groups competing for the same housing as the elderly, the trade-off of services for other public goods, and the market forces affecting land use and population patterns within a city or its neighborhoods. The central point to this discussion is that residents do not have to accept passively the transition of desirable neighborhoods into undesirable ones, or the inevitability of unsatisfactory neighborhood conditions

for the elderly. Current knowledge, if applied, can facilitate better decisions about how to maintain and develop more appropriate neighborhood and housing alternatives for the older population.

A Look Ahead

The remaining chapters in part 3 continue to examine the means for resolving some of the more critical issues that affect neighborhood quality and satisfaction among the elderly. In chapter 13, Frances Carp looks specifically at the issue of perceived and objective neighborhood quality. She outlines a very exciting approach to a refined measurement of quality and satisfaction, and interprets the neighborhood design implications arising from her work. In chapter 14, Jersey Liang, Mary Sengstock, and Melanie Hwalek direct attention to criminal victimization as a major factor in the residential dissatisfaction of the aged. They review environmental and other factors contributing to high actual and perceptual risk of victimization and offer suggestions for reducing both. In chapter 15, Michael Stegman examines the ways in which the phenomena of displacement and condominium conversion are affecting the life quality of the older population. In chapter 16, B. J. Curry Spitler and Robert Newcomer report findings from their national study of self-help groups among the elderly and discuss the varied importance of physical and social features in the formation and provision of a range of self-help services.

Finally, in chapter 17, Peggy Wireman and Antoinette Sebastian help operationalize the concepts and issues presented here. They outline a set of remedial actions which can be taken to compensate for or correct neighborhood limitations. Their review ranges across such environmental concerns as air quality, noise, security, and access to convenience and public services. Together these chapters summarize what is known about neighborhoods and their importance to the elderly, how these qualities are being threatened, and what can be done to help protect and enrich these settings.

References

Bohland, R., and L. Davis. 1979. "Sources of Residential Satisfaction Among the Elderly: An Age-Comparative Analysis." In *Location and Environment of Elderly Population.* Ed. S. M. Golant. Washington, DC: Winston.

Cantor, M. H. 1979. "Life Space and Social Support." In *The Environmental Context of Aging.* Ed. T. O. Byerts, L. A. Pastalan, and S. C. Howell. New York: Garland.

Carp, F. M. 1980. "Environmental Effects Upon the Mobility of Older People." *Environment and Behavior* 12: 139–56.

DeChiara, J., and L. Koppelman. 1969. *Planning Design Criteria.* New York: Van Nostrand Reinhold.

Gallion, A., and S. Eisner. 1963. *The Urban Pattern.* New York: Van Nostrand Reinhold.

Gutowski, M., and T. Field. 1979. *The Graying of Suburbia.* Washington, DC: Urban Institute.

Jacobs, J. 1970. "The Uses of City Neighborhoods." In *Neighborhood, City and Metropolis.* Ed. R. Gutman and D. Popenoe. New York: Random House.

Keller, S. 1968. *The Urban Neighborhood: A Sociological Perspective.* New York: Random House.

Lawton, M. P. 1970. "Ecology and Aging." In *Spatial Behavior of Older People.* Ed. L. A. Pastalan and D. H. Carson. Ann Arbor, MI: Univ. of Michigan.

———. 1977. "The Impact of Environment on Aging and Behavior." In *Handbook of the Psychology of Aging.* Ed. J. E. Birren and K. W. Schaie. New York: Van Nostrand Reinhold.

Lawton, M. P., and L. Nahemow. 1973. "Ecology and the Aging Process." In *Psychology of Adult Development and Aging.* Ed. C. Eisdorfer and M. P. Lawton. Washington, DC: American Psychological Assn.

Lawton, M. P., et al. 1976. "Psychological Impact of Crime and Public Housing." In *Crime and the Elderly: Challenge and Response.* Ed. J. Goldsmith and S. S. Goldsmith. Lexington, MA: Heath.

Lawton, M. P., E. M. Brody, and P. Turner-Massey. 1978. "The Relationships of Environmental Factors to Changes in Well-Being." *Gerontologist* 18:133–37.

Lawton, M. P., M. Greenbaum, and B. Liebowitz. 1980. "The Lifespan of Housing Environments for the Aging." *Gerontologist* 20:56–64.

Lindblom, C. 1980. *The Policy-Making Process.* 2nd ed. Englewood Cliffs, NJ: Prentice-Hall.

Louis Harris and Associates. 1975. *The Myth and Reality of Aging in America.* Washington, DC: National Council on Aging.

Molozemoff, I. K., J. G. Anderson, and L. V. Rosenbaum. 1978. *Housing for the Elderly: Evaluation of the Effectiveness of Congregate Residences.* Boulder, CO: Westview.

Myers, D. 1978. "Aging of Population and Housing—New Perspectives on Planning for More Balanced Metropolitan Growth." *Growth and Change* 9:8–13.

Newcomer, R. 1976. "An Evaluation of Neighborhood Service Convenience for Elderly Housing Project Residents." In *The Behavioral Basis of Design, Book I.* Ed. P. Suefeld and J. A. Russell. Stroudsberg, PA: Dowden, Hutchinson and Ross.

Newcomer, R. J., and E. F. Bexton. 1978. "Aging and the Environment." In *The Social Challenge of Aging.* Ed. D. Hobman. London: Croom Helm.

Newman, O. 1972. *Defensible Space.* New York: Macmillan.

Pollack, L. M., and A. H. Patterson. 1980. "Territoriality and Fear of Crime in Elderly and Nonelderly Homeowners." *Journal of Social Psychology* 111: 119–29.

Regnier, V. A. 1975. "Neighborhood Planning for the Urban Elderly." In *Aging: Scientific Perspectives and Social Issues.* Ed. D. Woodruff and J. E. Birren. New York, NY: Van Nostrand Reinhold.

———. 1982. *Final Report: Glendale, California Sub-Sample.* Prepared for U. S. Department of Health and Human Services, Office of Human Development Services, Administration on Aging. Grant No. 90-AR-2116/01.

Struyk, R. 1981. *The Housing and Neighborhood Environment of the Elderly: Challenge for the 1980's.* Washington, DC: Urban Institute.

Suttles, G. 1972. *The Social Construction of Communities.* Chicago: Univ. of Chicago.

Toseland, R., and J. Rasch. 1978. "Factors Contributing to Older Persons' Satisfaction with Their Communities." *Gerontologist* 18:395–401.

U.S. Department of Housing and Urban Development (DHUD). 1979. *How Well Are We Housed? The Elderly.* Washington, DC: U.S. Government Printing Office.

Ward, R. A. 1979. "The Implication of Neighborhood Age Structure for Older People." *Sociological Symposium* 26:42–63.

Warren, R., and D. Warren. 1977. *The Neighborhood Organizers Handbook.* South Bend, IN: Univ. of Notre Dame.

Windley, P. G., T. Byerts, and G. Ernst, eds. 1975. *Theory Development in Environment and Aging.* Washington, DC: Gerontological Society.

CHAPTER 13 Neighborhood Quality Perception and Measurement

Frances M. Carp

City planners and social welfare and public health practitioners have found behavioral science research difficult to use, one obstacle being that investigators tend to deal in theoretical constructs while planners and managers are confronted with the real world of people and things. This chapter reports an effort to bridge that gap by studying the neighborhood in terms of its factual characteristics, many of which are amenable to manipulation in planning and programs.

The chapter deals first with the importance of the neighborhood in people's lives and with definition of the term. Attention then turns to the need for objective measures of neighborhood quality, the development of scales of perceived neighborhood quality to serve as standards for developing objective measures (and, as well, to provide practitioners and researchers an understanding of residents' perception and definition of neighborhood quality), and on to the objective measures themselves. The topic then shifts to people's description of the "ideal" neighborhood.

The Importance of Neighborhood Quality

Marans (1976, p. 123) reports that "contemporary planners and designers have often suggested that improving the quality of the residential environment can profoundly affect the quality of people's lives." On the other hand, several empirical studies into determinants of life quality suggest that living environment is less important than are other aspects of life such as health, friendships, work, marriage, and financial status (Andrews and Withey, 1976; Campbell, Converse, and Rogers, 1976; Zehner and Chapin, 1974). However, these considerations are interdependent. The living environment may affect well-being not only directly, but also through its impact upon health, friendships, work, financial status, and possibly even marriage.

Many studies of neighborhood attributes seem to document their importance in residents' experience. Residents' assessments of their neighborhood influence their desire to move (U.S. DHUD, 1978). Studies of the behavior of residents within their neighborhoods show important relationships between places where activities take place and satisfaction with those activities (Fried and Gleicher, 1961; Gans, 1962; Lansing, Marans, and Zehner, 1970; Michelson, 1971; and Newman, 1972).

Galster and Hesser (1981, p. 748) claim that "there are certain physical and social features of

The author's research reported in the chapter was supported by research grant #1 RO1 AG 02433 from The National Institute on Aging of The National Institutes of Health and by research grants #1 RO1 AG/MH 32668 and #1 AG/MH 01291 from the National Institute on Aging of the National Institutes of Health and by the Center on Aging of the National Institute for Mental Health. Graphic materials in the chapter were prepared by David Christensen M. Arch.

neighborhood which people generally need or to which they aspire, and that people cannot adapt to the absence of these features." Neighborhood characteristics are more amenable to change by public efforts than are other situational influences on well-being. This "offers planners the opportunity to improve the quality of the physical surroundings and, in a very direct way, the livability of metropolitan area residents" (Marans, 1976, p. 123).

As people age and mobility is constricted, the influence of the neighborhood increases. For older people the neighborhood may be as important to general quality of life as the home (Carp, 1966; Lawton, 1975), which seems to be second in importance only to the spouse. The increasing incidence of widowhood in later life means that well-being will be even more dependent upon qualities of the living unit and neighborhood.

Neighborhood, Defined

For city planners the neighborhood "has been conceived as a building block in creating larger communities and has been defined by particular physical boundaries and a specific number of people" (Marans, 1976, p. 132). Some researchers (Ganz, 1962; Lee, 1970) suggest that this conception may be less meaningful to residents than would a group of houses, or one or two blocks. Other researchers focus on small areas such as four to six houses facing one another (Lansing, Marans, and Zehner, 1970; Mandell and Marans, 1972; Zehner and Chapin, 1974). For Regnier, Murakami, and Gordon (1979), neighborhoods were areas of approximately 800 to 1000 acres.

In order to determine residents' definitions, Carp and Appleyard (1972), Marans (1976) and Regnier (in press) had people outline their own perceptions of their neighborhoods, and all these researchers found that the results varied widely. The idiosyncratic definition of "neighborhood" by those who live in a seemingly homogeneous or meaningful area complicates the task of relating objective environmental characteristics to residents' perceptions. One approach is to note the

environmental elements within each person's "neighborhood." Another approach is to use the dwelling unit as the focus and measure the distances of environmental objects from it.

In addition to physical attributes, characteristics of the population in the area are an important aspect of the neighborhood. This "suprapersonal environment" (Lawton, 1980) comprises factual information about neighborhood residents (such as age and gender distributions, socioeconomic status, and ethnicity). It is not to be confused with each individual's social network or support system, which is highly personal and subjective.

The Need for Objectivity and Specificity

When the goal is assessment and improvement of neighborhood quality, it is necessary to know objective characteristics as well as perceptions that are amenable to manipulation through planning, design, and programs (Craik, 1981; Gans, 1967; Moos and Lemke, 1980). For example, if fear of street crime limits the activities and, therefore, the life quality of older people (Goldsmith and Goldsmith, 1976), efforts to ameliorate the situation must be enlightened by knowledge of the source of the fear—whether it is the actual crime rate or incorrect belief about that rate. In some instances, older people are not particularly subject to victimization (Antunes, Cook, and Skogan, 1977), and the appropriate intervention is to alter their perceptions of the street scene. If the danger is real, however, such an intervention would be irresponsible.

Objective measurements of neighborhoods have two bases: observer judgments and technical assessments (such as measured distances, noise levels, and land uses). Many observer-based indices of physical and social-institutional environments have been used in a variety of studies (Craik, 1981). Technical assessment procedures have been less prevalent. Assessment of the land and water characteristics (Burton, Kates, and White, 1978; Zube, Pitt, and Anderson, 1975), physical indices of air quality (Barker, 1976), water quality (Coughlin, 1976), and noise (Weinstein, 1976) have been used for large-scale environmental studies. Evaluations of lighting (Berglund, 1977), and interior and exterior colors (Kuller, 1971; Sivik, 1974; Whitfield and Slatter, 1976) were used for studies within the built environment. Such studies have demonstrated relationships between environmental attributes and human reactions. They do not provide knowledge of the dimensions of objective environmental quality that affect people in the course of everyday living in their neighborhoods.

Salient Characteristics of Perceived Neighborhood Quality

What physical and suprapersonal characteristics of a neighborhood are relevant to the well-being of its residents? Efforts to develop measures of objective environmental qualities are impeded by a lack of measures of people's perceptions of those qualities (Craik and Zube, 1976). Perceived neighborhood quality obviously is a multidimensional concept. Many neighborhood studies have not aimed to define the concept but were concerned with a single aspect such as noise or safety. Efforts to define the concept of perceived neighborhood quality in terms of the number and nature of its dimensions generally have relied on expert judgment. However, the opinions of environmental experts such as managers and planners often do not coincide with those of users (Carp, 1976, in press; Kaiser, et al., 1970; Lansing and Marans, 1969; Michelson, 1966; and Troy, 1971). The observer and the resident have different orientations toward a neighborhood. One works there temporarily; the other lives there. When interest lies in environmental impacts upon residents, indicators based on nonresident observations may be inappropriate.

In order to determine the reactions of residents to neighborhood quality, the author administered a questionnaire, addressing about 150 neighborhood characteristics, to people aged eighteen years and older. Responses were consolidated into perceived environmental quality indices (PEQIs) using factor analysis (Carp and Carp, 1982a). These PEQIs can also serve as criteria in developing objective measures of neighborhood quality (Craik and Zube, 1976).

The meaning of each PEQI factor is defined by the content of questions comprising it. For convenience and to avoid long lists of items, the factors are given labels suggested by their component items. Most of these PEQIs reflect judgments on a positive-to-negative scale of specific environmental attributes: aesthetics; safety; air quality; privacy; city maintenance; maintenance by neighbors; personal characteristics of neighbors; noise from neighbors' and own homes; noise from traffic, industry and construction; noise disturbing activities inside one's own home; and noise disturbing outdoor activities. Two are more general: general quality compared to other neighborhoods; and feelings about living in this neighborhood. The latter appears to resemble overall well-being since, in another study, scores on this factor correlated with those on several traditional measures of morale and life satisfaction (Carp and Carp, 1983). These factors represent the dimensions underlying neighborhood quality as perceived by residents, and they provide planners, environmental impact assessors, and researchers with an understanding of some major dimensions of neighborhood environmental quality as it is perceived by residents.

Neighborhoods are not randomly prescribed for people nor are residents randomly assigned to neighborhoods. Quite to the contrary, each neighborhood and resident are linked together by a selection process; certain kinds of people choose or remain in certain kinds of neighborhoods. Conversely, some kinds of neighborhoods are more open to certain kinds of people. Persons who can exercise options make residential choices that result in person-neighborhood "fit." Lack of options among population segments concentrates some groups (such as elderly people of low socioeconomic status) in certain types of neighborhoods, often those with old dwellings and poor maintenance. Thus, by choice or necessity, persons with certain traits are sorted into neighborhoods with certain characteristics.

In addition, individual characteristics influence judgments such as those involved in the PEQIs.

The same neighborhood may be rated as noisy by those who are sensitive to noise and quiet by those who are not, and the same contradiction may be true for other personal traits such as sensitivity to air quality and the importance of aesthetics and the other PEQIs.

Development of Objective Environmental Measures

The real test of the utility of objective assessments of the physical and suprapersonal characteristics of a neighborhood is whether they add to an understanding of people's perceptions of environmental quality. In order to assess fairly the potential utility of objective environmental measures, it is necessary to develop objective measures independent of environmental perceptions and then test their influence on PEQI scores, in competition with personal traits. This approach has the additional advantage of showing that there is a meaningful structure underlying items of objective environmental information that can be measured. These dimensions can be thought of as more abstract qualities of the objective environment that enable us to see better the underlying structure of the vast array of concrete aspects of the neighborhood environment.

An analysis by Carp and Carp (1982b), similar to that used in developing the PEQIs, was used to create Technical Environmental Assessment Indices (TEAIs). Twenty-one items about the physical environment (such as measured distances of facilities from home) and eight items descriptive of the suprapersonal E—environment (taken from census data describing characteristics of the residents of city blocks) produced nine TEAI dimensions.

TEAI 1 describes, at one extreme, a local milieu of mostly single-family, owner-occupied dwellings, in uncrowded sections of the city, which are not close to freeways, arterials, railroads, or fixed-rail public transit. Dwelling-unit values tend to be high, there is no overcrowding in terms of ratio of people to units or within units, and there are few single-person households. Figure 13-1 suggests

in pictorial form the opposite ends of components of TEAI 1, which might be labeled a suburban/inner-city dimension. TEAI 2 describes an area in which household heads tend to be women or black, much of the population is under age eighteen, and there is crowding within households. TEAI 3 represents a situation in hilly areas, far from both railroads and a fixed-rail transit line or station. TEAI 4 describes the distance from home to a fixed-rail transit system and one or more of its stations. TEAI 5 indicates that there is or is not a land barrier between home and the fixed-rail system. TEAI 6 includes the distance to arterials and amount of vacant land use within a quarter mile of home. TEAI 7 comprises the number of different land uses; and the presence/absence of open vegetation or water, and of industrial land-use within a quarter mile. TEAI 8 consists primarily of the distance from home to the nearest freeway. TEAI 9 includes home construction type and the percentage of units in the census block area lacking some or all plumbing.

To complete the attempt to learn more about the interrelationships between the PEQIs and TEAIs, dimensions pertaining to the people who made the PEQI judgments were sought. Twenty-six items of information about the respondents sorted themselves into nine dimensions, and age and gender were added to these dimensions as representatives of P. Both the nine TEAIs and the eleven personal characteristics contributed significantly and meaningfully to understanding perceptions of neighborhood quality. These results suggest that P—personal traits—and E—environmental—characteristics are not redundant but can be used together to understand what leads people to evaluate their neighborhood environments as they do (Carp and Carp, 1982b). This is a useful finding as observer judgments have been criticized for lack of specificity in suggesting environmental changes. The TEAIs may be applied more directly to city planning, and they gain meaning by virtue of their demonstrated relationships with people's judgments.

For example, the relationships of population to housing units, and of the percentage of units with more than one person per room to the PEQIs document the negative effects of crowding on subjective environmental responses with geographic areas and within living units. Economic factors can of course influence perceptions, however, in this study income was one of the P descriptors; therefore, the analysis with P dimensions partialed out suggests that, above and beyond the effects of income level, the environmental characteristics of single-family versus multiunit residence, of density of dwelling units in a given space, and of crowding within living units influence perceptions of environmental quality. Land barriers between home and the rapid-transit system (TEAI 5) provide an example favorably affecting PEQIs. Land contours are the best but not the only effective barriers against visual and auditory intrusions. Walls or dense plantings might ameliorate negative impacts of rapid-transit systems and other E intruders. The negative effects of several items (number of different transportation elements nearby; and distance to nearest railroad, rapid-transit, arterial, and freeway) on PEQIs suggest that the location of existing and projected transportation systems should be considered in zoning residential areas. The adverse effects on PEQIs of the number of different land uses and the presence of industrial land-use are similarly relevant to residential zoning. Residents of buildings constructed of wood were generally more negative in their perceptions of the quality of the neighborhood, which suggests that other construction types offer more effective buffering from such negative environmental impacts as noise and privacy invasion. This might have implications for design and construction decisions.

The Ideal Neighborhood

So far, the chapter has been concerned with attempts to define the parameters of neighborhood quality by comparing objective information and personal characteristics with individuals' responses regarding the neighborhoods in which they live. Another approach is to find out what people consider desirable. Such an approach may avoid some of the rationalization and the ostrich-like responses of those "trapped" in bad situations that influence responses about one's own situation. Carp and Carp (1982c) asked adults aged twenty-five to ninety-eight years about considerations they would deem important if they were to look for another neighborhood in which to live, and through the fifteen items, formulated three dimensions that might be labeled access to services and facilities, relationships with other people, and aesthetics. In regard to items relating to access, not surprisingly, school and work were more important to the young. Proximity to food stores was consistently "very important" for all age groups. There is some ambiguity about a tendency for the young to attach more importance to the proximity of restaurants and theaters since it was statistically significant for only one of the two subsamples used. As age increased, the importance of proximity to a freeway declined and the importance of nearness to a bus stop rose. There were no age differences regarding the importance of nearness to a rapid-transit station or having good walking conditions. The former was "not at all important" to nearly half the people, while the latter seemed "very important" to the majority, regardless of age (see fig. 13-2).

Regarding personal relationship items, age had no effect on the importance of having friends and relatives in the neighborhood. This attribute was "not at all important" to over a third, regardless of age. Neither was there an age difference in regard to the importance of having friendly people in the neighborhood. Nearly two-thirds of all ages considered this "very important" (see fig. 13-3).

There was no age trend regarding the importance of any of the aesthetic items: generally attractive, clean and unlittered, minimal air pollution, quiet, and nicely landscaped (see fig. 13-4). All five were "very important" to most respondents and had high importance ratings for all ages relative to other items.

For the majority of characteristics considered important in viewing a potential new neighborhood, results suggest that older people have the same concept of desirable neighborhood charac-

Suburban Pole

a. single-family dwellings

b. uncrowded

c. far from transportation

Inner-city Pole

f. multifamily dwellings

g. crowded

h. close to transportation

Suburban Pole

d. high property values

Inner-city Pole

i. low property values

e. family oriented

j. single-person households

13-1. Suburban and inner-city environmental dimensions.

teristics as younger adults do. The four clear age trends are consistent with life-stage phases: older people are less concerned with access to freeways and more concerned with access to bus stops, and they attach less importance to having schools and jobs in the neighborhood.

Investigators tend to ask for ratings or rankings on the importance of environmental attributes. This highly structured approach may not allow adequate opportunity for people to express their opinions. In particular, it does not allow expression of a trade-off between positive and negative as-

pects. A trade-off function with regard to financial considerations is implicit in Regnier's (in press) study, which provided residents of housing for middle- and upper-income elderly with negative as well as positive response options regarding additional services. The "negative preferences" for some services were related to the increased cost. The real issue was not the desirability of the services but whether they were wanted in view of the additional fees that having them would require. A similar cost-benefit trade-off was observed by Smit and Joseph (1982), who used a game method to have people reallocate the funds available in their municipalities and counties, indi-

a. schools more important for young

c. food stores important for all

b. work more important for young

d. restaurants perhaps less important with age

13-2. *Access to services and facilities.*

cating their view of the optimal distribution of funds among services provided by those agencies.

Trade-offs may not be limited to services versus cost but may include balances between service or other resource provision and negative impacts on neighborhood quality. For example, having schools and jobs nearby are understandably less important to older people since these facilities no longer provide needed resources. However, it is equally possible that having places of work and schools close to home have negative connotations in terms of such considerations as safety, noise, air quality,

e. freeways less important with age

f. bus stops more important with age

13-3. *Friendly people in the neighborhood are "very important" for most.*

g. rapid transit important for few

i. good walking conditions important for all

and traffic. During early adult years, the positive effects because of need may outweigh the negative concomitants of proximate schools and work places. Conversely, when needs for work places and schools are gone, the negative environmental quality considerations become dominant.

Carp and Carp (1982c) asked elderly women living alone for negative as well as positive responses regarding potential components of an ideal neighborhood. Because proximity is such a powerful influence on resource utilization and activity rate (Lawton, 1980), the women were asked separately about facilities "within easy walking distance" and "within a block of your home." To further clarify the meaning of their answers, they were given two additional response options: "it wouldn't matter one way or the other" and "I have no opinion or don't know."

Within easy walking distance in an ideal situation, the majority would include the stop for the bus that takes you where you need to go (91 percent), favorite grocery store (79 percent), own bank (68 percent), favorite library (67 percent), own place of worship (65 percent), senior center (65 percent), favorite drug store (62 percent), favorite restaurant (56 percent), nutrition site for seniors (55 percent), another drug store (55 percent), own doctor (53 percent), another bus stop (51 percent),

a. general attractiveness

c. minimal air pollution

b. clean and unlittered

d. quiet area

13-4. Some "very important" aesthetic elements.

favorite beauty shop (51 percent), and fire station (51 percent). The high level of "wouldn't matter one way or the other" was striking, while "don't know or have no opinion" was very infrequent. Practically everyone had an opinion in regard to every item, and for many that opinion was that it was irrelevant to the ideal situation. This was the majority response for a preschool (71 percent), lawyer other than own (68 percent), other beauty shop (67 percent), tax preparer's office (67 percent), movie other than favorite (63 percent), elementary school (62 percent), savings and loan other than favorite (60 percent), place of worship other than

e. nicely landscaped

own (60 percent), bar other than favorite (60 percent), library other than favorite (57 percent), other dentist (54 percent), favorite bar (55 percent), high school (54 percent), and own lawyer (52 percent).

With regard to the ideal block, responses were strikingly different. For only one item, the stop for the bus that takes you where you need to go, was the majority (72 percent) opinion that ideally it would be within a block of home. For no item was "it would not matter" the majority view. On the other hand, for many items the majority opinion was that ideally it would *not* be within a block of home. This was true for police station (73 percent), high school (65 percent), fire station (64 percent), other bank (63 percent), other drug store (61 percent), other doctor (58 percent), other dentist (60 percent), college (60 percent), elementary school (59 percent), own doctor (58 percent), own bank (58 percent), own savings and loan (58 percent), other savings and loan (58 percent), other-than-favorite library (58 percent), other restaurant (58 percent), other grocery store (55 percent), tax preparer's office (55 percent), other movie (55 percent), other lawyer (54 percent), senior center (54 percent), preschool (53 percent), favorite library (52 percent), other bar (52 percent), and other beauty shop (52 percent).

The trade-off process that determined the answers was clear. The positive resource aspects of a facility were weighed against the negative environmental-quality implications, and the balance was influenced by distance from home. Within walking distance, the resource aspects can be used as desired, and the negative impacts on the quality of the residential environment are less immediate. Within one's own block, the negative connotations become overriding. It may seem surprising, in view of the fear of crime among the elderly (Goldsmith and Goldsmith, 1976), that nearly three-quarters of these elderly women, living alone, would not, in the ideal situation, locate a police station within a block of their homes, while only 10 percent would. Nearly half (48 percent) would put one within walking distance, because they would feel safer if police were that close. However, for all but a few, the noxious effects of noise, traffic, "dan-

gerous people," and "unresidential appearance" would make one's presence far from the ideal within one's own block.

Up to the college level of education, people seemed to be negative rather than positive about having schools even within walking distance and, the older the school population, the greater the negativity. Junior high and high school students are perceived as noise-makers, litterers, graffiti-producers, purse-snatchers, general nuisances, or worse. The older the students, the greater their freedom to move into the older woman's territory of sidewalks and shops. The only resource value of schools was for a few women who would like the opportunity to watch young children play— but not within a block of home.

Responses were favorable toward the resources in programs for the elderly, but the women perceived negative impacts on the residential quality of a neighborhood. Inclusion of meal sites and senior centers has a strong positive valence in provision of needed services and desired activities and sociability. However, there are negative valences with regard to the "nonresidential appearance" and the attraction of strangers, including "a lot of [poor] old people" into the neighborhood. If the meal site or senior center was housed within an apartment house, that would take care of the "appearance" problem. However, it would not solve the negative impact of the influx of outsiders and, if the facility was in their own building, would accentuate it. Services for seniors should be within easy walking distance but not on one's block.

In brief, the majority view is that one's own block should include only other residential buildings and a stop for the bus that goes where you need to go, while the area beyond a block but within easy walking distance should be rich in facilities and services.

Conclusion

There has long been a cry for development of indicators of perceived environmental quality to provide guidelines for development of objective environmental measures. Neighborhood PEQIs have been developed, and their utility in helping create measures of objective environmental quality at the technical assessment level has been demonstrated. The PEQIs have potential utility to planners, in that they display aspects of neighborhood quality relevant to residents. The person-in-the-neighborhood may be more sophisticated in environmental perceptions than is ordinarily thought. For example, "noise" turns out not to be a simple matter; rather, ordinary people distinguish four dimensions of noise. Two relate to its interference with activities—inside the home and outdoors. The other two distinguish noise sources: equipment and appliances in one's own home and sounds from neighbor's homes; and noises from traffic, industry, and construction. The separation of "noise considerations" can alert the planner to the sensitivities of residents; it can also specify the steps that need to be taken in particular neighborhoods to improve conditions.

Scales were developed to measure qualities of the neighborhood based on objective technical assessment data, which can be useful in suggesting specific ways to improve neighborhoods. Despite the forces that link neighborhood quality to residents' characteristics and the influence of personal characteristics on such ratings as the PEQIs, the TEAI scores explained PEQI scores as well as resident characteristics did, and the TEAI contribution was additional to, rather than redundant with, those of respondent traits.

Proximity is well documented as the most powerful positive influence on resource utilization. There is new evidence that it may also be a powerful negative influence with regard to environmental quality dimensions such as aesthetics, maintenance, and characteristics of people in the neighborhood. There is need to investigate further the trade-off function between resource utilization and environmental quality in the context of proximity to home.

During the past decade, neighborhood improvement efforts have been undertaken across the country. Unfortunately, "neighborhood improvement" may set in motion forces that negatively affect older residents. However, many institutions "are responding imaginatively and energetically to the dual needs of improving city neighborhoods and responding to the special housing needs of older people" (Myers, 1982, p. ix). These programs should be evaluated in terms of their effects on older people. The neighborhood PEQIs and TEAIs and improved versions of them should be useful in studies to provide solid, objective, practical bases to assist designers, planners, and practitioners to improve the quality of life for older people by improving that of their neighborhoods.

References

Andrews, F. M., and S. B. Withey. 1976. *Social Indicators of Well-Being: Americans' Perceptions of Life Quality.* New York: Plenum.

Antunes, G. E., T. D. Cook, and W. G. Skogan. 1977. "Patterns of Personal Crime Against the Elderly." *Gerontologist* 17:321–27.

Barker, M. L. 1976. "Planning for Environmental Indices: Observer Appraisals of Air Quality." In *Perceiving Environmental Quality.* Ed. K. H. Craik and E. H. Zube. New York: Plenum.

Berglund, B. 1977. "Quantitative Approaches in Environmental Studies." *International Journal of Sociology* 12:111–23.

Burton, I., R. W. Kates, and G. F. White. 1978. *The Environment of Habit.* New York: Oxford.

Campbell, A., P. E. Converse, and W. L. Rogers. 1976. *The Quality of American Life: Perceptions, Evaluations, and Satisfactions.* New York: Russell Sage.

Carp, F. M. 1966. *A Future for the Aged.* Austin, TX: Univ. of Texas.

———. 1976. "User Evaluation of Housing for the Elderly." *Gerontologist* 16, No. 2:102–11.

———. In press. "The Effect of Planned Housing on Life Satisfaction and Mortality of Residents." In *Housing for the Elderly: Satisfactions and Preferences.* Ed. V. Regnier and J. Pynoos. New York: Garland.

Carp, F. M., and D. Appleyard, 1972. "Pre-BART Interview Method and Data." Interim Report No. 2. Berkeley, CA: Institute of Urban and Regional Development, Univ. of California.

Carp, F. M., and A. Carp. 1982a. "Perceived Environmental Quality of Neighborhoods: Development of Assessment Scales and Their Relation to Age and Gender." *Journal of Environmental Psychology* 2, No. 4:295–312.

———. 1982b. "A Role for Technical Assessment in Perceptions of Environmental Quality and Well-Being. *Journal of Environmental Psychology* 2:171–91.

———. 1982c. "The Ideal Residential Area." *Research on Aging* 4, No. 4:411–39.

———. 1983. Structural Stability of Well-Being Factors Across Age and Gender, and Development of Scales of Well-Being Unbiases for Age and Gender. *Journal of Gerontology*, 30, No. 5: 572–81.

Coughlin, R. E. 1976. "The Perfection and Valuation of Water Quality." In *Perceiving Environmental Quality*. Ed. K. H. Craik and E. H. Zube. New York: Plenum.

Craik, K. H. 1981. "Environmental Assessment and Situational Analysis." In *Toward a Psychology of Situations*. Ed. D. Magnussen. Hillsdale, NJ: Erlbaum.

Craik, K. H., and E. H. Zube. 1976 "The Development of Perceived Environmental Quality Indices." In *Perceiving Environmental Quality*. Ed. K. H. Craik and E. H. Zube. New York: Plenum.

Fried, M., and P. Gleicher. 1961. "Some Sources of Residential Satisfaction in an Urban Slum." *Journal of the American Institute of Planners*, 27:305–15.

Galster, G. C., and G. W. Hesser. 1981. "Residential Satisfaction." *Environment and Behavior*, 13:735–58.

Gans, H. J. 1962. *Urban Villagers*. Glencoe, IL: Free.

———. 1967. "Planning—and City Planning—for Mental Health." In *Taming Megalopolisic*. Vol. 2 Ed. W. Eldridge. Garden City, NY: Doubleday.

Goldsmith, J., and S. S. Goldsmith. 1976. *Crime and the Elderly*. Lexington, MA: Lexington.

Kaiser, E., et al. 1970. *Neighborhood Evaluations and Residential Satisfaction*. Durham, NC: Center for Urban and Regional Studies, Univ. of North Carolina.

Kuller, R. 1971. "The Perception of an Interior as a Function of Its Color." In *Architectural Sociology*. Ed. B. Honikman. London: Riba.

Lansing, J. B., and R. W. Marans. 1969. "Evaluations of Neighborhood Quality." *Journal of the American Institute of Planners* 35:195–99.

Lansing, J. B., R. W. Marans, R. B. Zehner. 1970. *Planned Residential Environments*. Ann Arbor: Institute for Social Research, Univ. of Michigan.

Lawton, M. P. 1975. *Planning and Managing Housing for the Elderly*. New York: Wiley.

———. 1980. Residential Quality and Residential Satisfaction Among the Elderly. *Research on Aging* 2:309–28.

Lee, T. 1970. "Urban Neighborhood as a Socio-Spatial Scheme." In *Environmental Psychology: Man and His Physical Setting*. Ed. H. M. Proshansky, W. H. Ittelson, and L. G. Riulin. New York: Holt, Rinehart and Winston.

Mandell, L., and R. W. Marans. 1972. *Participation in Outdoor Recreation: A National Perspective*. Ann Arbor: Institute for Social Research, Univ. of Michigan.

Marans, R. W. 1976. "Perceived Quality of Residential Environments." In *Perceiving Environment Quality*. Ed. K. H. Craik and E. H. Zube. New York: Plenum.

Michelson, W. 1966. "An Empirical Analysis of Urban Environmental Preferences." *Journal of the American Institute of Planners* 32, No. 2:355–60.

———. 1971. "Some Like it Hot: Social Participation and Environmental Use as Functions of the Season." *American Journal of Sociology* 76:1072–83.

Moos, R. H., and S. Lemke. 1980. "The Multiphasic Environmental Assessment Procedure." In *Community Mental Health: A Behavioral Ecological Perspective*. Ed. A. Jegar and B. Slotnick. New York: Plenum.

Myers, P. 1982. *Aging in Place: Strategies to Help the Elderly Stay in Revitalized Neighborhoods*. Washington, DC: The Conservative Foundation.

Newman, O. 1972. *Defensible Space*. New York: Macmillan.

Regnier, V. In press. "Preferred Services, Amenities, and Design Features in Housing for the Middle to Higher Income Elderly." In *Housing for the Elderly: Preferences and Satisfactions*. V. Regnier and J. Pynoos. New York: Garland.

Regnier, V., E. Murakami, and S. Gordon. 1979. "The Relationship of Goods and Services Retrieval Patterns to the Perceived Neighborhood Context of Four Los Angeles Communities." Paper presented at the 7th National Conference on Elderly and Handicapped, Orlando, FL.

Sivik, L. 1974. "Colour Meaning and Perceptual Colour Dimensions." *Göteborg Psychological Reports*, 4, No. 11.

Smit, B., and A. Joseph. 1982. "Trade-off Analysis of Preferences for Public Services." *Environment and Behavior* 14:238–58.

Troy, P. 1971. *Environmental Quality in Four Suburban Areas*. Canberra: Urban Research Unit, Australian National Univ.

U.S. Department of Housing and Urban Development (DHUD). 1978. *The 1978 HUD Survey on the Quality of Community Life.* Washington, DC: Office of Policy Development and Research, U.S. DHUD.

Weinstein, M. D. 1976. "Human Evaluations of Environmental Noise." In *Perceiving Environmental Quality.* Ed. K. H. Craik and E. H. Zube. New York: Plenum.

Whitfield, T. W. A., and P. E. Slatter. 1976. "The Effects of Categorization and Prototypicality: An Esthetic Choice in a Furniture Selection Task." *British Journal of Psychology* 70:65–76.

Zehner, R. B., and F. S. Chapin. 1974. *Across the City Line.* Lexington, MA: Lexington.

Zube, E. H., D. G. Pitt, and T. W. Anderson. 1975. "Perception and Prediction of Scientific Resource Values of the Northeast." In *Landscape Assessment: Values, Perception and Resources.* Ed. E. H. Zube, R. O. Brush, and J. Fabos. Stroudsburg, PA: Dowden, Hutchinson and Ross.

CHAPTER 14 Environment and Criminal Victimization of the Aged

Jersey Liang · Mary C. Sengstock · Melanie A. Hwalek

Crime against the elderly is a national problem of great concern. As early as 1971, the White House Conference on Aging deemed that protection of the elderly should be a top priority and that physical and environmental security standards must be developed as basic elements of all housing projects serving the aged. As one form of social intervention, housing programs not only provide physical shelters but also aim to improve the quality of life (Carp, 1976). Given that safety or freedom from criminal victimization represents an important aspect of the quality of life, it is important for housing or environment planners to learn the relationships between criminal victimization and characteristics of the environment. This chapter presents a brief review of the research concerning criminal victimization in relation to environmental characteristics. In addition, policy implications of current research will be discussed.

The lifestyle or routine activity perspective (Hindelang, Gottfredson, and Garofalo, 1978) perhaps provides the best theoretical rationale for examining the relationships between environmental characteristics and the risk of criminal victimization. According to this perspective, the risk of criminal victimization is largely dependent on the lifestyle and routine activities of persons that bring them and/or their properties into contact with potential offenders in the absence of a guardian

(Hindelang, Gottfredson, and Garofalo, 1978; Cohen, Kluegel, and Land, 1981).

Briefly, the risk of criminal victimization is strongly related to five factors. The first factor is *exposure*, the physical visibility and accessibility of persons or objects to potential offenders. In general, an increase in exposure leads to an increase in victimization risk. The second factor is *proximity*, the physical distance between areas where potential targets of crime reside and areas where relatively large populations of potential offenders are found. All else being equal, the closer the residential proximity of potential targets to relatively large populations of motivated offenders, the greater the risk of criminal victimization. *Guardianship* is the third factor which refers to the effectiveness of persons (such as housewives, neighbors, pedestrians, private security guards, law enforcement officers) or objects (such as burglar alarms, locks, barred windows) in preventing violations from occurring, either by their presence alone or by some sort of direct or indirect action. It is assumed that offenders prefer targets that are less well guarded to those that are more well guarded. Therefore, the greater the guardianship, the less the risk of criminal victimization. The fourth factor involves the *attractiveness of the target*. It is the material or symbolic desirability of persons or property targets to potential of-

This chapter was written on the basis of research supported by the AARP Andrus Foundation and the National Institute on Aging (Grant No. AG 03483). The assistance provided by Becky Warfel, Sara Barrett, and Jorge Tapia is gratefully acknowledged.

fenders. If crimes are motivated by instrumental ends such as property crimes, the greater the target of attractiveness, the greater the risk of victimization. The effects of the above four factors may differ depending on the fifth factor, the *properties of crime*. In particular, the effects of exposure, guardianship, and proximity on the risk of victimization are stronger in crimes motivated by instrumental means (such as burglary and personal larceny).

Given this perspective, environmental characteristics are important in determining the risk of victimization in that they are closely related to exposure, proximity, and guardianship. In fact, many environmental as well as personal characteristics have been employed by researchers as measures of these factors. For example, community size, inner-city location, marital status, labor force status, and activity level have been used as indicators of exposure while household composition, social integration, and isolation have served as measures of guardianship. In addition, proximity has been indexed by median income, demographic mix, and population density (Cohen, Kluegel, and Land, 1981; Hindelang, 1976; Lawton and Yaffe, 1980).

On the other hand, the link between environment and victimization is also consistent with the utilitarian model of criminal behavior (Becker, 1968). Based on this model, criminals are viewed as if they are responding rationally to incentives and deterrents within their environment. Characteristics of the environment conceivably would influence the potential cost and return associated with the commission of a crime and, thus, the probability of victimization.

In this chapter, criminal victimization includes: (a) personal victimization, (b) property victimization, and (c) fear of crime. Personal victimization refers to those crimes in which there is a direct contact between the offender and the victim. These include rape, assault, robbery and larceny with contact (purse snatching, pocket picking). Property victimization includes household larceny and burglary, those crimes without direct contact

between the victim and the offender. Victims of property crimes are neither physically attacked nor injured; financial loss and property damage are usually the only consequences. Furthermore, the victim is the whole household rather than the individual. Fear of crime, the third form of victimization, need not necessarily be a consequence of personal and/or property victimization. Due to their heightened vulnerability and potentially serious consequences of crime, the elderly are more fearful of crime than young persons (Clemente and Kleinman, 1976). This fear often leads to withdrawal from the community and a reduction in social activity (Midwest Research Institute, 1977), thus, adversely affecting the quality of life of the elderly. In a recent study, Lawton and Yaffe (1980) identified fear of crime as a central factor in affecting well-being which includes social space, satisfaction with housing and neighborhood, and morale.

The environment is viewed in terms of three dimensions. The first dimension is the type of community or the location of the residence. A community can be described as urban or rural on the basis of its total population. The second dimension entails the physical, demographic, and socioeconomic characteristics of the neighborhood. The third dimension includes housing characteristics which encompass structural features, the overall defensibility of the housing unit, and the community context in which they exist.

Criminal Victimization and the Community

In general, criminal victimization increases with the degree of urbanization or the size of the community. This is true for personal crimes, property crimes, and fear of crime. According to Liang and Sengstock (1981), with various social demographic characteristics controlled, urban aged are up to five times as likely to be victims of personal crimes as are rural aged. This is further supported by other studies of criminal victimization of the general population and the elderly. Adjusting for income, age, race, and lifestyle, Cohen, Kluegel, and Land (1981) reported that persons living in rural areas have a lower risk of suffering from crimes such as assault and personal larceny. Lawton (1980) also noted that the elderly in large cities including Boston, San Francisco, Washington, D.C., and New Orleans, suffered quite high rates of personal victimization, such as robbery and personal larceny.

The link between the risk of victimization and location of residence can be easily explained by the routine activity perspective. Specifically, the aged residing in urban areas are more likely than their rural counterparts to expose themselves to risky situations. They are also close to a large number of potential offenders; this is especially true for those who live in the inner city in high crime neighborhoods.

Fear of crime also increases as city size increases (Boggs, 1971; Brown, 1975; Lebowitz, 1975; Lawton and Yaffe, 1980). An illustration of this comes from a study recently conducted by Clemente and Kleinman (1976). According to their analysis of two nationwide surveys, 76 percent of the elderly residing in large cities were fearful of victimization compared with 68 percent of the aged in medium-sized cities, 48 percent in the suburbs, 43 percent in small towns, and only 24 percent reporting fear of victimization in rural areas. The percentage of elderly fearful of crime in each city size were consistently higher than their younger counterparts. Cook and associates (in press) reported that 75 percent of the urban elderly are afraid to walk the streets at night. Fear levels of the rural elderly, however, were extremely low.

On the other hand, Janson and Ryder (1983), in an analysis of fear of crime among the aged in Los Angeles, found that the observed greater fearfulness of the aged is actually a result of their income and residential pattern, since a large portion of the aged are poor and live alone in urban areas where the risk of victimization and concern for crime are very high among persons of *all* ages. In this study, age was not a significant factor in predicting fear of crime.

Criminal Victimization and the Neighborhoods

A number of neighborhood characteristics have been identified as correlates of crime rate or victimization risk. These include: (a) inner-city location, (b) socioeconomic status, (c) population density, and (d) the demographic mix of the population (Midwest Research Institute, 1977).

Some specific characteristics of the neighborhood were noted to be particularly dangerous in terms of promoting crime. Repetto (1974) noted that crimes were highest in areas with mixed land use and a high number of transients. Crime has also been found to be high near major thoroughfares (Feeney and Weir, 1974; Wilcox, 1973; Regnier and Hamburger, 1978). This is particularly serious in view of the fact that aged persons often reside in these high crime areas (Lawton et al., 1976). Cunningham (1976) notes that the aged tend to be concentrated in areas populated by large numbers of unemployed young men who have dropped out of school and who are known to commit most of the crime. He further declared that crime has assumed crisis proportions for the aged in these areas.

Fear of crime is also related to inner-city location. As Clemente and Kleinman's study (1976) points out, the aged living inside the city limits were more fearful of victimization than those living in the suburbs. This relationship was upheld even when the socioeconomic status of the neighborhood was controlled.

Lewis and Maxfield (1980) investigated "incivility" of the neighborhood in relation to fear of crime. Incivility of the neighborhood was defined as "people's perceptions of the problems of abandoned buildings, vandalism, kids hanging around on street corners, and illegal drugs in the neighborhoods" (Lewis and Maxfield, 1980, p. 162). In their study of four Chicago neighborhoods, these authors found a positive relationship between residents' perceptions of neighborhood incivility and their reports of fear of crime.

A principal correlate of crime rates is the socio-

14-1. *Abandoned and gutted buildings and vacant lots overgrown with weeds make a neighborhood difficult to secure.*

economic status of the neighborhood. While some researchers have reported that higher personal and property crime rates are associated with poor neighborhoods (Beasley and Antunes, 1974), generally it is believed that socioeconomic status has differential effects depending on the type of crime. In particular, street crimes which include assault and personal larceny occur disproportionately among low-income persons (Carrington, 1975; Wilson, 1975). On the other hand, socioeconomic status is parabolically related to the risk of household burglary (Cohen, Kluegel, and Land, 1981). That is, both low- and high-income households have a higher rate of burglary victimization than the middle-income households. As explained by Hindelang (1976), high-income urban residents make good burglary targets because their homes are perceived to contain valuable property. People with low family incomes are selected more often as targets for burglary because of proximity or greater accessibility.

The positive correlations between population density and crime rates have been reported by many ecological analyses of crime against the general population (Beasley and Antunes, 1974) as well as those against the aged (Midwest Research Institute, 1977). Such a link often has been interpreted as a result of crowding. In addition, population density is related to inner-city location and low socioeconomic status; therefore, it tends to increase one's exposure to potential offenders.

Another aspect of the neighborhood which affects the degree of safety of a housing project is the demographic mixture of the population. Victimization of the aged increases when the population includes residents of widely varying ages. Thus, age-segregated housing is associated with lessened crime against the elderly, since they are somewhat insulated from the juvenile and young adult population which commits most of the crime. Even a modest degree of age segregation (such as assigning the aged to a separate floor in an age-integrated building) decreases elderly victimization (Lawton and Yaffe, 1980; Van Buren, 1976).

The age composition of the housing structure and/or the neighborhood also has important consequences in terms of the fear of crime. Elderly who live in age-homogeneous housing reported less fear than those living in age-heterogeneous housing (Sherman, Newman, and Nelson, 1976;

14-2. *Age-heterogeneous social settings offer a greater threat to the elderly than age-homogeneous settings.*

Clarke and Lewis, 1982; Lawton and Yaffe, 1980). Neighborhoods can also be described according to age composition. Sundeen and Mathieu (1976a) found that the elderly in age-heterogeneous neighborhoods were more fearful than those living in age-homogeneous environments. This higher level of fear is certainly a reflection of the objective risk of victimization as mentioned before. It may also be due to the visibility of the elderly in age-heterogeneous environments. That is, an elderly individual is more likely to be picked out as an easy target when among people of all ages, while in an age-homogeneous environment each person has an equal chance of victimization.

Criminal Victimization and Housing Characteristics

While the relationship between the character of the dwelling unit and criminal victimization is by no means clear, it is also true that victimization which occurs at or near the home is especially threatening. The home is the last sanctuary for the aged person (Cunningham, 1976). Hence it is particularly important that aged persons be able to dwell in an apartment or home which has been made as free from the risk of victimization as possible.

Probably the most definitive work on the relationship between the character of the dwelling unit and criminal victimization has been written by Newman (1973a), who originated the term "defensible space" to refer to "an environment under the control of its residents." Newman points out that certain types of dwellings are highly unlikely to be defensible spaces. Chief among these are public housing projects, which tend to be in the innermost part of large cities, with their inordinately high crime rates. These buildings are often high-rise buildings with high population density, a characteristic which he also associates with high rates of criminal victimization. Further, Newman notes that high-rise public housing projects are often constructed to provide a number of places which are notably not open to surveillance by the residents and/or hired guards. These struc-

14-3. Tall apartment buildings with a great deal of public space are particularly difficult to secure against crime.

tural patterns which promote criminal activity include elevators, twisting passageways, fire escapes, banks of mailboxes, and blind stairways that allow a criminal to avoid detection. Consequently, he notes that there is a very low rate of arrest which occurs as a result of crime in such dwelling units. This pattern of high frequency of crime and a low detection rate in high-rise dwelling units has also been observed by Cunningham (1976).

Besides the elimination of the obvious structural patterns that make it difficult to prevent crime or apprehend criminals, Newman (1973b) suggests several patterns which would make for greater safety in public housing projects. These include the clear delineation between the space allotted to each individual or family, so that it would be easier to determine who is an intruder and the separation of vulnerable groups, such as the elderly, from other residents who are likely to commit crimes. He also cautions that residents should not rely upon guards for their safety, since this is both costly and ineffective.

It has also been found that the character of the dwelling unit has an effect upon the feeling of safety of the residents. Lawton and associates (1976) found that 94 percent of the aged in their study felt safe in their own apartments but the feeling of safety grew progressively less the farther one moved from the apartment itself. Thus only 70 percent of the respondents said they felt safe in the public portions of the buildings in which they lived; 41 percent felt safe in the outdoor parts of the property around the building, and 31 percent felt safe in the neighborhood which surrounded the building. We have indicated that Newman (1973a) recommends a clear demarcation of each resident's unit. Such "territorial marking" as the placement of nameplates or fences to delineate an individual's property also serve to decrease aged persons' fear of being victimized (Patterson, 1978).

One factor that must not be neglected in an analysis of the relationship between the housing characteristics and the crime rate is the social relationship or community that has been developed in a housing project or neighborhood. Certain types of physical structures may have quite different crime rates, depending upon the character of the people who live there and the relationships which they have developed with each other.

Gardiner (1976) states that control by the members of the community is necessary if crime is to be prevented in an area. They must establish clear boundaries and eliminate open, uncontrolled areas, such as vacant lots; and the members themselves must maintain surveillance over the area they call their own. Newman (1973a) has noted that one reason public housing projects are unsafe is that the residents feel little responsibility for any unit other than their own. The buildings and projects thus lack this vital sense of community control. Rosenthal (1974) has also stressed the importance of community control in crime

14-4. Public areas of buildings, such as elevators and common mailbox areas, offer a particular threat. Security guards alone are of limited value. They must be supported by an integrated social network.

14-5. The clear marking of property by such means as fences and nameplates makes it easier to limit the entry of strangers and, therefore, to control crime. Crime control is also facilitated by the existence of an integrated social network of neighbors who know each other, can recognize strangers, and will keep their own and their neighbors' activities and property under surveillance.

prevention in a process which he calls "turf reclamation." And Brill (1975) points out that controlled access to entranceways and hired guards are effective only if the community cooperates.

In a similar vein, fear of crime among the elderly has been associated with integration in the community. The elderly who are more integrated into the community tend to be less fearful of crime (Jaycox, 1978; Sundeen and Mathieu, 1976a). However, Hartnagel (1979) found no relationship between community integration and fear among the general population which he studied in Canada. He suggested that this lack of relationship was due to the general lack of integration present in American communities today. Skogan and Maxfield (1981) also found no significant relationship between community integration and levels of fear among the population they studied. As with the Hartnagel study, Skogan and Maxfield (1981) studied this relationship within the general population. Thus, the relationship between social integration and fear of crime may still hold for the older subgroups of the population.

Social isolation may be an important determinant of fear of crime among the elderly. Lebowitz (1975) found that the elderly living with at least one other person were less fearful than those living alone. This finding is important, given the fact that the elderly are more likely than any other age group to be living alone. Furthermore, this social isolation related not only to the fear of crime but also to the victimization itself. In a unique study of paroled offenders, the Midwest Research Institute (1977) determined that the characteristic which offenders looked for most in their victims was being alone. However, other researchers (Bishop and Klecka, 1978) did not find living alone to be an important determinant of fear of crime among the elderly living in New York City.

One's perception of neighborhood conditions may also be important in influencing the degree of fear of crime. Skogan and Maxfield (1981) surveyed 1,389 urban residents in three major U.S. cities where they found that the perception of the neighborhood as getting worse was significantly correlated with fear of walking in the neighborhood at night. Taub, Garthtaylor, and Dunham (1981) also found a relationship between perceptions of neighborhood deterioration and of safety in the neighborhood. Although these studies were not done separately for the aged, it is expected that the relationship between perceptions of neighborhood changes and fearfulness is true of the elderly also, given their greater fearfulness.

Another factor relating housing characteristics to fear of crime is the actual rate of crime present in the neighborhood. In Skogan and Maxfield's study (1981), the rate of crime in the neighborhood explained as much as 45 percent of the variability in fear of crime for the general population. Many other studies support this relationship (Furstenburg, 1971; Jaycox, 1978; McPherson, 1978; Lawton and Yaffe, 1980).

One may conclude, therefore, that alterations in the physical structure alone will not be sufficient to produce an environment which is safe from crime. The social setting must also be conducive to control of crime. This is produced primarily through the development of a strong sense of community, in which members of the community feel responsible for each other's welfare. They exhibit this concern by observing the activities which occur, reporting any suspicious behavior, making sure that doors are locked and entranceways are clear, and keeping children in control. It is also helpful if the most vulnerable members of the community, such as the aged, can be assigned a somewhat protected position. Studies have not only shown that crime tends to decrease in such settings but also that the aged are less fearful. Conversely, isolation tends to make them more fearful.

Conclusion

During the past decade, considerable effort has been devoted to the understanding of criminal victimization of the aged. Several findings have emerged as the result of such research. First, the elderly are the least likely age group to be victimized (Antunes et al., 1977; Cohen, Kluegel, and

Land, 1981). Second, elderly victims in general are no more likely to suffer more severe financial or physical hardships than younger victims (Cook et al., 1978). Third, the aged are most fearful of crimes despite their low probability of victimization (Garofalo, 1977). Fourth, there are wide variations in victimization rates among different subgroups of the elderly (Liang and Sengstock, 1981).

Two inferences can be drawn from these findings. First, criminal victimization is not an age-related problem but rather a situation-related problem (Cook et al., 1978). Since the aged have the lowest overall average victimization rate among all age groups, age should not be used as the sole indicator for vulnerability to criminal victimization. Furthermore, the risk of victimization may vary considerably among the aged depending on the characteristics of the individual and the environment. Consequently, crime prevention or control programs should be targeted for high risk subgroups of the elderly. Another implication of the research findings is that reducing the fear of crime among the aged should be a top priority. It should be noted that fear of crime would not be reduced significantly until the risk of victimization has decreased for those residing in high-crime areas.

Given these two factors, knowledge concerning the relationship between the environment and victimization is useful in helping policy-makers and service-providers design programs serving the aged. First, the various environmental features associated with high risk can be used to identify the individuals in need and subsequently to allocate resources and services. Second, the risk of victimization can be reduced by changing certain characteristics of the physical as well as the social environments. In particular, these include environmental design and various crime prevention programs which involve the elderly as participants.

Environmental design encompasses the design and modification of public buildings and individual dwellings to make them more crime proof. Changes as simple as removing high shrubbery and adding floodlights to the outside of a house can be shown to elderly people. Loans from the Department of Housing and Urban Development and the Farmers Home Administration are available for such undertakings. Thus, the elderly can be educated to make certain changes in their physical environments to reduce the risk of victimization.

Crime prevention programs have already been established in many cities and states. In these programs, citizens work with the criminal justice system to improve the saftey of their neighborhoods and communities. Examples of these programs include citizens' neighborhood watch groups and instructions on how to keep safe on the street, how to prevent residential crimes, and how to deal with the criminal justice system (Jaycox, Center, and Ansello, 1982).

One added value of the environmental design and the crime prevention programs is that once an old person is taught to avoid victimization personally the fear of crime diminishes, and frequently the individual is ready to take an active role in crime prevention in the community. Furthermore, it should be noted that a certain amount of fear is functional in the sense that it leads people to take reasonable precautions (Garofalo, 1981). However, findings concerning fear and its consequences are by no means conclusive. Using city-level data, Balkin (1979) suggested that the low rate of victimization for the aged may be a result of their fear which causes them to reduce their exposure to risky circumstances. However, this claim is not supported by other studies using individual-level data (Lawton and Yaffe, 1980; Garofalo, 1977). This discrepancy may be due to the different conceptualizations and measurement procedures of fear. Moreover, many of the actions insulating people from victimization are not primarily motivated by the fear of crime. A thorough discussion of these issues is contained in Garofalo (1981).

Finally, it is perhaps worth reiterating that environmental factors are not the only influences on the criminal victimization of the aged. Individual attributes, particularly one's lifestyle or routine activities, are also important. Consequently, environmental designs should be carried out in conjunction with crime prevention programs which capitalize on individual initiatives in reducing criminal victimization.

References

Antunes, G. E., et al. 1977. "Patterns of Personal Crime Against the Elderly." *Gerontologist* 17:321–27.

Balkin, S. 1979. "Victimization Rates, Safety and Fear of Crime." *Social Problems* 26:343–58.

Beasley, R. W., and G. Antunes. 1974. "The Etiology of Urban Crime: An Ecological Analysis." *Criminology* 11:439–59.

Becker, G. S. 1968. "Crime and Punishment: An Economic Approach." *Journal of Political Economy* 78:526–36.

Bishop, G. F., and W. R. Klecka. 1978. "Victimization and Fear of Crime Among the Elderly Living in High-Crime Urban Neighborhoods." Paper presented at the Annual Meeting of the Academy of Criminal Justice Studies, March 8–10.

Boggs, S. L. 1971. "Formal and Informal Crime Control: An Exploratory Study of Urban, Suburban, and Rural Orientations." *Sociological Quarterly* 12:1–9.

Brill, W. 1975. *HUD Technical Memorandum 1*. Washington, DC: U.S. Department of Housing and Urban Development.

Brown, E. 1975. "Fear of Assault Among the Elderly." Paper presented at the Annual Meeting of the Gerontological Society, Louisville, Kentucky, October.

Broderick, K. M., and Z. Harel. 1977. "Reducing Victimization and Fear of Crime." Paper presented at the Annual Meeting of the Gerontological Society, San Francisco, CA.

Carp, F. M. 1976. "Housing and Living Environments of Older People." In *Handbook of Aging and the Social Sciences*. Ed. R. H. Binstock and E. Shanas. New York: Van Nostrand Reinhold.

Carrington, F. G. 1975. *The Victims*. New York: Arlington.

Clarke, A. H., and M. J. Lewis. 1982. "Fear of Crime Among the Elderly: An Exploratory Study." *British Journal of Criminology* 22:49–62.

Clemente, F., and M. B. Kleinman. 1976. "Fear of Crime Among the Aged." *Gerontologist* 16:207–10.

Cohen, L. E., J. R. Kluegel, and K. C. Land. 1981. "Social Inequality and Predatory Criminal Victimization: An Exposition and Test of a Formal Theory." *American Sociological Review* 46:505–24.

Conklin, J. E. 1976. "Robbery, the Elderly and Fear." In *Crime and the Elderly*. J. Goldsmith and S. Goldsmith. Lexington, MA: Lexington.

Cook, F. L. 1976. "Criminal Victimization of the Elderly: A New National Problem?" In *Victims and Society*. Ed. E. C. Viane. Washington, DC: Visage.

Cook, F. L., W. G. Skogan, D. T. Cook, and G. E. Antunes. 1978. "Criminal Victimization of the Elderly: The Physical and Economic Consequences." *Gerontologist* 18:338–49.

———. In press. *Criminal Victimization of the Elderly*. New York: Oxford.

Cunningham, C. L. 1976. "Pattern and Effect of Crime Against the Aging: The Kansas City Study." In *Crime and the Elderly*. Ed. J. Goldsmith and S. Goldsmith Lexington, MA: Lexington.

Dowd, J. J., R. P. Sisson, and D. Kern. 1981. "Socialization To Violence Among the Aged." *Journal of Gerontology* 3:350–61.

Feeney, F., and A. Weir. 1974. *The Prevention and Control of Robbery*. Davis, CA: Univ. of California, Center on Administration of Justice.

Furstenberg, F. F. 1971. "Public Reaction to Crime in the Streets." *American Scholar* 40:601–10.

Gardiner, R. A. 1976. "Crime and the Neighborhood Environment." *Challenge* 7:9–13.

Garofalo, J. 1977. *Public Opinion about Crime: The Attitudes of Victims and Non-Victims in Selected Cities*. Washington, DC: U.S. Department of Justice.

———. 1981. "The Fear of Crime: Causes and Consequences." *Journal of Law and Criminology* 72:839–57.

Hartnagel, T. F. 1979. "The Perception and Fear of Crime: Implications for Neighborhood Cohesion, Social Activity, and Community Affect." *Social Forces* 58:176–93.

Hindelang, M. J. 1976. *Criminal Victimization in Eight American Cities: A Descriptive Analysis of Common Theft and Assault*. Cambridge, MA: Ballinger.

Hindelang, M. J.; M. R. Gottfredson; and J. Garofalo. 1978. *Victims of Personal Crime*. Cambridge, MA: Ballinger.

Hochstedler, E. 1977. *Personal Victimization of the Elderly in Twenty-Six Cities*. Washington, DC: U.S. Department of Justice.

Janson, P., and L. K. Ryder. 1983. "Crime and the Elderly: The Relationship Between Risk and Fear." *Gerontologist* 23:207–12.

Jaycox, V. H. 1978. "The Elderly's Fear of Crime: Rational or Irrational." *Victimology* 3:329–33.

Jaycox, V. H., L. J. Center, and E. F. Ansello. 1982. *Effective Responses to the Crime Problem of Older Americans: A Handbook*. Washington, DC: National Council of Senior Citizens.

Lawton, M. P. 1980. "Crime, Victimization, and the Fortitude of the Aged." *Aged Care and Services Review* 2:20–31.

Lawton, M. P., L. Nahemow, and J. Teaff. 1975. "Housing Characteristics and the Well-Being of Elderly Tenants in Federally Assisted Housing." *Journal of Gerontology* 30:601–7.

Lawton, M. P., et al. 1976. "Psychological Aspects of Crime and Fear of Crime." In *Crime and the Elderly*. Ed. J. Goldsmith and S. Goldsmith. Lexington, MA: Lexington.

Lawton, M. P., and S. Yaffe. 1980. "Victimization and Fear of Crime in Elderly Public Housing Tenants." *Journal of Gerontology* 35:768–79.

Lebowitz, B. D. 1975. "Age and Fearfulness: Personal and Situational Factors." *Journal of Gerontology* 30:696–700.

Lewis, D. A., and M. G. Maxfield. 1980. "Fear in the Neighborhoods: An Investigation of the Impact of Crime." *Journal of Research in Crime and Delinquency* 17:160–89.

Liang, J., and M. C. Sengstock. 1981. "The Risk of Victimization Among the Aged." *Journal of Gerontology* 36:463–71.

McPherson, M. 1978. "Realities and Perceptions of Crime at the Neighborhood Level." *Victimology* 3:319–28.

Midwest Research Institute. 1977. *Crimes Against the Aging: Patterns and Prevention*. Kansas City, MO.: Midwest Research Institute.

Newman, O. 1973a. *Defensible Space*. New York: Macmillan.

———. 1973b. *Design Guidelines for Creating Defensible Space*. Washington, D.C.: U.S. Government Printing Office.

Patterson, A. H. 1978. "Territorial Behavior and Fear of Crime in the Elderly." *Environmental Psychology and Nonverbal Behavior* 2:131–44.

Pollock, L. M., and A. H. Patterson. 1980. "Territoriality and Fear of Crime in Elderly and Nonelderly Homeowners." *Journal of Social Psychology* 111:119–29.

Regnier, V. A., and J. L. Hamburger. 1978. "Comparison of Perceived and Objective Crimes Against the Elderly in an Urban Neighborhood." Paper presented at the Annual Meeting of the Gerontological Society, Dallas, TX, November.

Repetto, T. 1974. *Residential Crime*. Cambridge, MA: Ballinger.

Rosenthal, E. J. 1974. "Turf Reclamation: An Approach to Neighborhood Security." *Challenge* 5:18–20.

Sherman, E. A., E. S. Newman, and A. D. Nelson. 1976. "Patterns of Age Integration in Public Housing and the Incidence and Fear of Crime Among Elderly Tenants." In *Crime and the Elderly*. Ed. J. Goldsmith and S. Goldsmith. Lexington, MA: Lexington.

Skogan, W. G., and M. G. Maxfield. 1981. *Coping with Crime: Individual and Neighborhood Reactions*. Beverly Hills, CA: Sage.

Sundeen, R. 1977. "The Fear of Crime and Urban Elderly." In *Justice and Older Americans*. Ed. M. A. Y. Rifai. Lexington, MA: Lexington.

Sundeen, R., and J. T. Mathieu. 1976a. "The Fear of Crime and Its Consequences Among Elderly in Three Urban Communities." *Gerontologist* 16:211–19.

———. 1976b. "The Urban Elderly: Environments of Fear." In *Crime and the Elderly*. Ed. J. Goldsmith and S. Goldsmith. Lexington, MA: Lexington.

Taub, R. P., D. Garthtaylor, and J. D. Dunham. 1981. "Neighborhoods and Safety." In *Reactions to Crime*. Ed. D. A. Lewis. Beverly Hills, CA: Sage.

U.S. Department of Justice. 1976. *Criminal Victimization in the U.S., 1974*. Washington, DC: U.S. Department of Justice.

Van Buren, D. P. 1976. "Public Housing Security and the Elderly: Practice Versus Theory." In *Crime and the Elderly*. Ed. J. Goldsmith and S. Goldsmith. Lexington, MA: Lexington.

Wilcox, S. 1973. *The Geography of Robbery*. Davis, CA: Univ. of California, Center of Administration of Criminal Justice.

Wilson, J. O. 1975. *Thinking about Crime*. New York: Basic.

Yin, P. P. 1980. "Fear of Crime Among the Elderly: Some Issues and Suggestions." *Social Problems* 27:492–504.

CHAPTER 15 Urban Displacement and Condominium Conversion

Michael A. Stegman

The elderly tend to be concentrated in old central cities and rural communities with populations of less than 2,500. This situation exists for a number of reasons: their long occupancy in older houses, the centrifugal growth pattern of cities, and the flight of young people from the countryside. In the cities, according to Struyk and Soldo (1980), these "gray ghettos" (Cowgill, 1978) typically exhibit high rates of building abandonment, inadequate housing, high unemployment, poverty, crime, poorly maintained streets and sidewalks, and limited municipal services. Most urban elderly who are dissatisfied with their area cite excessive street noise (39 percent), neighborhood crime (28 percent), industrial activities (27 percent) and airplane noise (24 percent) as reasons (Gutowski and Feild, 1979). Among suburban elderly, neighborhood crime (cited by 15 percent) is replaced by inadequate street lighting (19 percent) as one of the top four complaints. The *Annual Housing Survey* includes questions about the adequacy of six types of neighborhood services: transportation, schooling, shopping, police and fire protection, and medical care. According to Gutowski and Feild (1979, p. 79), suburban "households were far more likely to report inadequate services than central city households. . . . While neighborhood conditions may be better in the suburbs, neighborhood services appear to be better, or at least more widely available, in cities."

"By virtue of their location, housing units serve more than the simple need for shelter; . . . proximity to stores, recreational facilities, churches and neighbors is predicated on residential location" (Soldo, 1981, p. 15). Since the aged are estimated to spend between 80 and 90 percent of their time in the immediate home environment, access to a wide range of services may be even more important for them than for younger people (Soldo, 1981). Given the importance of location and convenience of the neighborhood in the elderly's quality of life, the displacement of the aged (their involuntary moves out of their homes and/ or neighborhoods) becomes another neighborhood concern. Because the elderly are attached to their familiar environments, the potential consequences of a forced move may damage their health and well-being more than those of the nonelderly. The aged face special problems when they are forced out of their homes and/or neighborhoods. Senator Dennis DeConcini, chairman of the Senate Special Committee on Aging, took note of these problems in a 1978 hearing on Older Americans in the Nation's Neighborhoods. Referring to the displaced aged as leading the ranks of the "new urban nomads," the Senator said that

older persons—so many of whom live on low, fixed incomes, have physical limitations and develop strong psychological needs for secure and

The author wishes to acknowledge the research assistance of Jean Crews and the editorial assistance of Anne Hafrey in the preparation of this chapter.

familiar environments—require the good housing; the ease of access to shopping, health care, and social services; and the informal support and assistance that can be summed up in the word *neighborliness* (U.S. Senate, 1978, p. 94).

Henig (1981, p. 68) cites the physiological evidence on which Senator DeConcini bases his concern for the displaced elderly. Because of such physiological changes associated with aging as diminished sight, hearing, and balance, and slowed response times, all of which may make "adjustments to environmental change more difficult," the elderly "have a more pronounced dependence on stable and predictable environments than other groups."

This essay provides an overview of the displacement issue with special emphasis on its effects on the elderly. The first section presents a glossary of terms used to define and describe the phenomenon of displacement and the processes that bring it about. Definitions can naturally depend on the context in which they are used and vary with the purpose for which they are used in discussion. This is very much the case with displacement. The second part of the paper addresses the question of how great the displacement problem is and summarizes various empirical estimates and anecdotal findings. There should be no doubt that many older people have been displaced through accelerated housing market activities in reviving neighborhoods throughout the country and that, "if the elderly are forced to compete head to head with others for continued occupancy in good neighborhoods, they will surely be forced out from the communities they have helped create" (U.S. Senate, 1978, p. 94). It must also be said, however, that we still lack reliable data on the size and extent of the problem nationwide.

The third section of the chapter focuses on the conversion of rental buildings into condominiums or cooperatives, and section four on the displacement caused by the demolition or redevelopment into luxury housing of old apartment hotels in which large numbers of elderly live. The conclu-

sion summarizes some important issues concerning the displacement of older people.

Defining the Problem

There are many definitions of displacement, with some being more operational than others. At one extreme is that of Hartman (1979), who defines the problem in terms of the political economy of urban communities and competing political interests. Displacement, in his view, is

> a political process at heart having to do with operant values and power in the society. Forced displacement results when one group of potential users of a piece of property has the motivation and power to force others out of the property (Hartman, 1979, p. 22).

The National Urban Coalition (1981) has defined displacement in somewhat less passionate terms, although it too thinks that the problem involves a competition for location in which the economically weaker are destined to lose. The coalition report states that the term *displacement* is often used to describe "the situation in reinvested urban neighborhoods in which low- and moderate-income residents are forced, for want of economic resources or the knowledge of alternatives, to leave their homes" (National Urban Coalition, 1981, p. 4).

The coalition writers define neighborhoods undergoing reinvestment as those "in which dwellings are purchased and/or rehabilitated . . . for middle- and upper-income occupants (p. 4). Clay (quoted in Henig, 1981, p. 67) speaks of gentrification and displacement as cause and effect, the former being "the gradual resettlement of some inner-city neighborhoods by a younger, wealthier, better educated elite," and the latter as "the forced movement by existing residents unable to compete in the accelerated housing market." Besser (1979) also attributes the problem to an increasing demand for housing by the new urban pioneers—young, affluent families who are "eager to experience the advantages of city living"—and to the real estate companies that "encourage and exploit home prices that soar at a dizzying pace" (Besser, 1979, p. 30). According to Besser, the displacement process is hierarchical:

> The first to go ... are the elderly, the countercultural, and the black and other minority poor who live in single-family houses converted to multiunit use.... Next, single-family houses renter-occupied homes and small apartment buildings are sucked into the current of exchange. Finally large apartment complexes and single-family owner-occupied houses are converted. Renters are forced out when new owners cease maintenance or evict them outright to begin renovation (Besser, 1979, p. 31).

One need look no further than to the U.S. Department of Housing and Urban Development (HUD) to illustrate the point that definitions vary with the purpose behind their use. For its report to the Congress on the magnitude and extent of the nation's displacement problem, HUD chose to emphasize that revitalization and reinvestment were just two among many causes of displacement, and that displacement "is a common and continual process in housing markets" (U.S. DHUD, 1979a, p. 5). To do this, HUD adopted a broad defintion of the phenomenon originally put forth in a study by Eunice and George Grier (cited in U.S. DHUD, 1979a). According to the Griers, displacement occurs when any household is forced to move from its residence by conditions that affect the dwelling or its immediate surroundings, and which (1) are beyond the household's reasonable ability to control or prevent; (2) occur despite the household's having met all previously proposed conditions of occupancy; and (3) make a continued occupancy by that household impossible, hazardous, or unaffordable.

This definition is broad enough to include displacement caused by reinvestment, disinvestment, abandonment, and the effects of government programs, and it suited HUD's purpose at that time. A more inclusive definition of the problem might reduce the likelihood that the Congress would restrict local community efforts to revitalize neighborhoods or that it would require cities to pay relocation benefits to families forced to move because of private market activities. In a later study on the impacts of condominium conversions delivered to the Congress, HUD chose to apply a particularly narrow definition to the phenomenon of displacement. Rather than including in its classification of displaced people all those who moved because their building was converted (perhaps including those who buy their unit because they are afraid of having to move), HUD classified as displaced only those moving to rental housing of similar or lower quality at higher cost, or lower quality at equivalent cost (U.S. DHUD, 1980, p. 5). This definition produces a far lower estimate of how many people are displaced by condominium conversions than would one of the broader definitions.

Magnitude of the Displacement Problem

There is no consensus on how much displacement is caused by neighborhood reinvestment, but there is a general recognition that the elderly probably make up a sizable number of those who are displaced. In its report, HUD sought to downplay the displacement caused by reinvestment by citing *Annual Housing Survey* data that less than 4 percent of all household moves made between 1974 and 1976 were forced ones, "which include moves due to evictions, closure of buildings by landlords for any reason, and mortgage defaults" (U.S. DHUD, 1979a, p. 17). An Urban Institute study (Gutowski and Feild, 1979) also based on the data from 1976, however, reported that 8 and 9 percent respectively, of all elderly central-city and suburban individuals who moved within the previous year had done so because they were displaced by private actions. Among nonelderly central-city households, only 4 percent cited private investment as the reason for their move. Younger suburbanites did not include displacement among their top eight reasons for moving. The high level of suburban displacement among old people is consistent with HUD's recent findings that elderly renters are disproportionately located in strong condominium conversion markets and that half of all conversions in the U.S. occurred in the suburbs (U.S. DHUD, 1980). Older people are more likely to move when their unit is converted than are younger ones (U.S. DHUD, 1981). Despite the displacement caused by conversions, HUD's official report on displacement concurs with the findings of several recent local studies that "housing abandonment and disinvestment account for a significantly greater proportion of displacement than . . . neighborhood reinvestment." Some analysts have placed this figure at "fewer than 100–200 families a year in declining neighborhoods in several major cities" (U.S. DHUD, 1979a, p. 4). In contrast, the Urban Coalition (1981) study of sixty-five neighborhoods in forty-four cities where reinvestment was occurring found evidence of more revitalization-induced displacement. In the view of the coalition such displacement is a national problem requiring national solutions:

> An extensive study in Seattle, for example, recently found that 25 percent of all renters, 27 percent of all low-income families, and 34 percent of all elderly people who moved during the study period did so because they were displaced (U.S. DHUD, 1979a, p. 3).

As in the case of the coalition's work, many existing displacement data are based on local estimates, case studies, and anecdotes, where methodological bases, definitions of terms, and/or quality of data are often lacking. Hartman (1979) cites one example, a study carried out by the District of Columbia Rental Accommodations Office, which concluded that "over the next four years 100,000 persons—one-seventh of the entire city's population—will be displaced by market forces" (Hartman, 1979, p. 24). Despite this extraordinarily high estimate, which is mainly due to the quickening pace of condominium conversions in Washington and other major cities in the late 1970s, HUD's national condominium conversion study produced very modest estimates of conversion-induced displacement. Using the restrictive HUD definition of the term, the report to the Congress found that just 18 percent of all households that moved from converted buildings had been displaced (U.S. DHUD 1980). Since 58 percent of all the original residents in converted buildings move out of them, around one in ten families living in converted buildings are, HUD believes, likely to be displaced (58 percent of 18 percent).

As implied above, much of the available information on displacement comes from municipal and private social service agencies that offer support and help displaced families, and from anecdotal and journalistic accounts. In a 1978 Senate hearing in California on the housing problems of the elderly (U.S. Senate, 1978, p. 105), the executive director of San Francisco's Commission on Aging testified that

> the Commission's information and referral service receives a monthly average of 300 telephone calls that are related to housing needs of the elderly. As property speculation continues unabated, the statistics of tragedy mount . . . 'Elderly tenants, some of whom have lived in the same apartment twenty or thirty years, are being forced to move because of rent increases as high as 100 percent . . .' Many landlords are enforcing these drastic rent increases with eviction proceedings. In the first five months of this year, landlords have gone to court 649 times; . . . over the last two years, evictions of senior citizens have risen 400 percent (U.S. Senate, 1978, p. 118).

The California Commissioner of the Department of Housing and Community Development spoke about his agency's recent hearings on housing problems of the elderly:

> We took testimony from an eighty-nine-year-old woman in Oakland a few months ago that she had been displaced three times. She was a retired teacher on $375 a month Social Security and a $300-a-month teaching pension. She had moved into apartment after apartment only to find that they were being converted into condominiums;

. . . She sat at the witness table and said, "I moved with two other teachers I retired with. We asked if they were going to convert to condominiums and they said no. They were ill and not as strong as I was." She said that in three successive moves her two friends had died. They simply couldn't cope with the trauma and tragedies of these moves and disruptions. She was alive and hanging on by a thread. (U.S. Senate, 1978, p. 105).

Despite the obvious technical limitations of some research studies and the lack of generalizable content to anecdotal case accounts, there is a growing consensus that the magnitude of rein-vestment-induced displacement is sufficiently great to warrant explicit policy concern and that the elderly are among the most vulnerable to displacement caused by increased housing market activity. Even HUD recognizes that "out-movers generally characterized as 'displaced' are repeatedly reported to be elderly households, minority households, and renters" (U.S. DHUD, 1979a, p. iii). While Henig's (1981) careful, systematic analysis of neighborhood moving patterns in 967 census tracts in nine cities does not support the Senate Special Committee on Aging view that "if we fail to understand what is happening in our cities . . . we face a future marked by stratification by age and income and wholesale displacement of the elderly" (U.S. Senate, 1978, p. 94), his research findings do

> provide some new support to the contentions that gentrification does exist, that gentrification-induced displacement is a threat to the elderly, that the elderly may be more at risk than other groups and that the threat may be increasing over time (Henig, 1981, pp. 67–68).

Although the debate on how many people are affected continues, there are signs that the discussion is beginning to shift to the issue of how one might systematically identify the conditions under which gentrification does occur and the conditions under which it does or does not have undesirable effects (Henig, 1980). There are three reasons why this important need is likely to be

met only by systematic local studies of neighborhood markets: neighborhood data are needed to identify various forms of reinvestment; controls for environmental changes during the study period must be included; and national studies of neighborhoods, which would permit reliable generalizations about causes and effects to be made, cost too much to be feasible.

Condominium Conversions

As previously noted, the recent rise in condominium conversions in the United States has probably caused a substantial number of families to make involuntary housing choices, such as undesired moves. Few conversions took place before 1970. Between 1970 and 1979, however, approximately 366,000 units were converted nationally, about 71 percent of them between 1977 and 1979 (U.S. DHUD, 1980). Conversions occur throughout the country, but nearly 75 percent of them have taken place in the thirty-seven biggest metropolitan areas, and 59 percent have been concentrated in twelve Standard Metropolitan Statistical Areas (SMSAs). The geographic unevenness of condominium conversions is frequently at the heart of policy conflicts over the appropriate public role in regulating them, with those living in areas with many conversions favoring a greater government role than those not threatened by conversion. According to HUD,

> by the end of 1979, 1.3 percent of the nation's occupied rental housing stock had been converted. However, there is considerable variation from one metropolitan area to another, as well as within each area. For example, in the New York City and Los Angeles areas, 1 percent of all rental units were converted during the 1970s, compared to 6 percent or more in Chicago, Denver, and Washington, D.C., areas. There are some atypical suburban communities and smaller cities where as much as 20 to 30 percent of the rental stock has been converted, and a few sections of cities where more than 30 percent of the rental stock has been converted (U.S. DHUD, 1980, p. ii).

With the onset of the economic recession and the resulting housing slump, conversions have declined sharply since 1980. The result is that HUD's trend-line estimates of future conversions, derived under the assumption that 1977–79 rates would continue over the next five years, no longer hold. Nevertheless, it is important to note the HUD estimate that, were past trends to continue through 1985, around 1.1 million additional rental units would be converted. This would mean that "five percent of all elderly renters in the nation . . . will face conversion at least once (U.S. DHUD, 1981, p. iii). The prolonged recession, high interest rates, and slowing of inflation may stretch out the projected five-year period for these conversions, but neither demographics nor the housing market give one any reason to believe that the numbers of expected conversions and displaced elderly might be wrong.

Nationally, around one-fifth of all households in buildings that are targeted for conversion are old, but not all of them are either poor or forced out of their homes. Nevertheless, HUD's restrictive definition of conversion-induced displacement probably greatly understates the number of elderly people harmed by conversion (U.S. DHUD, 1981). As of January 1, 1980, 23 percent of all aged households whose buildings were converted between 1977 and 1979 bought their unit, 29 percent continued to rent, and 49 percent moved. If 20 percent of the renters in buildings that were converted to condominiums were aged, and if the 49 percent who moved because of the conversion is applied to the total number of conversions for the decade (366,000), one finds that conversion induced 36,000 elderly to move between 1970 and 1979, and 26,000 of those moves probably occurred between 1977 and 1979. How can the official HUD report on reinvestment-related displacement all but ignore the problem of conversion when there were probably over 8,000 aged households forced to move in each of the last three years of the decade? There are two answers to that question. First, the report on displacement was completed sixteen months before the national study on condominium conversion, and there were neither reliable

national data on the number of conversions nor on the characteristics of the housing stock and its inhabitants before the latter study was done. Second, and more important, HUD found that conversions were occurring independent of other private reinvestment and most often outside of revitalizing neighborhoods (U.S. DHUD, 1980). Approximately 75 percent of all structures converted by 1980 were less than twenty years old; those in central cities were predominantly mid- to high-rise structures, and those in the suburbs were predominantly low-rise. Rents in these buildings exceeded the median for their respective markets. Consistent with this finding,

conversions are concentrated in nonrevitalizing neighborhoods characterized by above-average median incomes, rent levels, and housing values, and by rental vacancy rates equal to or below the city average. . . . Conversion has occurred in nonrevitalizing suburban locations in twenty-seven of the thirty-seven largest metropolitan areas; . . . these are nearly always close-in, economically stable suburbs, whose residents are typically middle- to upper-middle-income whites (U.S. DHUD, 1980, p. vii).

In short, it is important to keep in mind that HUD's official displacement analysis ignores the involuntary moves caused by condominium conversions and that these are more likely to take place in economically stronger neighborhoods and to involve higher-quality housing than other forms of reinvestment. The characteristics of the aged displaced by revitalization and conversion are likely to vary in important ways: for example, those affected by conversion are likely to have higher incomes and more assets than the other set.

One group of aged households that is obviously not classified as displaced is the 23 percent who purchase their converted apartments, and yet many of them must be considered "distressed buyers." Only one-fifth of older tenant-buyers reported buying their apartments for economic or financial reasons, in contrast to nearly half of all tenant-buyers (U.S. DHUD, 1981). Half of all elderly tenants who bought their converted apartments did so because of a reluctance to move. Seventy-five percent of old tenant-purchasers bought units that cost over two and a half times their incomes, compared to 56 percent of younger tenant-buyers. Housing costs generally increase less for the former group:

> The before-tax median percentage increase in shelter costs for elderly tenant-buyers is 11 percent, compared to 40 percent for all tenant-buyers. About one-third of all elderly tenant-buyers experience increases of over 25 percent. These increases occur despite the fact that approximately 20 percent of all elderly tenant-buyers pay more than 50 percent of total costs at their closing (U.S. DHUD, 1981, p. 16).

Many elderly households buy their converted apartments because they feel they have no other practical choice and use liquid savings to cover enough of a down payment to make the monthly mortgage costs affordable. As even the HUD report concludes, "the process of conversion increases manyfold the rate by which elderly renter households normally become homeowners. Only 6 percent of all elderly renters who move, in an average year, change tenure from renters to owners" (U.S. DHUD, 1981, p. 13).

For a short time, at least, the 29 percent of all elderly who rent in converted buildings will be less harmed by the conversion than other tenants. Many of them will benefit from various state and/or local tenant protection measures that give them security of tenure. In New York, the elderly are guaranteed lifetime tenure in their apartments. The combination of these measures in high-activity markets (such as New York, Washington, San Francisco, and Oakland) and rent regulation (in New York and Washington) are mainly responsible for the very low one percent increase in postconversion rents of elderly residents. Where there is no rent regulation, rents could increase substantially when current leases expire. Many old households that continue to rent occupy converted units that the converter will sell whenever market conditions allow. Finally, tenant protection measures benefit many older people who would

otherwise be victimized by conversion, but some people argue that these safeguards might backfire if owners of rental properties that could be converted refused to rent to aged householders because they would get security-of-tenure benefits upon conversion of the building (Dreier and Atlas, 1981).

In an average year less than 10 percent of all aged renters in high-conversion areas move compared to 50 percent of all old renters in converted buildings (U.S. DHUD, 1981). HUD reports that around 75 percent of all elderly and low-income former residents moved out of their neighborhoods after conversion. Despite the general belief that involuntary moves are traumatic and the fact that 70 percent of all older former residents of converted properties express anger at the conversion, HUD reports that 85 percent of movers find their new neighborhoods to be as good as, or better than, the old ones. HUD is therefore reluctant to define all conversion-induced moves as displacement.

If, however, we adopt HUD's narrow definition of displacement as a move to housing of similar or lower quality at higher cost or to housing of lower quality at equivalent cost, this produces a baseline displacement rate of 27 percent of all elderly movers (U.S. DHUD, 1981). Further adjustments to include all the old tenants who purchased their apartments because they did not want to move and all those who were forced to move to less desirable areas to find acceptable housing would further intensify this situation. It is fair to say that condominium conversions would adversely affect over one-quarter of all elderly households in buildings facing conversion.

The Demise of Housing

In one of its most socially disruptive forms, the revitalization of downtown neighborhoods may involve the redevelopment or conversion of single-room occupancy hotels (SROs). While this topic is discussed more completely in chapter 19, it is important to view the threat to SRO housing as part of the same urban change process that underlies other forms of displacement (see also Stegman, 1985; Eckert, 1979). These hotels house people "who don't have the money or the family support to live anywhere else, especially the single, pension-dependent elderly; . . . when these people are displaced, as increasingly is happening, they have no place else to go" (Hartman, Keating, and Legates, 1981, p. 54). In New York City, for example, the number of SRO hotel rooms, most of which rent for under $50 a week, dropped from around 50,000 in 1975 to 28,000 in 1978. Unless the city makes concerted efforts to protect this housing stock, the combination of inflation and the pressure of economic development could eliminate the SRO hotel in New York before 1990. Similarly, pressures from tourism and industrial development in San Francisco have contributed to the decline of the SRO hotel there. Between 1975 and 1979, nearly 6,000 SRO hotel rooms were converted to tourist accommodations (Hartman, Keating, and Legates, 1981). HUD scarcely addresses this issue in its reports on displacement.

The decline of the SRO hotel disrupts the social networks made up of occupants and management that enable tenants to maintain their independence. According to Lally and associates (1979), hotel employees are largely sympathetic to their tenants and often provide them with care, attention, and special factors, including delivering meals and rent reductions. Eckert (1979) reinforces this view in his case study of the redevelopment of an SRO-hotel district in San Diego where elderly and younger tenants took care of themselves despite high levels of functional impairment. In a third study, Cohen and Sokolovsky (1980) report that, general impressions to the contrary, SRO-hotel residents are not social isolates. Many of these self-proclaimed loners have social networks that extend beyond the hotel and can be permanently damaged if the housing is lost.

The combination of unique support systems, cheap rent, and central locations, which provide access to inexpensive eating places, second-hand clothing outlets, discount drug stores and so on, enable most SRO-hotel tenants to remain independent despite their poverty and physical and psychological disabilities. Thus, according to

Eckert, SRO hotels serve as semiinstitutional facilities which "provide numerous services to their residents at a price and in some cases with a finesse that is not available in many formal extended-care facilities" (Eckert, 1979, p. 501). The loss of inexpensive residential hotels in central cities throughout the country could not only mean the loss of affordable housing to marginally independent people but also the loss of their ability to survive outside of an institution.

Conclusion

The problem of reinvestment-induced displacement poses a more serious dilemma for federal policy than does displacement caused by government-encouraged urban renewal (which eventually formed the basis for the Uniform Relocation Act). The dilemma arises not only because the federal role in private reinvestment that causes displacement is frequently indirect (such as federally insured mortgages), or because displacement can result when owners with property next to successful renovation projects raise their rents to unaffordable levels. The problem goes beyond those examples or the considerable cost of extending full relocation benefits to everyone displaced by reinvestment, and its causes are reflected in HUD's conflicting mandates. The housing mission entrusted to HUD should lead it to take a strong position on the preservation of low- and moderate-cost housing in revitalized communities; the provision of rental and financing assistance to families who risk being priced out of their homes because of reinvestment; the extension of full relocation benefits to families displaced by private actions; strict controls on condominium conversions; and support for the full funding of deep-subsidy construction programs where there is a serious shortage of low-cost housing (Hartman, 1979). On the other hand, HUD's responsibility for urban development requires it to support the establishment and maintenance of viable urban communities as social, economic, and political entities, and this in turn requires that it pay attention to general housing problems rather than those of the poor alone. After nearly two decades of urban decline, the partial depopulation of major northeastern and midwestern cities, the abandonment by landlords of hundreds of thousands of unprofitable rental units, and the erosion of local economic bases, HUD in particular, and the federal government in general, are properly reluctant to impose costly and burdensome relocation requirements on private reinvestment that will benefit whole communities.

Ambivalence, combined with the problem of inadequate data which has prevented the development of reliable estimates of the nature and size of the displacement problem, has led HUD to conclude that

> neither the forces underlying revitalization and displacement nor the development and implementation of relocation remedies once displacement occurs are exclusively amenable to the control of the federal government; ... one of the most effective federal roles in minimizing displacement is to assist states, local governments, neighborhood organizations, and the private sector to develop and implement their own, locally appropriate antidisplacement strategies (U.S. DHUD, 1979b, p. 19).

HUD has declared that HUD-assisted projects leading to displacement will not be approved unless "an affordable, decent, safe, and sanitary replacement dwelling is available," but cautions that "because of the administrative complexity of some programs, as well as resource limitations, the department cannot guarantee that in every instance the goal will be achieved" (U.S. DHUD, 1979b, p. 19).

Although we are not likely to see a consistent and comprehensive federal antidisplacement policy and program, HUD has modified several regulations to lessen the probability of displacement and has increased the effective coverage of the Uniform Relocation Act by mandating equivalent protection for families displaced because of rehabilitation financed by direct federal loans. HUD (U.S. DHUD, 1979b) has also increased reporting requirements and responsibilities for local communities receiving federal Community Development Block Grant (CDBG) funds to plan for the housing needs of households displaced by publicly aided reinvestment. Since these requirements were incorporated into the CDBG application process and local housing assistance plan regulations, both of which have been all but eliminated by the Reagan administration, it is unlikely that any federal initiatives will be forthcoming in this area for some time.

There may be some action at the state and local levels, particularly in the regulation of condominium conversions and the protection of low-income, elderly, and handicapped individuals living in converted buidlings. More than twenty-five states have enacted some form of tenant protection for residents of buildings undergoing conversion (U.S. DHUD, 1980). These measures often involve extended notification requirements to tenants of the pending conversion, various safeguards to prevent premature eviction, and the right of first refusal (the tenants' right to buy their apartment before it is placed on the open market). At least three states, Connecticut, Minnesota, and New York, have enacted special protections for aged renters. The most comprehensive of these is New York's, which offers elderly tenants who do not buy a condominium and who have annual incomes of less than $30,000 a form of life tenancy, with rents set under any applicable rent regulations (U.S. DHUD, 1980).

Benefits granted by conversion legislation would be available to SRO-hotel tenants if the hotel were turned into luxury condominiums. If, however, SROs are demolished for new rental housing or commercial structures, tenant protection measures may not be available. In a somewhat belated recognition of the connection between the existence of SRO hotels and the health of people living in them, New York City recently ruled that the rehabilitation of SRO hotels is not eligible for tax abatements. The city has also taken steps to turn city-owned buildings (abandoned properties taken for back-taxes) into SRO hotels, rehabilitating them with CDBG monies. Continued state and local leadership on solutions to the problem of displacement is largely contingent upon continued availability of federal funds, which will be severely cut in the coming years. But since it is likely that official government concern over displacement caused by private reinvestment will decline, initiatives on this issue will have to come at the state and local levels.

References

Besser, J. D. 1979. " 'Gentrifying' the Ghetto." *The Progressive* 43, No. 1:30–32.

Cohen, C. I., and J. Sokolovsky. 1980. "Social Engagement Versus Isolation: The Case of the Aged in SRO Hotels." *Gerontologist* 20:6–44.

Cowgill, D. O. 1978. "Residential Segregation by Age in American Metropolitan Areas." *Journal of Gerontology* 33, No. 3:446–53.

Dreier, P., and J. Atlas. 1981. "Condomania." *The Progressive* 45, No. 3:19–22.

Eckert, J. K. 1979. "Urban Renewal and Redevelopment: High Risk for the Marginally Subsistent Elderly." *Gerontologist* 19:496–502.

Gutowski, M., and T. Feild. 1979. "The Graying of Suburbia." Washington, DC: Urban Institute.

Hartman, C. 1979. "Displacement: A Not So New Problem." *Social Policy* 9:22–26.

Hartman, C., D. Keating, and R. Legates. 1981. *Displacement: How to Fight It.* Berkeley, CA: National Housing Law Project.

Henig, J. R. 1980. "Gentrification and Displacement Within Cities: A Comparative Analysis." *Social Science Quarterly* 61:638–51.

———. 1981. "Gentrification and Displacement of the Elderly: An Empirical Analysis." *Gerontologist* 21:67–75.

Lally, M., M. Black, M. Thornrock, and J. O. Hawkins. 1979. "Older Women in Single-Room Occupant Hotels: A Seattle Profile." *Gerontologist* 19:67–73.

National Urban Coalition. 1981. *Neighborhood Transition Without Displacement.* Washington, DC: National Urban Coalition.

Soldo, B. J. 1981. "Impact of Neighborhood Change and Age-Related Adaptations." In *Long-Range Research Agenda for Elderly Housing and Related Services.* Ed. P. S. Taylor. Washington, DC: Gerontological Society.

Stegman, M. A. 1985. "Housing and the Elderly." In *Aging and Public Health.* Ed. H. T. Phillips and S. A. Gaylord. New York: Springer.

Struyk, R. J., and B. J. Soldo. 1980. *Improving the Elderly's Housing.* Cambridge, MA: Ballinger.

U.S. Department of Housing and Urban Development (DHUD). 1979a. *Interim Displacement Report.* Washington, DC: U.S. DHUD.

———. 1979b. *Final Displacement Report.* Washington, DC: U.S. DHUD.

———. 1980. *The Conversion of Rental Housing to Condominiums and Cooperatives. A National Study of Scope, Causes and Impacts.* Washington, DC: U.S. DHUD.

———. 1981. *The Conversion of Rental Housing to Condominiums and Cooperatives: The Impacts on Elderly and Lower-Income Households.* Washington, DC: U.S. DHUD.

U.S. Senate Special Committee on Aging. 1978. Hearing: *Older Americans in the Nation's Neighborhoods.* Field Hearings in Oakland, CA, 4 December. Washington, DC: U.S. Government Printing Office.

CHAPTER 16 Neighborhoods and Self-Help Programs among the Elderly

B. J. Curry Spitler • Robert J. Newcomer

The continuing growth in the number of older people, coupled with the occurrence of problems related to income, health, housing, and social isolation, has given rise to a variety of public and private actions. Formal programs range from income subsidies to homemaker/chore services. Informal services include the many forms of care and attention provided by family members and friends. While much remains to be learned about the efficacy and the trade-offs associated with formal and informal care, there is an apparent recognition by professionals and policy-makers that informal systems should be strengthened. Traditionally, families and neighborhoods have been considered as two bases for the development of informal support organizations and as an arena for the development of mutual aid (Litwak, 1961; Warren, 1976). Most of the research upon which these observations are based come from studies of ethnic minorities and low-income populations (Gans, 1962; Warren, 1975; Tamney, 1975; Hojnaki, 1979). Majority members of the society *and* those with middle-class incomes are generally more cosmopolitan and less oriented to neighborhoods in their social behavior (Warren and Warren, 1977; Craven and Wellman, 1974). Consequently, for them an assumption could be made that neighborhoods would not serve as a relevant base for the development of support organizations and mutual aid.

The ambiguity about the role and efficacy of neighborhoods as a basis for building informal systems increases when considering the older population. Current knowledge about the factors affecting neighborhood definition, use, and satisfaction among the elderly (as discussed in chapters 12 and 13) suggest that neighborhood-oriented programs could be a viable approach for delivering informal services. On the other hand, the extra neighborhood orientation of the majority population suggests that neighborhood-based strategies may not be the most effective stimuli in organizing the genesis of these delivery systems. This is illustrated by a variety of self-help groups which have formed to overcome problems such as alcoholism, obesity, mental illness, or the effects of surgery (mastectomy, colostomy, or amputee groups). Shared need rather than geographic proximity has been a common element in all these groups (Killilea, 1976). Is this also true among the elderly? From a public policy perspective, how much effort should be directed toward neighborhood-based strategies for building care systems versus delivering informal care?

To begin answering these questions, this chapter focuses on one form of informal support—self-

The information presented here is based on a national study of self-help and advocacy groups (Spitler and Newcomer, 1982), which was funded by the U.S. Department of Health and Human Services, Administration on Aging, under grant number AoA 90-AP-0013, and conducted at the Aging Health Policy Center, University of California, San Francisco.

help groups. In particular, we discuss the extent to which the elderly are forming self-help groups, the type of programs developed, and the elements leading to this development.

Three characteristics define self-help groups. The first is that control of the group rests with the members rather than with an external authority. Personal participation is also central to the concept of self-help. Finally, the origin of self-help groups has generally been found to be spontaneous and to occur because the participants perceive their needs are not, or cannot be, met by existing programs (Katz and Bender, 1976b; Levy, 1979; Gartner and Reissman, 1980).

The activity of self-help groups may be directed to personal change, growth, and satisfaction (inner-focused), or to the community and social institutions (outer-focused) (Katz and Bender, 1976a). Often these perspectives occur together and are self-reinforcing.

The prevalence of self-help programs among the elderly is growing nationally but the exact number is not known. The discussion in this section is based on the findings from our community survey of self-help programs (Spitler and Newcomer, 1982).

As identified by our study, the services provided or concerns addressed by self-help groups formed by the elderly generally fall into at least one of eight broad program categories: health, mental health, cooperative or consumer groups, nutrition programs, employment or craft groups, education, senior centers, and advocacy. Most of the programs identified by our study were formed by either paid or retired professionals who helped older people to come together. As the program matured, the participants assumed more (and often all) leadership responsibilities of the day-to-day program management. Professionals tended to remain involved as consultants and to help in obtaining program funding.

While there are many similarities in the origin and operation of the self-help programs, each type has its unique purposes. For example, mental health groups assist those who have been hospitalized or who have experienced a traumatic event (such as the loss of a spouse) to cope with emotional problems and to acquire the necessary skills to function in the community. Cooperatives or consumer groups, on the other hand, provide a way for older people to *increase* their limited financial resources. Health programs enable the elderly to accept responsibility for and gain some control over their own health.

Following is a brief description of the services and activities provided by these self-help programs. This presentation illustrates both the types of programs available, and some of the elements leading to their development.

Health

Self-help groups involving older people have developed to address a range of both personal health concerns and those of caregivers. These programs reflect three models of self-help: health promotion, access and service, and support groups.

Health Promotion

The purpose of health promotion programs is to help participants develop a sense of control over their own bodies and ultimately their own lives through involvement in improving their general physical and mental health. Several methods are used. These include informal classes on the principles of general health, nutrition, and the management of stress; exercise to control weight, reduce stress, and increase physical endurance; assertiveness training to develop a proactive stance, a sense of power and control over one's life; and support groups to reinforce gains and positive life changes as they are made.

Generally, professionals with expertise in health education, nutrition, physical fitness, and assertiveness training are necessary at the onset of these programs, and while funding is often necessary, leadership shifts and external funding needs diminish as the group gains experience. Although health promotion programs do not necessarily begin as traditional self-help groups, their final form can be unquestionably self-help.

Access and Service Programs

These programs identify the health and support needs of the frail elderly and link them to existing community services when possible. A typical form of this program is to train senior volunteers to locate the frail elderly in their neighborhoods, identify their needs, and activate the appropriate resources or provide the necessary resources, such as chore services.

Health Support Programs

The health support groups focused on specific illnesses, such as Alzheimer's and related disorders, stroke, and arthritis. Support groups are found in urban, suburban, and rural areas, but membership seems to be based primarily on identification with a particular problem rather than on neighborhood or other geographic location. Most often, health support groups are started by victims or their spouses in consultation with professionals.

The primary purpose of these groups is mutual support to those afflicted and their care-givers. Whether the focus is on the victim or the care-giver depends in part on the extent to which the illness affects the victim's functioning. The goals common to most of these groups are to develop a greater understanding of the disease and its long-term effects, resocialization of the victims, and social activities for both the victims and the care-givers.

Mental Health

Mental health programs attempt to serve a number of purposes, such as addressing the problems of alcohol and drug abuse, assisting hospital patients to reintegrate into the community, and helping the widowed to work through their grieving process. Groups are also organized to provide peer counseling, reduce isolation, and prevent emotional problems.

Each of the mental health groups identified was relatively small, with membership ranging from five to forty participants. The small size is conducive to and consistent with self-help goals of sharing information and feelings in face-to-face interaction. In general, group activities consist of education, socialization, mutual support, and peer counseling, but there are differences in emphasis reflective of the unique needs of the members.

The widowed groups, for example, are largely composed of women whose husbands had managed the family's financial affairs. Consequently, speakers are invited to provide information on such subjects as financial management, writing a will, and settling an estate.

Cooperatives and Consumer Groups

Variants of community gardens, buyers clubs, service exchanges, and retail outlets for craft products were found as examples of cooperative and consumer self-help programs. Community garden activities include the provision of food, area beautification, and opportunities for exercise and socialization. Service exchanges are essentially a barter mechanism to help the elderly obtain the services needed to maintain themselves and their own homes. These programs operate by developing and maintaining listings of people wishing to provide services and of the services needed by others. Buyers clubs or cooperatives enable people to benefit from the economies of group/high-volume buying. The groups studied generally focus on the provision of fresh produce and quality sources of protein. Some also offer nutrition education.

Employment or Craft

Employment-craft groups are formed to develop, find, and create employment opportunities. Usually this latter activity takes form in handcrafted objects made for sale, but the concept can be applied to any marketable products, such as electronic components or small machine subassemblies. Programs also serve as a clearing-house for part-time employment. For example, some programs maintain contact with employers for seasonal employment such as Santa Clauses or clerks; part-time employment for mail-order companies and other businesses with a need for part-time employees.

Nutrition Programs

Inadequate nutrition is intimately linked with inadequate income, poor physical health, social isolation, and limited knowledge of the principles of sound nutrition. Consequently, any program that addresses one or more of these problems might be thought of as being a nutrition program. Although publicly subsidized on-site nutrition programs and home-delivered meal programs are available in many areas (through the Older Americans Act or other funding), they are not often of sufficient size to serve the nutritional and social needs of all the elderly residing in those areas. In response to this, congregate and home-delivered meal programs, operated by the elderly, have emerged. In the congregate programs studied, meals are prepared at the site by volunteers/participants who are active in all the aspects of the program such as purchasing food, meal planning, food preparation, serving, and cleaning up.

Home-delivered meal programs are generally contracted with another organization such as a hospital or school. Volunteers are involved in the administration of the organization and the delivery of meals.

Senior Centers

Most senior centers are publicly established programs, run under parks and recreation departments or other auspices. Not all senior centers have this origin; many were started by a group of older people and were "bootstrap" operations in that they obtained private or public funding only after the center was in operation as a group effort. The following list of programs illustrates the activities available within self-help senior centers: exercise and fitness programs, support groups, cooperatives, consumer groups, employment-crafts, nutrition programs, access services, recreation, and transportation. In other words, a senior center is not a single activity; rather it is an umbrella organization and physical location which provides opportunities for social participation, recreation, and services. Self-help actions may produce the umbrella organization and its component parts, or provide the means for developing programs that are incorporated into existing (perhaps publicly funded) senior centers.

Illustrative self-help services include:

- *Education*, which may include classes devoted to academic concerns or take the form of current-events discussion groups. Art and craft classes are also popular and often focus on activities that can be continued in the older person's home. Some of the larger centers have elaborate woodworking equipment, pottery kilns, and other large equipment.
- *Volunteer opportunities*, an important part of every senior center. There are many volunteer opportunities just to keep the center's programs going. Most centers also serve as clearing-houses for volunteer opportunities in the community, such as tutoring children, assisting at hospitals, or long-term-care facilities.
- *Financial assistance*, most commonly involving assistance with tax forms, social security forms, and other insurance or government forms. A few centers make outright loans or grants from an endowment fund for which bequests are encouraged.
- *Legal services* directed to the issues of rental disputes, contracts, wills, conservatorship, and rights under entitlement programs. Law students act as legal counselors (under the supervision of professors), and center members are trained as paralegal counselors.
- *Housing services*, such as programs to assist members in locating affordable housing. Some centers have developed shared housing programs by linking those with larger homes with those who need housing. Moving assistance, home repairs, and modification of homes to assist older people in adapting to a recently acquired handicap are often operated by volun-

teers. Some clearing-house activity to inform participants of available housing is generally offered.

Advocacy Programs

The past twenty years have seen a remarkable increase in advocacy activity focused on the needs of the elderly. Nationally, organizations such as the Gray Panthers and the Older Women's League have contributed to consciousness raising and to legislative efforts to benefit the elderly, while the large membership organizations such as the American Association of Retired Persons, and the National Council of Senior Citizens have repeatedly demonstrated their ability to lobby effectively for the interests of their membership. At the state and local levels there has also been growth in the number of advocacy units addressing the needs of the elderly. Two broad types of self-help advocacy groups were identified: those that directly and primarily involve the elderly, and coalitions comprised of representatives from organizations whose primary function is the provision of services to the elderly.

Advocacy Groups of Elders

Advocacy groups approach the task of affecting the legislative process in many ways. One approach is to select groups of elders, involve them in classes, and arrange visits to legislative sessions as a means of educating members to the processes of the legislature and the current issues affecting older people at the state and local level. The elders who attend the classes agree to form groups in their own communities. In this way, a statewide network is established to track legislation and to react to the issues directly affecting older people. Another approach involves active lobbying, primarily at the state level. Information about pending bills is provided to older people by means of a telephone tree. As the bills are being considered by legislative committees, people are encouraged to advocate on an individual basis.

Coalitions

The coalitions tend to be formed by the service-providers, placing the elderly in the role of service recipient. However, many of the coalitions have been effective in promoting and obtaining local support for programs serving the elderly. Some coalitions also encourage or educate older people to self-advocacy.

Conclusion

To answer the primary question posed by this chapter—is the geographic or neighborhood orientation of a program a central factor in the formation and/or implementation of a self-help program?—two definitions of neighborhood-based programs are used. First, there are those that have their impetus for formation from the neighborhood residents and the participants, rather than some outside organization or professional, and second are those in which the majority of the program participants live within walking distance of the program.

These distinctions are important for differentiating between formation and delivery. Few of the programs studied claimed to be neighborhood-based. The groups instead tended to be organized by the problem addressed. Participants traveled to the programs and identified with the groups, but the groups generally were not identified with the neighborhoods in which they were located. In spite of this, most of the programs made some use of a neighborhood, or at least a geographic area, in the organization or participation in the program. For example, the health programs, buyers clubs, home-delivered meal programs, and several of the mental health groups and senior centers had organized service and/or participation by neighborhood. In other organizations that covered the entire state, volunteers functioned within their own church parish or neighborhood. This application of neighborhood orientation as a program catchment area is useful in identifying program delivery issues and is consistent with the service-use findings from other studies of neighborhood activity discussed elsewhere in this volume.

How is it that geography can be important for delivery but not program formation? One explanation seems to lie in the fact that people tend to relate to each other more out of mutual concerns than spatial proximity. Regardless of social class, ethnicity, and age, people are able to extend their informational ties and support network through telephone calls, traveling to other areas, or calling on groups outside their neighborhood. The idea that people help each other through loosely knit information networks mitigates the importance of neighborhood or geographic proximity (Laumann, 1973; Craven and Wellman, 1974).

Perhaps further contributing to this lack of neighborhood connection in program formation can be a stigma involved with the problem to be addressed (such as mental or other health problems). In such cases there may be a desire on the part of the participants to seek help outside of their neighborhood (Spiegel, 1976). Another practical consideration seems to be the number of people who share a problem. With the small out-patient mental health groups and the health support groups for example, it seemed that a "critical mass" was lacking in the neighborhood. This necessitated seeking others with a common need across a wider community.

Recognizing the factors that operate against neighborhoods being the stimulus for self-help formation, two other considerations can be raised from our findings. These have potential bearing on the role of community organizers and others interested in expanding self-help program efforts. The first issue is the comparative involvement of minorities in self-help groups. Three-fourths of the programs studied had less than a 20 percent minority participation. And only seven of the programs studied were predominantly minority groups. This racial representation is roughly proportionate to the distribution of minority aged to the total aged populations in the areas studied.

Two factors seemingly account for this level of participation. First, while minority individuals were involved in the formation of about one-third of the groups, coalitions of minorities were evident in the formation of only two groups. Second, it should be recognized that many of today's elderly reached young adulthood and established their values long before the civil rights movement, consequently it is possible that their values favor racial homogeneity in the formation of self-help groups. Such an attitude would be particularly problematic for group formation in racially mixed neighborhoods. Data from our interviews suggests, however, that language rather than color may be the major barrier to more integration. Of the ethnic minority programs studied, all drew their membership from the entire city and considered themselves organized by race. Moreover, in each case the program was situated in an ethnic neighborhood. Meeting days allowed for shopping for ethnic foods, socializing in a common language, visiting the neighborhood doctor, and in a very real sense returning to the cultural neighborhood.

The final issue is the extent to which self-help groups assist the frail and most dependent elderly. Generally, it is the able elderly who are attracted to self-help groups. This also helps explain their geographic independence as the more mobile and affluent elderly can become involved in relevant groups wherever they find them. The self-help groups expressly focused on support and service for the frail home-bound elderly or the disabled elderly, and their care-givers (spouse and adult children) were geographically independent too. For these groups participation may be widely drawn because of the reasons of stigma or critical mass noted earlier.

The major conclusion from this analysis of self-help programs among the elderly is further clarification of the role and function of neighborhoods in the development and operation of these activities. Seldom is the neighborhood in and of itself the genesis for self-help program development. Individuals, including professionals, focused on meeting a particular need, are the most common stimuli for program formation. However, the viability of most programs can be enhanced when the service delivery operation is neighborhood-based. In other words, both the self-help program and neighborhood development movements will be enhanced if a clear distinction is made between the basis for program formation and its mechanism for service delivery.

Note

1. The survey included eight planning and service areas selected from the states of California, Florida, Missouri, Pennsylvania, Vermont, Washington, and Wisconsin. The states were selected to provide variation in state taxing, decentralization, and state public program generosity to aging. The planning and service areas were selected to provide a range of urban, suburban, and rural settings. An inventory of self-help programs in each of these communities was developed by contacting representatives of agencies serving the elderly in each community and others identified as knowledgeable about aging programs. Particular attention was given to finding ethnic minority groups. In total, sixty-five groups met our selection criteria for defining self-help activity and of having been in existence for at least six months. All of these were contacted to obtain information of their origin, function, and current operation.

References

Craven, P., and B. Wellman. 1974. "The Network City." *Sociological Inquiry* 43:57–88.

Gans, H. 1962. *The Urban Villagers.* New York: Free.

Gartner, A., and F. Riessman. 1980. *Help—A Working Guide to Self-Help Groups.* New York: New Viewpoints.

Hojnaki, W. P. 1979. "What Is a Neighborhood?" *Social Policy,* 10:47–52.

Katz, A. H., and E. I. Bender. 1976a. *The Strength in Us.* New York: New Viewpoints.

———. 1976b. "Self-Help Groups in Western Society: History and Prospects." *The Journal of Applied Behavioral Science* 12:265–82.

Killilea, M. 1976. "Mutual Help Organizations: Interpretations in the Literature." In *Support Systems and Mutual Help: Multidisciplinary Explorations.* Ed. G. Caplan and M. Killilea. New York: Grune and Stratton.

Laumann, E. O. 1973. *Boards of Pluralism.* New York: Wiley.

Levy, L. H. 1979. "Process and Activities in Groups." In *Self-Help Groups For Coping With Crisis: Origins, Members, Processes, and Impact.* Ed. M. A. Lieberman, L. D. Borman and Associates. San Francisco: Jossey-Bass.

Litwak, E. 1961. "Voluntary Associations and Neighborhood Cohesion." *American Sociological Review* 26:258–71.

Spiegal, D. 1976. "Going Public and Self-Help." In *Support Systems and Mutual Help: Multidisciplinary Exploration.* Ed. G. Caplan, and M. Killilea. New York: Grune and Stratton.

Spitler, B., J. Curry, and R. J. Newcomer. 1982. *Self-Help and Advocacy Groups Among the Aged: A Manual for Area Agencies on Aging, Final Report.* U.S. Department of Health and Human Services, Administration on Aging, Grant No. 90-AR-0013. San Francisco, CA: Aging Health Policy Center, Univ. of California.

Tamney, J. B. 1975. *Solidarity in a Slum.* New York: Wiley.

Warren, D. J. 1975. *Black Neighborhood: An Assessment of Community Power.* Ann Arbor, MI: Univ. of Michigan.

———. 1976. *Helping Networks, Neighborhood and Community Patterns, Final Report,* Grant number 5R01-24982, National Institute of Mental Health. Washington, DC: U.S. NIMH.

Warren, R. B., and D. J. Warren. 1977. *The Neighborhood Organizers Handbook.* South Bend, IN: Univ. of Notre Dame.

CHAPTER 17 Environmental Considerations for Housing Sites for the Elderly

Peggy Wireman • Antoinette G. Sebastian

Good housing and neighborhoods for the elderly must accommodate the physical, social, economic, and other changes that may occur as part of the aging process. This chapter considers certain physical, social, and demographic facts about the elderly in terms of their implications for environmental review and planning and recommends possible mitigations and alternatives where conditions are not ideal. Our principal focus is on the independent, mobile elderly, but we have been sensitive to the dynamic functional status changes in the elderly population. The environment for any new housing development must take into consideration not only the characteristics of the incoming residents, but also the changes that can be expected during a ten-to-twenty-year residency.

Building in certain communities inevitably involves certain environmental problems such as air pollution, steep slopes, or crime because these environmental conditions affect all or large parts of certain communities. The range and quality of public and nonprofit agency services available depend upon the resources of the community in which the housing is to be located as well as the location of the particular site. Nevertheless, the needs of the elderly in each category of environmental concern must be addressed and mitigation measures developed when the suggested criteria for one category cannot be fully met.

It may be impossible to obtain the most desirable solution for each environmental factor and planning consideration. The site most desirable for

Colleagues at HUD and over thirty individuals from a variety of private organizations, government agencies, and universities generously worked with us in reviewing an earlier version of this material. None are responsible for any errors or limitations of this version, nor would they each agree with all of it. Nevertheless, without their insights, their knowledge, and their support, our efforts would not have been successful. Their help is gratefully acknowledged. Among those who contributed are: Paul Taylor, Gerontological Society; Wilma Donahue, Tom Beall, Mark Olshan, International Center for Social Gerontology; Mary Nenno, National Association of Housing and Redevelopment Officials; Shirley Patterson, Department of the Interior; Thomas Woodstock, National Council of Senior Citizens; Joe Eaglin, National Caucus and Center on the Black Aged; Samuel Simmons, National Center for Housing Management; Jessie Gertman, National Institute on Aging; Jose Garza, National Hispanic Housing Coalition; Jack Ossofsky, National Council on the Aging; Leo Baldwin, American Association of Retired Persons; Jeanne Kinnard, American Association of Homes for the Aging; Janice Caldwell, Gerontological Society; Robert Aldrich, University of Colorado; Judith Bernstein, The Wright Institute; Norm Blackie, National Policy Center on Housing and Living Arrangements for Older Americans; Marilyn Block, University of Maryland; Thomas O. Byerts, Gerontology Center, University of Illinois; Galen Cranz, University of California; Lorraine Hiatt, American Foundation for the Blind; Sandra C. Howell, the Massachusetts Institute of Technology; M. Powell Lawton, Philadelphia Geriatric Center; Eugene Litwak, Columbia University; Janet MacLean, Indiana University; Leon A. Pastalan, University of Michigan; and Victor Regnier, University of Illinois at Urbana.

The statements, opinions, and conclusions contained in this chapter are those of the authors and do not necessarily reflect the U.S. government in general or the departments of Housing and Urban Development or Commerce in particular.

one factor, such as proximity to public transportation and stores, may be least desirable for another, such as outdoor air quality or security. The cost and long-range implications of any decision must be considered carefully. Decisions regarding location, site design, obtaining services from outside agencies, internal house design, management, and costs must be made in relationship to each other so that the result of all of the decisions is an appropriate environment. If, for example, the housing is located in an area with no recreational opportunities, one planning alternative would be to arrange with a local agency to transport residents to recreational events. Another alternative could be to purchase a bus and expect the managers to arrange for volunteer drivers. A third might be to provide increased opportunities onsite or nearby (within "easy" walking distance). Each mitigation measure and planning alternative has design, management, and both long- and short-term cost implications. If the site is already on a bus route providing public transportation, negotiating with local authorities might result in a willingness to reroute the bus so that it would stop in front of the housing. The developer in turn might design the lobby of the housing to include an appropriate waiting area. In considering mitigations and planning alternatives, developers should consider that appropriate actions during early planning and design stages may reduce later management problems and maintenance expenses.

Given the dynamics of providing elderly housing at an affordable cost, some less-than-ideal sites are selected. However, appropriate mitigation of environmental factors and careful planning usually make it possible to produce acceptable housing on such sites. The mitigations suggested include some that require changes in site design, some that require negotiations to obtain services from public and private agencies, and others that require management actions once the construction has been completed. All parties ultimately to be involved in developing or providing services to the establishment should be contacted as early as possible. This enables coordination and also allows each organization the lead time necessary for ob-

taining money for comprehensive planning and necessary budgeting.

Following is a series of the more important environmental conditions known to affect neighborhood and housing quality for older persons. Under each we briefly review the condition, the reasons for its importance in site selection, and the actions that developers or sponsors might take when the chosen site varies from the ideal site.

Air Pollution

Housing for the elderly should be located in areas with good air quality. *Air Quality Considerations in Residential Planning* by Thuillier (1978) gives standards and methods for evaluating overall air pollution in an area and pollution specifically caused by a source near a potential site, such as a highway, parking garage, or a polluting industry. The publication can be obtained from the U.S. Department of Housing and Urban Development (HUD) or the Government Printing Office (GPO).

Air quality is important for several well-documented reasons. The U.S. Surgeon General's Report (1979) lists bronchitis, emphysema, and asthma, collectively, as the eighth leading cause of death among those over age sixty-five. Almost one-half of the persons over sixty-five must limit their activities because of chronic health conditions. The report states that respiratory conditions such as chronic bronchitis and emphysema often limit activity. The report also cites air pollution as aggravating to respiratory conditions.

Possible Mitigation Measures

1. Careful location and orientation of the building on the site can reduce exposure to pollutants, especially if the pollution is from a nearby source such as an adjacent highway. Landscaping can also shield the site from pollutants.
2. Report pollution from a site-specific or stationary source, such as a factory, to local and state authorities to see if plans and a schedule have been developed for eliminating the problem and to urge appropriate action.

3. Include air conditioning in the building design to filter and purify the air. The air-conditioning system should have thermostats in each unit, because the elderly are sensitive to cold, and a cold environment can aggravate respiratory problems. Provision of air conditioning should not lead to inoperable windows, however, since many of the elderly like fresh air and it is beneficial for some respiratory problems (Zeisel, Epp, and Demos, 1977).

4. Arrange for an air-conditioned bus or van to transport the elderly to shopping, libraries, and recreational facilities on air pollution alert days. Such vehicles can be included in the costs of the housing or may be obtained from the locality or a nonprofit agency.

5. Include indoor recreational space or an on-site convenience shopping facility within the complex to enable the elderly to stay home on air pollution alert days. If carried to the extreme, however, this solution may result in undesirable social isolation.

Noise Pollution

Housing for the elderly should be located in areas that at least meet and preferably exceed the HUD noise standards (HUD Regulation 24 CFR Part 51 [Subpart B and Subpart D] Environmental Criteria and Standards). For instructions on how to evaluate a site in accordance with the standards, see HUD *Noise Assessment Guidelines*, 1983. Copies of both publications may be obtained from HUD.

The majority of the elderly have normal hearing and would be as bothered by noise pollution as anyone else. People with partial hearing loss may experience pain or discomfort when exposed to a very loud noise (EPA, 1978). In addition, individuals with hearing impairments are bothered by high noise levels since they cannot easily distinguish individual sounds such as voices or telephone bells from background noise (Pastalan, 1979). The fact that the elderly are disturbed by noise is indicated in their responses to questions asking whether there were any neighborhood conditions bothersome enough so that the respondent

wanted to move. Suburban elderly listed street noise and crime as most important. Central-city elderly ranked street noise second behind crime. Even for central-city residents, the combination of rankings for street noise and airplane noise was almost as great as that for crime (Gutowski and Feild, 1973). Being in a "quiet neighborhood" is a frequently cited reason given by older people for liking where they live (Lawton and Byerts, 1973).

The sleep patterns of the elderly make them especially susceptible to noise disturbances. They have difficulty sleeping, wake up more frequently during the night than younger people, and have more trouble returning to sleep. "As a group, the elderly require special protection from the noises that interfere with their sleep" (EPA, 1978, p. 4). Older persons also often nap during the day. Therefore, daytime noises from aircraft, heavy traffic, and even children playing nearby can disturb the rest that older persons need to maintain good health.

Possible Mitigation Measures

1. Locate areas such as parking lots next to any sources of noise pollution to increase the distance between sources of noise-sensitive uses such as recreation and the dwelling itself.

2. Design the building so that non-noise-sensitive areas such as bathrooms or kitchens buffer the noise-sensitive areas such as bedrooms.

3. Appropriate selection of building materials and construction methods, as well as location and type of windows, can enhance insulation from noise.

4. Build barriers or berms. A berm is an earth mound that offers protection from noises from some sources but not from sources located higher than the berm. Neither berms nor barriers are effective protection from aircraft noise.

Floodplains

Housing should not be located in or adversely affect the 500-year floodplain, especially in the floodway or coastal high-hazard area (those areas closest to the source of a flood), or in an area prone to flash flooding. For most localities the flood insurance rate and other maps and studies necessary to determine the location of these problem areas can be obtained by calling the National Flood Insurance Program (toll free, 800-638-6620) or the state or local planning agency, or they can be examined at the office of the community's building inspector.

Evacuating the elderly in case of floods can be very difficult. For example, one-sixth of the residents of projects built under the Section 202 housing program are frail. This means they need assistance with at least two of the activities of normal living such as dressing or eating (U.S. Senate, 1984). One study of 15 million elderly-headed households reported that at least one person had activity limitations or health problems. These problems included arthritis or rheumatism, asthma, emphysema or chronic bronchitis, blindness, or deafness. These would make evacuation, especially into small boats, difficult (Struyk and Zais, 1982).

People evacuated from floods are frequently housed in churches and schools until alternative accommodations can be found for them. Heat, blankets, and hot food are often unavailable. Such conditions could aggravate existing health problems, such as respiratory difficulties. In addition, the elderly are particularly susceptible to influenza and pneumonia, the fourth leading cause of death among the elderly (Allan and Brotman, 1981). Moreover, people with high blood pressure and heart problems are often advised not to get upset, but being evacuated from a flood would cause stress for many people.

The elderly may suffer damage to their health and well-being if permanently relocated. Several studies over a twenty-year period have indicated that relocation can have long-lasting adverse effects. Some studies have found higher rates of death among elderly relocatees. Among the factors that seem to influence the effects of relocation are: whether or not the move was voluntary or involuntary, the amount of preparation for the move,

the environment in the new home, the continuity of social contacts, and the destination, whether to another home or an institution (Bourestom and Pastalan, 1981). For each of these factors, relocation because of a flood is likely to be inappropriate relocation because the time for careful planning will not be available.

Possible Mitigation Measures

1. Avoid locating housing for the elderly in the floodplain, especially in the floodway of a coastal high-hazard area.
2. Elevate the basements of buildings above the flooding level. Floodproof the building, the access road, and utilities serving the building.
3. Design and implement a flood evacuation plan for building occupants.

Hazards: Commercial/Industrial Facilities

There is an acceptable safe separation distance (ASD) between any proposed project site and a hazardous operation that handles petroleum products or chemicals of an explosive or flammable nature. This distance is calculated using HUD Regulation 24 CFR Part 51C and the HUD hazards guidebook, *Urban Development Siting with Respect to Hazardous Commercial/Industrial Facilities*. For problems associated with potentially hazardous toxic sites consult the local or state health department or the Environmental Protection Agency. The criteria are designed to minimize danger and injury to the occupants, damage to the building, and to provide a reasonable time for persons to flee from the heat caused by explosions or fire.

Possible Mitigation Measures

1. Barriers, building setbacks, and other special measures in design and materials in building construction can reduce damage and provide some protection.

Public Transportation

Housing sites for the elderly should have reliable, accessible, regular, barrier-free, and affordable public transportation. Accessible means nearby (preferably within a block) with sheltered waiting areas and barrier-free walkways.

Mobility is critical to the physical, social and psychological well-being of all people. Transportation facilitates social contacts and independent living by allowing the elderly to do their own shopping, make trips to doctors' offices, hospitals, community service agencies, and cultural and recreational facilities. Without good public transportation, the elderly may be isolated from needed services and social contacts. In fact, adequate affordable transportation has been listed as one of the three most serious problems of the elderly in various studies (Carp, 1979).

Possible Mitigation Measures

1. Negotiate with local transit authorities to provide convenient bus stops and shelters equipped with benches with backs, vehicles that can handle wheelchairs, and convenient scheduling.
2. Some services, such as convenience store, bank, stamp machine, drug store, and cleaners, can be provided on-site. Space can be available for lease by service providers, such as doctors or beauty parlors, or for residents to use in organizing cooperative services. Some transportation services are still necessary; otherwise the elderly will be limited to a few, possibly expensive, services and will be isolated from the larger community.
3. Arrange for special transportation services from local government or community agencies. Or provide special transportation services through purchase of a small bus or van. Such purchases can be included in the development cost or may be obtained from the locality or other funding sources. If the development is too small to justify such a purchase, pool resources with another development or a community service agency. The extent and frequency of service needed will depend upon the extent of services on-site or within walking distance and upon other available transportation.
4. Encourage the development of shared transportation arrangements among tenants, so that the few who drive can assist those who do not.

Personal Transportation

Housing location and design should assure safe access for the elderly to their homes and nearby facilities. Sidewalks should be well lighted, kept free of ice and snow, and in good repair without settling or other irregularities. Streets should have crosswalks, barrier-free curb cuts (although poorly designed curb cuts can be dangerous to blind persons), stop signs, and traffic lights geared to the time needed for the elderly to cross without hurrying. Traffic lights should have sound devices. In some cases bilingual signs will be needed.

Such precautions are important because a person over sixty-five years old is much more likely to have a pedestrian accident than a younger adult (Carp, 1979). The elderly's ability to cross streets safely is lessened by their reduced vision, hearing impairments, slower reaction times, and slower movements. Even minor accidents or falls can be disastrous for the elderly because their brittle bones break more easily than those of a younger person and they recover more slowly and less completely. A broken hip can result in permanent pain and loss of mobility. In addition, walking can provide good, safe exercise and recreation, and the elderly, like everyone else, need exercise for good health.

Possible Mitigation Measures

1. Obviously providing sidewalks, lighting, curb cuts, markings, and stop signs as described above is essential. Local traffic engineers can assist with the installation and appropriate timing of traffic lights and signs around the

housing and on the routes to nearby facilities. Sidewalks should be located where they will receive maximum sun in winter to reduce snow removal problems or located in maximum shade in hot climates.

2. Use appropriate site planning to separate vehicular/pedestrian routes.
3. Provide transportation for the elderly to shopping and other facilities and provide on-site space for walking for exercise.
4. Provide convenient, well-lighted, patrolled or otherwise secure parking for those elderly who do drive.
5. Do not use prefabricated concrete or wood wheel stops (wheel blocks) in parking areas or as pavement edging because of danger of trips and falls.
6. Provide convenient, well-lighted places with waiting benches for picking up and dropping off residents obtaining rides from others.

On-Site: Slope

The parts of the site to be used for entrances, walkways, or recreation should not have more than a 5 percent grade. Up to 20 percent of older persons are handicapped in their ability to move about freely (U.S. Public Health Service, 1979), and it is difficult or impossible for them to walk up steep grades. Although many residents will be among the younger and more mobile elderly population, they will age and their ability to climb grades will gradually decrease. Up to 80 percent of people in their seventies suffer from arthritis or rheumatism (Hendricks and Hendricks, 1977). Even elderly without mobility problems will have difficulties on slopes in bad weather, both winter and summer. Finally, slopes of drastic nature make using wheelchairs, walkers and other ambulation aids difficult and hazardous.

Possible Mitigation Measures

1. Provide resting areas with benches, ramps and handrails, and stairways with small elevations between steps.

2. The site should be designed so that any unavoidable steep slope on the walkway will be for only a short distance.

Community Services

Since the elderly differ in terms of the facilities and services used and frequency of their use, no list of desired services can be applied rigidly. However, residents must be able to buy food and medicine, cash checks (sometimes done by grocery stores), and perform other everyday chores. Medical, religious, and cultural activities may also be important, but they tend to be less frequently used. Housing should also provide varied opportunities, both on- and off-site, for residents to enjoy leisure activities with others and should include opportunities for physical exercise and mental stimulation necessary for proper health. At least some on-site facilities must be provided. Outdoor space is needed for fresh air, exercise, a chance to sit in the sun and enjoy nature, and simply for a change of scenery from a small apartment. Indoor space is needed for resident meetings, parties, and such activities as doing crafts, playing cards and pool, and dancing. Chapters 12 and 13 discuss service use more fully.

Social contact and interaction is greatly increased through community services. Independent living and the normal life functions do not cease with age; the elderly continue to shop, engage in recreation, use banks, post offices, and libraries (Regnier, Murakami, and Gordon, 1979; Regnier and Rausch, 1980). For many elderly the principal modes of travel are walking and public transportation. Consequently, proximity to services is important. Relatively independent elderly are able to walk fifteen to twenty minutes nonstop, and many can walk about one-half mile without undue fatigue. Thus, most would be able to walk to and from facilities located one-quarter of a mile away (Lawton, 1973). The accesibility of facilities depends not only upon the distance to be walked but also such factors as weather, slopes, and resting places.

Leisure activities of the elderly, as for everyone else, vary widely, so a variety of choices will be needed to ensure that all residents have an opportunity to do something they like. Some desirable types of opportunities based on surveys of what elderly people do include: having places to walk, to observe nature—especially birds, to fish, picnic, garden, visit senior centers, and attend sports events (Heritage, 1979). Nearby facilities are needed because the elderly, like everyone else, spend most of their leisure time around their own home. They are far more likely to enjoy a garden outside their door than one in a community park several blocks away.

Possible Mitigation Measures

1. Assure that the housing site is within a safe, negotiable walking distance to critical neighborhood facilities and services.
2. Provide tailor-made routes and transportation services to critical neighborhood facilities and services.
3. Provide, or arrange with others to provide, certain facilities on-site, such as a convenience store, hairdresser, or check-cashing service. In some cases this may mean providing space at low or no cost.
4. Provide additional on-site community space to accommodate indoor recreation and outside activities such as walking, gardening, and observing nature.
5. Establish a working relationship with a social agency or volunteer group to offer transportation (escort/friendly companion services for particular tenants with particular needs) to get to facilities that are neither local nor available by the other measures listed above.
6. Encourage local merchants to provide delivery services.
7. Use a combination of the above. The diversity of the elderly population and their increased physical limitations that accompany the aging process may require a plan that combines several means of assuring access to the various services; that is, walking to nearby facilities,

scheduled transportation, or special arrangements for more distant facilities.

Emergency Health Services

Housing for the elderly should be located where the response time of an emergency treatment vehicle with advanced life support service is not more than three to five minutes away, even in heavy traffic conditions. This service can be provided through the local police or fire services, rescue squads, hospital emergency rooms, and private ambulance services. The trip to a hospital for follow-up treatment should be no more than fifteen minutes.

Elderly persons are particularly subject to health problems, such as heart attacks and strokes, that cause them to stop breathing. Appropriate emergency medical treatment must be given quickly, as irreversible brain damage can occur after the brain has been deprived of oxygen for approximately four minutes.

Possible Mitigation Measures

1. Inform the local providers of emergency health care of the location of the housing project. Negotiate whatever adjustments, such as those suggested below, that are necessary to provide adequate service to the site.
2. Provide a "direct line" emergency signal system in residents' apartments or hallways. It will "flag" the manager's office or the local emergency services—police, fire, or ambulance.
3. Insure that staff or physically capable residents are trained to provide cardiac pulmonary resuscitation (CPR) and are available on a twenty-four-hour basis. Oxygen should be on-site with trained people to administer it.
4. Provide a list of emergency telephone numbers, establish a regular emergency procedure, and where possible, coordinate this procedure with the local police and fire departments and others providing emergency health care. Emergency medical information on each tenant, such as allergies and life-sustaining medication, should be available.

Personal and Residential Security

Ideally housing for the elderly should be located in low-crime areas. However, virtually no areas, whether in central cities or suburbs, are absolutely crime free.

The elderly are particularly vulnerable to street crimes because they are perceived by offenders as an easy target. Many walk or take public transportation and thus are more exposed than the person who drives from place to place and parks in his own driveway. Moreover, even though older people are statistically not victimized as often as younger persons, they are more likely to be seriously hurt (Smith, 1979). Even being pushed to the ground can result in serious harm because an older person's bones are brittle, break easily, and mend more slowly, with a greater chance of lingering pain or impairment than those of a younger person. And, since many elderly have limited money, losing it if robbed means they cannot buy proper food or medicine. Finally, fear of crime inhibits movement. Many elderly report that they do not go out at night, or even during the day, because of fear of crime. This prevents them from enjoying social activities and exercise (Smith, 1979; Lester, 1981). Among central-city residents who wanted to move because of inadequate neighborhood services, inadequate police and fire protection were cited frequently as reasons for wanting to move (Gutowski and Feild, 1979).

Possible Mitigation Measures

1. Design the site to ensure real and perceived security by applying principles such as those described in Oscar Newman's *Defensible Space* (1972). Provide good lighting for the entire site. Provide such security equipment as one-way doors, television monitoring, and buzzer arrangements for entrances.
2. Negotiate with the police for regular surveillance and for periodic visits with tenants to discuss how to improve and increase personal safety and security.
3. Negotiate with the transportation company to place a bus stop immediately in front of the entrance.
4. Install a security monitoring system and such other safety measures as dead-bolt locks and peepholes.
5. Locate parking in well-lighted, observable areas in close proximity to buildings.
6. Hire security guards or ask tenants to provide twenty-four-hour desk coverage.
7. Limit the number of entrances to the building: one main entrance, with all other entrances locked from the interior. If necessary, the main entrance should be locked twenty-four hours a day. Residents should have a key or card to enter. Visitors should use a phone or an intercom system. Explicit instructions concerning the security system should be posted in bold, easy-to-read print (signs should be bilingual, if appropriate).
8. Arrange for a course of self-protection and individual crime prevention measures.

Police and Fire Services

Housing for the elderly should be located in areas that meet the national and local standards for police and fire protection services. Response time should be rapid and location of hydrants and water pressure should have the capacity to serve the building.

Elderly housing developments should be a part of the community, thereby receiving all and any public safety services normally made available to the entire community. However, the age-related physical changes that increase the probability and frequency of serious medical emergencies (such as heart attack, blackouts, and falls) and the elderly's fear of crime and their vulnerability to it indicate that special attention should be given to providing emergency and regular police service to elderly housing sites and their residents. Moreover, the elderly have a high death rate from burns (Haddon and Baker, 1981). Some of the tactile limitations experienced by the aged (Pastalan, 1979) decrease their ability to safely handle stoves, cigarettes, and electrical equipment. In case of fires, the elderly also are more vulnerable since their ability to escape may be restricted by slow movement, deafness, and other physical limitations.

Some, for whom English is a second language, may revert to their native language when panicked. This hinders their ability to read signs or follow directions quickly in an emergency.

Finally, the elderly are uniformly concerned about security, and fear of crime, whether realistic or not, can significantly alter behavior.

Possible Mitigation Measures

1. During planning and construction stages, contact police and fire departments for safety suggestions.
2. Provide automatic telephone dialers or direct lines to local police and fire stations.
3. Design the site to ensure easy, safe access for emergency vehicles, especially taking into consideration the differences in the space requirements of the various vehicles. For example, a fire truck needs considerably more space to negotiate turns than a squad car or ambulance.
4. Install emergency equipment that will take into consideration the users. The elderly usually experience a loss in sensory perceptions; consequently the type of smoke detector being considered may need a large flashing light as well as an alarm. All emergency equipment should be inspected and tested at regular intervals.
5. Provide an emergency response system that can be activated from each unit; systems can be tied directly to local police and fire departments.
6. For fire emergencies, have the fire department and residents periodically conduct fire drills.
7. Arrange with authorities for routine police patrols.
8. Pay particular attention to the legibility and placement of signs and directions relating to

safety measures. Whenever possible provide both visual and auditory signals. If appropriate, provide bilingual signs.
9. Arrange for police community instruction or seminars to encourage residents to protect themselves and each other.

References

Allan, C., and H. Brotman. 1981. *Chartbook on Aging in America.* Washington, DC: White House Conference on Aging.

Bourestom, N., and L. Pastalan. 1981. "The Effects of Relocation on the Elderly: A Reply to Borup, J. H., Gallego, D. T., and Heffernan, P. G." *Gerontologist* 21, No. 1:4–7.

Carp, F. M. 1979. "Improving the Functional Quality of Housing and Environments for the Elderly Through Transportation." In *Environmental Context of Aging: Life-Styles, Environmental Quality, and Living Arrangements.* Ed. T. O. Byerts, S. C. Howell, and L. A. Pastalan. New York: Garland.

Dannenberg, G., G. O. Gioglio, and E. Fuccello. 1979. "The Utilization of the Elderly in Child Welfare Services." Paper presented at the 32nd Annual Scientific Meeting of the Gerontological Society, Washington, DC.

Environmental Protection Agency (EPA). 1978. *Noise: A Health Problem.* Washington, DC: Environmental Protection Agency, Office of Noise Abatement and Control.

Gutowski, M., and T. Feild. 1979. *The Graying of Suburbia.* Washington, DC: Urban Institute.

Haddon, W., and S. P. Baker. 1981. "Injury Control." In *Preventive Medicine.* Ed. D. Clark and B. MacMahon. Boston: Little, Brown.

Harris, L. 1976. *The Myth and Reality of Aging in America.* Washington, DC: National Council on the Aging.

Hendricks, J., and C. D. Hendricks. 1977. *Aging in Mass Society: Myths and Realities.* Cambridge, MA: Winthrop.

Heritage Conservation and Recreation Service. 1979. *The Third Nationwide Outdoor Recreation Plan: Appendix II, Survey Technical Report 3.* Washington, DC: U.S. Department of the Interior.

Howell, S. C. 1980. *Designing for Aging: Patterns of Use.* Cambridge, MA: MIT.

Lawton, M. P., and T. O. Byerts. 1973. *Community Planning for the Elderly.* Washington, DC: U.S. Department of Housing and Urban Development.

Lester, D. 1981. *The Elderly Victim of Crime.* Springfield, IL: Charles C. Thomas.

Lopata, H. Z. 1979. *Women as Widows: Support Systems.* New York: Elsevier.

Newman, O. 1972. *Defensible Space.* New York: Macmillan.

Pastalan, L. A. 1979. "Sensory Changes and Environmental Behavior." In *Environmental Context of Aging: Life-Styles, Environmental Quality, and Living Arrangements.* Ed. T. O. Byerts, S. C. Howell, and L. A. Pastalan. New York: Garland.

Regnier, V., E. Murakami, and S. Gordon. 1979. "The Relationship of Goods and Services Retrieval Patterns to the Perceived Neighborhood Context of Four Los Angeles Communities." Paper presented at the 7th National Transportation Conference of Elderly-Handicapped, Orlando, FL.

Regnier, V., and K. Rausch. 1980. "Spatial and Temporal Neighborhood Use Patterns of Older Low-Income Central City Dwellers." Paper presented at the Environmental Design Research Association Annual Meeting, Charleston, SC.

Smith, R. 1979. *Crime Against the Elderly: Implications for Policy-Makers and Practitioners.* Washington, DC: International Federation on Aging.

Struyk, R. J., and J. P. Zais. 1982. *Providing Special Dwelling Features for the Elderly with Health and Mobility Problems.* Washington, DC: Urban Institute.

Thuillier, R. H. 1978. *Air Quality Considerations in Residential Planning.* Volumes 1 and 2. Washington, DC: U.S. Government Printing Office.

U.S. Public Health Service. 1979. Office of the Surgeon General. *Healthy People: Surgeon General's Report on Health Promotion and Disease Prevention.* Washington, DC: U.S. Department of Health, Education and Welfare.

U.S. Senate, 1984. Special Committee on Aging. *Section 202 Housing for the Elderly and Handicapped: A National Survey.* Washington, DC: U.S. Government Printing Office.

Zeisel, J., G. Epp, and S. Demos. 1977. *Low Rise Housing for Older People: Behavioral Criteria for Design.* Washington, DC: U.S. Department of Housing and Urban Development.

PART IV

HOUSING ALTERNATIVES AND OPPORTUNITIES

CHAPTER 18   Housing and Shelter for Frail and Nonfrail Elders: Current Options and Future Directions

Joel P. Weeden • Robert J. Newcomer • Thomas O. Byerts

Throughout the earlier sections of this book, the needs, preferences, satisfactions, and benefits associated with a rather wide range of housing alternatives are presented. A common theme is the importance of recognizing the implicit ongoing matching process between the capability of the residents and the demands of the housing environment. A second theme is the fragmented, static approach of public policy to the dynamic nature of the older person-environment fit. The programs historically produced by public policy work best when applied to specific targeted groups: those capable of living independently, those needing short-term, in-home assistance, and those in institutions. These programs have worked much less effectively for people in transition from one level of capability to another.

Within part 4, attention shifts to the various public and private approaches emerging to respond to service needs and income maintenance problems not adequately resolved by formal national housing policy. Some of these approaches—such as residential care, single-room-occupancy hotels, mobile homes, adult foster care, and continuing-care retirement communities—have been available for some time. Others—such as home equity conversion, accessory apartments, and homesharing—are either relatively new or have had such limited application that little is known about their feasibility and widespread utility.

This chapter briefly introduces each of these housing alternatives. Particular attention is given to those alternatives for which there is less extensive evaluative background. This is done to highlight both their potential strengths and limitations. Single-room-occupancy hotels, rooming houses, continuing-care retirement communities, and mobile homes, which have a reasonably well-developed evaluative literature, are also more fully discussed elsewhere in part 4.

Income Assistance Programs and Other Low-Cost Alternatives

Traditionally, publicly assisted housing programs have tended toward financial assistance to independent households. For the elderly this has taken the form of rental assistance programs (see chapters 1 and 6), property tax relief, and home-repair loans and grants. The private sector has tended to respond to low-cost housing needs by emphasizing the adaptation of existing housing stock. Among these adaptations are accessibility modifications, accessory apartments and ECHO (Elder Cottage Housing Opportunities) housing conversions, homesharing arrangements, and home equity conversion plans. Each of these topics is covered here.

Another approach taken by the housing industry has been to develop low-cost housing using modular construction, prefabrication, and other material- and labor-saving devices. Such technologies are more fully discussed elsewhere, but one dimension of this issue is examined by Haley in chapter 22. She examines the viability of mobile homes in meeting housing needs of low- and moderate-income elderly. Her chapter provides an extensive treatment of the demographic, design, and planning perspectives of mobile homes and also voices concerns about access to services, financing, safety, and mobile home park policy. She concludes that without considerable subsidy, the mobile home market cannot respond adequately to the housing needs of the poor and, often, minority elderly. Nevertheless, she shows that the market for and acceptance of mobile home living by the middle-class elderly population continues to grow as homeowner equity is converted to retirement housing.

Property Tax Relief

Property tax relief is largely provided by state rather than federal government. In many cases this relief may apply to renters as well as homeowners by imputing the percentage of an individual's rent payments going for property tax. Benefits usually take the form of a credit on state personal income taxes, or a lien against the property to be collected when the property is sold. Elderly homeowners are also able to claim property tax and mortgage interest deductions on their federal and state income taxes, although roughly only 15 percent of all elderly homeowners filed itemized returns in 1979 (Newman, Zais, and Struyk, 1984).

Home Repair

The primary orientation of existing home-repair programs is weatherization and structural maintenance. The major federal programs benefiting the elderly are the Farmers Home Administration (FMHA) Section 504 Program and Community Development Block Grants. Both provide low-interest loans or grants. Elderly homeowners constitute about 60 percent of the households receiving funds under the Section 504 program (Cohen, 1983). In fiscal year 1983, 3,845 grants were made

at a cost of $12.5 million. Approximately $3.5 billion is available nationally for all aspects of the Community Development Block Grant program. Data are not available on the proportion of these funds going to home repair for elderly households. Nor are data available on the number of persons (low-income or not) who would be interested in loans or grants for structural repairs on their homes (U.S. Senate, 1984).

Accessibility Modifications

An area largely overlooked by home-repair programs is the need for renovation or other modifications to make the living unit more usable by residents whose functional capabilities have changed. Existing housing repair programs could be expanded to finance these adaptations. Structural changes that meet the special needs of impaired elders include installing a stair lift or ramp, modifying appliance and electrical controls for easier manipulation, and widening doorways. Comprehensive data on the number of persons who could benefit from or would be interested in such programs are not available. However, Newman (1985), using data from the 1978 *Annual Housing Survey*, has found that roughly 13 percent of the elderly population has at least one mobility limitation that may necessitate potential demand for in-home services. Among this subgroup of elderly about 17 percent live in dwelling units that fail the Department of Housing and Urban Development's test for physically adequate housing (by having, for example, incomplete kitchens, unusable kitchen facilities, or incomplete plumbing facilities). In spite of this apparent potential demand, the utility of living unit modification programs has not been tested for success in improving the appropriateness of a dependent person's housing environment and delaying the need for a more dependent setting.

Accessory Apartments and ECHO Housing

Accessory apartments and ECHO housing present two living unit modifications that can allow frail elders and others to live in a neighborhood setting close to family care-givers. An accessory apartment is usually installed in surplus or converted space (a basement or garage) in a single-family home. An ECHO house, also known as a "granny flat," is a separate, movable, small unit usually installed in the side or rear yard of a single-family home. Both options permit two households to live close enough to each other to exchange services and still maintain privacy. These living arrangements claim to maximize the potential of informal network support and make detection of health problems easier (Hare, 1983).

The cost of building an accessory apartment or ECHO housing unit is far less than the cost of other forms of planned housing for the elderly. Accessory apartments, along with ECHO housing, typically cost from $10,000 to $20,000 depending on their size, quality of construction, and location (Hare, 1984). Both options appear to be relatively untapped housing resources, but there are no national data available on the number of such units or of their benefits or abuses. Zoning regulations in many communities prohibit the development of these units within single-family neighborhoods, because of the assumption that they will adversely affect property values, overload street parking capacity, and overcrowd housing. These assumptions apply more to potential nonelderly users of these conversions than to the elderly themselves. Enforcement of conversions restricted to use by the elderly or disabled is likely to be a major local problem.

In communities that have made zoning changes to permit the use of accessory apartments or ECHO housing, there has been a surprising lack of interest on the part of homeowners. Explanations include public unfamiliarity with the concept and an unknown demand for this type of housing at any time period (Hare, 1985). Land use regulation as applied to various elderly housing issues is given a much fuller discussion by Hopperton in chapter 23. He describes the impact on the elderly made by various kinds of land use regulations. Specific references are made to both positive and negative aspects of a variety of zoning

approaches. Examples are drawn from selected judicial and legislative case studies focusing on age-neutral zoning, age-restrictive zoning favorable to the elderly, and zoning unfavorable to the elderly. Hopperton argues that most senior citizens have benefited greatly from the majority of zoning practices. However, he notes that efforts at community change have been slowed in many localities as poorly informed citizen groups and authorities use zoning to oppose many of the housing alternatives discussed elsewhere in this book. Hopperton, nevertheless, documents the legal viability of zoning practices that could enhance the feasibility of these various housing types.

Homesharing Arrangements

A shared household, in this context, is usually defined as a living unit, housing at least two unrelated people, and in which common living spaces are shared (Dobkin, 1983). Agencies in many communities have taken on the responsibility of pairing potential home-sharers with home-seekers. Although this arrangement has been utilized primarily by independent elderly homeowners who are seeking to augment their incomes, some arrangements have been made that involve an exchange of chore services needed by frail elders. Service arrangements with younger home-seekers include cooking, housework, gardening, or companionship in exchange for room and board or some financial consideration such as rent reduction.

The strength and durability of the market demand for the home-seeker either living in the elder's home, or the elder's willingness to have a nonrelative move in, is not really known, but it is thought to be limited. Agencies involved in facilitating homesharing arrangements usually have limited budgets for either counseling or for the solicitation of homesharers. In spite of this, many programs claim to be unable to keep pace with the potential demand by homeowners wanting assistance in the home, especially those elders who are "house rich and cash poor." The amount of funding for these services nationally is not known.

Most programs are privately funded; a few receive state or federal Community Development Block Grant monies.

Home Equity Conversions

A dominant characteristic of the elderly homeowner population is that they own their homes without any mortgage. For the majority of these homeowners, the equity they have accumulated in their homes represents their single largest asset. There are two different ways to utilize the equity in one's home: older homeowners may sell the property outright, or they may convert their equity to cash without having to leave their dwellings. The need to pay for in-home care has become a primary reason to seek a home equity conversion plan (Belling, Kenny, and Scholen, 1985).

Home equity conversion plans are essentially variations of three familiar financial transactions: loans, sales, and deferred payments. Reverse mortgage loan plans differ from conventional loans because they do not require the older person to repay any principal or interest for many years, or in some versions, for the rest of the individual's life. The sales plans, unlike conventional sales, allow the elder to remain in the home and retain occupancy rights as long as they live. Deferred payment plans enable the elder to use housing equity for home improvements, tax deferrals, and other purposes (Scholen, 1984).

A great deal of attention is being given to the various home equity conversion plans. Private sector participation has expanded as a result of a newly created market. Unfortunately, there has probably been an overestimation of the number of people who could substantially benefit from these programs. Careful analyses have shown that only about 20 percent of elderly homeowners could obtain as much as $2,500 per year in extra income from a standard home equity conversion plan (Struyk, 1985). A smaller percentage of homeowners appear to be willing to participate. To be widely successful, it is likely that a variety of options will have to be available to meet a range of needs.

Supportive Housing Options

A number of supportive housing alternatives have been available for decades within the private housing market. Interest in housing for the semi-dependent elderly has increased in recent years due to a number of factors. Paramount among them is the growing number of people over the age of seventy-five and their proportionately higher likelihood of need and interest in supportive living arrangements. Favorable tax provisions encouraging construction is another factor. Public policy interest is also influenced by the expectation that these forms of housing may offer a relatively low-cost approach to long-term care. Within this section several approaches to meeting the supportive housing needs are briefly discussed. Several of these topics are given much fuller treatment elsewhere in part 4.

Life-Care Retirement Communities

Life care is an option for financially secure elders who are interested in a living arrangement that provides a full range of accommodations, including congregate housing, personal care, and nursing facilities. Residents generally move from one level to another as their needs change. Historically, life-care retirement communities have used basically a prepaid long-term-care insurance plan to help capitalize this full range of housing options. More recently developed plans are electing to use a fee-for-service arrangement to finance the health service components. In chapter 24, Powell and MacMurtrie review current knowledge about this type of housing and discuss in some detail the viability of developing an acturially sound fee structure for these facilities.

Board-and-Care Facilities

Board-and-care facilities have existed for many years to provide food, shelter, and some degree of protection for chronically impaired, semidependent and dependent elderly. Terms used to describe board-and-care housing include boarding homes; residential-care facilities; and community, personal, and domiciliary-care homes.

The board-and-care arrangements of low-income individuals are often financed by the federal income maintenance programs (such as SSI) or state supplemental payments (SSP). In chapter 20, Stone and Newcomer examine recent trends in the development of board-and-care housing and describe the regulatory structure affecting this industry. Special attention is given to the innovations taking place as state governments attempt to resolve the dilemma of upgrading the quality of these facilities without regulating them out of operation.

Adult Foster Care

Another form of residential care is foster care. This type of living arrangement serves people who are unable to continue independent functioning in their own homes and who need and desire the support and security of family living. The provider, supervised by a sponsoring agency such as a local department of social services, is responsible for providing the client with housing, meals, and custodial care as needed. In most states these homes are legally defined as having no more than three or four nonrelated paying residents. Due to the small number of residents, the private home facility, and its family characteristics, this housing generally conforms to community zoning regulations. Adult foster care programs exist in twenty-nine states plus the District of Columbia and Puerto Rico (Bogen, 1979).

The biggest barrier to further development of this housing is the expectation that the compensation received by providers is unlikely to keep pace with other employment opportunities (Brockett, 1984).

Small Group Residences

The small group residence is known by as many different names as there are programs. Labels include share-a-home, small congregate home, cooperative house, community housing, and shared elder house. Living arrangements vary from private bedrooms with all other facilities shared to efficiency apartments and a shared living room. A nonprofit agency usually sponsors the shared living residence in existing or newly built housing. Sponsor arrangements may include the provision of shopping and cooking, maintenance and housekeeping, and access to medical and social services. Residents are provided opportunities for social contacts and services in an environment that is more involvement-oriented than protective.

The interest of the Department of Housing and Urban Development in this concept has to date been limited to the chronically mentally ill. Approximately 2,000 newly constructed or rehabilitated units have been financed under the Section 202 and similar programs. Small, scattered site projects, such as group homes for twelve or fewer chronically mentally ill individuals or independent living complexes of six to ten apartment units for no more than twenty individuals have been the norm (U.S. Office of Management and Budget, 1983). Within the private sector there have been few notable uses of this housing model for the elderly. Approximately seventy-five shared residences of between three to fifteen persons have been identified nationally (Day-Lower, Bryant, and Mullaney, 1982).

SRO Housing Hotels and Rooming Houses

On the opposite end of the income spectrum from life-care retirement communities are single-room-occupancy (SRO) hotels. The term is used to describe the age-mixed, commercial hotels and rooming houses serving a diverse population with low-income elderly constituting the single largest group. Approximately 400,000 elderly live on a relatively permanent basis in SROs (Haley, Pearson, and Hull, 1981).

Although SRO accommodation is an important component of the housing stock in many communities (for example, in San Francisco such housing accounts for about 25 percent of all low-income rental housing), these units frequently stand in disrepair. Only a few communities have taken steps to maintain this housing stock, usually depending on federal rehabilitation funds or private syndication sources. In general, this housing stock is disappearing rapidly as buildings are either torn down or rehabilitated and converted to other uses.

In chapter 19, Ehrlich discusses the types of residents typically occupying SROs, rooming houses, and other low-income supportive housing, and the effect these facilities have on residents' quality of life. She also calls attention to the public policy and private sector initiatives needed to facilitate the maintenance of these approaches.

Counseling Component

Regardless of the form and financing structure available for housing arrangements and services, there is an apparent need for housing counseling programs. Many communities have housing referral offices. These agencies maintain records of available rental housing. Other needed counseling includes assessments of an individual's ability to perform the activities of daily living, the impact of the living environment on these activities, and the amount of such support already being provided by family and friends (the informal network) to assist the individual. Case management and hospital discharge-planning programs provide some of these functions in their attempt to meet supportive service needs. Neither housing referral programs nor case management has given much attention to living unit modifications or temporary placement in semidependent living arrangements.

Emergency Shelter and Transition Housing

This housing is intended for frail elderly and disabled older adults who are victims of a traumatic disruption in their lives. Referrals—coming from fire and police services, aging network providers with drop-in emergencies, and case management workers whose clients unexpectedly agree to leave a traumatic situation—include:

- Elder abuse—any elder receiving physical abuse, fiduciary abuse, custodian neglect, custodian abandonment, or psychological abuse
- Homeless—any frail elder or disabled older adult facing a forced-to-move situation because of eviction, housing market change (rent increase, sale of property, lock-out, or conversion), or functional level change that results in the current living arrangement no longer being accessible
- Emergency respite—individuals who are temporarily homeless such as frail elders or disabled older adults found wandering the streets not knowing where they live, and individuals under custodial care whose custodian, as a result of an emergency, is unable to provide care for a period of time

Existing emergency shelters provide nightly shelter and food. They have been developed largely to respond to the needs of the chronically homeless adult and the adult abuser of alcohol or drugs. Much less attention has been given to the shelter and counseling of others requiring emergency respite or transition housing.

Current planners see this housing as parallel to women's abuse centers. The emergency respite shelters and transitional housing tend to be small-scale programs situated within a communal and therapeutic environment. Staff are sensitized and trained to respond to the specific needs related to the frail elder or older impaired adult. Live-in staff provide ongoing counseling and maintain a secure, stable environment. Staff, in cooperation with the ongoing formal and informal supports, counsel those individuals needing to evaluate new housing options. Current settings for these programs include a floor of a residential hotel and the upstairs of a senior center (Elston and Slavin, 1985). With so few programs available, the impact and demand for this service is not known.

Conclusion

Judged from the vantage point of the historical federal policy responses to the continuum of housing needs among the elderly population, it appears that the housing market is becoming increasingly more responsive to needs across a full spectrum of capability.

Less encouraging is that this "market response" to the housing continuum continues to be highly fragmented. Each approach is motivated by different economic forces. For example, life-care retirement communities are responsive both to higher affluence among the elderly and to tax incentives. Board-and-care housing supply is apparently most affected by income maintenance programs. SROs and rooming houses, on the other hand, seemingly exist because of the absence of other market forces competing against the current residents. Many of the other approaches, such as homesharing and home equity conversions, reflect individual attempts to accommodate income or support service needs.

Is this piecemeal and fragmented approach to housing a problem? The answer is somewhat ambivalent. The approach has, after all, allowed innovation; and people are benefiting from the programs in place. On the other hand, there is also inefficiency and a time lag inherent in the current process. For example, much more needs to be learned about interest and demand across a range of communities, income levels, and racial makeups for the various private sector housing approaches. Such experience and knowledge may not be gained quickly if reliance is placed only on "naturally" occurring innovations.

In chapter 21, Gollub and Chmura outline one strategy for stimulating local initiatives. They discuss both some innovations they have observed across the country and a community organization process that has helped bring local government officials, community groups and private entrepreneurs together to expand housing alternatives for the elderly.

Even with the presence of these local innovations, it is still likely that public financing, particularly in the supportive housing arena, will be needed to expand the development and diffusion of housing options across all income groups.

Tax incentives, public bond issues, and mort-

gage insurance are presently the most common approaches used to encourage private investment. These strategies however mostly affect the supply of units. Health or other insurance with benefits that could help finance some of the care received in facilities or in one's own home is an emerging approach that affects the demand for services.

Is it asking too much to have public policy pursue complementary strategies in fostering both the supply and demand for housing services? We do not think so. This book, by synthesizing current knowledge about the housing continuum, tries to identify the needed and likely directions of further innovation and exploration, in order to better coordinate efforts to house an aging society.

Note

1. HUD recently issued a new regulation permitting FHA mortgage insurance for retirement service centers under the Section 221(d) (4) program. The department has received an increasing number of requests from prospective developers for a mortgage insurance program that covers the gap between the totally independent living arrangement of noncongregate housing for the elderly and the health-care-oriented nursing home. Facilities under this new program would be limited to market rate elderly tenants.

References

Belling, B., K. Kenny, and K. Scholen. 1985. "Home Equity Conversion for the 'House Rich, Cash Poor.' " *Generations* 9, No. 3:20–21.

Bogen, H. 1979. "The History of Adult Foster Care." In *Readings in Adult Foster Care.* Ed. K. Nash and D. Tesiny. Albany: Continuing Education Project, State University of New York.

Brockett, R. G. 1984. "Issues in Promoting Adult Foster Care as an Option to Institutionalization." *Journal of Housing for the Elderly* 2, No. 1:51–63.

Cohen, J. 1983. "Public Program Financing Long-Term Care." Interim report prepared for the National Governor's Association. Revised edition. Washington, DC: Urban Institute.

Day-Lower, D., D. Bryant, and J. Mullaney. 1982. *National Policy Workshop on Shared Housing: Findings and Recommendations.* Philadelphia: Shared Housing Resources Center.

Dobkin, L. 1983. *Shared Housing for Older People.* Philadelphia: Shared Housing Resource Center.

Elston, L., and L. Slavin. 1985. "Safe Shelter for Homeless Elders." *Generations* 9, No. 3:48–49.

Haley, B. A., M. Pearson, and D. A. Hull. 1981. "Urban Elderly Residents of Single Room Occupancy Housing (SROs), 1976–1980." Paper presented at the 34th Annual Meeting of the Gerontological Society of America, Toronto, Canada.

Hare, P. 1983. "Innovative Living Arrangements and the Role of Agencies Serving the Elderly." *Human Development News,* January.

———. 1984. "ECHO Housing." In *Housing Options for Older Americans.* Ed. L. Hubbard. Washington, DC: American Association of Retired Persons.

———. 1985. "Accessory Apartments: Who Can Afford to Market the Concept?" *Generations* 9, No. 3:43–45.

Newman, S. 1985. "Housing and Long-Term Care: The Suitability of the Elderly's Housing to the Provision of In-Home Services." *Gerontologist* 25:35–40.

Newman, S. J., J. Zais, and R. Struyk. 1984. "Housing Older America." In *Elderly People and the Environment.* Ed. I. Altman, M. P. Lawton, and J. F. Wohlwill. New York: Plenum.

Scholen, K. 1984. "Home Equity Conversion." In *Housing Options for Older Americans.* Ed. L. Hubbard. Washington, DC: American Association of Retired Persons.

Struyk, R. J. 1985. "The Big Housing Picture." *Generations* 9, No. 3:18–21.

U.S. Office of Management and Budget (OMB). 1983. *Catalog of Federal Domestic Assistance.* Washington, DC: U.S. Government Printing Office.

U.S. Senate. 1984. Special Committee on Aging. *Developments in Aging: 1983.* Volume 1. Washington, DC: U.S. Government Printing Office.

CHAPTER 19 Hotels, Rooming Houses, Shared Housing, and Other Housing Options for the Marginal Elderly

Phyllis Ehrlich

Adequate housing to meet the idiosyncratic needs of an aged and aging population is a goal still out of reach. Demographers are projecting both a growing and more long-lived elderly population, implying an increase in population heterogeneity that, in turn, should be reflected in more flexible housing characteristics. It has been suggested that social planners should avoid monolithic solutions that would eliminate options for the healthy exercise of individual choice (I. Ehrlich, 1976).

The investigation of optimal environments has received much attention in recent social gerontological research. From a theoretical perspective, support for housing options arranged on a continuum that recognizes modal needs of the majority as well as differing needs of selected minorities can be found in gerontological literature. Both Kahana's (1975) multidimensional "person-environment congruence" model and Lawton's (1980) "adaptation" model conceptualize the need for a goodness-of-fit between the person's characteristics and needs and the properties of the environment. Carp's (1968) studies of Victoria Plaza, an early high-rise congregate housing project for the low-income elderly in San Antonio, Texas, documented that both satisfaction and adjustment depended upon congruence between person and situation mediated by individual history.

Elderly persons should be able to live according to the lifestyle that best fits their developmental needs and within the least restrictive environment. Figure 19-1 (Lawton, 1981) presents a housing continuum designed to provide varying levels of support. Mangum (1980) defines support, as "the degree to which the housing environment provides for the routine and special needs of the resident, as well as the extent to which the resident is freed of responsibility for maintaining the housing environment" (Mangum, 1980, p. 196). While figure 19-1 suggests that a wide range of housing options ordered on a continuum of support exists, in actuality, only the "least deprived" are able to take advantage of these options. As Carp (1976) has pointed out, the least deprived are frequently the most favored.

In a recent study, Turner (1982) summarized the paradox in the housing scene. He describes the elderly of today as well housed in comparison with earlier periods of U.S. history. Moreover, most seniors are in good health and live in noninstitutional housing. Nevertheless, a significant fraction of the elderly either cannot afford adequate housing or live in a residence that is inappropriate for their present needs.

This chapter addresses the issue of housing options for some of Turner's "significant fraction" who will be called here the marginal elderly. The term marginal is defined as "on the bordering edge"; the population of concern in this chapter can be described as living on the fringe of com-

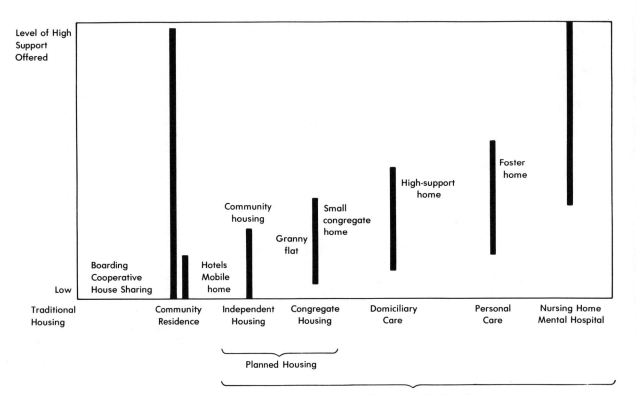

19-1. *Level of support offered by traditional housing and alternative housing.*

munity life and presenting one or more of the following characteristics: (1) poverty, (2) atypical lifestyles, (3) frailty in terms of physical or mental disorders.

Housing options that allow the marginal elderly to live in community settings include hotels, rooming houses, modular homes ("granny flats"), shared (group) housing, and foster homes. Each provides an alternative in varying degrees within the independent, self-care range and supportive range for those frail elderly wishing to avoid institutionalization. In spite of their diversity, these housing alternatives have a great deal in common. On one hand, they respond flexibly to atypical lifestyles. On the other hand, they are frequently perceived as incompatible with "social progress" expressed in terms of gentrification, zoning regulations, urban planning and redevelopment, welfare regulations, and federal low-income housing legislation.

Planners and providers must understand that the policy issues in alternative housing for marginal elderly include the provision of housing that respects lifestyle needs as well as the preservation of diverse housing stock. To realize this two-fold goal, the issue of alternative housing for the marginal elderly must stop being the social workers' problem and start becoming the social planners'.

SRO Housing—Hotels and Rooming Houses

The term *single room occupancy* has been used to describe not only the structure but also the common characteristics in lifestyle of residents of single-room accommodations. Less than ten years ago the terms *invisible, unseen,* and *hidden* were used synonymously with SRO to describe both the housing types and the resident population.

During the 1970s ethnographic studies in diverse metropolitan areas—San Diego (Eckert, 1980); St. Louis (Ehrlich, P., 1976; Ehrlich and Ehrlich, 1982); Syracuse, New York, and Charleston, West Virginia (Rubenstein, Schuster, and Desiervo, 1976); Detroit (Stephens, 1975); New York (Shapiro, 1971; Siegel, 1977), San Francisco (McKay, 1976)—have brought this housing type out of obscurity, distinguished it from "skid row" accommodations, and established it as a viable alternative for marginal segments of the elderly population.

Haley, Pearson, and Hull (1981) proposed three alternative SRO definitions based on U.S. Census Bureau housing unit criteria:

- Single-room units—renter-occupied one-room housing units in an apartment building, a rooming house, a residential hotel or a permanent unit in a transient hotel
- Partial single-room units—renter-occupied one-room housing units with no or shared access to kitchen and/or bath facilities in a rooming house or residential hotel
- Family unit—renter-occupied room in a single-family house

Recent reanalyses of national *Annual Housing Survey* data indicate that: more than 80,000 units in hotels were occupied by people sixty-five years and older in 1975 (Goode, Lawton, and Hoover, 1980); although SRO housing stock decreased by 12 percent, there were still 397,000 elderly people identified as residing in partial or single-room units in 1976 (Haley, Pearson, and Hull, 1981).

Residential hotels and smaller rooming houses vary widely according to price and conditions.

However, the early ethnographic studies (referenced above) of low-priced hotels serving poor people suggested common environmental features and services. General characteristics of SRO accommodations include:

- Furnished rooms with or without self-contained bathrooms
- Rooms usually without kitchens (may have communal kitchen or hot plate in room)
- Some management services (desk, linens, housekeeping)
- Permanent occupants (at least half the tenants)
- Commercial establishment (neither subsidized nor licensed for institutional care)
- Frequently an old or deteriorated physical facility with systems needing replacement

Usually these facilities are located in commercial areas (U.S. Senate 1978). Overall these accommodations provide a minimum of formal organization and a maximum of freedom, tolerating a broad range of behaviors.

While the demographers have described SRO residents as a heterogeneous group (Haley, Pearson, and Hull, 1981), the ethnographic studies have identified behavioral characteristics that are essential to a basic understanding of the SRO environment. However, the findings refer only to poorer elderly in low-priced urban accommodations; no case studies have been done of permanent, older residents of higher-priced hotels. Observations by this author when assisting in the relocation of elderly persons from one costly hotel also suggest similarities of residents' attitudes, behaviors, and needs (P. Ehrlich, 1976).

The ethnographic studies identified an elderly population that is primarily male, single, mobile, and nontraditional. Though minimal services are offered in these environments, an independent, self-reliant lifestyle is typical. A study of a sample of sixteen elderly SRO women in Seattle revealed a "population with work histories in trades and a lifestyle based on mobility, extreme individualism and independence" (Lally et al., 1979, p. 67).

Individualism is frequently expressed as "loner-type" behavior implying not isolation but few, if any, confidant relationships. Yet, the environment supports the development of informal support networks particularly for assistance in instrumental tasks of daily living. Cohen and Sokolovsky's (1980) analysis of the social networks has further documented the presence of such networks. Eckert (1982) identified three SRO network sectors: (1) nonkin networks in hotels; (2) nonkin networks in neighborhoods; and (3) kin networks. Many in the first two sectors are role-identified and task-related connections; kin networks, though infrequently activated, are considered affective supports. In general, Eckert found networks characterized by minimal density with a high degree of privacy and noninvolvement.

The early studies viewed the SRO as the environment of choice for many. Permanence rather than transience is suggested by two facts. First, residents whose housing was demolished tended to relocate within the area. Second, the lengths of residence indicated that many had moved in before old age. Though low income as well as lifestyle may have contributed to the choice of SRO housing, this outcome should not be construed as a preference for deteriorating housing. Eckert (1982) has documented that approximately 70 percent of elderly relocatees chose to move to similar hotels located in the downtown area.

From a social service perspective, the network intervention demonstrations of Cohen and Sokolovsky (1981) are significant. Only 19 percent of the problems of SRO residents (50 percent of whom were over age sixty) were successfully handled by project social workers using formal network interventions exclusively. Impediments to attempted network interventions appeared to include lack of trust, loner lifestyles, unwillingness to confide, absence of a network, and frequently, the immediacy of the problem. From a practice perspective this may suggest the need for neighborhood workers who are as familiar and trusted as the bartender and the desk clerk (Cohen and Sokolovsky, 1981; P. Ehrlich, 1976). It is also possible that the informal support network of this environment remains effective only if it functions independently of the formal service system.

Two recent national studies using *Annual Housing Survey* data (Goode, Lawton, and Hoover, 1980; Haley, Pearson, and Hull, 1981) provide current and comprehensive descriptions of SRO housing and its population. The findings of Goode and associates, while strongly supporting those of the above ethnographic studies, provide a new data base particularly in relation to urban-rural differences. "The socioeconomic profile of the nation's elderly hotel and rooming-house dwellers reveals that they were more likely than the community-based elderly to be never-married or widowed, living alone, over seventy-five, and living in poverty" (Goode, Lawton, and Hoover, p. 152). This study further identified an "at risk" population as living in unsound structures with undependable utilities. The low-cost housing reflected lower incomes. Of interest also is the surprisingly large female population, many of whom are still married, living in all types of SRO accommodations in rural areas. The study concluded, "At a minimum, this report has provided evidence of an extremely 'high-risk' elderly population which is easily identifiable by their type of residence" (Goode, Lawton, and Hoover, 1980, p. 155).

The national estimates of Haley and associates indicated a larger and more diverse SRO elderly population in 1976 than anticipated from the literature of the ethnographic studies (Haley, Pearson, and Hull, 1981). The heterogeneity of the population was reflected in demographic measures such as age, employment, education, and number of public assistance recipients. These findings of a more diverse population may be an outcome of Haley's three alternative definitions, which include SRO housing stock not previously examined. Nevertheless, the need for national concern is suggested by the identification of a larger, more diverse elderly population along with findings such as (a) a drop of 18 percent in SRO housing stock in standard metropolitan statistical areas (SMSAs) and 12 percent overall, (b) 397,000 elderly persons (12 percent of all older people) had chosen some form of SRO living arrangement on a permanent basis, (c) 25 percent of elderly SRO dwellers had occupied the same room for twelve or more years, (d) slightly over half (51 percent) resided in partial rooms, and of these one-third moved more frequently than elderly in other housing types (probably related to the transiency of the accommodations or to the changing functional status of these people).

The Haley study also included five urban community case studies in Massachusetts, New York, and Oregon. Their findings replicate those of the earlier ethnographic studies and attest to the value of the SRO housing type while underscoring conflicting policy issues such as zoning, gentrification, commercial encroachment, condominium conversion, greater demand for student housing, and lack of private or federal funds for renovation of this housing stock.

SRO accommodation is a viable part of community housing stock. Generally inexpensive, it is one option for the community's very poor unattached citizens including a disproportionate number of elderly residents. However, whether large hotel or small rooming house, the SRO does not constitute planned housing for the elderly in the same sense that the retirement villages or life-care centers that serve the more affluent do. Frequently SROs stand in disrepair because of the disinterest of community leaders or are torn down because they stand in the way of community change or mores. Both SRO housing and SRO tenants often appear expendable.

Testimony before the House Subcommittee on Housing and Community Development (Bryson and Werner, 1981) reported on successful steps some communities have taken to maintain this housing stock and recommended, as well as justified, changes in federal and local housing legislation. This testimony was based on the assumption that "SRO buildings can be managed and maintained well and can provide decent places to live for the people who choose them" (Bryson and Werner, 1981, p. 5). Throughout the country, in cities as diverse as Denver, San Francisco, Portland, Seattle, and Venice, CA, newly formed not-for-profit organizations, private long-term property owners, or local government agencies are successfully maintaining single-unit housing. Werner and Bryson (1982) have provided an excellent SRO "how-to" manual with descriptions of successful SRO projects as well as guidelines for (a) making SRO housing eligible for federal housing program funds; (b) affirmative SRO programs; (c) local legislative strategies to prevent conversion and demolition; and (d) litigation on behalf of SRO tenants.

> The SRO is perhaps the best of all available examples of person–environment congruence built around marginal individuals. Though the deprivation and sometimes unasked-for isolation are less than ideal, were it not for these environments, many of these elderly would be dealing with stronger press than their competence could tolerate (Lawton, 1981, p. 68).

The financially secure elderly person seeking single-room unit living will probably always be able to find such accommodations. The greater problem is to preserve this housing stock for the poor marginal elderly as well.

Modular Housing—Granny Flats

Modular, movable, unattached homes for the elderly in their own or kin's backyard (as distinguished from mobile home parks) is a concept developed in Australia (Nusberg, 1978) and only recently brought to this country. Terms such as *granny flats, elder cottage,* and *ECHO housing* (Elder Cottage Housing Opportunities) have been coined to describe this housing alternative. Such modular units of reduced living space designed to meet the elderly's physical needs provide the opportunity to live independently or semiindependently but near kin or close friends. They reduce the stress of relocation while maximizing the potential of informal network support.

From a community-planning perspective, there are many positive aspects to this housing alternative. It responds to the community's need for larger homes by putting such homes previously occupied by the elderly back on the rental or sale market. Through this change to ownership by younger people, the potential for home improvements is increased. The cost of building a modular unit is far less than the cost of other forms of planned housing for the elderly. The movability of the homes among neighborhood sites as needed provides neighborhood flexibility while recognizing the life space of and ensuring the stability of familiar surroundings for the elderly. Proximity to care-givers reduces the demand for public services.

Restrictive zoning regulations in many communities prohibit the placement of these units on the grounds of single-family homes. Neighborhood integrity could be maintained if the aesthetics of the housing were controlled and the building approved for use by elderly residents only. Though the value to individual, family, and community is clear, one must wonder whether there will be a shift in public and private attitudes toward this housing option in the future. Demonstration projects have been developed in Pennsylvania and Maryland; the American Association of Retired Persons (AARP) has commissioned a study of zoning ordinances throughout the country in a beginning effort to expand modular housing.

Shared (Group) Housing

Affordable housing for the financially marginal single person is more elusive than ever in the present housing market. If this person is also elderly with a limited informal network, the housing problem is compounded by the cost and non-availability of support services provided on a one-to-one basis and by the fear of social isolation in private home/apartment living. The Share-a-Home movement, which is attracting a great deal of attention today, grew out of these issues. A shared elder household is defined as "a facility housing at least two unrelated people, where at least one is over sixty years of age, and in which common living spaces are shared" (Day-Lower, 1981, p. 1).

There are two basic methods of developing shared housing: agencies or individuals provide a matching service and pair potential home sharers with home seekers; or a private not-for-profit agency sponsors a shared living residence in existing or newly built housing. The first type (matching or assisting home sharers/seekers) is more appropriate for those at the independen⸰ ⸰nd of the shared housing continuum; the second, sponsored housing, serves the more dependent elderly. The *Shared Housing Quarterly* (1982, p. 1) reports that "for every established shared housing project three projects are aborted." This may to some extent be a function of the newness of the concept for elderly and the lack of a central information source. The Shared Housing Resource Center in Philadelphia is a response to this need.

Shared housing increases an older person's option by establishing a cooperative extended-family type of living arrangement. In such settings active peer and/or intergenerational groups often form natural cooperatives or corporations to alleviate financial, home maintenance, and sociability problems. Agency-assisted or sponsored shared housing for the "in-between" elderly provides opportunities for social contacts and services in an environment that is more involvement oriented than protective. It is this characteristic that distinguishes shared housing for the frail elderly from boarding and foster homes, the more traditional group home settings. Furthermore, shared housing for the frail elderly is generally considered an alternative to institutionalization rather than a post-institutional placement. "Philosophically speaking the shared residence seeks to promote self-determination and independence through interdependence and complementarity with other residents" (Day-Lower, 1981, p. 2).

Streib (1978) and Streib and Hilker (1980) discuss the positive and negative aspects of this new form of housing. The benefits include coping with loneliness, maintaining the helping role, saving money through shared costs, having a greater sense of security, avoiding the stigma of institutionalization, providing an alternative to living with children, and maintaining normal neighborhood living and freedom of activities. Drawbacks include the partial loss of privacy and autonomy, the necessity for accepting some responsibility for the more handicapped in the setting, risk-taking regarding housing mates, and the uncomfortableness of change—in this case, change to a very new and unfamiliar housing concept.

Benefits and drawbacks exist from a community perspective as well. Shared housing renovation is extremely cost-effective compared to new construction; the remodeling upgrades the housing and the neighborhood and avoids the problems related to clusters of high-rise apartments for geriatrics. Though there appears today to be greater social acceptance of alternative family constellations for the elderly, federal subsidies benefit primarily the traditional household. Supplemental Security Income (SSI) and food stamp benefits are reduced for the resident of shared housing; Section 8 housing subsidies are not available at all. Moreover the Department of Housing and Urban Development's definition of a full housing unit constitutes a roadblock to successful shared housing residency.

Documentation of and research on shared housing is sparse, although descriptive case studies, particularly of agency-sponsored supportive housing, are available (Brody, 1979; Wax, 1976). These studies describe successful projects and the methods used to handle interpersonal and management problems. All recommend a modus operandi that focuses on minimal protection and maximum participation. Day-Lower (1981) outlines staffing needs for shared residences based on target population characteristics. For nonfrail households he suggests a management consultant or group facilitator as administrator. Households serving the frail should involve homemaker, nursing, and transportation services realizing the cost-effectiveness of providing support services for several people in one shared home rather than in multiple scattered units.

The most salient finding in a pilot study of twenty-one shared housing residences conducted by the Shared Housing Resource Center (*Shared Housing Quarterly*, 1982) was the wide variety of housing types than can be developed within this concept. Other observations hold that: (1) households in single-family dwellings rather than apartments appeared to have fewer problems; (2) occupants' satisfaction was expressed in terms of "caring," "dignity," "price," and "maintenance of independence"; (3) two-thirds of the households required resident activity and chore participation according to ability; (4) zoning was generally not a problem; and (5) neighborhood response was mostly "supportive" and "friendly."

The findings of the national elderly-housing study (Turner, 1982) suggest that the frail and poor appear to be less interested in house sharing than the mobile and well elderly. For the frail this resistance is attributed to fear of change, lack of familiarity with this housing form, and concern about the potential of elderly abuse in a shared residence. For the poor it is suggested that because of the inflexible housing and welfare legislation the financial risks far outweigh the benefits. Turner recommends that house sharing be pursued as a viable option for the elderly in general and that new local and federal regulations be prepared to support this concept and open up its potential to the marginal elderly as well as to the more independent and financially secure. There is much to be learned, however, about the proportion of people willing to make shared homes available or to move into such housing.

Foster Homes

A foster home is a community sheltered-housing facility providing social, psychological, and physical support services within a family context. In most states these homes are legally defined as having no more than three to four nonrelated paying residents. Foster homes provide a placement option for the physically and/or mentally frail elderly person who is frequently single, with a weak or nonexistent support system. The concept is based on the belief that (1) participation in the life of a family is superior to institutionalization (Newman and Sherman, 1979; 1980); (2) it provides opportunities to the residents for community participation; and (3) it increases the tolerance of the community for the frail elderly (Newman and Sherman, 1979). It is the orientation based on these three beliefs that distinguishes foster home programs from boarding homes and institutions. Because of the small number of residents, the private home facility, and its family characteristics, this housing alternative generally conforms to community zoning regulations.

Evaluative or case studies in this area have been sparse. The major contributions have been those of Newman and Sherman, who examined one hundred foster homes serving the elderly in the case loads of the New York State Departments of Mental Health and Social Services. In the area of "familism," it was found that family integration did occur, although more frequently between the caretaker and the residents than among residents, and that the majority of these homes could be termed "surrogate families" (Newman and Sherman, 1979; 1980). Newman and Sherman (1977) suggest that "familism" may be defined in terms of attitudes and tasks. Their sample of caretakers was predominantly female (93 percent), and only slightly more than half (58 percent) were married. The traditional family including children at home was found in only 36 percent of the homes. Thus the addition of the elderly residents definitely contributed to the concept of "family."

Community opposition to the homes was low, which is contrary to the experiences of other types of group homes serving younger mental retardees or mentally ill clients. Resident participation in the formal (senior centers) or informal (walks or visits in the neighborhood) life of the neighborhood was minimal. In light of the frailty of the residents, a reevaluation of the relevance of such activities as a goal for this population is suggested (Newman and Sherman, 1979).

Inadequate recruitment and training of caretakers was documented as was the need for ongoing professional supervision of both caretakers and residents by agency social workers. The researchers recommend that future efforts to strengthen foster-home care should focus on the interaction among case worker, caretaker, and client (Sherman and Newman, 1979). They conclude that foster-family care should be considered

a viable option for community placement of the frail elderly. Though this recommendation is frequently implemented on a case-by-case basis in local communities, Brody stresses the need for further study of basic issues such as definitions, standards, enforcement, psychosocial and environmental factors, and financial assessments, in order to ensure that "foster homes are not to become the newest inadequate institutional solution albeit masquerading under a new, palatable name" (Brody, 1977, p. 522). Of course, these same considerations also apply to shared housing.

Housing Legislation Update

Recent developments suggest that the prospects for positive legislative changes may be more favorable today than had been anticipated by concerned researchers and practitioners a few years ago (U.S. Senate, 1978). HUD's present position was described by Abrams (1981), who stated that, with inflation making the per-unit cost of new housing too expensive, HUD "intends to emphasize rehabilitation of existing units where it is administratively feasible. We must utilize the nation's standing housing stock, upgrade it within cost limitations, and get these people into an acceptable living environment" (Abrams, 1981, p. 4). There seems, however, to be a discrepancy between the full implications of this statement and present regulations. The need for wary and educated advocates remains urgent.

In 1980 a provision of the federal housing legislation (U.S. PL 96-399) made SRO units eligible for rehabilitation loans under Section 312 (Loans to Owners of Single Family and Multifamily Properties). The Reagan administration subsequently withdrew the regulations for this statute; they have since been reinstated but the program is only minimally funded.

Until 1981 the Section 8 Rehabilitation and Rent Subsidy program was unavailable for SROs. Eligibility was based on a full housing unit including a kitchen and bathroom. The 1981 Housing and Community Development Act Amendments (U.S. PL 97-35, Section 324) were specifically designed to broaden the definition of eligibility to include SROs; regulations to implement these amendments have since been issued (Section 8, 1982). Through these new regulations, HUD has taken steps to implement the statutory changes of 1981 by waiving the statutory limit on the percentage of single persons who may participate in the assisted housing programs within a single multiunit structure. On the other hand, they imposed an eligibility criterion requiring that the units must be in a structure consisting of more than twelve units. This severely limits participation of small hotels and rooming houses in urban and rural areas; moreover, it has no support in the statutory language (Bryson, 1982). Although the amendments as adopted are not as broad as those sought by SRO advocates, the regulations need further interpretation, and Section 8 funds have been cut back, the 1981 amendments represent a major legislative advance for the single-housing-unit resident. It is interesting to note that three West Coast communities with strong SRO planning advocates, San Francisco, Portland, and Seattle, have also enacted local legislation to delay or hinder conversion and demolition of SRO structures. These statutes can serve as models for other communities (Werner and Bryson, 1982).

Turner (1982) expects that the Section 8 changes for SROs will eventually be applied to the rehabilitation of other forms of alternative housing. The Housing and Urban-Rural Recovery Act of 1982 (HR 6296) provides in Section 208 that Section 8 Existing and Moderate Rehabilitation Programs be made available to elderly families electing to live in shared housing. Commentary on the bill suggests that regulations should limit eligibility to single-family dwelling units and require separate bedrooms for each family unit in home sharing.

Section 311 of HR 6296 provides $50 million for a demonstration program to assist communities and nonprofit organizations in creating temporary or basic shelter for people subject to life-threatening situations because of their lack of housing—the homeless. If enacted, this will provide a small but beginning response in housing legislation to these marginal elderly who are most at risk.

Conclusion

The majority of elderly persons prefer and will undoubtedly choose to remain living independently and privately in their own single-family homes. The community's ability to support this decision is the key factor in the interface of the elderly and their environment. At the same time it should be recognized that there will always be elderly in need of a full range of housing options that respond to differing lifestyles, declining physical and mental health, inadequate social networks, and limited incomes.

The housing options for the marginal elderly—hotels, rooming houses, modular homes, shared housing and foster homes—represent a continuum of alternatives within the total housing scheme (see fig. 19-1). Most of the housing stock needed for these alternatives already exists. The concepts distinguishing this broad range of housing types are also known. What is needed are more flexible definitions of our ideas about family constellations and housing-unit needs and continued advocacy for legislation that supports rather than deters the providing of housing alternatives.

Although alternative housing for the marginal elderly serves only a minority, it is important for social planners and practitioners to consider not only the aggregate but the needs of each individual. Surely it should be possible to reverse the situation noted by Carp (1976) that the least deprived are frequently the most favored.

References

Abrams, P. 1981. Statement Before the Subcommittee on Housing and Consumer Interest of the Select Committee on Aging, 29 July.

Brody, E. 1977. "Comments on Sherman/Newman Paper." *Gerontologist* 17:520–22.

———. 1979. "Service Supported Independent Living in an Urban Setting." In *The Environmental Context of Aging.* Ed. T. Byerts, S. Howell, and L. Pastalan. New York: Garland.

Bryson, D., and F. Werner. 1981. "Single Room Occupancy Buildings and the Federal Housing Program." Supplemental statement of the National Housing Subcommittee on Housing and Community Development of the House Committee on Banking, Insurance and Urban Affairs, 14 April.

Bryson, D. 1982. "Comments to HUD Regarding Interim Regulations for the Section 8 Moderate Rehabilitation Program." *Federal Register,* Docket #R-82-995, 8 October.

Carp, F. 1968. "Person–Situation Congruence in Engagement." *Gerontologist* 8:184–88.

———. 1976. "Housing and Living Environments of Older People." In *Handbook of Aging and the Social Sciences.* Ed. R. Binstock and E. Shanas. New York: Van Nostrand Reinhold.

Cohen, C., and J. Sokolovsky. 1980. "Social Engagement Versus Isolation: The Case of the Aged in SRO Hotels." *Gerontologist* 20:36–44.

———. 1981. "Social Networks and the Elderly: Clinical Techniques." *International Journal of Family Therapy* 3:281–94.

Day-Lower, D. 1981. Testimony Before the Select Committee on Aging, Subcommittee on Housing and Consumer Interest, 17 November.

Eckert, J. K. 1980. *The Unseen Elderly: A Study of Marginally Subsistent Hotel Dwellers.* San Diego: Campanile.

———. 1982. "Dislocation and Relocation of the Urban Elderly: Social Networks as Mediators of Relocation Stress." *Human Organization* 42:39–45.

Ehrlich, I. 1976. "The Politics of Housing the Elderly." In *The Politics of Housing in Older Urban Areas.* Ed. R. Mendelson and M. Quinn. New York: Praeger.

Ehrlich, P. 1976. "A Study: Characteristics and Needs of the St. Louis Downtown SRO Elderly." In *The Invisible Elderly.* Washington, DC: The National Council on the Aging.

Ehrlich, P., and I. Ehrlich. 1982. "SRO Elderly: A Distinct Population in a Viable Housing Alternative." In *Aging and the Human Condition.* Ed. G. Lesnorr-Caravaglia. New York: Human Sciences.

Goode, C., M. P. Lawton, and S. I. Hoover. 1980. *Elderly Hotel and Rooming House Dwellers.* Philadelphia: Philadelphia Geriatric Center.

Haley, B., M. Pearson, and D. Hull. 1981. "Urban Elderly Residents of Single-Room Occupancy Housing (SROs), 1976–1980." Paper presented at the 34th annual meeting of the Gerontological Society of America, Toronto, Canada, November.

Kahana, E. 1975. "A Congruence Model of Person–Environment Interaction." In *Theory Development in Environment and Aging.* P. Windley and G. Ernst. Washington, DC: Gerontological Society.

Lally, M., E. Black, M. Thornock, and J. D. Hawkins. 1979. "Older Women in Single Room Occupant (SRO) Hotels: A Seattle Profile." *Gerontologist* 19:67–73.

Lawton, M. P. 1980. *Environment and Aging.* Monterey, CA: Brooks/Cole.

———. 1981. "Alternative Housing." *Journal of Gerontological Social Work* 3:61–80.

Mangum, W. 1980. "Housing for the Elderly in the U.S." In *Geographical Aspects of an Aging Population.* Ed. A. M. Warnes. London: Wiley.

McKay, J. 1976. "The Invisible Elderly in San Francisco." In *The Invisible Elderly.* Washington, DC: National Council on the Aging.

Newman, E., and S. Sherman. 1977. "A Survey of Caretakers in Adult Foster Homes." *Gerontologist* 17:436–39.

———. 1979. "Community Integration of the Elderly in Foster Family Care." *Journal of Gerontological Social Work* 1:175–86.

———. 1980. "Foster-Family Care for the Elderly: Surrogate Family or Mini-Institution?" *International Journal of Aging and Human Development* 10:165–76.

Nusberg, C. 1978. "Granny Flats"—Increasing Housing Options for the Elderly." *Aging International* 4:8–10.

Rubenstein, D., K. Schuster, and F. Desiervo. 1976. "A Study of Older Persons Living in Inner City SRO Hotels and Boarding Houses." Final Report. Syracuse, NY: School of Social Work, Syracuse Univ.

Section 8 Housing Assistance Payments. 1982. "Program for Moderate Rehabilitation, Interim Regulations." *Federal Register,* Docket #R-82-9951, 9 August.

Shapiro, J. 1971. *Communities of the Alone: Working with Single Room Occupants in the City.* New York: Association Press.

Shared Housing Quarterly, 1982. July, p. 1.

Sherman, S., and E. Newman. 1979. "Role of the Caseworker in Adult Foster Care." *Social Work* 24:324–28.

Siegel, H. 1977. *Outposts of the Forgotten: N.Y. City's Welfare Hotels and Single Room Occupancy Tenants.* New Brunswick, NJ: Transaction.

Stephens, J. 1975. "Society of the Alone: Freedom, Privacy and Utilitarianism as Dominant Norms in the SRO." *Journal of Gerontology* 30:230–35.

Streib, G. 1978. "An Alternative Family Form for Older Persons: Need and Social Context." *The Family Coordinator* 27:413–20.

Streib, G., and M. Hilker. 1980. "The Cooperative 'Family.'" *Alternative Lifestyles* 3:167–84.

Strozier, A. 1976. "SRO and the Health Care System: Case Study." In *The Invisible Elderly.* Washington, DC: National Council on the Aging.

Turner, L. 1982. *Housing Options for the Community Resident Elderly.* Report prepared for the Administration on Aging. Washington, DC: Office of Human Development Services, U.S. Department of Health and Human Services, March.

U.S. Senate. 1978. Special Committee on Aging. *Single Room Occupancy: A Need for National Concern.* Washington, DC: U.S. Government Printing Office.

Wax, J. 1976. "It's Like Your Own Home Here." *The New York Times Magazine* 21 November: 38–40, 87–102.

Werner, F., and D. Bryson. 1982. "A Guide to the Preservation and Maintenance of Single Room Occupancy (SRO) Housing." *Clearing House Review: National Clearinghouse of Legal Services,* (15 April), No. 12:999–1006; (16 May), No. 1:1–25.

CHAPTER 20 Board-and-Care Housing and the Role of State Governments

Robyn Stone · Robert J. Newcomer

Board-and-care facilities have existed for many years to provide food, shelter, and some degree of protection for chronically impaired, dependent elderly and disabled individuals. During the past decade a combination of factors, including increasing fiscal constraints on state and local governments, deinstitutionalization of mental hospital patients, and the serious consideration of community-based alternatives to nursing homes has stimulated interest in board-and-care housing. Maintenance of the chronically impaired elderly and disabled in such housing is seen as a means to reduce the costs of institutionalization, promote independence, and enhance quality of life (Harmon, 1982).

While board-and-care housing represents a potentially large resource in the long-term-care service continuum, the diverse and frequently elusive nature of the board-and-care "industry" also poses a dilemma for state and local governments. This dilemma can be attributed, in large part, to the fact that the typical home, inconspicuously located among private dwellings, tends to be a "mom and pop" operation with provider(s) often lacking the requisite administrative skills and substantive knowledge to address the special needs of residents (Harmon, 1982). While far from providing sophisticated environments, many offer truly homelike caring qualities and familylike in-

formality not found in institutions. However, the housing stock and staff frequently fail to meet appropriate safety and care standards.

These problems began to receive national attention in the early 1970s, after a rash of boarding home fires and the exposure of substandard conditions and resident abuse and exploitation (U.S. GAO, 1979; U.S. House, 1981; U.S. Department of Health and Human Services [U.S. DHHS], 1982b). A series of federal initiatives was designed to help ameliorate these problems. The first of these was the Keys Amendment to the Social Security Act in 1976 (Section 1616[e] of the Act). The Keys Amendment, though not providing for direct federal regulation of quality of care or life safety standards, attempted to stimulate state efforts to regulate and monitor board and care by requiring states to set and enforce standards concerning admission policies, life safety, sanitation, and civil rights protection for board-and-care facilities where three or more SSI recipients reside (U.S. House, 1981). These are individuals receiving federal income support through the federal Supplemental Security Income program.

While this legislation encouraged many states to clarify the language in their standards and regulations (Stone, Newcomer, and Saunders, 1982; Reichstein and Bergofsky, 1983), there appears to be little demonstrable improvement in life safety

The contents of this chapter are drawn from research supported by the U.S. Department of Health and Human Services, Administration on Aging, under cooperative agreement No. 90AP0003.

or quality of care. For example, in 1979 an investigation of boarding homes (U.S. GAO, 1979) cited unsafe and unsanitary living conditions in facilities housing SSI recipients. Several studies found that existing regulations largely exclude personal care and social needs, areas which are often more subject to abuse or quality variability than physical features of the housing (Mellody and White 1979; Dittmar and Smith, 1983). The U.S. Select Committee on Aging, through its hearings, has also reported "widespread instances of poor living conditions and negligent care for a population which is, for the most part, indigent or elderly, and many of whom are former mental hospital patients (U.S. House, 1981, p. 5).

Another federal measure designed to strengthen state capability in enforcement and monitoring of board-and-care housing was a 1978 amendment to the Older Americans Act (OAA) that encouraged nursing home ombudsman programs to include advocacy for board-and-care residents. Only a few states, such as Florida and New Jersey, officially expanded the responsibilities of their ombudsman programs to include board and care under this voluntary program (U.S. AoA, 1981). Congress has since added a provision in the 1981 OAA amendments requiring state nursing home ombudsmen to investigate complaints about board-and-care homes.

More recent federal efforts have been initiated in response to findings by the Office of the Inspector General of the U.S. Department of Health and Human Services (U.S. DHHS, 1982b), which continued to report a generally low state level of participation in the oversight of board-and-care housing. The emerging strategy includes: (1) the partial withholding of OAA funds to states that fail to certify that they maintain and enforce safety and quality of care standards as part of their OAA plan; (2) the provision of $400,000 to the National Bureau of Standards to complete development of fire safety standards for board-and-care; (3) the establishment of a board-and-care coordinating unit within DHHS; (4) the development of model statutes for dissemination to the states; and (5) the requirement that Medicaid waivers used for board-

and-care to be granted only to those states in compliance with the Keys Amendment (U.S. DHHS, 1982a).

While the DHHS plan has attempted to clarify the federal role in ensuring life safety and quality of care for board-and-care residents, no additional federal funds have been made available to the states to improve enforcement and oversight activities. The onus, therefore, rests with state and local governments to make creative use of existing resources and to design strategies for enhancing their regulatory and monitoring capabilities.

Any action taken by government to expand regulatory oversight of the board-and-care industry can have immediate effects on the supply and availability of this housing. Furthermore, the financing of this regulatory activity presents its own barriers to implementation. In spite of these problems, states are increasingly attempting to respond to the need for expanding the supply and accessibility of facilities, protecting the life safety and personal rights of board-and-care residents, and ensuring quality of care.

This chapter briefly discusses the status of current knowledge about board-and-care housing and its residents; it provides an overview of regulatory and financing mechanisms and examines the barriers reported by and actions being taken by state governments to effect changes in the quality and quantity of board-and-care housing. Much more effort will be needed to establish board-and-care housing as an important component of the long-term-care service continuum, but these state actions illustrate the strengths and weaknesses of emerging public policy.

This descriptive review draws heavily upon the findings of a recent study conducted by the Aging Health Policy Center (AHPC) (Stone, Newcomer, and Saunders, 1982). The study describes the major policy issues with respect to the regulation and administration of adult board-and-care programs serving the elderly, mentally ill, mentally retarded, and developmentally disabled in all fifty states and Washington, D.C., for the 1981–82 period. The major source of data was telephone interviews conducted with representatives of ninety-two state agencies involved in licensing, regulating, and monitoring board-and-care programs. In addition, supporting documents were gathered from each agency where available, including statutes and regulations, statistical reports and directories of facilities, administrative and budgetary information, and other data to complete the board-and-care policy picture. Follow-up interviews were conducted to obtain 1983 information on the supply of beds and facilities and important statutory and/or regulatory changes.

Board-and-Care Defined

Board-and-care housing refers to the provision by a nonrelative of food, shelter, and some degree of protective oversight and/or personal care that is generally nonmedical in nature (McCoy, 1983). The "personal care and oversight" responsibilities of board-and-care operators, as established by state regulations (Reichstein and Bergofsky, 1983), usually include assistance with activities of daily living (eating, bathing, grooming), help with transportation and shopping, supervision of residents' medication, and assistance in obtaining medical and social services.

A variety of terms are used to describe board-and-care housing. These include residential-care facilities, community-care homes, personal-care homes, domiciliary-care homes, supervisory-care homes, sheltered-care facilities, adult foster care, family homes, group homes, transitional living facilities, and halfway houses. Board-and-care facilities also vary in terms of size, ownership, resident population, administrative or regulatory auspices, services, and funding sources. For example, a national survey of state regulatory programs for board-and-care housing (Stone, Newcomer, and Saunders, 1982), identified 142 distinct board-and-care programs administered and regulated by ninety-two state government agencies. Several researchers have attempted to develop a taxonomy of board-and-care programs based on such factors as level of care (foster care, personal care, and so on), target population (children, adults, mentally ill, developmentally disabled, aged),

facility size (Dittmar and Smith, 1983), and degree of functional impairment (Rutman, 1981). However, the lack of consensus among either researchers or regulators regarding a common taxonomy or definition continues to be problematic.

The diversity of board-and-care categories has contributed to a wide variation in estimates of the number of both facilities and residents. A report issued by the Office of the Inspector General (U.S. DHHS, 1982b), estimates that there are approximately 300,000 boarding homes and 30,000 board-and-care homes in the United States housing between 500,000 and 1.5 million residents. While the vast majority of residents live in unlicensed facilities, studies of adults in licensed homes give some indication of the size of the population currently served by board-and-care providers. According to a study completed at the Center for Residential Community Services at the University of Minnesota (Lakin et al., 1982), there are approximately 90,000 mentally retarded persons in "private community-based" residences. One national survey of group homes for the mentally retarded (Janicki, Mayeda, and Epple, 1982), estimates that 49,000 mentally retarded adults now reside in 6,300 facilities of this type. Sherwood and Seltzer (1981) estimate that between 60,000 and 80,000 mentally ill adults reside in board-and-care homes in the United States, with the largest subgroup housed in foster-care facilities. A recent nationwide survey of board-and-care facilities for the aged (Reichstein and Bergofsky, 1983) identifies approximately 25,000 licensed and 5,000 unlicensed facilities housing a primarily elderly population. Another study (Teresi, Holmes, and Holmes, 1982) estimates the board-and-care population of persons sixty-five years or older to be about 285,000.

The Aging Health Policy Center's (AHPC) nationwide survey of board-and-care programs serving a variety of dependent adult populations estimates that there were approximately 454,000 state-licensed board-and-care beds in 1983; these housed about 114,000 mentally disabled and 340,000 aged and physically disabled adults.

Regulation and Administration

Formal regulation involves a number of activities, including the licensing and/or certification of board-and-care facilities, the enforcement of explicit rules and regulations through both formal and informal sanctions, and the monitoring of these facilities to ensure that operators adhere to the regulations. All states have some type of statutory authority and regulations addressing board-and-care concerns, but states vary tremendously in the level of effort invested in licensing and regulation (ABA, 1983). In addition, standards frequently vary by type of facility within and between states. Some states use general licensing standards for all board-and-care facilities, while others have promulgated different standards by size and type of facility, with special requirements for each target population.

The regulatory process and administrative structure of board-and-care programs nationwide forms a continuum from total control of residential-care programs (in which both the supply of and demand for facilities are determined by state policies) to a pure market model in which supply and demand are subject to competition and choice (Harmon, 1982; Stone, Newcomer, and Saunders, 1982). Programs targeted specifically for the mentally retarded adult tend to be the most formally and strictly regulated, with state and local agencies controlling recruitment and financing of providers as well as placement and oversight of residents. Board-and-care programs for the mentally ill that are part of the state mental health system also appear to be heavily controlled by state policy.

Board-and-care facilities housing the elderly and/or a mixed adult population have been traditionally subject to minimal regulation and oversight. However, the past decade has witnessed a variety of state initiatives to formalize board-and-care programs and strengthen state regulatory and oversight functions. Reichstein and Bergofsky's (1983) nationwide survey of 118 state-administered board-and-care programs serving the aged or a mixed population identifies three common functions performed by a single state agency or combination of agencies: (1) regulation of facilities; (2) case management or placement of residents; and (3) financial functions including eligibility determination and reimbursement.

Board-and-care policy research points to the existence of a two-tiered system of board-and-care programs (Sherwood, Mor, and Gutkin, 1981; Stone, Newcomer, and Saunders, 1982; Dittmar and Smith, 1983). Residential-care facilities for the mentally retarded and, to a lesser extent, the mentally ill, are usually small group homes with a strong therapeutic orientation. In contrast, facilities housing the elderly or a mixed adult population tend to be larger and institutional in character with little attention paid to rehabilitation or services. Data from an analysis of thirty-one sets of board-and-care regulations (Sherwood and Seltzer, 1981) indicate that as compared with regulations addressing facilities for the mentally retarded, standards focusing on board and care for the elderly emphasize maintenance rather than rehabilitation or training. Moreover, Dittmar and Smith (1983) argue that the goals of deinstitutionalization are being met to a much higher degree with the mentally retarded than with the elderly, and that the care being provided to the latter population is really just a form of "reinstitutionalization."

Financing Mechanism

The primary source of public reimbursement for board-and-care programs is the federal Supplemental Security Income (SSI) program (Title XVI of the Social Security Act), which provides a guaranteed minimum income to persons who are aged, blind, or disabled. States have the option of supplementing these federal payments through State Supplemental Payments (SSP). The SSI benefit levels are established nationally and provide uniform minimum payments in all states. The maximum benefit levels in 1982 were $264.70 for an individual and $397.00 for a couple. The SSP income is more varied with different possible income levels depending on household size, housing type, and whether the person is aged, blind, or disabled. Thirty states provide SSP specifically for persons receiving some form of personal care or supportive housing. Twenty-nine states offer SSP to individuals living independently. Twenty states offer SSP benefits to both independent living and supportive housing populations, while nine states do not offer SSP benefits to either subpopulation (U.S. SSA, 1982).

The income levels provided through the SSI/ SSP program operate as a direct income supplement to the low-income aged, blind, and disabled population. Recipients can use these funds to help pay the rent in board-and-care housing. This approach, especially for the aged, relies largely on a "market" approach to influencing the supply, rent levels, and demand for board-and-care housing. A few states have adopted procedures which more directly affect the supply and access to this type of housing. Such procedures are most commonly used to purchase board-and-care services for low-income clients who are not eligible for SSI (as in New Jersey) or for residents of states that do not offer optional supplementation payment. Washington state, for example, does not provide an SSP benefit to board-and-care residents, but pays for these placements directly by contracted arrangements using other state and Social Service Block Grant funds.

Barriers to Effective Regulation and Oversight

Formal standards and regulations have been promulgated in each state; yet the 1982 AHPC survey found that implementation has been extremely problematic for most regulatory agencies. A variety of major barriers were identified by state agencies (Stone, Newcomer, and Saunders, 1982).

Lack of Funding and Personnel

Perhaps the most pervasive problem is the failure of the states to commit adequate resources to regulatory and monitoring activities. The AHPC survey of state agency officials (Stone, Newcomer, and Saunders, 1982) found that 75 percent of the agencies reported inadequate funds or personnel to license, inspect, or enforce regulations. While all state agencies are usually required to inspect facilities at least annually, several states noted that budget cuts and reduction in staff have seriously curtailed visits to many board-and-care homes. An earlier survey by Ruchlin (1979) suggests that states have understaffed their regulatory programs for some time.

Weak Statutory and Enforcement Authority

Statutes governing board-and-care programs are generally regarded as weak. While requirements for the inspection and regulation of the physical plant are usually explicit, the language regarding the monitoring of quality of care is ambiguous (Stone, Newcomer, and Saunders, 1982; ABA 1983). In addition, the absence of intermediate sanctions, especially civil penalties and fines not subject to lengthy administrative and judicial review, impedes the enforcement capabilities of state agencies.

The Encumbered Legal Process

The lengthy and costly formal procedures involved in revoking a license or closing a facility have been found to impede effective regulation and enforcement (Ruchlin, 1979). Such drastic measures are rarely used because inadequate funds usually preclude this expensive course of action. Another factor operating to reduce enforcement is the judicial protection afforded for owners' property rights over residents' rights to quality of care. Even when the operator of a facility has been convicted of a felony and the state actively attempts to remove the operating license, legal obstacles and appeals can prevent or delay the facility's closing.

Inadequate Data Base to Facilitate Regulation and Oversight

Few state and local resources have been made available to support the maintenance of adequate records regarding changes in bed supply, client placement and turnover, and enforcement actions (Reichstein and Bergofsky, 1983). Consequently, there are no mechanisms for ensuring accountability or for assessing the impact of state discretionary policy changes on the supply, availability, or accessibility of board-and-care facilities.

Fragmentation of Agency Responsibility

Compounding other barriers to effective regulation and oversight of board-and-care programs is the fragmentation of administrative and regulatory responsibility. These responsibilities are frequently spread among a number of agencies, encouraging duplication of effort and allowing clients and facilities to become lost in a bureaucratic maze. For example, local as well as state departments of health are often responsible for sanitation and other physical environment considerations. Furthermore, state and/or local health and social service offices may share responsibility for programmatic review. The division of authority between state and local government, and among categorical service populations (such as aged versus mentally retarded), helps contribute to fragmentation. Most states lack formal intergovernmental coordination mechanisms. Informal coordination usually depends upon such factors as proximity of agencies and the degree to which a "problem" facility or program is perceived as a common threat.

Inadequate Knowledge and Skills among Regulatory Officials and Operators

Board-and-care housing inspectors have been described in many states as having little knowledge of the unique problems of the elderly or disabled target populations and of not being specifically trained to evaluate the quality of care in board-and-care facilities (Ruchlin, 1979; Stone, Newcomer, and Saunders, 1982).

Many board-and-care operators have been found to lack the administrative skills and/or substantive understanding of the needs and concerns of their residents to provide adequate and appropriate care (U.S. DHHS, 1982b; Harmon, 1982). "Mom and pop" operators, in particular, are frequently unskilled in such areas as bookkeeping and records management and are often confused by the intricacies of state and local regulatory changes (Dittmar and Smith, 1983).

Inadequate Reimbursement Policies

The current reimbursement method for board-and-care housing, which relies primarily on SSI/SSP benefit levels, has been described as an inadequate mechanism for encouraging the expansion of supply and the upgrading of facilities to meet life safety and quality-of-care standards (U.S. GAO, 1979; U.S. DHHS, 1982b; Stone, Newcomer, and Saunders, 1982). One particularly important consideration is the ability of low-income (publicly subsidized) persons needing board and care to compete with private (nonsubsidized) individuals seeking such housing. Access to this care is especially problematic in situations where there is a high demand from private payers and a limited bed supply. Without public subsidies that are high enough to compete with private payers, low-income persons can be expected to have limited access.

While no study has investigated how reimbursement levels affect supply and access on a national scale, the experience of Washington state (Peguillan-Shea, Wood, and Newcomer, 1983) illustrates the potential interaction between reimbursement levels and access. Rather than providing an SSP benefit to board-and-care residents, this state pays for these placements by contracted arrangements using other state and Social Service Block Grant funds. The Washington State Department of Health and Human Services views these reimbursement rates as low in comparison to private market rents. In 1980 there were 16,000 licensed supervised housing (board-and-care) beds within Washington meeting an estimated 59 percent of the need for this housing. Because of the relatively low reimbursement level, less than one-third of these beds were occupied by SSI-eligible persons; the balance were occupied by residents who pay privately.

Alternative State Strategies

Recognizing the various obstacles to regulation and enforcement, several states have begun to explore nonregulatory alternatives to expanding the supply and availability of facilities and ensuring life safety and quality of care. These strategies make use of existing resources and attempt to provide low-cost, less threatening mechanisms to facilitate provider compliance. Recent reports (U.S. DHHS, 1982b; Harmon, 1982; Stone, Newcomer, and Saunders, 1982) have identified some of these activities as "best practices." Following are examples of ways in which state and local governments might address their board-and-care problem. Given the newness of most of these programs and the myriad changes and reorganizations occurring in state agencies, formal evaluations have not been conducted.

Coordination among Agencies

The lack of coordination among agencies involved in regulating and administering board-and-care programs has been addressed by policies requiring all agencies responsible for licensing, inspection, placement, and monitoring activities to share information (Stone, Newcomer, and Saunders, 1982). Several states (such as California, Oregon, Minnesota) have developed formal information-sharing agreements among the appropriate agencies. New Jersey has even used a state statute to mandate the establishment of a formal communication network.

Consultation/Technical Assistance

Recognizing that a purely adversarial approach to noncomplying board-and-care operators may result in unnecessary reductions in the availability of needed beds (Harmon, 1982), many state agencies have adopted technical assistance strategies to encourage operators to comply with standards and to upgrade physical plant and quality of care (U.S. DHHS, 1982b; Stone, Newcomer, and Saunders, 1982). While most of the state regulations include, at best, minimal training requirements, a number of state agencies have instituted formal training programs in issues such as financial management, home improvement, cardiopulmonary resuscitation, and nutrition. A few states offer formal courses for operators to receive certification. Curriculum for operators is also being tested to include gaining access to community resources, establishing case management, and handling medications. While these activities reflect an increasing recognition of the benefits of formal training, this strategy requires a strong financial commitment from the state in order to be successfully executed.

Financial Incentives

The provision of financial incentives beyond board-and-care reimbursement rates is another major nonregulatory device for encouraging the supply of board-and-care facilities while simultaneously ensuring quality of care and life safety among residents. Among a few states, these incentives have taken the form of low-interest loan and grant programs to assist operators in upgrading their physical plants. This upgrading can include the installation of sprinklers and smoke alarm systems or more elaborate remodeling. One state has even appropriated funds to help finance the upgrading and new construction of facilities for the developmentally disabled and the mentally ill, as well as for conversion of motels into group homes.

Establishment of Complaint Offices

Several states have attempted to capitalize on informal existing sources to strengthen state enforcement efforts. These include encouraging the general public, through advertising in the mass media, to report complaints. Another state operates a twenty-four hour hotline with complaints investigated within twenty-four to seventy-two hours and results reported to county welfare agencies for action. A Central Referral Bureau to control placement and monitoring of any individual receiving board-and-care assistance represents an even more stringent attempt by a state agency to improve life safety and quality-of-care oversight.

States have also used their nursing home ombudsman programs to strengthen monitoring activities. Though most of these efforts are still on an ad hoc basis, at least three states require their ombudsmen to investigate all complaints related to board-and-care facilities.

External Participation in Inspection and Monitoring

The use of provider and consumer groups represents a low-cost strategy for inspecting and monitoring board-and-care facilities. Provider organizations have begun to assume some responsibility for enforcing standards in several states. These include offering bimonthly training sessions for operators and monitoring the quality of care in member facilities. In addition, some provider groups have begun to help the state identify unlicensed facilities.

Integration of Board-and-Care with the Continuum of Care

Several states, committed to the dual goals of cost containment and the provision of appropriate levels of care, have attempted to incorporate board-and-care into their broader long-term-care strategy (Sherwood, Mor, and Gutkin, 1981; Harmon, 1982; Stone, Newcomer, and Saunders, 1982). This has been done by provider recruitment and training, direct control of placement by restricting SSI and/or other state funds to clients determined eligible by the program agency, formal needs assessment, case management, and linkages to community services (Harmon, 1982).

Conclusion

State and local governments have been hindered by a number of serious barriers in their policy attempts to encourage the expansion of supply and accessibility to board-and-care facilities while at the same time ensuring life safety and quality of care for board-and-care residents. To date such diverse factors as the definitional ambiguities surrounding the concepts *board and care* and *quality of care*, insufficient state and local resources for programs, weak statutory authority and an encumbered legal process, fragmentation of responsibility, and an inadequate data and knowledge base have impeded effective regulation and oversight of the board-and-care industry.

Several states have attempted to overcome these barriers by expanding their statutory authority and/or by promulgating stricter and more explicit regulations. Others have begun to explore alternative strategies to strengthen their administrative and oversight capacities. The development of financial incentives for board-and-care operators and the expansion and upgrading of technical assistance and formal training programs for providers and licensing and inspection personnel represent two promising approaches. Formal evaluations of these various regulatory and non-regulatory innovations are needed, however, to assess the impact of these activities and to ascertain the feasibility of replicating them.

Particular attention must be paid to the costs of alternative strategies and their potentially adverse effects on the supply of licensed beds. For example, one course of action might require the licensing of all group housing facilities but would also increase the regulatory costs for state and local governments. A countervailing strategy might entail federal, state, and local government experimentation with alternative reimbursement policies beyond the SSI/SSP benefit levels. Options would include tax incentives, subsidized construction, and bond issues.

Regardless of the approach adopted, the AHPC review of board-and-care programs (Stone, Newcomer, and Saunders, 1982) suggests two factors which will help to determine the relative success or failure of state strategies. One is that the future of board-and-care policy depends, in large part, on the level of financial commitment from state and local governments to support the development and coordination of board-and-care programs. In addition, the design and monitoring of effective policy requires more complete national and state data documenting client and facility characteristics, changes in board-and-care regulations and standards, enforcement activities, and utilization patterns. In spite of the presence of these problems, states have been innovative in their attempts to establish greater administrative oversight of this industry. Although board-and-care services potentially have a key role to play in the long-term-care service continuum, it is apparent that approaches to financing and regulating this industry need to be reformulated. Without such action, it is likely that state and local government will continue to have problems ensuring availability, accessibility, and quality of care in board-and-care housing.

References

American Bar Association (ABA). 1983."State Laws and Programs Serving Elderly Persons and Disabled Adults". *Mental Disability Law Reporter* 7, No. 2 (March–April): 158–209.

Dittmar, N. D., and G. P. Smith. 1983. *Evaluation of Board-and-Care Homes: Summary of Survey Procedures and Findings.* Denver: Denver Research Institute.

Harmon, C. 1982. *Board and Care: An Old Problem, A New Resource for Long-Term Care.* Washington, DC: Center for the Study of Social Policy.

Janicki, M. P., T. Mayeda, and W. A. Epple. 1982. *A Report on the Availability of Group Homes for Persons with Mental Retardation in the United States.* Albany, NY: New York State Office of Mental Retardation and Developmental Disabilities.

Lakin, K. C., R. H. Bruininks, B. K. Hill, and F. A. Hauber. 1982. *Sourcebook on Long-Term Care for Developmentally Disabled People.* CRCS Report No. 17. St. Paul, MN: Univ. of Minnesota.

McCoy, J. L. 1983. "Overview of Available Data Relating to Board-and-Care Homes and Residents." Unpublished memo. Washington, DC: U. S. Department of Health and Human Services.

Mellody, J. F., and J. G. White. 1979. *Service Delivery Assessment of Boarding Homes, Technical Report.* Washington, DC: U.S. Department of Health and Human Services.

Peguillan-Shea, V., J. Wood, and R. Newcomer. 1983. *Washington: State Discretionary Policies and Services in the Medicaid, Social Services, and Supplemental Security Income Programs.* San Francisco: Aging Health Policy Center, Univ. of California.

Reichstein, K. J., and L. Bergofsky. 1983. "Domiciliary-Care Facilities for Adults: An Analysis of State Regulations." *Research on Aging* 5, No. 1: 25–43.

Ruchlin, H. S. 1979. "An Analysis of Regulatory Issues and Options in Long-Term Care." In *Reform and Regulation in Long-Term Care.* Ed. V. La Porte and J. Rubin. New York: Praeger.

Rutman, I. D. 1981. "Community-Based Services: Characteristics, Principles, and Program Models." In *Planning for Deinstitutionalization.* Human Services Monograph Series, No. 28. Ed. I. D. Rutman. Rockville, MD: Project Share.

Sherwood, C. C., and M. M. Seltzer. 1981. *Task III Report—Board-and-Care Literature Review, Evaluation of Board-and-Care Homes.* Boston: Boston Univ. School of Social Work.

Sherwood, S., V. Mor, and C. E. Gutkin. 1981. *Domiciliary-Care Clients and the Facilities in Which They Reside.* Boston: Hebrew Rehabilitation Center for Aged, Department of Social Gerontological Research.

Stone, R., R. J. Newcomer, and M. Saunders. 1982. *Descriptive Analysis of Board-and-Care Policy Trends in the 50 States.* San Francisco: Aging Health Policy Center, Univ. of California.

Teresi, J., M. Holmes, and D. Holmes. 1982. *Sheltered Living Environments for the Elderly.* New York: Community Research Applications.

U.S. Administration on Aging (AoA). 1981. Office of Program Development. *The Long-Term-Care Ombudsman Program: Development from 1975–1980,* Washington, DC: Administration on Aging.

U.S. Department of Health and Human Services (DHHS). 1982a. *HHS News,* 21 April.

———. 1982b. Office of the Inspector General. *Board-and-Care Homes: A Study of Federal and State Actions to Safeguard the Health and Safety of Board and Care Home Residents.* Washington, DC: Department of Health and Human Services.

U.S. General Accounting Office (GAO). 1979. *Identifying Disabled: A Major Step Toward Resolving a National Problem, Report to the Congress by the Comptroller General of the U.S.* Washington, DC: U.S. General Accounting Office.

U.S. House of Representatives. 1981. Select Committee on Aging. Hearing: *Fraud and Abuse in Boarding Homes*, 25 June. Washington, DC: U. S. Government Printing Office.

U.S. Social Security Administration (SSA). 1982. Unpublished data.

CHAPTER 21 Using Public and Private Policy Options to Meet the Housing Needs of the Aged

James O. Gollub • Thomas J. Chmura

The availability of shelter for older adults is influenced by many forces. Some forces, such as inflation or interest rates, are typically beyond the range of state and local action. Other forces may be more local such as land costs, and real estate and banking practices. The focus of this chapter is on how state and local government, through means other than public spending powers, can improve the availability of shelter for housing older people. These efforts have taken a variety of forms such as strategies to reduce the withdrawal from the market of housing units typically used by older adults (older apartments, SROs and so on), as well as actions to stimulate the availability of new units (by encouraging use of planned unit developments and development of below market rate units for example). Such actions involve a shift in thinking — the development of new options. This chapter will review key tools used by both the public and private sectors, discuss how they can combine to influence the forces affecting housing for the elderly, and present a process for effectively applying these tools.

Local governments have begun a systematic use of their governance tools and of new relations with the private sector to help meet the housing needs of the aged. Often these efforts emerged in reaction to problems—such as assisting the elderly displaced from an urban renewal area. In other instances they have consisted of innovative ideas learned from nonprofit organizations or local government in other communities.

One stimulus for innovation is the recognition that if the problems are in part due to market forces, then alternative markets can be developed to respond to needs. Thus, if problems arise from the actions of public or private institutions (such as real estate investors), then new relationships with these institutions can be developed to improve the situation. When problems are due to the needs of the individual or family—poor health for example—then actions to reinforce or support individual needs can be developed.

Beginning in 1978 the Public Policy Center at SRI International began a series of research and demonstration studies focusing on how state and local government and the private sector have developed policies which influence the actions of markets, institutions, and individuals. Each study involved examination of policy activities in over thirty cities and counties. The findings indicated that policies were very often formed in a reactive,

The contents of this chapter draw from research carried out by SRI International for the Office of Human Development Service and the Administration on Aging, Department of Health and Human Services (HHS), and for the Office of Community Development, Department of Housing and Urban Development (HUD).

ad hoc manner, and frequently in isolation with one policy sometimes contradicting or nullifying another. This work (Waldhorn and Gollub, 1980) also found that the prospects for exerting a greater impact on social and economic needs were better when a systematic process for developing and implementing policy strategies was used. These research efforts found that a set of problem-solving principles were evolving among communities (Chmura et al., 1981; Gollub and Waldhorn, 1981). These principles include the following:

- Defining a mutuality of interest among sectors, which creates a basis for business, government, and community collaboration
- Taking a fresh look at problems by moving away from traditional needs assessments to more purposeful analysis of the supply and demand forces in community markets
- Using traditional policy tools in new ways—bringing the policies and practices of business, government and the community to focus on issues in a deliberate and concerted manner
- Moving toward redesign of community systems by looking beyond expenditure of public dollars alone to mobilizing the entire set of fiscal and policy resources in a community

Subsequently, several demonstrations were carried out to test the principles observed in these earlier studies (Chmura et al., 1983). Three efforts were underway in 1983 involving over twenty local communities. These efforts all focused on using the motivation for collaborative problem solving, such as a shared interest in housing, to build new coalitions or partnerships that conducted market and institutional analyses and laid the foundation for new strategies for local changes. These strategies for change called for a wide range of public and private sector actions by problem-solving partners.

Public and Private Policy Options

Six basic approaches or tools have been identified through the six-year study and consultation with state and local governments. These tools are the primary means for public, private, and community sectors to "redesign" local systems or influence the forces causing housing problems for older adults. They have typically been used independently and ad hoc, but it is through their concerted use that market and institutional factors can best be influenced. These tools are regulation and deregulation, tax policy change, administrative reform, public-private sector collaboration, promotion of self-help, and advocacy by the public sector. Each of these tools is briefly summarized below.

Regulation and Deregulation

State and local governments regulate activities in the housing market as part of their mission to protect the health and safety of citizens. These powers can be purposefully used to stimulate development in ways that benefit the elderly. Local policies include use of zoning ordinances; building, health and safety codes; and development permit processes. These can be applied either to stop harmful actions (condominium conversion ordinances, rent control, inclusionary zoning practices, or antidiscrimination ordinances) or to encourage helpful ones (flexible zoning and code enforcement, density incentives, permit streamlining, and group home location policies).

Tax Policy Change

Most state governments enable local governments to impose and collect property and other taxes under their state constitution. The use of tax powers can create incentives or disincentives for action. High property taxes can force older homeowners on fixed incomes out of their homes, and assessment formulas can prevent landlords with older tenants from making significant repairs. Enforcement of tax collection can also be used as a tool either to confiscate the tax-delinquent property of negligent absentee landlords or to encourage them to bring properties up to code. The use of tax reduction—through homeowner exemptions, deductions, credits, tax freeze, and deferrals—allows state and local governments to shift some burden away from elderly homeowners. Local government can also use tax abatements as incentives for improvements that might add to the housing stock, such as encouraging accessory units (so-called mother-in-law apartments).

Administrative Reform

Local governments regularly make decisions that involve personnel, facilities, and programs. Decisions redefining how existing resources are used—as opposed to development of new programs funded by line items in the budget—can help provide housing for older adults. Multiple use of schools or conversion of surplus school property to housing, directing social welfare agency staff to develop home-matching services for older clients, and streamlining housing development permit processing are examples of changes in ways of doing business within government that can help expand alternatives, improve efficiency, and reduce the time needed to produce housing units.

Public-Private Sector Collaboration

The involvement of the private sector in solving community housing problems has grown over the last few years. Businesses can do much to help beyond charitable giving. Firms have policies that determine how they operate their business, such as whether they will hire older workers or keep older workers on the payroll, and whether they will provide flexible schedules for employees with older family members, so they can take time to care for elders living with them. In addition, firms make investment decisions that can affect housing. Some firms, particularly insurance companies, manage large real estate portfolios that may include various forms of housing for the elderly. Banks and savings-and-loan institutions can also help older adults utilize the equity in their homes to supplement their current incomes through a variety of equity conversion instruments. The lending of corporate expertise and facilities for local efforts in organizing housing projects of dif-

ferent types is another example of corporate involvement. Finally, business leaders often have the ability to marshall others in an effort to address housing problems.

Promotion of Self-Help

Promoting self-help is an activity to which local government, nonprofit organizations, and business can all contribute. Promoting self-help involves creating opportunities for community resources to be pooled—as when a senior center or social service agency matches people for home sharing, a business volunteer helps prepare the front-end paperwork for a reverse equity mortgage, a nonprofit organization leases a home that can be shared by a group of frail older persons, or a utility trains seniors to do energy conservation checks and those elderly train others to continue the work. Promoting self-help is a means of expanding resources by using existing people and materials in new ways.

Advocacy by the Public Sector

Few community organizations have the staff capacity to analyze and frame housing policy questions, or translate them into regulatory, tax, administrative, or public-private initiatives. However, collaboration with local officials and community leadership can often marshal this expertise. For example, local government social service, housing and planning agency staff can work with and help formulate housing policy issues and intervention strategies. Local advocacy can be targeted on state laws such as those affecting nursing homes or the licensing of domiciliary care, as well as local private sector directions such as those concerning new developments and provisions for older, low-income citizens.

Applying Policy Options in Housing

There is much debate about how to resolve the difficult shelter problems confronting the aged. However, these problems are complex and their solutions depend on such factors as society's ability and willingness to subsidize housing, prevailing interest rates, the structure of the housing industry, federal income tax policies, demographic changes, and the demand for housing. Although these factors cannot be fully resolved at the local level, some constructive policy and programmatic options can be developed locally, as indicated above. These approaches should not be seen as easy answers to complex problems. They are often difficult to undertake, and they are not equally effective in all local situations. However, many of them can be made to work successfully in a community and, in the absence of other alternatives, they may represent the best opportunities available to the elderly and their advocates. Table 21-1 outlines key areas of need and examples of how the policy tools discussed above can be applied to meet housing needs of older adults.

While the policy options described in table 21-1 can be helpful when used alone, the optimal benefit comes when a community is able to develop a concerted strategy for addressing a particular shelter issue.

Key Actors in Developing Shelter Strategies

The development and implementation of policy options requires a willingness on the part of all sectors to work with a local community's housing system. In essence, this means identifying the key actors in this system: state government, local government, state and area agencies on aging, the business community (particularly financial institutions and real estate firms), and the elderly themselves. The potential roles of these actors are shown in table 21-2.

Elements of Strategy Development

Although each of the actors described above can undertake individual initiatives, a concerted strategy involving efforts across sectors can have a greater impact on the shelter needs of the elderly.

TABLE 21-1. Examples of Policy Options in Meeting Shelter Needs

Making Housing More Affordable
- State and local tax relief (e.g., tax freezes, deferrals, exemptions)
- Reverse annuity mortgages
- Rent control and rent mediation boards
- Lifeline utility rates
- Loans for tax payments or weatherization improvements

Facilitating Home Maintenance
- Sensitive code enforcement
- Tax abatements and building permit fee waivers
- Maintenance sharing
- Volunteer and community group maintenance
- Corporate caring for senior housing

Protecting against Market Pressures and Discrimination
- Downzoning
- Antispeculation tax
- Condominium conversion controls
- Antidiscrimination ordinance
- Eviction controls

Expanding the Supply of Affordable Housing
- Inclusionary zoning
- Use of public lands and buildings for housing (e.g., schools)
- Tax-exempt revenue bonds
- Targeted corporate investments
- Pension fund investments

Developing More Supportive Alternatives
- Homesharing
- Group living arrangements
- Accessory apartments
- Adult foster care
- Use of volunteer guardians

The key to developing such a strategy is establishing a process whereby members of each sector can come together to develop collaborative efforts.

Results from prior demonstration efforts show that five key steps can help in the process of addressing the shelter needs of the elderly. These are discussed next.

TABLE 21-2. Illustrative Roles of Local Actors and Institutions in Developing Housing Policy Options

State Government
- Enact enabling legislation allowing localities to grant property tax relief to the elderly.
- Remove banking restrictions in state banking laws that inhibit development of reverse annuity mortgages.
- Provide tax and other incentives to spur corporate involvement in housing for the elderly.
- State Pension Commission can enable targeting of pensions to housing investment.
- Department of Housing and Community Development can enable use of surplus and facilities.

Local Government
- Local council or commissioners can enact property tax relief for elderly homeowners and renters; lobby state if enabling legislation needed.
- The zoning board can reform zoning regulations to allow accessory apartments, group homes, and other housing alternatives.
- The Housing and Community Development Department can develop legal means to protect the elderly from displacement, evictions, and discrimination.
- Local administrators and school districts can make available surplus public lands and buildings for elderly housing development.
- Develop neighborhood housing corporations and volunteer home repair and maintenance programs.
- Focus local foundation resources to the needs of vulnerable groups, such as the frail elderly.
- Place a portion of union pension monies into housing development funds.

State and Area Agencies on Aging
- Raise priority awareness and articulate the need for housing for the elderly.
- Organize community volunteer programs to provide housing assistance for the elderly.
- Work to stimulate the development of homesharing and group home programs.
- Lobby for new public and private sector initiatives in elderly housing.

The Business Community
- Develop and promote new banking instruments such as reverse annuity mortgages.
- Use realtors to organize programs to help the elderly find affordable housing.
- Place a portion of business investment portfolios into funds for the development of elderly housing.
- Encourage corporations to "adopt" a senior housing project as a community activity.

The Elderly Themselves
- Advocate for public policy reforms before state and local legislative and administrative bodies.
- Organize self-help maintenance-sharing programs to barter needed skills and services.
- Use volunteers to organize and develop homesharing and other programs.

Forming Partnerships

When local officials decide to help older adults increase available housing, a public-private partnership effort can be initiated. Local officials and community members will often recognize that many of the forces affecting the ability of the elderly to live in their own homes or pay for housing are related to real estate and financial industry practices. Therefore, the active involvement of local savings-and-loan institutions and real estate firms, and lawyers should be sought for the partnership, in addition to community groups serving the elderly. Strong leadership by a local official, community leader, or corporate executive will be essential to initiating and managing such a partnership.

Diagnosing the Problem

To gain a better understanding of the forces that may affect housing, a problem diagnosis using local data generated by the city or county, universities, local banks, and real estate offices would be helpful. The diagnosis should examine demand factors affecting the shelter needs of the elderly, including where the elderly live, what their incomes are, and the expenses required to live alone. The group should also look at forces affecting the supply of shelter, including competition for rental housing in neighborhoods with large concentrations of elderly, difficulties and cost of home maintenance, and the financial pressures of living at home. In addition, there should be a review of current service delivery approaches in the area and their deficiencies. The diagnosis can provide the partnership group with a useful, realistic picture of the forces that need to be changed and the potential options they could use to make those changes.

Formulating Policy Options

Following the problem diagnosis, the public-private group can begin to develop a set of appropriate policy options to help local elderly. Many of the options identified may draw from the experience of other communities. These may include reverse annuity mortgages (RAMs), tax exemptions and deferrals, new facilities for independent group living, and development of a shared housing program.

Negotiating Action Agreements

The partnerships can then negotiate an "action agreement" covering the options developed to address the housing issue selected by the partnership. The agreement specifies the commitments of the various actors involved in the partnership. Involvement of the banking and real estate groups in a partnership effort can help to facilitate the development of a RAM program for example. The involvement of community groups helps make the development of group living, shared housing, and other options more viable and accepted by each sector.

Implementing Action Agreements

The process of joint diagnosis, strategy development, and implementation is perhaps the most difficult phase of the collaborative problem-solving process. To assist each sector in carrying out their respective agreements the partners should develop support roles that will gather political and technical resources as they are needed. Table 21-3 lists a set of self-assessment questions a community can use as a guide through this process.

TABLE 21-3. Checklist of Questions for Developing Policy Options in Shelter

Forming a Broad-based Community Problem-solving Partnership
- Who are the key public, private, and community actors involved in issues of housing?
- How have business groups (board of realtors, savings and loans, property insurers) been involved in discussions about housing for the elderly?
- How do state and local planning, taxation, building, and code enforcement agencies relate to these issues?
- Which community organizations (neighborhood groups, tenants' organizations, homeowners' associations, etc.) have a vested interest in housing?
- Does some sort of organized housing coalition exist in the community, or can a new one be organized to focus on shelter needs of the elderly?

Diagnosing the Problem
- What kinds of difficulties are faced by elderly homeowners and tenants?
- What is the current state of the local housing market in terms of average costs? Vacancy rates? Interest rates? Extent of abandonment?
- What kinds of supportive, noninstitutional housing alternatives exist for the elderly?
- What external factors are influencing the local housing market (economic conditions, interest rates, declines in subsidy programs)?
- What local factors are influencing the local housing market (demand for housing, constraints on new housing development, age and condition of housing, changing demographics)?
- What are the current government housing programs and policies relating to older persons?
- What are current private sector practices and policies regarding housing for the elderly?

Identify Potential Policy Options
- What uses of local governance powers could help address the problem (tax policy changes, code reform, zoning initiatives, regulatory protections)?
- How do private sector policies relate to the problem (lending practices of banks, the practices of realtors and insurers, the investments of corporations, and union pension funds)?
- What opportunities exist for community involvement and volunteerism in resolving elderly shelter needs?
- How can the elderly themselves, through self-help and mutual support, be involved in the problem-solving process?

TABLE 21-3. *(Continued)*

- What kinds of incentives (e.g., tax, zoning) could state and local governments provide or what barriers (e.g., regulatory, administrative) could they remove to encourage greater private and community involvement?
- What advocacy and supportive roles could the aging network play with respect to other local actors?

Negotiating Action Agreements

- What are the expected impacts (costs and benefits) of the various policy options being considered?
- What are the implementation considerations (timing, obstacles, legality, special approvals) involved with each option?
- What are the political considerations involving local elected officials and the local financial and real estate community?
- Is there a consensus among the participants about the preferred options? Can there be trade-offs or compromises among the participants? How can government encourage changes in banking and realty practices?
- Is the negotiated agreement clear and understood by all parties? Are roles well defined? Objectives established? Commitments secure? Schedules agreed to?

Implementing Action Agreements

- What vehicle will be used for implementing the agreements?
- What assurance is there that the agreements will be carried out?
- What responsibility does each partner in the agreement (the local government, banks, community groups) have for implementation?
- What measures (e.g., number of new housing units, percentage of elderly placed) will be used to determine if the approach is working?
- Who will monitor and report on the progress of the agreement to see that it is realized?
- What mechanism will be used to keep the lines of communication open among partners during the implementation of the agreement?
- What is the contingency plan if the initiative fails or goes awry?

Conclusion

Communities, in their attempts to meet shelter needs of the aged, increasingly seek to use the widest range of public and private resources available. As this chapter describes, there are many public and private policy tools that can be used to accomplish these objectives. Six general approaches beyond traditional financial assistance programs have been discussed: regulation and deregulation, tax policy, administrative reform, public-private collaboration, self-help, and advocacy. The effectiveness of these approaches can be enhanced if several tools are used in concert. The best means for doing this is the development of a process that brings public, private, and community actors together (collaborative problem solving). Involvement of state, local, community, and business groups and the systematic application of problem-solving approaches should produce a positive influence on the local economic and social forces that both cause and solve housing problems facing the aged. While the procedures reviewed here will not by themselves resolve all problems, they reflect a creative and productive alternative to the narrow conceptualization of housing solutions represented by traditional federal housing programs. The full potential of various public and private policy options approaches is only beginning to be tested.

References

Chmura, T., et al. 1981. *Using Policy Options to Address Needs of Older Americans: An Overview.* Menlo Park, CA: Public Policy Center, SRI International.

Gollub, J., and S. Waldhorn. 1981. *Nonservice Approaches to Problems of the Aged—A White House Mini-Conference.* Menlo Park, CA: Public Policy Center, SRI International.

Gollub, J., et al. 1981. *Using Nonservice Approaches to Address Local Social Welfare Problems—A Guide for Local Officials.* Menlo Park, CA: Public Policy Center, SRI International.

———. 1983. *Promoting Indirect Services: Lessons from Seven Local Demonstrations.* Menlo Park, CA: Public Policy Center, SRI International.

Waldhorn, S., and J. Gollub. 1980. *Using Nonservice Approaches to Address Local Social Welfare Problems—A Guide for Local Officials.* Menlo Park, CA: Public Policy Center, SRI International.

CHAPTER 22 Are Mobile Homes a Solution to the Housing Problems of Low-Income Elders?

Barbara A. Haley

Soaring housing costs in the 1970s have helped exacerbate a situation in which many low-income elderly and other low-income families face the prospect of being unable to pay for decent, safe housing (U.S. House, 1982). At least 30 percent of the elderly live in substandard, deteriorating or dilapidated housing (U.S. Senate, 1977). As discussed elsewhere in this book, government programs through the years have been either ineffectual or too underfunded to redress these conditions adequately. Since 1980, the reduced commitment by the federal government to federal housing programs has been accompanied by a search for alternatives in the private sector to replace federal rent subsidies. Mobile homes have gained recognition by the President's Commission on Housing as a "significant source of affordable housing for American families," especially for the elderly and low- and moderate-income families (U.S. President's Commission on Housing, 1982, p. 85). This chapter explores the question of whether privately purchased mobile homes can be reasonably expected to replace subsidized housing as a source of shelter for the low-income elderly. A brief overview of who is currently served and a discussion of barriers to wider utilization are included.

A National Profile

Mobile homes were first introduced to the U.S. housing market in 1930.[1] By 1963, every tenth new house in the United States was a mobile home (Clark, 1972); by 1971 this figure had increased to one in every three (Drury, 1972). Currently, mobile homes and other manufactured housing constitute nearly all of the new housing that costs under $40,000 (U.S. DHUD, 1982). These dwellings have been used primarily by young families and the elderly, who were attracted to mobile homes because of a perception of easy maintenance and the gregarious social environment of many mobile home parks as well as by their relatively low sale price (Edwards, Klemmack, and Hatos, 1973; Johnson, 1971). These dwellings have offered greater privacy and open space than apartments and have satisfied a desire for single-family home ownership (Drury, 1972).

The 1980 Annual Housing Survey, sponsored by the U.S. Department of Housing and Urban Development, provides data on which to base a profile of the characteristics of mobile homes and the households in them headed by a person sixty-five years of age or older.[2] The 1980 survey,

The author wishes to thank Ann Alfaro-Carrea, Winston Punch, Ronald Monrony, Franz Seitz, Lois Starkey, and Gloria Schroeder for their encouragement and assistance in the preparation of this chapter.

planned and conducted by the U.S. Census, also provides information on the households that were living at or below the federal poverty level.[3]

In 1980, 836,300 households headed by persons sixty-five years or older lived in mobile homes, an increase of 67 percent since 1975. The total population of these households was 1.2 million people. The graying of the entire mobile home population continued in the late 1970s: in 1975, 17 percent of the people living in mobile homes were elderly (Rausch and Hoover, 1980); by 1980, this proportion had increased to 21 percent. These increases in the elderly mobile home population parallel the increase in the number of elderly households nationally. Thus, the proportion of all older people in mobile homes has remained constant since 1975 at about 5 percent (Rausch and Hoover, 1980).

Ownership of mobile homes was nearly universal, with 90 percent being owned or bought. Ownership of the land occupied by the home was comparatively rare, with slightly less than one-quarter (23 percent) owning the site itself. This low percentage is partly the result of the extensive use of mobile home parks for sites. More than half (59 percent) of the homes are located in parks (defined by the AHS as any group of six or more mobile homes). The wide use of parks is partly due to more than half (52 percent) being located in SMSAs, which typically lack large tracts of land. As discussed below, towns and cities place very tight restrictions on the location of mobile homes within their boundaries. Elders living in mobile homes are slightly less likely to endure inadequate plumbing facilities than their counterparts in conventional housing were, with 2 and 4 percent, respectively, reporting this problem.

Mobile homes are apparently favored by younger elders. Only 14 percent of the household heads were aged eighty or older, whereas 39 percent of the heads of conventional households were this old. The elderly in mobile homes were almost exclusively white. Only 3 percent had nonwhite heads, whereas 10 percent of the elderly households in conventional housing were headed by nonwhites.

Of the four census regions, nearly half the elderly-headed mobile home households were located in the western region (table 22-1). Nearly three-quarters of these households were located inside an SMSA. The southern region contained nearly a third of the households. Many of these units (58 percent) were located in rural areas. The southern mobile home households were least likely of all regions to be located in mobile home parks, with only 39 percent in groups of six or more units. These households were also least likely to own their units, with 5 percent renting for cash and an additional 9 percent living in their units without cash rent. However, owners were the most likely in all regions to own their site, with 35 percent owning the land on which they were located. Southern households were most likely to live in deficient units, with 4 percent lacking complete plumbing. More than three-quarters (78 percent) of all elderly blacks living in mobile homes were located in the south.

The northeastern region (8 percent) and the northcentral region (15 percent) make up the balance of all households. Nearly half of these households (41 percent) in each region were located in urban areas. And, about half (44 and 45 percent, respectively) of the households were located in mobile home parks.

Differences by Gender of Head

The characteristics of elderly mobile home households vary widely depending on the gender of the head of the household. Female-headed households—those containing a woman with no adult male present—comprised two-fifths (41 percent) of the households. Males usually live in households with a spouse and no other relatives (table 22-2). The vast majority (88 percent) of the female-headed households contain a single woman. However, as with female-headed households in conventional housing, other relatives (not including spouses) were occasionally present; 7 percent contained other relatives. As in conventional housing, owners tended to be male. But unlike conventional housing, the households in very

TABLE 22-1. Comparison of Selected Characteristics by Census Region for Households in Mobile Homes with Head 65 Years or Older for 1980 (In thousands)

	Northcentral		Northeast		South		West	
	No.	%	No.	%	No.	%	No.	%
Total	125.6	100	65.3	100	263.8	100	381.6	100
Metropolitan Location								
Inside SMSA	52.6	42	26.9	41	75.9	29	282.8	74
(Urban)	(47.6)	(38)	(21.4)	(33)	(68.0)	(26)	(275.3)	(72)
(Rural)	(5.0)	(4)	(5.4)	(8)	(7.9)	(3)	(7.5)	(2)
Outside SMSA	73.0	58	38.4	59	187.9	71	98.9	26
(Urban)	(3.2)	(3)	(4.6)	(7)	(42.2)	(16)	(14.2)	(4)
(Rural)	(69.8)	(56)	(33.8)	(52)	(145.7)	(55)	(84.6)	(22)
Tenure								
Own or buying	113.4	90	60.8	93	229.1	87	353.4	93
Rent for cash	6.0	5	3.8	6	12.3	5	14.5	4
No cash rent	6.2	5	.7	1	22.3	9	13.7	4
Ownership of Site, For Owners of Units								
Owned	27.8	22	21.6	33	93.0	35	48.4	13
Not owned	71.7	57	38.5	59	115.6	44	286.9	75
Ownership of Site, For Renters of Units								
Owned	—	—	—	—	1.6	1	—	—
Not owned	8.4	7	3.8	6	25.3	10	27.6	7
Location in Park								
Group of 1–6 units	69.1	55	37.0	57	160.9	61	75.5	20
Group of 7–98	16.2	13	17.5	27	55.6	21	138.0	36
Group of 100+	40.3	32	10.9	17	47.3	18	168.2	44
Plumbing Facilities								
Complete	123.2	98	65.3	100	252.6	96	376.6	99
Incomplete or shared	2.4	2	—	—	11.2	4	5.0	1
Size of Household								
1 person	66.5	53	30.7	47	125.3	48	183.8	48
2 people	52.8	42	33.9	52	125.3	52	188.5	49
3 people	5.5	4	.8	1	6.2	2	6.0	2
4 or more people	.8	1	—	—	6.8	3	3.3	1
Race of Head								
White	125.6	100	63.8	98	246.3	93	376.4	99
Black	—	—	1.5	2	13.4	5	2.2	1
Other	—	—	—	—	4.1	1	3.0	1

SOURCE: *U.S. Department of Housing and Urban Development. 1980 Annual Housing Survey.*

219

TABLE 22-2. Differences by Gender of Head for Selected Characteristics of Households with Head 65 Years or Older in 1980 (in thousands)

	Mobile Homes				Conventional Housing			
	Male-Headed		Female-Headed		Male-Headed		Female-Headed	
	No.	%	No.	%	No.	%	No.	%
Total	495.2	100	341.2	100	8,700.7	100	6,680.5	100
Size of Household								
1 person	106.6	22	300.0	88	1,493.0	17	5,128.5	78
2 people	371.9	75	28.5	8	5,892.7	68	1,090.3	16
3 people	11.9	2	6.7	2	841.2	10	208.2	3
4 or more people	4.7	1	6.2	3	473.7	6	163.3	3
Number of People Aged 65+ Years in Household								
1 person	245.4	50	334.0	98	4,093.9	47	6,204.0	93
2 people	249.7	50	4.3	1	4,495.6	52	446.5	7
3 people	—	—	2.9	1	107.8	1	25.1	—
4 or more people	—	—	—	—	3.2	—	4.8	—
Presence of Relatives (nonspouse)								
No relatives	486.5	98	314.2	92	7,843.6	90	5,711.5	86
Other relatives present	5.6	1	24.0	7	735.9	9	820.9	12
Nonrelatives present	3.1	1	3.0	1	9.5	1	141.1	2
Ownership of Unit								
Own or buying	466.5	94	289.3	85	6,864.3	76	4,084.7	61
Rent for cash	15.5	3	21.1	6	1,643.2	19	2,373.5	36
No cash rent	13.2	3	29.8	8	193.1	2	222.2	3
Number of Rooms								
1	6.7	1	—	—	171.1	2	113.3	2
2	26.0	5	22.4	7	192.3	2	323.8	5
3	75.6	15	88.1	26	678.3	8	1,168.7	18
4	243.9	49	155.2	46	1,660.2	19	1,553.6	23
5	114.1	23	70.5	21	2,366.2	27	1,598.7	24
6	28.9	6	3.6	1	2,035.8	23	1,103.1	17
7	—	—	1.5	—	879.6	10	453.6	7
8 or more	—	—	—	—	716.6	8	365.8	5
No Telephone	50.6	10	23.8	7	522.6	6	323.1	5
Plumbing Facilities								
Complete	480.3	97	337.4	99	8,374.6	96	6,451.8	97
Incomplete or shared	14.8	3	3.8	1	325.9	4	228.7	3

SOURCE: *U.S. Department of Housing and Urban Development. 1980 Annual Housing Survey.*

Raw data are unadjusted for missing values.

small mobile homes with one room (these are likely to be converted travel trailers) were almost exclusively male-headed. Almost no differences were present in the likelihood to have telephones. Male-headed households were more likely to lack complete plumbing. Female-headed households were most likely to pay cash rent. As with conventional housing, female-headed households were most likely to live in poverty. One-fifth of the female-headed households had poverty incomes, while one-twelfth (8 percent) of the male-headed households lived at this level.

Poverty among Mobile Home Households

In 1980, 13 percent of the households in mobile homes with heads sixty-five years and older had incomes that were at or below the federal poverty level (table 22-3). This concentration of elders in poverty was slightly lower than for conventional housing, in which 15 percent of the households of elders were living in poverty. The distribution of low-income mobile home households by region generally followed the distribution of mobile home units with 7 percent of the elders in poverty in mobile homes living in the northeastern census region, and 13 percent in the northcentral census region. Poverty households (47 percent) were represented in the southern census region, and underrepresented (33 percent) in the west. Except for in the west, low-income mobile home households tended to be located outside of mobile home parks. About half of the low-income elders in mobile homes live in rural areas. By contrast, three-quarters of the elders in poverty in conventional housing live in urban areas.

Nearly all (94 percent) of the poverty-level elders in mobile homes are white, whereas only three-quarters of the poverty-level elders in conventional housing are white.

TABLE 22-3. Selected Characteristics of Elderly-Headed Households with Income at or Below the Poverty Level in 1979 (In thousands)

	Mobile Homes		Conventional Housing	
	No.	Percent	No.	Percent
Total Region	110.3	100	2,231.7	100
Northeast—Total	7.3	7	373.2	17
(not in park)	(4.3)	(4)		
Northcentral—Total	14.8	13	552.0	25
(not in park)	(10.1)	(9)		
South—Total	51.6	47	1,074.2	48
(not in park)	(37.8)	(34)		
West—Total	36.5	33	232.4	10
(not in park)	(7.4)	(7)		
Metropolitan Location				
Inside SMSA	54.4	49	1,332.0	60
Outside SMSA	55.9	51	899.8	40
Urban Location				
Urban (pop = 2,500+)	56.4	51	1,683.4	75
Rural (farm)	3.1	3	57.1	3
Rural (nonfarm)	50.8	46	491.2	22

TABLE 22-3. *(continued)*

	Mobile Homes		Conventional Housing	
	No.	**Percent**	**No.**	**Percent**
Ownership				
Own or buying	85.8	78	1,235.4	55
Rent for cash	12.3	11	838.3	38
No cash rent	12.2	11	158.0	7
Presence of Mortgage, For Owners				
Mortgage	8.4	8	134.5	6
No mortgage	71.1	65	863.4	39
Size of Unit				
1 room	1.7	2	83.9	4
2 rooms	10.7	10	121.0	5
3 rooms	36.6	33	402.4	18
4 or more rooms	61.3	56	1,624.4	73
Plumbing Facilities				
Complete	100.2	91	1,987.9	89
Incomplete or shared	10.0	9	243.9	11
Presence of Telephone				
Telephone	88.4	80	1,923.6	86
No telephone	21.9	20	308.1	14
Household Composition				
Male head with wife present	23.7	22	459.9	21
Other male head	.8	1	73.8	3
Female head	9.2	8	276.2	12
Single male	16.4	15	265.1	12
Single female	60.1	55	1,156.7	52
Presence of Children Under 18 Years				
No children	105.4	96	2,202.5	99
Children	4.9	4	29.2	1
Race of Head				
White	103.2	94	1,688.3	76
Black	7.1	6	509.6	23
Other	—	—	33.8	2
Ownership of Site, For Owners				
Owner	14.7	13	—	—
Not owned	63.4	58	—	—

TABLE 22-3. *(continued)*

	Mobile Homes		Conventional Housing	
	No.	**Percent**	**No.**	**Percent**
Ownership of Site, For Renters				
Owned	.7	1	—	—
Not owned	21.4	19	—	—
Location in Park				
Group of 1–6 mobile homes	59.6	54	—	—
Group of 7–99 mobile homes	27.3	25	—	—
Group of 100+ mobile homes	23.3	21	—	—

SOURCE: *U.S. Department of Housing and Urban Development. 1980 Annual Housing Survey.*

As with conventional housing, about half (55 percent) of the poverty-level households contained single females. A fifth of all the single females in mobile homes lived in poverty, while only 6 percent of all the households containing a married couple were in poverty. Many of the female-headed households in mobile homes with poverty-level incomes paid an excessive proportion of their incomes for housing. The mean proportion of this group's income used for housing expenses was 45 percent.

The poverty-level elders in mobile homes were much more likely to live in small dwellings than poverty-level elders in conventional housing. Nearly half lived in three or fewer rooms while a quarter of the elders in conventional housing lived in three or fewer rooms.

Barriers to Access

A variety of factors have contributed to the present distribution of older people in mobile homes. Several of these are reviewed here for both their applicability as barriers to wider use by the low-income elderly and as areas for policy intervention.

Affordability

It appears that many elders in mobile homes sold their conventional dwellings, bought their mobile homes outright, and used the difference in price as funds to supplement their incomes (Davidson, 1973). The expectation that poverty-level elders can follow this pattern lacks an appreciation of their limited asset position. Only half of this group are homeowners. Moreover, in 1976, half of the low-income homeowners lived in houses that were valued at less than $15,000 (Struyk and Soldo, 1980). In that year, the average price of a manufactured dwelling was $12,740, excluding the cost of transportation, land, site preparation, or installment onto the site (Nutt-Powell, 1982). These costs can easily add several thousand dollars to the purchase price. Thus, the low-income elder is likely to have no other option but to acquire a mobile home with installment credit. Mortgage credit is not available unless the owner has land and sufficient resources to attach the unit to a permanent foundation (U.S. DHUD, 1983).

Mobile homes that are not fixed to permanent foundations are legally defined as personal property; consequently these purchases are financed through consumer credit rather than mortgages. Usually consumer credit from a bank is much more expensive than mortgage credit. For example, Nutt-Powell (1982) found that in order to purchase a $12,000 mobile home (at 16.5 percent interest for a seven-year period) and pay a low $80 per month rent on a site, a family would need an annual income of $14,220, an amount that far exceeds the poverty level for nearly all elderly-headed households. The problem of affordability of mobile homes is nothing new. More than a decade ago, MacFall and Gordon (1973) observed that, coupled with high downpayment requirements, even inexpensive models were out of reach of most low-income families.

Used mobile homes are considerably less expensive than the new homes, but the alternative of purchasing used units necessitates the consideration of the question of durability. Mobile homes belong to two classes: those built according to the HUD Manufactured Housing Construction and Safety Standards (see *U.S. Federal Register*, 1975) and those built prior to 1976 when these standards became law. Estimates of the expected average life span of a mobile home built before 1976 range from seven to sixteen years (MacFall and Gordon, 1973; Center for Auto Safety, 1975; Drury, 1972). The result is an investment with rapidly depreciating value. Thus, an elder at age sixty-five who purchases one of these older units could easily find him/herself at age eighty without a decent home and without a major asset that could be converted into suitable housing. The life span of the newer units built under the HUD code has not yet been determined.

Availability of Sites

The second problem a prospective park resident must face is finding a space for their unit. Due to zoning restrictions, very few available sites near urban areas exist (Rausch and Hoover, 1980; Center for Auto Safety, 1975). This shortage is exacerbated by the common practice of park operators reserving vacant spaces for mobile homes that they or approved dealers have for sale. The shortage of space is especially acute for the owners of the less expensive, single-section units. Many new parks and older parks that are attempting to "upgrade" themselves will only admit the larger, multisection units.[4]

Mobile home parks have usually been banned from residential areas and zoned into fringe, commercial, or industrial areas. Local officials have often contributed to the unattractiveness and lack of safety in many parks by relegating them to flood plains or next to highways and by refusing responsibility for streets and sewage systems (Center for Auto Safety, 1975). Only a few states have acted to outlaw complete exclusion of parks from their communities (Nutt-Powell, 1982), and the New Jersey Supreme Court (1983) has set a precedent in that state by ruling that communities cannot use zoning to exclude low-income people.

Further complicating these problems is a trend for some older parks in commercially zoned areas to be sold for other uses (Nutt-Powell, 1982). The residents of such older parks are themselves usually elderly. They have often had to bear complete losses for they rarely have had the capital to purchase their parks, and the units themselves have often been unmovable. In fact only 2 percent of all mobile homes are ever moved after the initial installation.

An elder with low income (or anyone else) who wishes to live in a mobile home outside of a park is likely to be left no choice but to move to a rural area that is far from services.[5] The Center for Auto Safety (1975) estimated that due to zoning, no private lots have been available in 60 percent of all rural and urban communities. As of 1982, a majority of jurisdictions continued to exclude mobile homes and other manufactured housing. The minority that allowed these dwellings in residential districts subjected them to "aesthetic controls" (U.S. DHUD, 1982). These controls typically require that the mobile homes look like conventional units, with such amenities as sloping roofs, a minimum width and/or minimum amount of interior square footage. All these requirements have the effect of precluding the use of the least expensive units. A HUD-sponsored demonstration aimed at showing that mobile homes and other manufactured housing could look like conventional housing was completed in 1982 in Elkhart, Indiana. The total price of the least expensive unit (including delivery, installation, and utilities but excluding the cost of land) was $33,000. Elimination of landscaping and the use of a smaller unit could lower the total cost to an estimated $25,000 (excluding land). In 1980 and 1981, other mobile home sub-divisions in California, Washington, and Illinois contained homes costing $49,000 to $69,000, including land (Nutt-Powell, 1982).

According to Bernhardt (1980), very few states are expecting to decrease their present zoning restrictions. Without such changes any federal government efforts to encourage the production of mobile homes and other manufactured housing, especially that looking like conventional housing and attached to a permanent foundation, may stimulate mobile home ownership among middle-income families. However, prices of mobile homes made to look like conventional housing are well beyond the means of a low-income household.

Race and Park Admission

Mobile homes continued to be used almost exclusively by whites, especially among the elderly. While 93 percent of the heads of all mobile home households were white, 97 percent of those with elderly heads were white. These proportions are not consistent with either the total population or the low-income population. According to the U.S. Census (cited by Wallace, 1981), of the total black population sixty-five years and older, 36 percent lived below the poverty level in 1975. Among elderly whites, only 13 percent lived in poverty. Black elders have been more likely to live in substandard or deficient dwellings than white elders (Hoover, 1981).

One reason for the low representation of minorities in mobile homes has probably been their relatively low rates of homeownership: 57 percent of the elderly black households were owners in 1975. By contrast, 72 percent of the white households were owners in that year (Hoover, 1981). Low-income nonwhite elders are more likely than whites to have had low incomes for their entire adult lives.

Racial and ethnic discrimination on the part of mobile home park operators may also play a role in proportion of minority persons in mobile home units (Center for Auto Safety, 1975; and Smith, 1976). The 1980 Annual Housing Survey contains data that supports this assertion. It shows that all or nearly all of the black elders in mobile homes lived outside of parks. Whether consumption preferences also act to limit the acquisition of mobile homes is unknown, for studies that compare black and white attitudes toward mobile homes do not exist.

Rents and Rules

The elder who chooses to live in a park faces additional problems. In many parks, the resident has the status of "tenant-at-will" (Nutt-Powell, 1982; Center for Auto Safety, 1975). The usual laws that govern landlord–tenant relations do not apply here; a resident can be evicted for no reason with only a few days' notice. In many more parks, only short-term (one to three years) leases are available. Rent controls on park sites are rare. No states have legislated guidelines that protect a resident from rent increases that are not accompanied by increases in park services. This can create significant hardship in areas such as the southern two-thirds of Florida where park vacancies are nonexistent and there is a high demand for spaces. In southern Florida annual increases have often exceeded 50 percent.[6]

In addition to rents, mobile home parks are also likely to have rules covering permissible activities of residents that invade the privacy that is taken for granted by tenants of conventional housing. A resident can be told when to water her lawn, how late in the evenings she can use her television, or whether she can hold a paying job. In Florida, a resident can be evicted for the second infraction of any rule, no matter how petty it might be. The Center for Auto Safety (1975, p. 65) concludes that the effects of overzealous rule making is often the creation of "a virtual police state." Legal remedies are unlikely, for the courts have shown a reluctance to infringe on long-held property rights of park owners.[7] Because sites are difficult to obtain, market mechanisms will not correct these problems. States have the authority to set guidelines or standards for park operators, yet few of them have adopted such statutes.

Safety

The mobile homes built prior to 1976 have shown themselves to be far less safe than conventional housing. The extensive use of polyvinylchloride and other plastics, plywood coated with highly combustible materials, and light-weight construction in long, narrow building designs, have rendered these older mobile homes easily destructible by fire, wind, and other natural disasters (Clark, 1972). These mobile homes burn rapidly when they catch fire. Data from both pre– and post–1976-building-code homes show that the fatality rate for mobile home fires was at least two times greater than that for conventional homes (Center for Auto Safety, 1975; Schaenman and Herrin, 1982). According to the Center for Auto Safety (1975) the rate of destruction by wind was thirty times greater than for conventional homes. These mobile homes have had death rates from windstorms that are ten times the death rate in conventional houses. Winds that are sufficiently strong to overturn an unanchored mobile home— gusts to seventy miles per hour—occur in every state. While tie-downs afford some protection from wind damage, their use is not required in the HUD code or the laws of most states (Center for Auto Safety, 1975; *U.S. Federal Register*, 1975).

Conclusion

In 1980, almost 1.2 million elderly persons lived in mobile homes. Between 1975 and 1980 the percentage of households headed by elders living in mobile homes remained constant at about 5 percent. This constancy during a period of rapidly escalating housing costs suggests that the problems associated with mobile home ownership may be so severe that little confidence can be placed on the prediction that 8 percent of the elderly will live in mobile homes by the year 2000 (Struyk, 1981). Moreover, the growth and availability of this housing has not generally followed the distribution of the total population. The west has overtaken the south as the region containing the highest percentage of these households. Nearly half were in the west, and an additional third lived in the south. The areas with the oldest housing stock, the northeastern and northcentral regions, combine for less than one-quarter of the units.

The skewed geographic distribution of this housing, its cost, and the apparent orientation of park managers to whites are indications that the use of privately purchased mobile homes to replace subsidized housing for elders with poverty-level incomes has not yet emerged as a strong market-driven response to this housing need. These dwellings have been somewhat available as a source of low-cost housing for rural elderly residents, but this is much less true for urban residents, particularly those in large cities of the northeastern and northcentral regions of the country. There is no reason to believe that new units will be affordable to these elders in the future without some kind of financial assistance. Used units are often not available because of the selling practices of mobile home park operators and because of a high level of risk of damage associated with moving these units. Units built prior to 1976 (a potential low-cost alternative) and perhaps even those since that date offer limited durability, wind damage potential, and fire hazards that far exceed those of conventional housing. Even if mobile homes were affordable, a lack of available sites in most communities would leave most new owners no option but to move to rural areas that are far from services and family-support networks. To assume that this kind of location is suitable for most poverty-level elders is to ignore their wide diversity of needs and preferences.

In short, the viability of mobile home housing for the elderly, especially the low-income elderly, will require changes in financing, changes in zoning laws and land-use policies, less restrictive mobile home park location practices, improvements in design and construction, incentives to attract in-movers, and sanctions aginst park operators who raise site rents excessively, discriminate against nonwhite in-movers, or impose other practices that invade privacy or inhibit the availability of qualified residents. Actions in these areas will involve mobile home manufacturers, park operators, federal, state, and local governments and the court system. However, even if changes could be made quickly and uniformly across the country, shortages of large tracts of urban land and the well-documented attachment of the elderly to their neighborhoods (Speare, 1970; Pickvance, 1973; Lawton and Cohen, 1974) suggest that mobile homes cannot by themselves meet the housing needs of the majority of urban low-income elderly because they live in urban areas.

Notes

1. The mobile home is defined here as a detached single-family dwelling unit that has been designed for long-term occupancy. Resting on its own chassis, it contains sleeping accommodations and a complete kitchen and bath. It is designed to be transported after fabrication in a factory on its own wheels or on a flat-bed trailer. It arrives at its site as a complete dwelling, usually including major appliances and furniture. It is not usually permanently fixed onto a conventional foundation; usual installation is on a concrete pad. Unlike a travel trailer, it is not easily moved and cannot be towed by an automobile. Few are moved after the initial installation because of high costs, high risk of permanent damage, and a lack of available units. The producers of this kind of dwelling now refer to these units as "manufactured housing." However, since this term also applies to other varieties of factory-built housing, the older term "mobile home" will be used in this essay.

2. All mobile homes with occupants whose usual residence was elsewhere are excluded from this discussion.

3. Questions on income in the 1980 Annual Housing Survey asked about income during the preceding year. Poverty, therefore, was defined in terms of the federal poverty standard for 1979. A poverty-level income varies according to the number of persons in a household and location in an urban area. For example, the poverty level for a single person outside an urban area was $3,400, but poverty for a two person household in an urban area was $4,500.

4. Telephone interview with Kelly Mione, Director of Communications for the Federation of Mobile Home Owners of Florida, Largo, Florida; June 8, 1983.

5. In some states, county zoning ordinances require that the mobile home in a rural area be placed on a large parcel of land. For example, Kelly Mione reports that in rural Florida a minimum of five acres is required for each mobile home.

6. Telephone interview with Kelly Mione; June 8, 1983.

7. To further illustrate this issue, Kelly Mione in a telephone interview reports that rules in Florida must be "reasonable." This is legally determined by the presence of similar rules in other parks in one's general vicinity. A circuit court in that state recently ruled that it is "reasonable" to have a rule that requires a tenant sign a lease or be evicted, even if the lease contains provisions that are illegal. This ruling is being appealed. Other examples of "reasonable" rules include a stipulation regarding the maximum number of people who can live in a home, a requirement to register one's overnight guests, charges for overnight guests, stipulations regarding the number of people who can live in a unit, a ban on working on one's auto in the park, a ban on hanging out one's laundry to dry outside the unit, the requirement that a resident can only sell his/her unit to a buyer who qualifies for tenancy in the park, the requirement that a resident be "retired," and a ban on "disturbing activities."

References

Bernhardt, A. D. 1980. *Building Tomorrow: The Mobile/Manufactured Housing Industry.* Cambridge, MA: MIT.

Center for Auto Safety. 1975. *Mobile Homes: The Low-Cost Housing Hoax.* New York: Grossman.

Clark, M. L. 1972. *The Illusion of Mobile Homes as Supplemental Housing for Low Income Families.* Monticello, IL: Council of Planning Librarians, No. 349.

Davidson, H. A. 1973. *Housing Demand: Mobile, Modular, or Conventional.* New York: Van Nostrand Reinhold.

Drury, M. J. 1972. *Mobile Homes: The Unrecognized Revolution in American Housing.* Rev. 1972 Ed. New York: Praeger.

Edwards, J. N., D. L. Klemmack, and L. Hatos. 1973. "Social Participation Patterns Among Mobile-Home and Single-Family Dwellers." *Social Forces* 51, No. 4:485–89.

Hoover, S. L. 1981. "Black and Spanish Elderly: Their Housing Characteristics and Housing Quality." In *Community Housing Choices for Older Americans.* Ed. P. Lawton, and S. L. Hoover. New York: Springer.

Johnson, S. R. 1971. *Idle Haven.* Berkeley, CA: Univ. of California Press.

Lawton, M. P., and J. Cohen. 1974. "The Generality of Housing Impact on the Well-being of Older People." *Gerontologist* 29, no. 2: 194–204.

MacFall, E. A., and E. Q. Gordon. 1973. *Mobile Homes and Low Income Rural Families.* Washington, DC: U.S. Office of Economic Opportunity.

New Jersey Supreme Court. 1983. *So. Burlington N.A.A.C.P. et al. v. twp. of Mount Laurel.* Text of Mount Laurel II. Trenton, NJ: New Jersey Manufactured Housing Association.

Nutt-Powell, T. E. 1982. *Manufactured Homes: Making Sense of a Housing Opportunity.* Boston: Auburn.

Pickvance, C. G. 1973. "Life Cycle, Housing Tenure and Residential Mobility: A Path Analytic Approach." *Urban Studies* 117: 171–88.

Rausch, K. J., and S. L. Hoover. 1980. *Mobile Home Elderly: Structural Characteristics of their Dwellings.* Philadelphia, PA: Philadelphia Geriatric Center.

Schaenman, P. S., and C. L. Herrin. 1982. *Evaluation of Mobile Home Fire Safety: 1979–1980.* HUD-7005-

82. Washington, DC: U.S. Department of Housing and Urban Development.

Smith, R. A. 1976. "An Analysis of Black Occupancy of Mobile Homes." *Journal of American Institute of Planners* 42:410–18.

Speare, A., Jr. 1970. "Home Ownership, Life Cycle State and Residential Mobility." *Demography* 7, no. 4: 449–58.

Struyk, R. J. 1981. "The Changing Housing and Neighborhood Environment of the Elderly." In *Aging: Social Change.* Ed. March, Kiesler, Morgan, and Oppenheimer. New York: Academic.

Struyk, R. J., and B. J. Soldo. 1980. *Improving the Elderly's Housing.* Cambridge, MA: Ballinger.

U.S. Bureau of the Census. 1980. *Annual Housing Survey: 1980.* Washington, DC: U.S. Government Printing Office.

U.S. Department of Housing and Urban Development (DHUD). 1982. *Affordable Housing: A National Symposium.* Proceedings of the Event. Washington, DC: U.S. Departmennt of Housing and Urban Development.

———. 1983. *More Favorable Mortgage Insurance Allowed by HUD for Manufactured Homes.* News Release, 24 February. Washington, DC: U.S. Department of Housing and Urban Development, Office of Public Affairs.

U.S. Federal Register. 1975. "Mobile Home Construction and Safety Standards." *Federal Register*, 40, No. 244, (December): 58752–92.

U.S. House of Representatives. 1982. Select Committee on Aging. Subcommittee on Housing and Consumer Interests. Hearing: *Housing the Elderly: Present Problems and Future Consideration,* 29 July 1981. Washington, DC: U.S. Government Printing Office.

U.S. President's Commission on Housing. 1982. *The Report of the President's Commission on Housing.* Washington, DC: U.S. Government Printing Office.

U.S. Senate. 1977. Special Committee on Aging. *Developments in Aging: 1976.* Part 1. Washington, DC: U.S. Government Printing Office.

Wallace, E. C. 1981. "Housing for the Black Elderly—the Need Remains." In *Community Housing Choices for Older Americans.* Ed. P. Lawton, and S. L. Hoover, New York: Springer.

CHAPTER 23 Land-use Regulations for the Elderly

Robert Hopperton

The title of this paper suggests a point frequently overlooked in discussions of older Americans and land-use control devices such as zoning. Most discussions focus on the obstacles and problems (and their solutions) and overlook the fact that most elderly live in noninstitutional settings and, therefore, are directly benefited and protected rather than injured by existing land-use regulations.

In other words, a land-use control such as zoning, which is a very effective device for conserving existing land uses and lifestyles, operates to protect the elderly just as it protects the lifestyle and property values of nonelderly residents of a residential area. When the existing zoning is age-neutral (does not explicitly take the age of the users into account) and when that existing zoning is designed "to establish a quiet place where yards are wide and people few, and motor vehicles are restricted, . . . where the blessings of quiet seclusion and clean air make a sanctuary for people,"[1] then young and old alike benefit from that protection. Just how and why the elderly benefit in these ways is discussed in the first section of this chapter.

The second section looks at some recent judicial and legislative developments that point the way to land-use laws that are specifically and explicitly favorable to the elderly. It is noteworthy that local and state land-use decision-makers often look favorably upon regulations that benefit the elderly. Local officials commonly view land uses in basic monetary terms. Is a land use a good ratable or a bad one? Will it generate income or act as a drain on community resources? Senior citizen developments, with their absence of school-age children, are good ratables. Also, the perceived disruptive influence of, for example, a student commune or a halfway house for parolees, is totally lacking with a housing development for senior citizens. Thus, housing for the elderly will usually be viewed as economically and politically desirable to a local constituency.

All of this is not to say, however, that local zoning never excludes housing for the elderly or creates significant problems for older Americans. It can and does. Section three discusses appropriate responses to solve these very real problems.

Land-use Planning and Age-neutral Zoning

Land-use planning is generally viewed as the process that formulates on a coordinated basis a community's basic policy decisions regarding physical layout and the distribution of land uses. Naturally, zoning is also concerned with physical layout and land distribution, but it is the implementing tool, the legal device to carry out the policy decisions. Said simply, zoning is the means to carry out land-use planning ends.

What sorts of land-use policies does zoning normally achieve (Williams, 1974)?

1. Diverse land uses are to be segregated, industry is excluded from commercial areas, and both industrial and commercial uses are excluded from residential zones. This prevents negative spill-

overs (smoke, noise, traffic) from disrupting residential settings.

2. Within residential zones, there is also a hierarchy from apartment zones at one end to two-family and, at the apex, single-family zones. Maximum protection in terms of lifestyle, aesthetics, privacy, and safety is provided to single-family areas.

Once a community has made its policy decisions such as those just summarized, its legislature enacts the appropriate implementing mechanisms. Zoning is a proper function of elected legislatures because land-use decisions are among the most significant the community has to make. Few decisions affect the character of the town or the property rights of its residents more than the designations of areas appropriate for residential, commercial, and industrial uses.

Zoning functions as an implementing device in three ways (Williams, 1974): it regulates the use of land, the size of structures, and the location of structures in relation to parcel lines.

The principal operating features of a zoning ordinance are the zoning districts it establishes. Typically zoning ordinances include basic use districts as well as height and area districts which are overlayed upon the use districts. The combination of these districts ensures that within each zone land uses are compatible with each other and that a commercial use of tremendous height and bulk (such as the World Trade Center in New York City) is not placed among single-family homes.

The zoning ordinance normally includes two components (Williams, 1974). The text of the ordinance establishes the district regulations while a zoning map illustrates the location of each zone within the community. Using the text and map in conjunction, a property owner or interested party can determine the zoning regulations for any parcel. The parcel or lot is the typical unit of regulation in zoning ordinance.

Local governments get their authority to zone from the state, either from the state constitution or a state zoning enabling act. This delegated authority flows from the state police power, the power to exercise controls to protect health, safety, morals, and general welfare. The power to zone in the public interest was upheld by the U.S. Supreme Court in 1926 in the landmark decision, *Village of Euclid* v. *Ambler Realty*.[2] The court held that the Euclid zoning ordinance which classified the village into residential, commercial, and unrestricted zones did not violate the Fourteenth Amendment of the U.S. Constitution.

The *Euclid* decision also established what has become the dominant judicial approach to reviewing the constitutionality of zoning laws. First, the court granted a presumption of validity to the local government's legislative decision (i.e., the zoning regulation adopted by the local legislature). Second, the burden of proving constitutional invalidity was placed on the party challenging the ordinance. Third, the standard of proof established by the court was "beyond fair debate."[3] This standard of proof, first articulated for zoning litigation in *Euclid*, is almost impossible for a challenger to meet. Thus, the dominant judicial approach, the one usually followed by the U.S. Supreme Court and also adopted by most state courts, makes existing zoning almost immune to successful challenge (Williams, 1974).

This immunity is the judicial shield that protects benefits offered by existing zoning legislation to the elderly. When zoning regulations that are age-neutral benefit senior citizens in the ways enumerated above, those regulations will not easily by invalidated by litigation. Thus, zoning generally gives stability, protection, and predictability to the neighborhood and to the lifestyle and property values of the elderly who live within it, while the dominant judicial approach gives stability, protection, and predictability to the zoning. In these ways, the elderly living in typical housing, in typical residential zones, can be and are benefited by local zoning.

Age-restrictive Zoning Favorable to the Elderly

The term *age-restrictive zoning* is used to describe land-use regulations that explicitly take into account the age of the users of land. The age restriction may affect elderly citizens in either favorable or unfavorable ways. In the leading case on zoning by age, *Taxpayer's Association* v. *Weymouth Township*,[4] the New Jersey Supreme Court held that the defendant township's zoning ordinance, which limited use of mobile units within a mobile home park to families in which the head of household or his spouse was fifty-two years of age or older, was within the zoning power delegated to the township by the state. Moreover, the court took note of the growing percentage of the population which is elderly, the needs of the elderly for lower cost housing, and the special physical and social needs of the elderly related to housing. The court then concluded that the township regulation violated neither constitutional equal protection nor substantive due process requirements.

The plantiff taxpayer's association in *Weymouth* wished to stop a mobile home development proposed by the defendant developer and approved by the defendant township. The proposal complied with the township's age-restrictive regulation, and plaintiffs hoped to kill the entire project by attacking the validity of that age classification. The court rejected the plaintiff's contentions that zoning cannot regulate land uses but only land users. Activities by different groups of users affect the community differently, and, therefore, the age restriction was, in the court's opinion, within the ambit of the New Jersey state zoning-enabling act.

The court also held that, because housing is not a fundamental right and because age is not a suspect criterion under the New Jersey Constitution, only a rational basis was required to sustain the ordinance against the plaintiff's equal protection attack.[5] Finding that rational basis, the court held that the ordinance did not violate equal protection.

Finally, the court held that the age restriction promoted the general welfare, concluding that zoning for a planned senior citizen housing development is presumptively valid, not presumptively invalid, as plaintiffs had argued, and that it, therefore, did not violate substantive due process.[6]

Other state judicial decisions also provide strong precedents supporting the proposition that age-restrictive zoning favorable to senior citizens promotes the general welfare and is legally and constitutionally permissible. (See the New York case, *Maldini* v. *Ambro*,[7] and the New Jersey case, *Shepard* v. *Woodland Township Committee and Planning Board*.[8])

While judicial trends favor zoning helpful to elderly citizens, a recent legislative enactment in New Jersey is also promising. The New Jersey legislature passed, as part of a general overhaul of its zoning-enabling act, specific permission for local governments to provide senior citizen housing. The New Jersey legislation provides an example of a very useful amendment that can be added to state zoning-enabling acts in other states in order to make clear that local governments may provide specifically favorable zoning treatment for senior citizen housing. As in the area of judicial developments, New Jersey provides leadership with regard to legislation favorable to senior citizens. (For more discussion, see Williams, 1974; Moskowitz, 1977; and *Land-Use and Zoning Law Digest*, 1983.)

Zoning Unfavorable to the Elderly

Although existing zoning may benefit the elderly, there are various specific zoning obstacles that often confront senior citizens. Parking requirements, density allowances, and exclusion of board-and-care homes through narrow definitions of "family" are three widespread examples.

Parking Requirements

Parking requirements in multifamily zones are designed to ensure parking spaces for younger working couples or families with children and, therefore, for more autos. These requirements can add significantly to a builder's development costs as more land is needed to provide the parking spaces. The same requirements imposed upon apartment developments for senior citizens, which are more likely to have few or no autos, add unnecessarily to development costs and rents. Some housing developments for the elderly might even become economically unfeasible and, therefore, not be built due to onerous and unnecessary parking requirements. For this reason, some local legislatures provide specific relief by reducing or eliminating parking requirements for senior citizen housing developments.

Density Allowances

Density requirements can make construction of housing for the elderly economically unfeasible. For this reason, many cities have solved this problem through legislative amendments to their zoning regulations that increase density allowances for senior citizen housing. There are various ways of doing this; for example, apartment zone regulations allowing fifteen units per acre might be modified to allow twenty-five or more units per acre of housing for the elderly. Other examples of solutions include concessions with regard to open space, floor area ratio, lot area per room and setback requirements.

Housing Restrictions

Many senior citizens require some assistance and supervision in their daily activities and, therefore, cannot live independently in a detached, single-family home or apartment. Various types of facilities offer such assistance to the elderly. These facilities receive varied treatment in local zoning ordinances. Not infrequently, the zoning ordinance will define "family" in such a way as to prohibit more than two or three unrelated adults from living together in a single unit in a desirable residential area of a city. This prohibition also excludes board-and-care homes for the elderly from areas in which most elderly will want to live.

Other zoning ordinances treat rooming or boarding houses as undesirable uses with all the negative connotations such terms carry.[9] Rooming and boarding houses are then excluded from desirable, residential neighborhoods and forced into commercial zones, "institutional zones," or rapidly declining multifamily residential districts.[10]

Exclusion from desirable residential neighborhoods is neither necessary nor appropriate for board-and-care homes or shared housing serving the elderly. Such homes do not negatively affect their surroundings as do rooming and boarding houses which serve transient clienteles. Therefore, such small group homes for senior citizens, which serve a stable, nondisruptive, and contributing segment of the population merit discerning zoning treatment.

For example, group homes can vary in size. Smaller homes serving up to six or eight clients are appropriate for treatment by local governments as "permitted uses" in single-family zones because they are of a size commensurate with surrounding homes.[11] Larger homes of nine to sixteen residents are appropriately treated as permitted uses in lower density mulitfamily zones. Homes of seventeen to thirty should be either permitted uses or conditionally permitted uses in high-density multifamily zones.[12] Many communities provide the graduated zoning treatments suggested above. In other communities the elderly, as well as planners and advocates on behalf of the elderly, need to lobby for improved zoning treatment of group homes.

In some cases, it may even be necessary to lobby for state legislation regarding zoning for such homes. Certain state legislatures, concerned about the exclusionary tendencies of local governments have preempted local land-use decision making in this area. For example, Vermont enacted legislation requiring local governments to treat board-and-care homes ("Registered Community Care Home") as permitted uses in single-family residential zones.[13] The state preemption of local decision making is also an approach that should be considered by the elderly and by planners and advocates for the elderly when confronted with widespread local intransigence relating to group homes (Hopperton, 1980).

It should be remembered that land-use barriers that have a negative impact on the elderly are most often a result of the legislative intent to solve problems unrelated to the use of land by senior citizens. Frequently, when it is pointed out to a local legislature that these unintended results have occurred, carefully drafted legislative amendments will be accepted and barriers removed.

Conclusion

Generally land-use controls in the United States pose neither widespread nor intractable problems for the elderly. For elderly Americans who reside in single-family detached housing, age-neutral land-use regulations commonly provide significant support and protection. In addition, this protection gets reinforced by prevailing judicial attitudes that presume that land-use regulations are constitutionally valid. Moreover, recent judicial and legislative trends, particularly in New Jersey, point the way to specifically favorable, age-restrictive zoning treatment for housing developments servicing the elderly.

On the other hand, where specific exclusionary barriers exist, particularized amendments that will remove obstacles to senior citizen housing can be offered to local decision-makers with the knowledge that such housing is customarily viewed in a sympathetic rather than hostile way. If, however, local opposition is unyielding, then the extraordinary device of preemptive state legislation should be considered. This is particularly true when important uses such as board-and-care and shared housing for the elderly are concerned.

Notes

1. Village of Bell Terre v. Boraas, 416 U.S. 1, at 9 (1973).
2. 272 U.S. 365 (1926).
3. 272 U.S. at 388.
4. 71 N. J. 249 (1976).
5. For a brief discussion of fundamental rights and suspect criteria as they relate to constitutional equal protection challenges to land-use regulations, see Godschalk, et al., (1979).
6. The plantiffs in *Weymouth* tried unsuccessfully to use the presumptive invalidity test that the New Jersey Supreme Court had developed in its first *Mount Laurel* decision. (Southern Burlington County NAACP v. Township of Mount Laurel, 67 N.J. 152 (1975). That decision found impermissible land-use regulations that excluded low- and moderate-income housing. For a discussion of the presumptive invalidity test see Moskowitz, (1977).

7. 36 N.Y. 2d 481 (1975).
8. 71 N.J. 230 (1976).
9. An example of a definition of a rooming or boarding house is as follows: "Boarding House" means a building other than a hotel, where room and board for three or more persons are served for compensation.
10. An "institutional zone" is not customarily used as an official zoning classification; it is a term used to describe districts, usually older, declining residential areas, where there exists a heavy concentration of uses such as, drug treatment centers, alcohol abuse facilities, nursing homes, and hospitals.
11. A "permitted use" is a use-by-right which is specifically authorized in a particular zoning district. See Meshenberg (1976).
12. A "conditionally permitted use" is a use authorized in a particular zoning district only if certain requirements or standards are met and only after approval is given by the local zoning appeals board or other public body. See Hopperton (1982).
13. Vt. Stat. Ann. Tit. 24, Section 4409 (Supp. 1982).

References

Godschalk, D. R, et al. 1979. *Constitutional Issues of Growth Management.* Chicago: Planners.

Hopperton, R. 1980. "A State Legislative Strategy for Ending Exclusionary Zoning of Community Homes." *Urban Law Annual,* 19 (Spring):47–85.

———. 1982. "Zoning for Community Homes Serving Developmentally Disabled Persons: Statutory Survey and Model Statute." In *Disabled Persons and the Law: State Legislative Issues.* Ed. B. D. Sales, and D.M. Powell. New York: Plenum.

Land-Use and Zoning Law Digest. 1983. No. 3. (March).

Meshenberg, M. D. 1976. *The Language of Zoning.* Planning Advisory Service Report No. 322. Chicago: American Society of Planning Officials.

Moskowitz, D. H. 1977. *Exclusionary Zoning Litigation.* Cambridge, MA: Ballinger.

Williams, N. 1974. *American Planning Law.* Vol. 1. Chicago: Callaghan.

CHAPTER 24 Continuing Care Retirement Communities: An Approach to Privately Financed Housing and Long-Term Care for the Elderly

Alwyn V. Powell • J. Alexander MacMurtrie

A relatively new and novel approach addressing the housing and health-care needs of the elderly is the Continuing Care Retirement Community (CCRC). The continuing care concept is founded primarily in the combination of the provision for housing and delivery of health-care services to the elderly. The financing mechanism used to fund these services is unique among housing alternatives for the over-age-sixty-five population. For purposes of this chapter, CCRCs (also known as Life-Care Communities) are defined to have the following characteristics:

- The physical plant consists of independent living units and generally has one or more of the following facilities: congregate living, personal care, intermediate nursing care, and skilled nursing care.
- The community guarantees housing and access to various health-care services under a contract with residents that lasts for more than one year.

- The additional fees for resident health care, if any, are less than the full costs of such services, implying an insurance approach to finance the health-care costs of contract-holders (Winklevoss and Powell, 1984).

A 1981 study conducted by the Wharton School of the University of Pennsylvania identified approximately 300 retirement communities nationwide that met the above definition (Winklevoss and Powell, 1982). A detailed twenty-four-page survey instrument was collected from 200 of these communities. Another 150 communities were identified as similar communities. The difference between these communities and CCRCs is the financing of health-care costs (fee-for-service versus risk pooling).

The median age for the CCRC institutions, as measured by the year they first offered a continuing care contract, is fourteen years. Because the industry is in its infancy, it is rather heteroge-

The authors would like to express their appreciation to the Pension Research Council of the Wharton School for allowing the use of statistics that were derived for *CCRCs: An Empirical, Financial, and Legal Analysis* (Winklevoss and Powell, 1984) and to a Delaware Valley CCRC for providing data on their historical population experience (see figs. 24-1 and 24-4).

neous, and dominant characteristics are difficult to discern. A summary of the general characteristics based on data collected in the 1981 survey (Winklevoss and Powell, 1984) is presented in the following section. The financial implications associated with continuing care contracts are discussed in the subsequent section.

General Characteristics

This industry has been characterized by rapid growth with over 40 percent of the communities surveyed opening during the 1970s. Many factors have contributed to this growth. One is the scarcity of comparable private and/or governmental programs providing a combination of housing and health care. Currently, Medicaid is the only public alternative that finances long-term nursing care (stays of over one year). The Medicaid option is available only after an individual has exhausted his or her assets. Therefore, it is not a desirable alternative for most of the elderly.

Another contributing factor is the changing demographic profile of the United States, with the over-age-sixty-five population growing fastest of all age groups. This results in an increasing need for the services offered by CCRCs. Due in part to the availability of construction monies, initially from conventional mortgage-lenders such as banks and insurance companies and currently through municipal revenue bonds, this concept gained rapid popularity. The growth rate slowed somewhat during the early 1980s because of unfavorable economic conditions. Nevertheless, one industry analyst predicts that 1,000 to 1,500 CCRCs or similar communities will be in operation by the end of the decade (Rose, 1982).

CCRCs are concentrated in states with the largest elderly populations such as California, Florida, Pennsylvania, Ohio, and Illinois. New York, with more than one million residents over age sixty-five, is missing from this list since the prepayment of future health care is legislatively prohibited there. However, there are several similar retirement facilities operating in New York

and elimination of the legislative barriers is being explored. Regionally, the northcentral area has the most CCRCs, corresponding to that region's high density of aged individuals. The South is currently the fastest growing region.

Almost all CCRCs are nonprofit (98 percent) and a substantial percentage have some type of religious affiliation, although this affiliation is not likely to include financial responsibility. CCRCs are relatively small with a median size of 245 residents. The trend among newer ones is toward larger populations so that the median for CCRCs opened since 1970 is 305 residents. The average entry age for admissions to CCRCs is fairly consistent, ranging from seventy-five to seventy-seven years and the average attained age in a demographically mature community (one that has been in operation for at least twelve years) is eighty-one years. Hence, these communities serve the "old-old."

Based on their mix of housing and health-care facilities, CCRCs reach two distinct elderly populations. One group is composed of ambulatory-independent residents who live in apartment units and whose average age is around eighty years (for a mature community). The other group consists of residents who require some type of supportive health-care service; their average age is around eighty-five years.

Services and security are the main selling points of CCRCs. There is a trend among newer communities to provide a "continuum of care," by offering services ranging from independent living to congregate care to personal, intermediate, and skilled nursing care on the same "campus." This is not typical, however, for older CCRCs (approximately 50 percent of the survey) which usually provided two extremes of care: independent living and skilled nursing.

Services and contract provisions offered to residents in exchange for the basic fees vary significantly among CCRCs. For example, 50 percent of the survey CCRCs include three meals with their basic fees, while 45 percent include one or no meals. Most of the CCRCs that include only one meal have opened since 1970, signaling a trend to offer services on an "à la carte" basis.

Policies regarding refund of entry fees upon the resident's death or withdrawal also vary. CCRCs consistently (90 percent) provide withdrawal refunds, usually prorated over five years. Refunds upon death are not as prevalent. Only 50 percent of CCRCs offer this type of refund, and the average period for eligibility is one year.

The primary distinctions among CCRC contracts are the fees paid for extended health care (this is mainly for nursing care services).[1] Although CCRCs by definition advance-fund (or repay) some portion of future costs, two distinct funding patterns have emerged. One is referred to as an "extensive health-care guarantee" which means that the resident does not pay additional fees for usage of the health-care center. Approximately 55 percent of existing CCRCs follow this traditional approach.

For the other 45 percent, the pattern is referred to as a "limited health-care guarantee" and implies that the resident will have to pay some additional charges for health-care usage over and above regular monthly fees. This occurs after transfer to a health-care facility lasting more than a specified number of days per year and/or per lifetime. There is no discernible trend among developing communities as to which option will be dominant in the future.

The fee structure is two-tiered, consisting of a one-time charge paid upon admission to the community and an ongoing monthly fee that is adjusted for inflation, but not for living status. The monthly fee is payable for as long as the resident remains in the community. One misleading impression about CCRCs is that they are affordable by only a small portion of the elderly population. A review of fees from two comprehensive directories listing over 200 CCRCs (Adelmann, 1980; Winklevoss and Powell, 1982) would seem to debunk this myth.

Admission requirements would appear to limit entrance to those persons who were in the upper-middle-and-above income levels during their working lifetime. The experience of the authors and discussions with many administrators indicate that a high percentage of their residents were middle income. Moreover, many communities have fund-raising programs to support residents who run out of money, and many accept and subsidize residents who would not otherwise be able to afford their fees. The authors know of no community that has ever asked a resident to leave due to inability to pay fees.

Median fee levels in 1981 called for a $35,000 entry fee for a single person and $35,900 for a two-person entry into a one-bedroom unit. Monthly fees that year were $594 for one person and $806 for two-persons. Based on a recent income and asset survey of the over sixty-five years (Turner et al., 1982) and assuming liberal admission policies, these median fees would be affordable by 40 percent of the over-sixty-five population who own their own homes free and clear of mortgages. Applying stricter admission requirements (for example, requiring a prospective entrant to have monthly income equal to twice the current monthly fee and assuming that the sale of their home covers the entry fee), these fees would be affordable by only 10 percent of the same population.

One drawback to the preceding analysis is that income statistics alone understate the financial status of the elderly. A better measure would be an individual's net worth which reflects other resources that could be used to pay monthly fees after inflation has increased them over monthly income. Although reliable statistics on the elderly's net worth are difficult to obtain, the authors believe that an individual with a net worth of more than $200,000 (taking into consideration future monthly income) would easily be able to pay for lifetime residence in a CCRC. Since many of the current CCRC residents are widows whose husbands left estates in excess of this amount, it is reasonable to assume that more than 10 percent of the elderly would meet this criteria. However, it should be noted that services provided by a CCRC are expensive, and a widespread expansion of the concept to serve lower economic levels is not possible without substantial outside subsidies.

With this general background, we can now discuss the financial implications of continuing care contracts.

Financing Continuing Care Contracts

Among the issues and factors that affect funding decisions for continuing care contracts are (1) controlling fee increases in light of increasing health-care utilization; (2) maintaining equity among different generations of entrants; (3) differentation of fees for demographic factors such as age, sex, and health status at entry; (4) equitable fee differentials among apartment types and for numbers of occupants; (5) inclusion or exclusion of various refund provisions; and (6) type of health-care guarantees to be offered (extensive versus limited). This section will concentrate on the first and most important issue, controlling fee increases. A more complete examination of the other issues is found among the references given at the end of this chapter (see Berry and Weaver, 1980; Cohen, 1980; Digard, 1978; Greene, 1981; Hewitt, 1982; Parr and Green, 1981; Sosnoff and Blumenthal, 1980; and Steinhauer and Ecker, 1980).

Developing a sound methodology for financing future costs of continuing-care contracts presents several unique problems that are not present elsewhere in the housing and health-care industries. On the one hand, the continuing care contract contains elements of real estate financing since long-term debt is used to construct and maintain the physical plant. Many communities have applied all initial entry fees to cover the "bricks-and-mortar" portion of costs (referred to as capital expenses). Others have reserved their entry fees and annually release a predetermined amount to cover debt service and other capital expenses. Monthly fees are not typically used to fund capital costs.

On the other hand, the continuing care contract has provisions similar to those of a small health insurance company due to the promise to provide long-term health care. Here, too, CCRCs vary in their financing practices with some communities using only monthly fees to cover their operating costs for housing and health care, while others

have used a combination of monthly and entry fees for this purpose.

An insight into the financial considerations of continuing care contracts must begin with the dynamics of their population. To illustrate this phenomenon, figure 24-1 presents a historical picture of an actual CCRC that opened in 1967. This community offered three levels of care: independent living in apartments; personal care; and nursing. During the first year of operation all contract holders were in apartments. The health-care beds (personal and nursing) were occupied by non–contract holders who were relocated elsewhere as these beds were required by the continuing care contract holders.

The transfer of continuing care apartment residents to personal and nursing care increased over time and by 1982 there were 271 apartment, 32 personal care, and 44 skilled nursing continuing care contract holders. The permanent health-care requirements for this community averaged 24.2 beds per 100 apartment contract holders (19.4 percent of the total population) during the period 1978 to 1982. The industry average for a facility offering three or more levels of care is 25.3 beds per 100 apartment residents (Winklevoss and Powell, 1982). This community, as do all CCRCs, has additional demands on its health-care facilities since some of the apartment residents will use the health-care center on a temporary basis with the expectation that they will return to their apartments after a short stay (usually less than thirty days).

The changing population mix has a significant impact on continuing-care costs since it is more expensive to care for those residents who transfer to the health-care center. To illustrate the financial consequences, it is necessary to make some assumptions about historical expenses since actual values are not available. We know that 1982 health-care expenses are approximately twice apartment expenses and will assume that operating expenses for apartment residents are $10,000 and are therefore $20,000 for health-care residents. Using this Consumer Price Index (CPI) as a measure of the community's internal inflation expe-

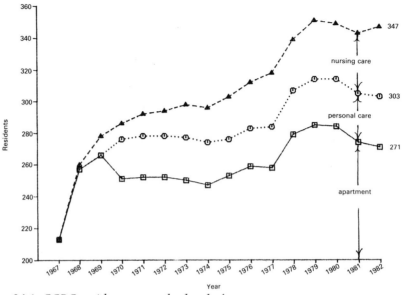

24-1. CCRC resident census by level of care.

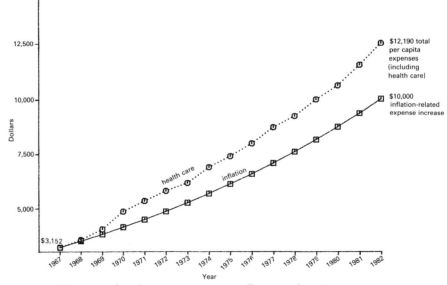

24-2. Health-care-related expenses versus inflation-related expenses.

238

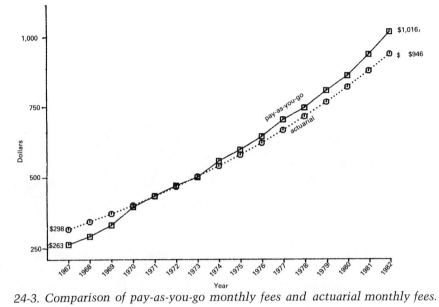

24-3. Comparison of pay-as-you-go monthly fees and actuarial monthly fees.

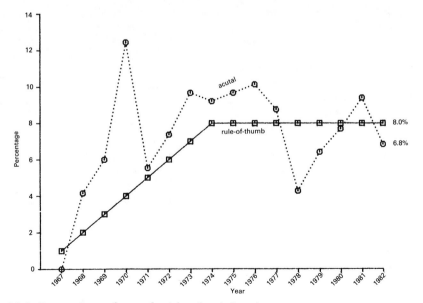

24-4. Comparison of actual with rule-of-thumb apartment turnover percentages.

rience, assume that the average inflation rate during the past fifteen years was 8 percent. Assume further that both apartment and health-care expenses were affected by the same inflation rate (this assumption will be removed later). Hence, 1967 expenses are generated by deflating the 1982 values. This procedure generates annual expenses of $3,152 ($10,000 divided by 3.172) for apartment residents and $6,305 ($20,000 divided by 3.172) for health-care residents.

Figure 24-2 shows the impact of increasing health-care use on total per-capita expenses for the retirement community. The solid line shows the expense increase due to inflation only. It begins at $3,152 for 1967 where all contract-holders are residing in an apartment and increases to $10,000 reflecting 8 percent annual inflation. The dotted line shows the combined effect of increasing health-care use on per-capita expenses. Per-capita expenses increased to $12,190, approximately four times the 1967 value. Inflation was responsible for 82 percent ($10,000 divided by $12,190) of that increase. Increasing health-care use was responsible for the other 18 percent; an additional 1.3 percent per year over and above normal inflation.

The preceding illustration shows one major financial policy issue facing continuing-care providers. This issue is the conflict between holding monthly fees at a minimum (along the same order of magnitude as their internal inflation) and providing for the increasing costs of health-care usage. At first blush, this may not seem feasible and in fact many communities cannot achieve this goal because their monthly fees are based on a current-cost or pay-as-you-go methodology. With pay-as-you-go methodology, monthly fees are set to cover projected expenses for the next year, with no attempt to accumulate reserves. Monthly fees under this approach will increase at the same rate as per-capita expenses.

The inflation-constrained increase in fees can be achieved by employing an actuarial methodology. This results in monthly fees that are initially higher than actual expenses in order to fund reserves for future health care. Alternatively, a portion of entry fees could be set aside to advance-fund those health care expenses.

Actuarially determined monthly fees are compared with pay-as-you-go monthly fees in figure 24-3. The actuarial fees are based on an open-group methodology where the initial and subsequent entrant cohorts are combined and assumed to pay the same fees. These fees were determined such that they would generate sufficient revenues to cover all operating expenses during the sixteen-year period taking into account interest earnings (assumed to be 10 percent) on reserves. Increases in actuarial fees are set equal to the inflation assumption of 8 percent. Entry fees for both pricing methodologies are assumed to be reserved for future capital expenses and do not affect monthly fees.

At startup, actuarial monthly fees are 13.5 percent higher than pay-as-you-go fees ($298 versus $263). Actuarial fees are higher for the next six years with the difference reducing dramatically over the next three years. After 1973, actuarial fees are always less. By 1982, actuarial fees are 6.9 percent less than the corresponding pay-as-you-go fees. It should be noted that after 1982, actuarial fees in this example would have to equal pay-as-you-go fees since the reserves would have been depleted. To avoid this problem, management would have to select a longer time horizon to develop its funding policy.

The preceding example shows that a community employing an actuarial funding policy will have lower fees for more years than one that does not, although the present value of fees in both cases is equal. The initial difference in fees is reduced if health-care inflation were assumed to be higher than apartment inflation as has been the case in the past. Sensitivity analysis on the backward health-care inflation assumption illustrates this point. Consider, for example, health-care inflation equal to 10 percent (apartment inflation and increases in actuarial monthly fees are still assumed to be 8 percent). Actuarial fees are only 10.8 percent higher than pay-as-you-go fees in 1967. They continued to be higher through 1973, but the difference is declining. By 1982, actuarial monthly fees are 9.1 percent lower than pay-as-you-go.

If health-care inflation were assumed to be 11 percent, then actuarial fees are 9.7 percent higher in 1967 and 10.1 percent less in 1982 with the crossover again in 1973. Assuming a 12 percent health-care inflation rate, actuarial fees are only 8.4 percent higher in 1967 and 11 percent less in 1982. One important conclusion affecting admission policies can be drawn from this analysis. Recently health-care inflation has exceeded general inflation. If this experience continues, a community that bases admission requirements on current monthly fees and employs actuarial principles in determining those fees is less likely to face the problem of monthly fees exceeding residents' resources as compared to a community employing a pay-as-you-go methodology.

Summarizing the preceding analysis, the advantages of using the actuarial funding methodology in setting monthly fees are: (1) a CCRC can exert some control over the increases in future monthly fees; (2) in the long run, actuarial funding will result in lower fees, which is desirable since most of a CCRC's residents will be on fixed incomes; and (3) this methodology provides a higher level of fiscal security during the early years of operation when a CCRC is more vulnerable to fluctuations in demographic experience. The disadvantages of actuarial funding are: (1) fees are higher initially which may present a marketing problem for a developing community (in this example, however, the higher fees lasted only four years); and (2) it may not be clear to residents that they are paying their fair share of expenses since some members of the current group will not survive to receive the benefits of lower fees in the future.

The second disadvantage is related to the policy issue of maintaining equity among different generations of entrants. The actuarial funding methodology can be applied so that, on average, all members of the current group are paying their fair share. However, for a given individual this average

may not be accurate (which is also the case in the pay-as-you-go methodology).

Another approach for applying the actuarial funding methodology is to increase entry fees so that a portion can be set aside to advance-fund future operating expenses. This approach has the same advantages and disadvantages that were raised in the preceding discussion. This approach has another disadvantage in that by relying on initial and subsequent entry fee receipts, the community experiences an added risk since entry fee receipts can be adversely affected by variations in apartment turnover occurring when a resident dies or permanently transfers to the health-care center. An illustration of the potential variation is given in figure 24-4. This figure shows the actual experience of a CCRC (dotted line) and an industry rule-of-thumb (solid line) (Wasser and Cloud, 1980). Apartment turnover is expressed as a percentage of the average apartment occupancy. Although the variations in this example are favorable since actual experience exceeded expected experience, they could just as likely have been unfavorable.

In summary, management must weigh the potential financial risks against marketing considerations (affordability and desire to pay fees by marketplace) in deciding where to set their pricing policies in the spectrum of pay-as-you-go to actuarial funding. After making that decision, appropriate methodology can be applied to address the other financial issues raised at the beginning of this section.

Conclusion

This chapter has defined and characterized a small but rapidly growing industry addressing the housing and long-term health-care needs of the elderly. This industry, referred to as Continuing Care Retirement Communities (CCRCs), currently consists of over 300 institutions serving approximately 90,000 elderly individuals nationwide. This figure represents only one-half of one percent of the over-age-sixty-five population and 5 percent of our *minumum* estimates of the portion of the elderly population who could afford fees charged by these communities.

The industry has doubled in size during the past decade. However, growth has slowed during the 1980s. Reasons for the decrease in new starts include poor economic conditions, cost of capital for financing a new facility ranging from 15 percent to 20 percent, and the high "seed money" requirements for planning a facility. These up-front costs are on the order of $500,000 and are not available to many nonprofit sponsors.

The authors believe that the growth rate will increase over the next few years, driven by the demand from a growing elderly population and more sensible interest rates. Moreover, we are observing a tremendous interest in this field from proprietary groups such as nursing home chains, hospitals, and other housing specialists. If the proper financing vehicle can be developed (minimizing the taxation disincentives), these groups will play a significant role in the future development of the industry since they have the financial resources for the planning phase. Our best information shows that ten to fifteen facilities are actually being financed annually which implies a 33-to-50-percent growth in this decade.

Funding the continuing care contract poses some unique financial problems. These problems are associated with the volatility of health-care usage among a small population (for CCRCs, 300 residents) and the extremely high costs of health care and rate of increase in those costs. This would apparently make continuing care a very risky proposition. In fact, the private insurance industry has yet to accept this challenge of insuring long-term nursing care for the elderly. Nevertheless, the authors believe that several characteristics of CCRCs lend themselves to a financially viable operation provided proper actuarial and financial planning is employed. For example, the underwriting process of admission screening and substantial lump-sum entry fees provides these communities with a select and relatively more healthy population. Also, there is typically an emphasis within CCRCs on prevention care (similar to an HMO) that attempts to maintain residents in the lowest level of care where costs for the community are the least. When some form of health care is needed, it is provided quickly and efficiently.

However, the preceding ideal characteristics do have their limitations. The costs of lifetime health care are expensive and can be independently financed by a minority of the elderly. Also, as a community ages, the average age of its resident population tends to increase, making it more difficult to attract younger residents who are necessary to reduce rising health-care usage. Despite these limitations, the continuing care concept appears to be an efficient health-care delivery system. Further research is needed to determine whether it is cost effective and whether the delivery system can be applied to the general public outside the confines of a retirement community. If the system is cost effective, then governmental policy might be changed to channel dollars into encouraging the development of CCRCs as well as to subsidize the application of the delivery system outside CCRCs.

Note

Almost all hospital costs, as opposed to health-center costs, are covered under Medicare Part A, and most physician's fees are covered under Medicare Part B. Since most CCRCs require supplementary insurance to Medicare, that combination covers all hospital expenses and most physicians' fees, leaving the costs of nursing care to the community. It is in this context that the authors suggest that CCRCs provide total health-care services.

References

Adelman, N. 1980. *Directory of Life-Care Communities*, 2nd edition. Kennett Square, PA: Kendal Crosslands.

Berry, R., and B. Weaver. 1980. *Life Table Estimation and Financial Evaluation for California Life-Care Homes*. Berkeley, CA: Teknekron.

Cohen, D. L. 1980. "Continuing-Care Communities for the Elderly: Potential Pitfalls and Proposed Legislation." *University of Pennsylvania Law Review* 128–849:883–936.

Dilgard, C. K. 1978. *Financial Management Guide for Nonprofit Homes for the Aging.* Evanston, IL: Health and Welfare Ministries Division, Board of Global Ministries of the United Methodist Church.

Greene, M. R. 1981. "Life-Care Centers—A New Concept in Insurance." *Journal of Risk and Insurance* 48:403–21.

Hewitt, D. L. 1982. "Actuarial Amortization of Entry Fees for Life-Care Communities." *1981–82 Proceedings of the Conference of Actuaries in Public Practice* 31:506–23.

Parr, J., and S. Green. 1981. *Housing Environments of Elderly Persons: Typology and Discriminant Analysis.* Clearwater, FL: Foundation for Aging Research.

Rose, A. M. 1982. *Lifecare Industry 1982.* Philadelphia: Laventhol and Horwath.

Sosnoff, H. D., and J. E. Blumenthal. 1980. "Accommodation Fees: Have You Earned Them?" *American Health-Care Journal* 6:23.

Steinhauer, M., and J. Ecker. 1980. "Life-Care Communities: Private Sector Involvement in Housing Alternatives for the Elderly." Paper presented at the annual meeting of the Gerontological Society of America, San Diego, November.

Turner, L., C. Schreter, B. Zetick, G. Weisbrod, and H. Pollakowski. 1982. *Housing Options for the Community Resident Elderly: Policy Report of the Housing Choices of the Older American Study.* Graduate School of Social Work and Social Research: Byrn Mawr.

Wasser, L. J., and D. A. Cloud (eds.). 1980. *Continuing Care: Issues for Nonprofit Providers.* Washington, DC: American Association of Homes for the Aging.

Winklevoss, H. E. and A. V. Powell. 1981. "Retirement Communities: Assessing the Liability of Alternative Health-Care Guarantees." *Journal of Long-Term Care Administration* 9:8–33.

———. 1982. *1982 Reference Directory of Continuing Care Retirement Communities.* Philadelphia: Human Services Research.

———. 1984. *Continuing-Care Retirement Communities: An Empirical, Financial, and Legal Analysis.* Philadelphia: The Pension Research Council of the Wharton School.

INDEX